Child Abuse and Neglect

A Guide with Case Studies
for Treating the Child and Family

Edited by
Nancy B. Ebeling
Deborah A. Hill

John Wright • PSG Inc
Boston   Bristol   London
1983

Library of Congress Cataloging in Publication Data
Main entry under title:

Child abuse and neglect.

Includes bibliographical references and index.
1. Child abuse—United States—Addresses,
essays, lectures. 2. Interviewing in child abuse
—Addresses, essays, lectures. 3. Abused children
—Services for—United States—Addresses, essays,
lectures. 4. Family psychotherapy—United States—
Addresses, essays, lectures. I. Ebeling, Nancy B.
II. Hill, Deborah A. III. Title. [DNLM: 1. Child
abuse. WA 320 C53413]
HV741.C4527 1982 362.7′1 82-11094
ISBN 0-7236-7040-4

Published by:
John Wright · PSG Inc, 545 Great Road, Littleton,
Massachusetts 01460, U.S.A.
John Wright & Sons Ltd, 823–825 Bath Road,
Bristol BS4 5NU, England

Printed in Great Britain by
John Wright & Sons (Printing) Ltd. at The Stonebridge Press, Bristol.

International Standard Book Number: 0-7236-7040-4

Library of Congress Catalog Card Number: 82-11094

Dedicated to all social workers, past and present,
who have pioneered
and persevered in the treatment of
child abuse and neglect.

ABOUT THE EDITORS

Nancy Brokaw Ebeling received her undergraduate degree from West Virginia University and a Masters in Social Work from the Case-Western Reserve University School of Applied Social Sciences. She is a licensed independent clinical social worker.

Ms. Ebeling has had extensive clinical experience in all areas of child welfare in both public and private social agencies as a caseworker, supervisor, and administrator and in teaching and consultation. For many years she was District Executive for the Boston Office of the Massachusetts Society for the Prevention of Cruelty to Children, a private child protective agency. She is currently in private practice and a consultant in family and child welfare. She has published in professional journals and co-edited and authored articles in *Child Abuse: Intervention and Treatment* (1975, Publishing Sciences Group, Inc.), a book arising out of the proceedings of two symposiums sponsored by the interagency committee, Children's Advocates, Inc. in Boston, Massachusetts.

Deborah A. Hill received her undergraduate degree from the University of Vermont and her Masters in Social Work from the Simmons College School of Social Work. She is a licensed independent clinical social worker.

As a staff member of the Social Service Department at the Massachusetts General Hospital, Ms. Hill's interest in child protective concerns included development of a trauma team at the hospital, consultation, teaching, and later the development of a Massachusetts Department of Social Services contracted protective service evaluation and treatment program within the Massachusetts General Hospital—Chelsea Memorial Health Care Center, itself. She currently administers and supervises this treatment and training program, called the Child Care Project, and functions as a social work consultant to and coordinator of the Massachusetts General Hospital trauma team. She co-edited and authored articles in *Child Abuse: Intervention and Treatment* (1975, Publishing Sciences Group, Inc.).

CONTRIBUTORS

Stephen Antler, DSW
Associate Professor of Social
  Welfare Policy
Chairman, Social Welfare Policy
  Sequence
Boston University School of
  Social Work
Boston, Massachusetts

Peter L. Appleton, MSc, ABPS
Senior Clinical Psychologist
Child Development Centre
Maelor General Hospital
Wrexham, Clwyd
Wales

Alan Bedford, MA, CQSW,
  Dip Crim
Team Leader
National Society for the Prevention
  of Cruelty to Children
Haringey Special Unit
London
England

Elizabeth Reynolds Bishop, MSW,
  LICSW
Caseworker
Massachusetts General Hospital
Chelsea Memorial Health Care
  Center Child Care Project
Chelsea, Massachusetts

Marybeth Bronson, MSW, LICSW
Caseworker
Massachusetts General Hospital
Chelsea Memorial Health Care
  Center Child Care Project
Chelsea, Massachusetts

Lillian Pike Cain, PhD, LICSW
Director of Social Work
Massachusetts Mental Health Care
  Center
Adjunct Assistant Professor of
  Social Work
Simmons College School of Social
  Work
Boston, Massachusetts

Helen Vye Daley, MSS, LICSW
Supervisor, Boston Office
Massachusetts Society for the
  Prevention of Cruelty to Children
Boston, Massachusetts

Ann J. Gegg, CQSW, Dip App Soc
  Studies
Royal Liverpool Children's Hospital
Liverpool
England

Herbert H. Hershfang, JD
Winer and Abrams
Counsel, Boston Office
Massachusetts Society for the
  Prevention of Cruelty to Children
Boston, Massachusetts

Deborah A. Hill, MS, LICSW
Supervisor and Coordinator
Massachusetts General Hospital
Chelsea Memorial Health Care
  Center Child Care Project
Chelsea, Massachusetts

Barbara A. Holleman, MSW,
  ACSW
Caseworker
Massachusetts General Hospital
Chelsea Memorial Health Care
  Center Child Care Project
Chelsea, Massachusetts

Irving Kaufman, MD
Child and Adult Psychoanalyst
Consultant, Boston Office
Massachusetts Society for the
  Prevention of Cruelty to Children
Faculty, Harvard University
  School of Medicine
Cambridge, Massachusetts
Faculty, Smith College
  School for Social Work
Northampton, Massachusetts

Marylou Kaufman, MSW, LICSW
Head Supervisor
Chelsea Area Office
Massachusetts Department of Social
   Services
Chelsea, Massachusetts

Eleanor C. Knox, MSW, LICSW
Child Guidance and Family Mental
   Health Specialist
Boston, Massachusetts

Robert M. Mulford, MSSW
Formerly General Secretary, Retired
Massachusetts Society for the
   Prevention of Cruelty to Children
Boston, Massachusetts

Richard A. Noonan, MSW
Private Consultant in Child and
   Family Services
Boston, Massachusetts

Sally T. Owen, JD
Winer and Abrams
Counsel, Boston Office
Massachusetts Society for the
   Prevention of Cruelty to Children
Boston, Massachusetts

E. G. G. Roberts, MB, FRCP,
   DCH
Consulting Paediatrician
Maelor General Hospital
Wrexham, Clwyd
Wales

Mary Scott, RSCN, CQSW, CPSW
Principal Social Worker
Maelor General Hospital
Wrexham, Clwyd
Wales

Diana Waldfogel, MSW, LICSW
Dean and Professor of Social Work
Simmons College School of Social
   Work
Boston, Massachusetts

Judith K. Williams, BA, CQSW
Former Senior Medical Social
   Worker
Royal Liverpool Children's Hospital
Liverpool
England

CONTENTS

PREFACE

The decade of the 1970s brought the problems of child abuse and neglect in our society sharply to our attention. These problems had existed for centuries and had been dealt with in partial fashion by professionals for many decades previously. There was, however, a dramatic rise in the general public's awareness of the problems in the 1970s and a more comprehensive response from professionals to the issues. The amount of written material and research on child abuse and neglect expanded rapidly. The problem was addressed from many vantage points. They included the development of public social policy, implementation of programs for service delivery, increased theory in child development and family relations, and the introduction of a variety of treatment approaches, including family treatment and self-help groups.

Important key concepts in dealing with the problem emerged and were addressed by almost all authors with somewhat varying emphases. These included the need for prevention, the need for interdisciplinary work, the need for treatment if change was to occur, the desirability of treating the whole family (as the abuse or neglect was seen as a symptom of family dysfunction), and the need for using and developing community resources.

The editors of this volume contributed to the general consciousness-raising process, to the development of theory, and to explication of program development and implementation in their book *Child Abuse: Intervention and Treatment* in 1975. Their extensive experience now leads them to offer their cogent views and a guide to those engaged in this demanding and compelling work.

The present volume addresses the needs of clinical social workers who give direct service to children and families. It should be particularly helpful to workers who are new to the field of child abuse and neglect. It presents a clarifying and welcome focus in a rapidly expanding field. The editors and the selected authors have a consistent, defined point of view. Their theoretical perspective is a psychodynamic one. They direct their attention to the treatment of the abusing parents and their children. They demonstrate that the same principles of good clinical work apply to these clients as they apply to others. The writers hope to show, particularly through the use of case studies, what actually happens between workers and clients and thus to help remove the mystique from the work in a field that may engender fear and discouragement. The authors believe that a primary individual relationship must be established with the abusing client before any other method of treatment is introduced if change is to occur. Differential diagnostic planning is then required to determine whether other additional modalities, such as family treatment, groups, and so forth, will be helpful. Throughout any additional help, they believe that the original individual relationship must be maintained, for the constancy of that primary relationship is most important.

The editors of this volume also have a firm position regarding the question now frequently raised as to whether the worker who may institute legal control through the courts, who may have previously or may in the future remove the child from the home, can also do the treatment with the abusing parent or family. Ebeling and Hill believe workers can and do so every day. I would go further and suggest that they should be the ones to do both. To do so would be an important and perhaps an essential component of the treatment. Parents (who themselves often have had less than adequate parenting) may not be able to tolerate their own ambivalence or control their impulsivity. They may benefit from the experience of having controls and limit-setting used as an expression of caring and not of punishment if they are to do the same with their children. They may need to see that the loving parent can protect through the use of authority and not do harm with its use. They surely do not need to further experience a split between the good parent and the bad one in the persons of a good and bad therapist, when they must integrate these aspects of themselves to deal more adequately with their own children.

As a social work educator, I find this volume particularly gratifying and important for it reclaims much social work territory that has seemed in danger of being relinquished or at least merged. The child welfare field is singularly a social work development with a long history and a specialized knowledge base. It has contributed greatly to an understanding of the needs of children and to the meaning of loss, deprivation, and separation in human development. It is in this field, of all fields in social work or the human services, that the greatest amount of practical experience exists in dealing with severely problematic families and their young children. Decisions regarding placement and adoption, decisions regarding separating or maintaining families, and decisions weighing the needs of all family members are daily occurrences. Problems of existing or potential child abuse and neglect and actions regarding them are also constant in this field. Thus child welfare workers are long used to dealing with child abuse and neglect cases.

As has happened in other areas of social work practice (for example, family treatment), there is a danger that social workers underestimate the knowledge and expertise they have and the contribution they can make to a field. This is particularly true when they encounter new and different approaches and knowledge in other professions. It is possible to overvalue the other professions' contribution to a point where one abandons one's own position. Aside from territorial and status issues, which cannot be ignored, there is the broader issue of losing unique and valuable perspectives and knowledge. Knowledge and expertise is not the exclusive property of any one profession. In a problem area as complex and difficult as child abuse, the knowledge, work, and support of every profession and sector of society is needed. Everyone agrees on the desirability of an interdisciplinary approach. However, interdisciplinary teamwork often becomes less, not more, effective when professional roles and responsibilities are blurred. Interventions may be duplicated, and the lack of boundaries can contribute to imprecise and confused thinking. When professionals operate from a secure base and identity, with a firm conviction of the special contribution they can make, it usually engenders mutual respect, less threat, and more breadth in the options, decisions, and possible actions. Thus a volume such as this, which explicates what social workers know and do in a field where they have expertise and long experience, should help immeasurably to solidify and reaffirm their position and value.

Clinical social work, of all the therapeutic professions, seems the best suited to deal with the treatment of child abuse and neglect. Some young workers have questioned whether the work is actually "clinical social work." If it is not, I believe that clinical social work does not exist. The distinguishing nature of clinical social work compared to other therapies is its emphasis in treatment of social as well as psychological aspects of the defined problem. The "person in the environment" is suggested by the National Association of Social Work task force charged with defining clinical social work in 1980 (Ewalt, *Toward a Definition of Clinical Social Work*), as a required cornerstone regardless of the theoretical perspective of the worker.

To do good work in the area of child abuse and neglect requires a coming together of all the knowledge, skills, and values of our profession. Knowledge of child development, life stages, and theories of family interaction are essential. Skills in treatment from beginning to end are necessary, including the special outreach skills needed to establish relationships with frightened and resistant clients; appropriate differential use of those relationships; use of support, education, clarification, modeling, insight; and eventually handling termination. Collaboration and consultation with a myriad of other professionals will undoubtedly be required. Often advocacy for the parents and/or the child will be necessary. Often broader social action on a policy level will be required, sometimes to be done by an agency specialist or administrator if not the individual worker. The use of community resources (and sometimes the actual development of some of them) will almost surely be necessary. The description is of clinical social work at its best and most comprehensive.

This book, through the example of its knowledgeable, effective, dedicated professionals, renews our commitment to the values and skills of clinical social work, to good, basic treatment principles and, most of all, to the clients who need us.

Diana Waldfogel, MSW, LICSW
Dean and Professor of Social Work
Simmons College School of Social Work
Boston, Massachusetts

ACKNOWLEDGMENTS

The editors wish to express their appreciation to the authors, without whose valued contributions this book would not have been possible, to Anne Lunt, BA, Dip. Soc. Admin., of Clwyd, Wales, for her interest and assistance, and to Debra Lavandier for her excellence in typing.

Authors acknowledge their gratitude to consultants for the following chapters:

To Evelyn Corsini, LICSW, Massachusetts General Hospital, for the chapter "The Initial Interview;" to Ms. Corsini and Louise V. Barry, LICSW, private practitioner, for "Ego Assessment and Treatment Planning;" to Matthew Dumont, MD, and Joseph Paretti, EdD, consultants at the Massachusetts General Hospital–Chelsea Memorial Health Care Center for "Child Treatment;" to the National Society for the Prevention of Cruelty to Children Director Dr. Alan Gilmour; and the National Society for the Prevention of Cruelty to Children child abuse consultant Ray Castle for "Aspects of Child Abuse in Britain."

INTRODUCTION

Take me away from all the pain
from corners so sharp and cold
and covered with grime
that in order to survive
you must leave who you are
and where you are
and change places with others
in your mind
and live in their lives
so that your life won't touch you.
I escaped the pain
but it fouls my mind with its
need to be heard
its clamour clouds my senses,
but if the pain comes
will I survive?
or just become a part of it?

Treatment for the pain and despair conveyed in this poem, written by a mother receiving protective services, calls not only for compassion, but for the highest level of professional knowledge and skill. Solid casework skills, an understanding of psychodynamics, and a specialized body of knowledge particular to child protective work are necessary in order to work effectively with the complexity of problems presented by abusing and neglecting families. This text, written by clinicians, deals in depth with the entire process of the worker–client relationship in child protective work. Based on a psychodynamic approach, the book integrates both theoretical and case material.

Defining what we believed to be a comprehensive approach to the treatment of families at risk, we asked authors to write chapters, each of which would address a specific part of the treatment process and would make extensive use of case material where appropriate. Thus, this book deals with diagnostic and treatment issues in the direct practice of child protective work after a child at risk has been identified.

The content of the book includes: understanding the etiology of a particular symptom, transference and countertransference, the impact of loss, skills involved in making assessments through home visiting, assessing families' coping mechanisms, dealing with separation issues, and formulating treatment plans utilizing a variety of methods. In addition, other chapters provide insight into legal, historical, research, and public policy issues which have an impact on child protective services. Finally, the book has been enriched by three chapters from England and Wales which describe the problem of child abuse and neglect and the approaches used in those countries.*

In the United States during the 1970s there has been a great increase in attention to the problem of child abuse and neglect through the literature and the media. The federal government has, in recent years, expended considerable sums toward developing understanding, knowledge, and new approaches through training and research projects, but while public and professional concerns have escalated and referrals have increased tremendously, the focus has been mainly on identification and reporting. Quick solutions and a smorgasbord of approaches have been sought to cope with the increased number of referrals. In many instances the rigidity inherent in bureaucratic institutions has resulted in an almost assembly-line-like approach with emphasis on "management" of the problem with little regard for individual needs and differences.

It is our hope, therefore, that this book will provide the reader not only with increased understanding but the foundation to develop therapeutic tools to perform this difficult work which we believe must focus on individual needs and differences. An individual's psychological functioning must be understood, further, in the context of his social environment. Poverty, violence, and other adverse social conditions have tremendous impact on individual functioning. The enormity of these societal problems and their impact on client and worker alike cannot be overemphasized.

On his/her part, the worker faces problems of high caseloads, lack of resources, bureaucratic snags, community expectations, lack of funding, and many more. In short, the enormity of these problems goes well beyond the resources of the individual worker. The worker does not operate in a vacuum. He or she requires not only an active, responsible community, but a supportive agency climate which is responsive to the needs of both client and worker. An agency which also strives to use its staff's thoughtful observations and questionings to expand the existing body of knowledge about child abuse and neglect enriches the workers' lives as well as the clients' and also, it is hoped, contributes to knowledge which can influence community attitudes and, ultimately, public policy. The impact of stress on the worker will be mitigated by that support and by an understanding of what is within his or her power to do and what is not. Increasing self-awareness, knowledge, and skill are essential as they provide the worker with a feeling of autonomy and clarity about his or

---

*Additionally, the appendix contains a translated summation of a proposal by the Swedish Committee on Children's Rights. This proposal, included because of its uniqueness, states a position prohibiting subjecting children to corporal punishment. This later was introduced into the Swedish Parenthood and Guardianship Code.

her own role. This in turn should help to alleviate some of the stress and feelings of helplessness.

Treatment of these troubled families requires every skill we can bring to bear to help them grow and develop their potential and not just to survive the pain.

NBE
DAH

1 Historical Perspective

Robert M. Mulford

"There is nothing new under the sun." Certainly this old saying is true as it relates to the problem of child neglect and abuse. History records practices of every form of neglect, abuse, and murder imaginable throughout the world and in primitive as well as so-called civilized cultures. In China girl babies were drowned; in Egypt children were buried alive to serve deceased persons in afterlife; in ancient Rome fathers had the right to sell, mutilate, or kill their children; and in the eighth century BC Roman citizens were ordered to bring up all healthy males and at least one female child. As late as 1204, "The Pope, moved by the frequency with which fishermen of the Tiber found bodies of children in their nets, dedicated part of a hospital to the care of abandoned children." Historians relate that in seventeenth century France, despite regulations and decrees of authorities, child murder increased. Some babies were thrown into sewers, others lay deserted on the highways, and the more fortunate were left at hospital doors. The apprentice system in England came into being during the sixteenth century as a result of the increase in numbers of vagrant children. Boys and girls were bound out between the ages of 5 and 14—boys until they were 24 and girls until 20. As a result of industrialization in England, cheap labor was in such demand that brokers sprang up to traffic in children who worked from five in the morning until ten at night. Inhuman overseers frequently goaded laggards with whips and prods, and any who dared to run away, and were caught, were chained to their work by their ankles. In 1833 Lord Shaftesbury secured legislation providing a 48-hour week for children from 9 to 13 and a 68-hour week for children 13 to 18. Employment of children under 9 was prohibited.

Nor was the United States immune from the abuse and exploitation of its children, for under Colonial Laws of Massachusetts 1672-1686, the attitude of early lawmakers toward children is clearly enunciated:

> If a man have a stubborn or rebellious son of sufficient years of understanding, viz., fifteen years of age, which shall not obey the voice of his father, or the voice of his mother, and that when they had chastened him, will not hearken unto them, then shall his father and mother, being his natural parents, lay hold on him, and bring him to the magistrates assembled in court, and testify unto them that their son is stubborn and rebellious, and will not obey their voice and chastisement, but lives in sundry and notorious crimes, such a son shall be put to death.

And as in England, the industrial revolution brought with it exploitation of young children in unregulated factory labor. In 1866, the year in which the first Society for the Prevention of Cruelty to Animals was organized in New York City, a report was made to the Massachusetts Legislature in which it was stated that representatives of the factories went about canvasing for small children. "Small help is scarce, a great deal of machinery has been stopped for want of small help, so that the Overseers have been going around to draw the small children from school into the mills, the same as a drive in the army." And when asked if there were any limit to the age at which they would take children, a witness replied, "They will take them at any age they can get them, if they are old enough to stand."

It was not until 1874 that a significant movement to recognize the rights of children in the United States became evident. It developed as a result of a situation in which a volunteer church worker, Mrs. Charles C. Wheeler, in New York City visited a poor woman who was dying of tuberculosis. The woman's only request was that something be done to help a child living in an adjacent tenement and whose cries for help she frequently heard. The child, 8-year-old Mary Ellen Wilson, had been brutally beaten by her guardian to whom she had been indentured at age 18 months. Mrs. Wheeler was advised by the charitable agency not to interfere and when she went to the police was told that since no law had been broken, there was nothing they could do. Her pastor and her attorney advised her to drop the matter lest she be involved in a civil suit. Finally she went to Henry Bergh, president of the New York Society for the Prevention of Cruelty to Animals, and persuaded him that since there was no law protecting Mary Ellen as a child, that she be reached by laws enacted for the protection of animals. Mr. Bergh considered the matter and decided that "If that child has no rights as a human being, she shall at least have the justice of a cur on the street." After conferring with the Society for the Prevention of Cruelty to Animals counsel, Elbridge Gerry, Mary Ellen was brought into court, placed with Mrs. Wheeler, and the guardian was sentenced to one year in prison. This was the first step accomplished in establishing the rights of children in the United States. As a result of the Mary Ellen case, so many cases were brought to Henry Bergh's attention that he and Mr. Gerry formed the New York Society for the Prevention of Cruelty to Children in 1875.

Following the establishment of the New York Society for the Prevention of Cruelty to Children, similar organizations were formed in other cities and states. In addition to providing instant protection for abused, exploited, and neglected children, these societies were actively engaged in publicizing the plight of these children and campaigning for child protective legislation which reflected their experience in dealing with specific cases. It is important to note that the work of these early pioneer agencies was supported totally by contributions for their efforts from interested citizens. For the most part they saw themselves as arms of the law, and prosecution of abusive parents and others resulted in many children being "rescued" and offenders being imprisoned. The early reports of these privately supported societies detailed gruesome stories of children who were savagely beaten or sold to so-called "baby farms" where they were neglected or beaten and allowed to die. Parents brought the children to the "baby farms," paid the proprietors to keep them, and abandoned them. It is reported that within a radius of one and a quarter miles of one such home bodies of 25 infants were found within a four-month period. Other children were intentionally maimed by abusive parents and sent out on the street to beg. It was to such extreme brutality that early child protective workers responded. Their response to such situations was to rescue the child and prosecute the parents. Less extreme situations were dealt with by warning parents and advising them not to repeat their neglectful treatment. It would appear that parental abuse and neglect were willful and premeditated in the opinion of the early workers. Thus, it was logical to adopt a prosecutory, punitive approach to the perpetrators. The contributions of psychology and psychiatry to the understanding of human motivation and behavior were unknown to these early protectors of children. Many of these workers were former law enforcement and military men who found it quite natural to identify themselves with agencies who saw themselves as "arms of the law."

It was not until 1903 that a new direction and philosophy came into being when the newly elected president of the Massachusetts Society for the Prevention of Cruelty to Children, Grafton D. Cushing, gave vigorous support to the move from prosecution and rescue work to the employment of preventive and remedial measures. This new direction was well described in his 1905 report:

> I believe that we must develop in a new direction, and take a more active part in all movements which look towards the betterment of the conditions under which children of the state live. This will bring us face to face with many of the problems affecting parents as well as the children. Where the evil is unremedied, we should exert ourselves to find a remedy. Where the enforcement of existing laws will further protect children, we should call to the attention of the proper authorities any lack in the enforcement of the laws which we know of. Whatever touches the welfare of children concerns us. Every movement for improved social conditions should find the Massachusetts SPCC an active participant.

This statement of broad concern and responsibility was significant not only for the new direction the agency was to take, but for the fact that it identified itself with social and charitable agencies. In 1907 Carl C. Carstens, who had studied at the New York School of Philanthropy and had been associated with the Philadelphia and New York Charity Organization Societies, was employed as the General Secretary of the Massachusetts Society for the Prevention of Cruelty to Children. He proceeded to carry out the new directions enunciated by Mr. Cushing. Under Carstens' leadership the agency rapidly moved away from the "arm of the law" concept of its function to a preventive and rehabilitative service with no diminution of its objective of protecting children from neglect, exploitation, and abuse. To carry out the new direction, personnel with college degrees were employed as "agents," and the emphasis was on helping parents to provide adequate care where possible rather than removing children through court action. Even so, a high percentage of the agency's case load were court cases involving removal of children from their parents. As late as the 1940s, the percentage of court actions was as high as 25% of the case load. And although the fields of psychology and psychiatry were developing in the 1920s and 1930s, it was not until the late 1940s that psychiatric consultation became a regular part of the treatment program of the Massachusetts Society for the Prevention of Cruelty to Children. It was at this time that the agency began employing graduates of schools of social work as caseworkers and providing professional training courses for staff.

In the brief review herein we have moved from a time when children were murdered with no penalty to the perpetrators to a time when laws for the protection of children provided both penalties and help to those who neglected or abused children. We have seen a change in attitude toward parents who neglect or abuse children. We have seen a move from the "arm of the law" function of the child protective agency to that of a treatment-oriented function. And we have seen a move from the employment of law enforcement and military personnel as child protective workers to the employment of graduate social workers. But what of public attitudes in regard to child neglect and abuse?

Throughout history, attitudes toward children have reflected the value society has put on them at a given time. In primitive societies female infants were of less value than male children because they could not hunt and fight. In agrarian cultures children were economic assets because they could work in the fields and help to produce, but in large urban areas they became a liability because they were not economic assets and thus were abandoned or murdered. Since children were considered the property of their parents (at one time the father only), they were subject to whatever treatment their parents chose to inflict, and without interference from anyone. The exploitation of children by parents prior to the passage of child labor laws and child protective laws included outright selling of them, maiming of them to make them pitiable objects who were put on the street as beggars, putting them into various forms of employment involving long hours, inadequate supervision, and sometimes dangerous conditions which included factory work, theatrical performances, and exhibitions. And it was not only parents who permitted these forms of exploitation. Children were seen as cheap labor in many forms of employment by unscrupulous employers.

It was natural that the response to such flagrant exploitation and cruelty would be to rescue children, punish the perpetrators, and pass legislation which was punitively oriented. It was several decades before parents who abused and neglected their children were perceived as people who could be helped. It was not until social casework came into being that treatment and prevention were seen as the responses which offered the best hope in dealing with these difficult situations. Even after the early child protective organizations adopted a casework philosophy and method, it was many years before they were seen by their colleagues as therapists rather than authoritative agents. Since the protective worker is given the authority to enter family situations by law or agency function which has community support and without the request of the parents, the question was raised as to whether or not casework was compatible with authority. This question was debated for a number of years, and it was demonstrated that it was the nonpunitive helping approach by a worker who accepted his right to be in the situation which produced successful treatment results. As more understanding of parental behavior became a part of the worker's knowledge, the skill in diagnosis developed and the approach to the parent was based on the perception of his needs as a person as well as his performance as a parent. Seeing the parent as a person in need of help and offering that help in a nonpunitive, nonthreatening way made it possible for parents to begin to trust the social worker and use that help in a constructive way. Recognition of the psychological factors involved in parents' acceptance or nonacceptance of casework help motivated child protective workers to change laws which were based on a punitive, prosecutory orientation, in favor of statutes which emphasized a treatment approach based on the assumption that parents could use help and did not abuse and neglect their children willfully.

As child protective laws were modified to reflect the new understanding of parental motivation and the possibility of treatment for neglectful and abusive parents, a new awareness on the part of the public came into being in the 1960s. Dr. Henry Kempe in Denver, Colorado, originated the diagnosis of "battered child syndrome," and the media as well as medical journals publicized the problem of child abuse nationwide. During the decade of the 1960s, all 50 states passed laws relating to the reporting and treatment of child abuse. For the first time legislation made it mandatory for those professionals who came in contact with children who they believed to be abused to report their condition to the designated authorities (in some states, law enforcement authorities and in others, the public welfare agency). Prior to the passage of this legislation physicians, teachers, and psychiatrists had been loath to make a report to the authorities and many could not believe that parents would abuse children. Many of the statutes mandate reporting by social service, guidance, police, educational, probation, and counseling personnel and provide for the investigation and treatment of neglect as well as abuse. These laws have resulted in an avalanche of reports throughout the country and a great increase in funding and staffing for child protective services. Since there had been a gradual reduction of the privately financed child protective organizations as public child welfare services began to develop specific child protective services in the 1940s and 1950s, the tremendous increase in reported cases of child neglect and abuse in the 1960s and 1970s necessitated the great increase in public funding on federal and state levels. Titles IV A and XX of the Social Security Act were major sources of funding which supported public welfare departments in the development of child protective services themselves and permitted them to purchase services from the private social work sector. A number of private social agencies negotiated purchase of service contracts which often resulted in over 50% of their operating income coming from these contracts.

The great increase in legislation in all 50 states, the substantial increase in the funding of child abuse programs, and the public support of efforts to combat the problem of child abuse were the result of a tremendous media campaign which publicized the incidence of cases of child abuse and neglect and shocking case stories. All the print media as well as radio and television brought to public consciousness the magnitude of the problem during the 1960s and 1970s. Although child protective agencies had been dealing with child neglect and abuse since 1875, it seemed as if the problem had just been discovered in the 1960s. Furthermore, while professionals in the fields of social work and mental health looked down on the field of child protection for years as being a prosecutory and punitively oriented function, it now became recognized as a professionally accepted part of the helping professions. Professionally trained social workers sought positions in the rapidly expanding public child welfare programs and the "old-line" private child protective agencies. Many new "inner city" agencies came into being as a result of federal funds for child protective services and were a source of employment for others. Even with the phenomenal increase in services and personnel, it has been impossible to provide adequate help for families reported to the designated agencies under the newly passed legislation. One might characterize the problem of child abuse and neglect as a problem out of control. In spite of the efforts to provide services to families reported under the statutes, the number of cases continues to increase and children suffer.

What of preventive efforts? The original child protective agencies had the word "prevention" in their titles. Most would agree that it would be more accurate to call them "societies for the prevention of *recurring* cruelty to children." Some attention has been given to the fact that there is community neglect of children — that when certain services are not available to parents, the community has failed. Does society in a highly industrialized urban community have a responsibility to provide certain medical, educational, and social services for all families irrespective of economic status? Is it significant that over 50% of neglect and abuse cases are families receiving public assistance — in many cases inadequate assistance? These families are not able to provide themselves with what, in our modern urban society, are necessities for healthy productive family life. It has been said that nowhere in the United States are all these necessities available to all families.

It has also been said that we live in a violent society. We know that under pressure people erupt into violent behavior. We know that our children see violence in the news, radio, and television as a regular part of life. And some of them see and experience it in their own lives and then as adults inflict violent behavior on their own children. Corporal punishment is a generally accepted form of discipline in our society and even approved by the Supreme Court. No reliable data are available to accurately indicate the effect of observed violence by parents and children on the incidence of child abuse and neglect. One can speculate that seeing abusive behavior frequently makes it less abnormal and thus easier for parents to perpetrate. This speculation seems to be supported by the well-established fact that children who have been abused frequently become abusive parents.

A critical review of current programs indicates that there is not any appreciable volume of preventive activity directly related to the problem of child neglect and abuse. Furthermore, it would seem from the continuing increasing incidence of the problem, as revealed by state and national statistics, that the problem is out of control—that neither personnel, funds, nor perhaps strategy are adequate to prevent the system from being completely overwhelmed. This is not to minimize the importance of what is being done by well-trained and well-intentioned practitioners to relieve the suffering of thousands of children throughout the country. But it is clear that thousands more are suffering with little hope of relief.

The above commentary is not meant nor should it be interpreted to indicate that there has been no progress in dealing with the problem of child abuse and neglect in the over 100 years of efforts on the part of dedicated people. What the data seem to say is that we have not yet found the effective means of preventing what has become a serious social problem, a problem which will not be solved by one-to-one treatment modalities after neglect or abuse has occurred in a family. To attack the problem on a preventive level would seem to require a new approach which deals with those behavior patterns of violence in society and provides the various services and supports which strengthen and stabilize family life—these on a mass basis reaching all those who need them. This approach would emphasize the importance of early diagnosis of symptoms of neglect and abuse and immediate intervention and provision of the necessary family supports and treatment. Although proposals of this nature have been made, none has ever been achieved on a massive, universal scale.

Our brief review of the history of child neglect and abuse and the attempts to ameliorate and prevent the suffering of children tells us that we have made progress in understanding and dealing with the problem, but that we have not been able to achieve the same success in eradicating it as have the medical scientists in eradicating certain diseases. Until we attack the root causes of this "social disease" on a massive level, history would seem to tell us that child neglect and abuse will continue to increase. And what makes it difficult is that changes in the attitudes of society toward violence to people must occur as well as the availability of supports and services. This is a large order, and unfortunately it will take time and a great deal of effort!

BIBLIOGRAPHY

Massachusetts Society for the Prevention of Cruelty to Children. *Crusading for Children,* 1943, and annual reports.

Mulford RM: *In the Interest of Children — A Century of Progress.* Denver, CO, American Humane Association, 1968.

Mulford RM: Protective services for children. *Social Work Encyclopedia,* Washington, DC, National Association of Social Workers Inc, 1977 pp 1115–1121.

Shultz WJ: *The Humane Movement in the United States 1910–1922.* New York, Columbia University Press, 1924.

2 Physical Abuse, Neglect, and Sexual Abuse: Dimensions and Frameworks

Marylou Kaufman

An historical survey of the problem of child maltreatment manifests the capriciousness of society's views about how its children should be nurtured and disciplined. Over the past 20 years, the United States has demonstrated a surge of interest in developing standards of child care to ensure its children's healthy development. This can be seen in the increase in scientific literature on this subject, focused media coverage of those tragic failures by society to prevent harm to its children, and the increase in official reports of child abuse and neglect which call for and encourage society's intervention.

The material presented here with regard to the incidence and the prevailing definitions of physical abuse, neglect, and sexual abuse of children has been brought together at a point in history when society's permission and financial support to public agencies to monitor families' care of their children has peaked. As economic problems deepen and political ideology increasingly favors limiting governmental involvement in family affairs, one can predict that definitions of child maltreatment will become increasingly restricted and statistical evidence of the maltreatment will diminish. The author only can hope that the framework for understanding and analyzing the phenomenon of child maltreatment presented here will not become a curious historical artifact too quickly but instead will be of long-term benefit to potential reporters and protective service workers alike.

DIMENSIONS

The report, *National Analysis of Official Child Neglect and Abuse Reporting (1978),* prepared by the American Humane Association in cooperation with the Denver Research Institute, is a description of the most current attempt "to provide the status of reporting on a national basis [and] to provide the profile of abuse and neglect as it is portrayed by official reports."[1] The analysis is valuable as much for gaining an appreciation for how difficult it is to obtain consistent data nationally as it is for the data it actually provides. It is based on a 1978 study of officially reported allegations of child abuse and neglect collected from 50 states, the District of Columbia, Puerto Rico, and the Virgin Islands. It documents a rapid increase in the rate of official reporting from 416,033 in 1976 to 614,291 in 1978, an increase of over 47%.[2]

Of the 614,291 reports collected in 1978, 191,739 were in the form of individual case data from 33 of the states. These reports were analyzed more closely, and the following statistics are based on the smaller sample. Of these allegations, 60% were unsubstantiated (ie, not proven at the time the data was collected), a national statistic which remained constant over the three-year period studied despite wide variation from state to state. The largest group of reporters were nonmandated reporters (38.4%), made up of family, friends, and neighbors. This is especially interesting in light of the fact that by the mid-1970s all states had enacted legislation requiring professionals, usually medical, school, social service, and law enforcement personnel, to report cases of suspected maltreatment. However, the rate of substantiation was higher for professional reports, ranging from the high of 60% for law enforcement sources to the low of 34% for the nonprofessionals.[3]

Of the 40% which were substantiated, 13.4% were counted as abuse, 24.2% neglect, and 2.4% counted as both. Statistics regarding the relationship between the perpetrators and the children indicated that the parent–child relationship predominates overwhelmingly in substantiated reports, with natural parents represented most frequently, 81.7%, and stepparents, adoptive, and foster parents adding an additional 8.9%. As the study states "this indicates that child maltreatment is a *family* problem and as such, a better understanding of the problem requires examination of the characteristics of those families that are reported to have been involved in maltreatment."[4] The statistics portray these parents as having limited education, 64.5% less than high school diploma; low income, 67% less than $9000 annually; and experiencing numerous other stresses including broken family, 45%, and inadequate housing, 20.6%.[5]

In contrast to this strongly consistent picture is the finding that "as a group (the victim children) did not seem to have any special characteristics that contributed toward their parents' maltreatment of them."[6] No patterns emerged whether examining abuse or neglect, even as to age or sex of the child. Some special characteristics examined were "premature birth," "mental retardation," "chronic illness," and "emotional disturbances." The most commonly noted was "emotional disturbance," but this was indicated for only 6.8% of the children reported, and all special characteristics taken together accounted for only 12.1%.[7]

Another major finding of the national study, that fits comfortably with the profile of socioeconomic hardship, is that "deprivation of necessities" accounted for 86.4% of the types of maltreatment substantiated.

"Major physical injury," including serious injuries like fractures and brain damage, represented only 1.9% of the reports. Other types of maltreatment noted were "sexual abuse," 6.2%; "minor physical injury" (bruises, welts), 20.7%; and "emotional maltreatment," 22.4%. (These figures add up to more than 100% because multiple responses exist.) These findings, like those regarding special characteristics of children, have remained constant during the three-year reporting period.[8]

While the types of services offered as a result of substantiating reports have remained constant too, there have been fewer reported instances of substantiated reports receiving no services. In 1976 46% of substantiated reports were marked "no action taken" as compared to 15% in 1978. Counseling is the most frequent service provided, 83.0%. In-home supportive services, such as day care and homemaker services, were provided in only 10.1% of the substantiated cases. Out-of-home care, such as foster or shelter care, was provided in 20.6% of the cases.[9]

The study offers an intriguing array of statistics in its effort to illustrate the status of national reporting and to provide a profile of abuse and neglect. If reliable, the data can be used to construct needed national policy and to lobby for increased resources to address the causes of child maltreatment. Unfortunately, the study indicates several problem areas which make interpretation of the raw data risky at best.

First, there is the question of how closely reporting statistics mirror the actual incidence of abuse and neglect. The report states: "It can be conclusively stated that these reporting statistics underrepresent the actual incidence of maltreatment on a national basis."[10] States vary in terms of who is mandated to report and in what is mandated to be a reportable condition. Kentucky showed a 432% increase in reports largely because its definition of reportable condition was expanded between 1976 and 1978 to include neglect. To complicate matters even more, there is considerable variation in state-to-state requirements for substantiation.

Another problem is found in the fact that some states list reports by individual children while others list reports by family. This can make one state's reporting statistics look ostensibly lower than another when in fact there may be no difference in the rate. To sum up, then, reporting statistics only can hint at the magnitude of the problem of child abuse and neglect and increases in reporting or differences in rates may suggest broadening of a state's definitions of reportable condition, increased public response, or differences in how cases are counted. These are vague underpinnings for sound national planning.

Second, there is the question of how reliable are the profiles. The profiles were established as a result of examining substantiated reports from a smaller sample of states which voluntarily completed either the study's form or its substituted state form. An analysis prepared by Westat, Inc., and Development Associates, Inc., for the National Center on Child Abuse and Neglect indicates the problems inherent in this approach.

"No doubt some children who were not substantiated by Children's Protective Service and some who were not accepted as in-scope because the data form contained insufficient information had actually experienced problems falling within the study definition."[11] The analysis of Westat also suggests another reason to suspect the sample of substantiated cases. "There is some indication in this study's findings that substantial numbers of reports are being unsubstantiated, not because the report was found to be invalid but because the problem was considered not urgent enough to require immediate attention, given the available staff and programmatic resources."[12]

It is apparent that the sample from which profiles were drawn is influenced by fluid definitions of what constitutes a reportable condition, by inconsistencies in the use of the reporting forms, and by the failure of many states to contribute statistics.

Despite the many ambiguities in the data, the number of substantiated reports is clearly rising dramatically and, at the same time, 15% of this sample of the most serious cases received no intervention. With all its flaws, the national effort to identify the incidence and severity of child abuse and neglect lead to the conclusions that reports are increasing rapidly and that as a nation we are not doing enough to address the problem of child maltreatment.

DEFINITIONS

The "battered-child syndrome," first described by Ambroise Tardier in Paris in 1860 and brought to the stunned attention of the American public in 1961 by C. Henry Kempe at the annual meeting of the American Academy of Pediatrics,[13] is a shibboleth that often stands for all forms of child maltreatment including abuse, neglect, and sexual misuse of children. Physical abuse receives more scholarly and popular attention in part because its effects are often more immediately obvious and severe. It also represents an act that is more easily defined, observed, and indeed, when compared to sexual abuse, discussed.

The statistics reported earlier indicate that physical abuse and neglect do not overlap very frequently. Of 70,717 substantiated reports, only 4470, or 6%, were cases involving both types of reports.[14] This suggests that careful delineation of the various types of child maltreatment is necessary to focus programmatic policy and to direct clinical intervention. An effort will be made here to identify various child maltreatment phenomena as separate entities, although it must be acknowledged that in this author's experience, all of it in Massachusetts, a state which did not contribute data for individual case study, these phenomena are more often than not seen together in families.

The Kempes' book *Child Abuse* describes physical violence this way: "Physical violence implies physically harmful action directed against the child; it is defined by any inflicted injury such as bruises, burns, head injuries, fractures, abdominal injuries or poisoning."[15] Wayne and Avery in their work *Child Abuse: Prevention and Treatment Through Social Group Work* state: "Physical abuse has been defined as any nonaccidental physical injury inflicted on a child by a parent (or other caretaker) deliberately or in anger."[16] Both definitions underscore the theme of intentional activity on the part of the parent or caretaker, as opposed to including acts of omission which may lead to physical harm.

Norman Polansky et al criticize a broader definition by Gil which includes "intentional, nonaccidental acts of omission aimed at hurting, injuring or destroying the child" because "operationally it presents difficulties: how to verify that an act of omission was intentional."[17]

In fact, even the simplest definition of child abuse presents operational problems because victims and perpetrators alike often present confusing and contradictory explanations of injuries. It is seldom clear initially how the injury occurred, who caused it, and whether it was inflicted accidentally or not. In practice, substantiation of reports of physical abuse and all other forms of child maltreatment usually depends on finding a host of patterns in the family's interaction which are associated with these phenomena.

Although there is more popular and scientific discussion and writing in the area of physical abuse, all research efforts indicate that child neglect is a more common and varied problem. Generally the emphasis in definition is on acts of omission. Polansky et al provided the following comprehensive definition: "Child neglect may be defined as a condition in which a caretaker responsible for the child either deliberately or by extraordinary inattentiveness permits the child to experience avoidable present suffering and/or fails to provide one or more of the ingredients generally deemed essential for developing a person's physical, intellectual and emotional capacities."[18]

The definition focuses on failure to act and obviates the need to look for intent. The phrase "ingredients generally deemed essential" is capable of being expanded or contracted to fit varying cultural values and our expanding knowledge of what constitutes the elements of essential child care. Generally counted among these elements are the following: proper food, clothing, shelter, medical care, supervision, education, physical and emotional stimulation, and discipline. The precise quality which each of these elements must show varies too with the particular attributes of the child being considered. For example, supervision required by the mature 12-year-old is of a different order from that needed by the 6- or 2-year-old. Still, as a practical matter, if confronted by a particular child, questions like these arise for reporters and assessors alike: "How do we sort out the effects of poverty?" "How do we recognize the consequences of emotional neglect without reporting every emotionally disturbed child?" "Do communities thoroughly share accepted norms regarding how much supervision children of specific ages require?" In many states (Massachusetts is one) a reporter need only suspect that neglect or abuse has occurred to bring apparent child maltreatment to protective service attention. For assessors, they will rely, as indicated earlier, on those patterns of family dynamics believed to be associated with the incidence of neglect and abuse in order to substantiate reports.

It can be argued that there is a wide continuum of acceptable child-rearing practices which makes identification of physical abuse and neglect extremely complicated. This is true as well of sexual abuse/misuse of children. Rayline A. DeVine describes the problem of definition this way: "It is clear that sexual abuse is not easy to define. Permissible childhood sexual behavior varies in accordance with cultural taboos and family and social tolerances." DeVine proceeds to offer this definition: "Sexual abuse can be defined as contacts or interactions between a child and an adult when the child is being used as an object of gratification for adult sexual needs or desires."[19]

This broad conception suggests that there need not be any physical contact between adult and child to qualify an experience as sexual abuse. Indeed, to acts of fondling and genital contact, should be added acts of exhibitionism, the taking of erotic photographs, and inciting children to be sexually active with each other for an adult's sexual gratification.

Renee S. Brant takes a somewhat different approach to the problem of definition. Brant places the problem of sexual abuse in this context: "Under usual circumstances, the loving caresses of a parent or close relative serve to increase a child's sense of self-esteem and feelings of being pleasing and lovable . . . There are a wide range of family patterns of affectionate interaction possible, ranging from patterns in which children are understimulated to patterns of 'appropriate' stimulation and patterns of overstimulation and inappropriate stimulation." Within this context, Brant prefers to label as sexual misuse "those instances in which the interaction between family members represents an exaggeration of family interactions which approaches the acting out of incestuous fantasies."[20] Brant reserves the term sexual abuse for cases where the child is an "object of an aggressive or sadistic attack which includes forced sexual contact."[21]

Brant's attempt to differentiate between the contexts of sexual abuse / misuse is in part an effort to distinguish which cases should be reported to government agencies, including protective workers and the criminal courts. There are experts in the field who argue strongly for criminal court involvement in all cases of sexual abuse of children.[22] Brant, on the other hand, believes that sexual misuse cases, being treated in a clinical setting knowledgeable about child welfare and guidance issues, are most effectively handled without protective service and/or criminal court involvement.[23]

FRAMEWORKS

Thus far, an attempt has been made to give the reader some sense of the enormity of the problem of child maltreatment in the United States. Definitions of physical abuse, neglect, and sexual abuse have been advanced with the acknowledgment that these definitions are operationally inadequate for assessing reports without a framework for analyzing those factors associated with child maltreatment. The remainder of this paper will discuss those symptoms and behaviors which are commonly believed to be evidence and/or causes of child abuse and neglect. Since reporting trends suggest that the phenomena of physical abuse, neglect, and sexual abuse occur isolated from one another, the discussion will begin with discrete descriptions and examples of each. Finally, the author will argue from her own experience in community-based protective service agencies that assessments more often disclose a variety of forms of child maltreatment occurring together within multiproblem families.

Identification of physical abuse, and all other forms of child maltreatment, depends on the integration of clinical and sociological models which highlight respective stressors in the family's interaction and environment.[24]

Richard Galdston, a psychiatrist, primarily focuses on the clinical factors which predominate in abusive and neglectful families; however, he also argues that environmental stress must be seen as a predisposing factor. He cites projection as the abusive parent's leading defense in managing intrapsychic stress. The parent's negative self-image is projected onto the child, and violence erupts as a result of the parent's inability to translate highly charged affective states into anything but physical activity directed against the child. Often one child in a family of many is the target as a result of that child's correspondence to the abusive parent in terms of age, sex, or position in the family which are unconsciously associated by the parent to earlier events which precipitated the negative self-image. Environmental factors like isolation, poverty, illness, and the lack of positive authority figures (including extended family) may prompt or fail to ameliorate abuse of the child.

Abused children are described as listless, apathetic, and unresponsive. Typically, they flee from interaction with others. In addition to the physical scars they bear, they are marked by an inability to trust anyone or anything in their environment.[25]

If confronted with a physically injured child then, we should look for projection involving the child as the parent's major defense and extreme withdrawal or hypervigilance in the child to make an assessment of child abuse as opposed to accidental injury. Clues about the use of projection are found in parental descriptions which ascribe adult abilities and intentions to the child. The 18-month-old is not seen as developmentally needing to assert his/her independence but as intentionally destroying the house to anger the parent.

Kempe and Kempe describe the withdrawal that is evidenced by the abused child as a need to "make themselves invisible and therefore safe from attack."[26] These children are characterized by their lack of spontaneity and their need to comply with adult demands to avoid anticipated rejection. In some cases, however, children identify so closely with the abusing parent that they themselves become aggressive. This distinction can most often be attributed to the seriousness of abuse and the child's age at onset. Extremely harsh abuse or consistent abuse of very young children will generally result in the child's withdrawal. A child who experienced some positive nurturance in infancy and less serious injury later is posited as the candidate for acting out. Most writers describe the former type because they either come from or are primarily influenced by studies conducted in hospitals where the most serious cases eventually are discovered or treated. Since statistics quoted earlier show that serious physical abuse is relatively uncommon, an example of the latter type is given.

Mother was 22 years old when she was first reported to a protective service agency for alleged abuse of her 4-year-old son. She had been divorced from the child's father since before his birth and said her son was exactly like his father. She described her marriage to this man as a "mistake."

The protective service worker noted bruises on the child's face and arms, and mother explained the injuries as the result of needed parental discipline to end the boy's excessive activity.

School also reported the boy was a behavior problem. During the worker's visits, the child would constantly interrupt his mother. Mother complained that her son continuously sought her attention, that he "spied" on her, and never permitted her "a moment's peace." Mother described an overly sexualized relationship with her father and voiced her worry that others might see incestuous implications in her relationship with her son if she permitted him to get too close. Although this family was totally dependent upon AFDC for support and lived in a community where the cost of living is unusually high, mother kept an immaculate and well-furnished home. The boy's physical care was excellent.

In this example the theme of projection is well illustrated. Mother's own sexual impulses are projected onto her son, and physical punishment serves to exorcise those impulses as well as to (however ineffectively) keep the boy at a safe distance. Mother's ambivalent feelings about closeness result in her son's constant attempts to move closer to prevent an ultimate abandonment.

While signaling projection as the hallmark of abuse, Galdston sees denial as the major defense mechanism in parents who neglect their children. In this case, parents unconsciously deny the existence of their children, who are seen as the embodiments of their negative self-image. They cut themselves off emotionally and/or physically from the child. These parents often express difficulty in naming their children and feel that they are being ignored by their children. When projection is evidenced, as when parents express the belief of being ignored, it is ameliorated by less impulsivity than one sees in abusive parents. Depression results instead of abuse.

Neglected children are marked by their failure to reach the normal weight or height expected for their age. They show a lack of interest in the environment, which is more traditionally a sign of withdrawal than the guarded, silent watchfulness of abused children. These children are unable to form significant object relationships and are often distinguished by their inability to take pleasure in their bodies. Here too, socioeconomic factors are addressed by Galdston as he recognizes that poverty and isolation may prevent other caretakers from assuming the nurturing functions the depressed parent has abandoned.[27]

Focusing on parent and child psychopathology is important in terms of its implication for treatment of child neglect cases. When discussing definitions of child neglect, the parent's intent was purposely left out because the failure to provide certain necessary supports like medical care, proper supervision, etc, can lead to disaster for children whether this failure is due to depression, denial, poverty, or ignorance on the part of the parent. However, in determining whether forms of neglect, like lack of sufficient clothing and poor hygiene, reflect neglect rather than poverty, the foregoing signs of psychopathology offer the best clue.

Again, the example that follows will not be of the grossest type of neglect (eg, failure to thrive) because what one more often sees are children whose chronic poor physical and emotional care have hampered their interactional abilities. These children either demonstrate a pseudomaturity as a result of role reversal in which parents look to them as caretakers, or they act out their parents' anger seemingly without reference to seeking adult attention.

> The Visiting Nurse Association (VNA) filed an allegation of neglect after visiting the N family to check on the progress of the family's 3-year-old son who had been born with congenital respiratory problems. In addition to the parents who are in their late 20s, there are six children including 3-year-old Bobby. Mary is 10, Tommy and Allen are twin 7-year-olds, Diane is 14 months, and Helen is 2 months old.
>
> The VNA noted that the younger children's care was good; however, Mary, Tommy, and Allen were described as "out-of-control." Mary is encopretic, both at home and at school. Her hair is always so tangled that she is constantly demeaned by her peers. Like her brothers, she is inattentive and underachieving at school. Tommy and Allen go from one endangering situation to another: climbing and jumping from high places, riding their bikes in the busy streets in their urban community, tying ropes around each other's necks while playing "hangman."
>
> Father is employed as a machinist. When not working, he is pursuing night classes meant to enhance his job opportunities. Father is rarely at home. Mother, on the other hand, is always at home and is totally absorbed by the infants. She is described as depressed, taking no enjoyment from life except that provided by her babies. She is most depressed when she is not pregnant. Mother provides no supervision of the older children and expresses little more than bewilderment at their problematic behaviors. Father expresses more concern, and the children will comply better to his limit-setting. He does not understand why mother does not control the children better during his frequent, lengthy absences.

The N family demonstrates accurately what one commonly finds in neglecting families. Mother reveals little of her history with her own family of origin, but her inability to handle separation as her children leave infancy and need more autonomy is striking and suggestive of separation anxiety which must have roots in the past. She married a man who is chronically unavailable to her and toward whom she never expresses anger. The anger around the issue of separation is denied, internalized, and depression results. Like the abusive mother in the earlier example, this mother, too, uses distance to protect her children from her feared impulses; however, she accomplishes this by withdrawal rather than physically pushing her children away. The children cannot engage their parents directly as the boy in the abuse example did. Their acting out is an expression of mother's anger and, while surely motivated to capture attention, appears to be unrelated to an interactional context.

Sexual abuse, particularly incest, as a subject of child welfare or protective service concern, has received less attention than either physical abuse or neglect. Galdston does not specifically address the issue in the article used as a reference here. However, it is attracting more interested researchers as the social climate has thawed from its embarrassed indifference to the problem. The focus here will be on sexual misuse or incest, in part because it is reportedly more common and in part because sexual assault by strangers is, in this author's view, a better subject of investigation for law enforcement agencies. Since father–daughter incest is the most commonly reported and frequently studied form,[28] the focus on incest will be further narrowed to that sphere.

There are few writers who analyze incest outside the context of the interrelationships among all family members. Father–daughter incest is commonly seen as a symptom of dysfunction in the marital relationship. Groth writes, "In assessing those family interrelationships in which father–child incest developed, we found the marital relationship between husband and wife to be characterized by dependent attachments on the part of one or both parents . . . unspoken expectations (are) met with frustration, and immature needs sabotaged the marital relationship."[29] Groth goes on to develop the familiar theme of father seeking maternal support from his wife whose frustration, at his inability to be the strong independent partner she thinks she meant to marry, turns to contempt and increasing indifference. Daughter steps into mother's role. First she may assume the housekeeping chores, eventually she assumes mother's abandoned sexual role as well. The family's problem is often discovered by the community as the daughter attempts to withdraw from her father's increasing dependence upon her. Often this cycle will begin as a result of environmental stress. Fathers who suffer a threat to self-esteem (loss of a job, for example) and who are unable to obtain needed support through the crisis from their wives will be at risk for incest, particularly if there is a parentified child already in place. Another frequent component in incest is the father's rigid bonding to the family as the source of all need gratification. He is unable to satisfy needs for dependency and sex outside the boundaries of the family.

There are a host of symptoms associated with children who have experienced incest. The severity of pathology will depend on variables like type of sexual activity, age at onset, type of coercion employed by abuser, and the reaction of the community when the incest is discovered. Symptoms of distress linked to sexual abuse include isolation from peer relationships, overly seductive behavior, disturbance of sexual identity, and pseudomaturity which breaks down under stress revealing more childlike coping mechanisms.[30]

> The T family was reported to protective services for alleged sexual abuse as a result of their 19-year-old daughter's expression of concern to her therapist. Elaine was convinced that her 13-year-old sister Terry was being misused sexually by their father who reportedly engaged in sexual intercourse with Elaine until she left home a year earlier. Elaine stated that her mother, a nurse who worked the night shift at a nursing home, refused to credit her story and blamed Elaine for being a "troublemaker."
> Father had a very unstable work history which appeared to be related to a growing drinking problem. Elaine had dropped out of school, was finding it impossible to settle on a career, and sought counseling around her failure to have satisfying sexual relationships with men.
> Terry was reportedly a quiet, shy girl at school who made frequent visits to the nurse's office with vague complaints of stomach upset. She engaged in little peer interaction at school, rushing home to perform the household chores including preparing father's dinner.

This example illustrates the points made earlier and suggests some others which should be added. Often mother's unavailability is both physical and emotional. She is as unavailable to her child as she is to her husband. She is unable to nurture either one, a fact that can lead daughters to respond to father's sexual attention as the only source of warmth. Another point which needs underscoring is that incest does not necessarily cease when the involved daughter leaves home. Frequently, a younger female child will take her place.

In reviewing some of the literature on child neglect and abuse and in attempting to identify cases with which the author has first-hand knowledge to illustrate the literature's major themes, it was striking to see how the typical community-based protective service family fails to conform to the literature's expectations. (This view reflects this author's experience, and while confirmed in discussions with other community workers, it remains to be verified by more rigorous scientific inquiry).

Statistics given earlier indicate that severe physical injury and neglect are relatively rare; nonetheless most of the literature is based on cases discovered and/or treated in hospitals. Pediatricians have taken the lead in analyzing child maltreatment, particularly as it affects infants who are extraordinarily sensitive to their parents' failures as caregivers. Given the infants' extreme vulnerability, society cannot be too vigilant about addressing parental difficulties in providing adequate care; however, concentration on the severe manifestations in this area has distracted society's attention from the chronic, less dramatic inadequacies of parents of older children which are more commonly treated by protective service agencies.

As noted earlier, the literature also suggests a dichotomy between abuse and neglect which, in less severe forms, rarely exists. This is not to suggest that teasing out the variables which are associated with specific forms of maltreatment is useless. What needs to be added is the broader context of the multiproblem family where abuse, neglect, and sexual misuse can occur concurrently with many other forms of social dysfunctioning.

Minuchin et al, in *Families of the Slums,* provide an effective framework for comprehending the family that is most often reported to protective service agencies. They describe the "impermanence and unpredictability" that distinguish these families as follows: "In home visits we encountered a world in which objects and events have a transient quality . . . a bed shared by two or more children can be turned over to a different child or to a semi-permanent visitor while its original occupants are crowded into a section of another bed. The geography of the home and its arrangements impede the development of a sense that 'I have my place in the world.' Meals have no set time, order, or place. A mother who prepares four individual and different dinners one day, according to the wishes of the children, will prepare nothing another day . . ."[31]

Unpredictability is also described as a strong feature of the interpersonal contacts within these families. Executive functions are not clearly assigned, so child care is a responsibility which shifts constantly back and forth from parent to grandparent to older child. A child may receive enormous amounts of attention one day and be permitted to wander the streets alone the next. Limit-setting is not consistent and depends on family members' moods which may or may not tolerate specific behaviors at a given point in time.[32]

The lack of consistency in a family's structure results in an absence of internalized rules. Minuchin et al note that rules must be "continuously stated only in terms of *immediate interpersonal control.*" This requires family members to reference their behavior to each other's shifting moods, which in turn leaves no room for individual autonomy.

Noncompliance to a parent's mood is seen as an insult, not as a violation of society's norms. By the same token, violation of society's rules outside the sphere of family interaction is not seen by parents as their responsibility because "they were not there."[33]

In families where roles are not clearly defined, boundaries between members are fluid, and where the events of everyday life are totally unpredictable, all forms of child maltreatment are possible. For example:

The R family was brought to the attention of a protective service agency as a result of a school nurse's report that the family's 6-year-old daughter had twice been seen with cuts on her face and that the second cut required medical attention which mother failed to secure. The report did not clearly indicate whether abuse or neglect was the chief worry.

Assessment revealed a mother in her mid-20s who for many months hid her alcoholism from the worker. It was also many months before it became apparent that mother's boyfriend resided off and on in the apartment and that he abused her and the children.

Tanya, the 6-year-old girl, was reportedly doing very poorly in first grade, and she was required to repeat that grade the next year. The school reported that Tanya was often tardy and fell asleep at her desk.

Sometimes she was extremely well dressed, other days she appeared very untidy. Tanya often took care of her 3-year-old brother, Michael, and in fact was said to be the only one with whom he interacted positively.

In addition to mother's boyfriend, other sometime residents in mother's sprawling, usually unkempt apartment were mother's two alcoholic younger brothers and occasionally their girlfriends. These adolescent boys were sometimes used as babysitters. Mother supported this household with AFDC; occasional work as a homemaker, maid, or waitress; and her boyfriend's infrequent contributions from his drug sales.

Mother's relationship with her mother was variously described as very positive, depicting maternal grandmother as someone who was readily available to offer support, and as thoroughly unhappy, with maternal grandmother viewed as an alcoholic herself who frustrated mother's wish to make a different life for herself. For a time, maternal grandmother took over her grandchildren's care by moving into her daughter's apartment while daughter lived in a rooming house close by.

This household, with its changing cast of characters who constantly interchange roles and responsibilities, is typical of the multiproblem families that Minuchin describes and that protective service agencies try to engage and treat.

These children are subjected to lack of appropriate supervision, harsh discipline by parents and substitute caregivers, medical neglect, and physical care which vacillates between being lavish and thoroughly inadequate.

They are extremely vulnerable to sexual misuse by the males who move in and out of the household. While rarely at risk of serious physical injury, they are at grave risk for school failure, delinquency, drug addiction, premature sex, early pregnancies, and a repetition of this cycle with their own children.

This style of family interaction is not offered as the only statistically significant model that protective service agencies encounter. Although disguised, the examples given of families which demonstrate isolated phenomena of abuse or neglect do exist. The potential reporter must be alert to a wide range of patterns, and the worker must be able to analyze psychological, sociological, and structural factors to plan interventions which will enable families to safeguard their children.

REFERENCES

1. US Department of Health and Human Services (DHHS), Office of Human Development Services, Administration for Children, Youth and Families, Children's Bureau, National Center on Child Abuse and Neglect: *National Analysis of Official Child Neglect and Abuse Reporting (1978),* Washington, D.C., 1978, p 3.
2. DHHS: p 6.
3. DHHS: pp 18–20.
4. DHHS: p 21.
5. DHHS: pp 26–33.
6. DHHS: p 37.
7. DHHS: p 29.
8. DHHS: p 34.
9. DHHS: p 55.
10. DHHS: p 4.
11. Burgdorf K: *Recognition and Reporting of Child Maltreatment: Summary Findings From the National Study of the Incidence and Severity of Child Abuse and Neglect.* Draft prepared for National Center on Child Abuse and Neglect, Children's Bureau, US Department of Health and Human Services, by Westat, Inc., of Rockville, Maryland, in affiliation with Development Associates, Inc., of Arlington, Virginia, October 14, 1980, p 7–12.
12. Burgdorf K: *Recognition and Reporting of Child Maltreatment,* p 7–12.
13. Kempe RS, Kempe CH: Child abuse, in Bruner J, Cole M, Lloyd B (eds): *The Developing Child.* Cambridge, Harvard University Press, 1978, pp 5–6.
14. DHHS: p 30.
15. Kempe RS, Kempe CH: Child abuse, p 6.
16. Wayne JL, Avery NC: *Child Abuse: Prevention and Treatment Through Social Group Work.* Boston, Charles River Books, 1980, p 8.
17. Polansky NA, Hally C, Polansky NF: Definition of neglect, reprinted in *Selected Readings on Child Neglect,* US Department of Health, Education and Welfare, Office of Human Development and Services, Administration for Children, Youth and Families, National Center on Child Abuse and Neglect, DHEW publication (OHDS) 80-30253, January 1980, p 1.
18. Polansky NA, et al: Definition of neglect, p 3.
19. DeVine R: Sexual abuse of children: An overview of the problem, in *Sexual Abuse of Children,* US Department of Health and Human Services, Office of Human Development Services, Administration for Children, Youth and Families, Children's Bureau, National Center on Child Abuse and Neglect, DHHS publication (OHDS) 78-30161, November 1980, p 3.
20. Brant RS: Manual on Sexual Abuse and Misuse of Children, uncopyrighted publication of New England Resource Center for Protective Services, Boston, Massachusetts, p 1.
21. Brant RS: Manual on Sexual Abuse, p 2.
22. Burgess AW, Groth AN, Holmstrom LL, et al (eds): *Sexual Assault of Children and Adolescents,* Lexington, Lexington Books, 1978.
23. Brant RS: Manual on Sexual Abuse, p 2.
24. Wayne JL, Avery NC: *Child Abuse,* p 9.
25. Galdston R: Dysfunctions of parenting: The battered child, the neglected child, the exploited child, in Howells JG (ed): *Modern Perspectives and International Child Psychiatry.* Edinburgh, Oliver and Reid, 1968, pp 571–574.

26. Kempe RS, Kempe CH: Child abuse, p 32.
27. Galdston R: Dysfunctions of parenting, pp 575–579.
28. DeVine R: Sexual abuse of children, p 26.
29. Groth NA, Patterns of sexual assault against children and adolescents in Burgess AW, et al, p 19.
30. Brant RS: Manual on Sexual Abuse, p 5.
31. Minuchin S, Montvalvo B, Guerney B, et al: *Families of the Slums.* New York, Basic Books, 1967, pp 193–194.
32. Minuchin S, et al: *Families of the Slums,* p 194.
33. Minuchin S, et al: *Families of the Slums,* pp 211–214.

PART II
Diagnosis and Treatment (with Case Studies)

3 The Professional Use of the Self: Transference and Countertransference

Irving Kaufman

The focus of this chapter will be on the use of the self. This includes an understanding of the transference and countertransference patterns in the client and the therapist. In addition, there will be a discussion of the associated identity issues in both the client and the therapist which result from the transference–countertransference interaction.

A particularly interesting discussion of the identity issues involved in the development of an abused child's personality was presented by Dr. Shengold[1] in his article "Child Abuse and Deprivation: Soul Murder." Dr. Shengold presented the concept that the abused child "is robbed of his identity and the ability to maintain authentic feelings." He also discusses some of the paradoxical identities these children may assume in order to survive, and these can include the development of unusual strengths and gifts. In my own experience the most frequent and also most paradoxical identity personification seen in the abused child is the precociously mature child who takes on the role of parenting the parent. Sometimes this supermature identity will collapse when the child is placed in a setting where he receives nurturance and care. The child at this juncture may then regress and become particularly infantile and hence elicit a different countertransference response, resulting in the necessary use of the appropriate treatment procedure.

The process of treatment is further complicated by the countertransference reaction of the other people in the facilities working with the abused and neglected child and his parents. For example, Hill,[2] in her discussion of the emotional reaction to child abuse within a hospital setting, pointed out the complicated feelings, reactions, and intervention involving hospital staff, protective case workers, court staff, etc, in their responses to the parents of the abused child and in the case management of the child.

Child protective services deal with cases of neglect, abuse, pedophilia, exhibitionism, and incest. Frequently all these forms of mistreatment of children are lumped together. The personality structures of the adults who mistreat children in these different ways can be very different, elicit extremely different responses from the therapist and, as a result, require different treatment, management techniques, and approaches.

In addition, the clients during the course of their treatment may undergo extreme changes in their personality and patterns of behavior. This has a major impact on the therapist's feelings and reactions to the client. This concept was described by Flanzraich and Steiner,[3] who delineated three phases in their treatment of abused children. First, there is a depressive phase where the child is lethargic, dull, fearful, and has difficulty communicating. The second phase is characterized by impulsivity, negativism, and narcissism. In the third phase the negativistic behavior subsides, and there is "aggressiveness, competitiveness, and controlling, power-oriented behavior." It has been my experience in working with children like this that the countertransference reaction in phase one, where the child is fearful and needs help to come out of his shell, is characterized by nurturance and encouragement to be more self-expressive. In phases two and three, where the child becomes aggressive, narcissistic, and in some ways obnoxious in his seeking of power and control, the therapist will often feel rejected, repelled, and frustrated. This occurs at a time when the child particularly needs help in dealing with these new feelings and identity posture. The therapist particularly needs a supportive network within his setting to help him with his feelings to enable him to maximally use his self which is now not viewed as nurturing but in an oppositional identity. The needs of the therapist to cope with his own feelings will be discussed further.

The major therapeutic instrument in the treatment of the abusing family derives from the relationship between the therapist and the client. In contrast to classical or psychoanalytically oriented psychotherapy, protective casework is much more active. This includes reaching out and giving to the client, rather than always waiting and expecting the client to come to the therapist. This technique of actively using the self requires an appropriate assertiveness, considerable self-confidence, and a strong belief in the validity of the process. In addition, it is necessary to define the developmental level of the client and gear the treatment process accordingly. Many of the clients will be relatively infantile, desperately needing parenting themselves, and overwhelmed by the task of being a parent and a spouse. There are two questions inherent in this conceptualization, "Who am I to the client?" and "Who is the client?" These identity issues will be discussed throughout this chapter.

There are several basic concepts relevant to the use of the self that are necessary to consider. The first is the concept of transference and countertransference. When Freud[4] started treating patients, he discovered that they reacted to him in their idiosyncratic fashion which had no or little reality base. He soon realized that the patients were reacting to him the way they reacted to the important people in their past. He termed this pattern of response in his patients "transference." His own feelings toward the patient, reactions of liking, disliking, etc, he termed "countertransference." The understanding and analysis of the transference and countertransference process and its content became one of the keystones of psychoanalysis. It is based on a concept that long predates psychoanalysis: people react according to the way they were brought up. Another related conceptualization is the idea that people take into themselves the mental images of the important people in their lives and, along with the myriad experiences, they have developed an identity which is in relation to their experiences and their introjects. The identity could be an identification or imitation of their parents, for example, or it could be a more complicated result of this reaction to their parents. For example, we frequently find that parents who neglect their children are often dependent and infantile. Some of the children take on a dependent, infantile identity. Others get pushed into a prematurely mature role and, at a remarkably early age, assume some of the parenting of their parents and siblings. The therapist needs to understand the personality of the client. In contrast to psychoanalysis, restitution of adequate parenting is more relevant as a treatment technique than an analysis of the origins of the client's current functioning. Studying the transference as well as observing the patterns of the client's daily life gives the information needed to understand the client's identity and then to gear the treatment approach accordingly. It is necessary with infantile, dependent parents to provide a restitutional experience which gives parenting to the parent and to continue this process long enough so that regression back to the original pathologic pattern does not occur. It is extremely difficult to evaluate how long this should continue. Many factors enter into such a decision, such as pressure on agencies often without sufficient staff to render service, administrative policy which attempts to maximize the cost efficiency of services, etc.

Kaufman[5] discusses the various pressures on the therapist to take action. This can stimulate considerable anxiety in the worker and may result in premature placement and not allow for the necessary resolution of the parent–child problem. The therapist's anxiety can cloud his ability to evaluate the degree of pathology and danger to the child. Sometimes the parent is acting out through the child, and the request is a cry for help on the part of the parent. Frequently referrals to a protective agency come from parents. So it is necessary to handle the anxiety around and stimulated by the referring source in order to be able to evaluate what the treatment request is and how best to deliver the appropriate service.

Another issue discussed in this article is the concept that going to the home, discussing the budget, or arranging a trip to the doctor's office is not dynamic and places the therapist in a lower professional status. "This kind of self-demeaning feeling has to be dealt with if the client is going to get the help he needs." To quote the article, "I do not know if it is possible to emphasize enough that for orally fixated acting out depressed patients of the type described here, the therapy has to be geared through communication which is meaningful to the patient." In other words, this type of therapy is not a negative reflection on the therapist but just the opposite. It is essential to view it as based on an understanding of the developmental level of the client and relating to the client in a way which he can comprehend.

This article pointed out that work with the children places the therapist in a very difficult position which can also be anxiety-provoking for the therapist. The therapist has to deal with problems in the family as well as the community's reaction to the family and their children. The family is seen as the undesirable "dirty" element. The therapist then has to cope with his own hostility, anxiety, and sense of frustration as well as the anger of the community demanding that something be done about these "undesirable" people and their "undesirable" children. This requires considerable forbearance, tact, and coolness on the part of the therapist.

The task of dealing with all these forces falls upon the therapist, who has to confront the parents and the child with the problems they are experiencing and incurring, as well as to develop a therapeutic relationship. A straightforward reality-oriented approach can be the only stability in an extremely chaotic situation. All this is extremely taxing to the therapist and requires maximal support to be able to carry it off.

Another factor in the countertransference feelings of the worker toward the client who improves with treatment and begins to function in a relatively adequate way at this juncture is that the therapist may feel useless and not needed and hence does not realize how necessary continued support is as a maintenance process. This often leads to cases being seen for a while and then closed, only to require further services over the years when the patient regresses.

The following illustrates an example of this process. The client was a 32-year-old woman with four children all under the age of 12. An investigation of the report of neglect led to the discovery of a horrendous home situation. The children were dirty and inadequately clothed and fed. There were newspapers all over the floor. Dried oatmeal was in a pot on the stove, and the mother was drunk in bed with many empty liquor bottles strewn about. The children were noisy, dirty, and difficult to manage. Their health care and school attendance were sporadic. A care and protection petition was brought before the court. Through court order the mother was helped with the realities of daily living including shopping, cleaning the apartment, and caring for herself and the children. With the help and influence of the court probation officer and the caseworker, the mother rapidly improved. The children were fed, got medical care, supervision, and attended school. The apartment was cleaned up. By the time she began putting up curtains, the case was closed. Within a few months the mother regressed back to her original pathologic style. The probation officer and the caseworker had both felt they had accomplished their objectives. The inability to see that such severe pathology requires long-term contact was affected by their countertransference feelings. All therapists need some gratification and feedback to feel that what they are doing has some usefulness and meaning. This is a major factor in determining whether the therapist's countertransference feelings are positive or negative. Because of the forces of a taxing and heavy case load, agency pressure, and a feeling that the case was no longer rewarding or progressing, it was closed. The transference feelings of the client can be presumed to be negative, and this creates or perpetuates an associated identity issue where she is struggling between being a child and an adult. If we assume that the mother was herself in great need of attention and mothering and that she felt that her only way to receive it was to regress, be inadequate, and alcoholic, then she gained the care and attention by being a neglecting parent. This is exactly the opposite of what the community is attempting to accomplish, but because of the complicated transference–countertransference and identity issues, the wrong kind of conditioning resulted.

Serrano et al,[6] discussing this same issue stated, "Most abusing families are long-term frustrating cases which are often a countertransference challenge. Even experienced clinicians struggle between not fostering excessive dependence or not precipitating premature termination after some initial improvement in their attempt not to act out their impatience and frustration in response to family resistance." Serrano et al concluded that the treatment was affected by this countertransference reaction and said, "Due to limited ability of abusive families to use intervention and external resources, it is more effective to intervene through the social system to mobilize an extensive family-rehabilitative network." He did say that the therapeutic team did provide direct therapeutic intervention but needed an external network to maximize their effectiveness. This article illustrates the tremendous influence of the countertransference feelings, and he gives some very important ways to help the therapist and the client. There are other additional ways to help which will be discussed.

There is another conceptual framework which can be used in considering the kinds of cases seen in protective casework. These are all cases where there is a breakdown in a major life function—the parent-child relationship. Kaufman,[7] using a psychoanalytic model, states that the abuse, neglect, or sexual molestation of the child can be viewed as a breakthrough of id impulses. The community sets up the standards by which this behavior is evaluated and the social and legal system to judge and enforce these standards. In this way the community functions like a superego. The caseworker has the task of evaluating the case, making the reality appraisal of the family, and determining whether any action is required. In this way the caseworker can be viewed as the ego in this system. The effectiveness of any treatment depends on a caseworker who can make a realistic appraisal and not have it distorted by the transference and countertransference feelings. Nancy Ebeling[8] described some of the transference and countertransference reactions and their effect on the treatment process.

Feelings of horror at the sight of children burned, bruised, and possibly mistreated can affect the worker's judgment and make it more difficult to carry out the necessary therapeutic intervention. Not being aware of the meaning of the client's behavior in light of the client's past life experience may lead the therapist to take actions which the client views as negative. The example given was a case where the client asked the therapist to see her neighbor. When the therapist did, the client became negative. It was only later that it was learned that the client was reliving her feelings that her foster sister was preferred to her. Joanne Lipner[9] discussed her experiences working with abusing families and described how the anxiety she felt about the parents abusing the child led to a series of complications. These included the family's hostility to the limit-setting. Despite the development of a beginning trusting relationship, the parents had to again reject the therapist because they needed to reenact the closeness-distancing process. With continued contact, the family could test out the trust, and the case was able to move successfully when the trust extended to greater inclusion of the collaborating professionals. This illustrated how the transference and countertransference feelings directly affected the work with the family and the relationship to other involved professionals.

Paul D'Agostino[10] discusses other factors involved in the relationship between the abusing family and the therapist. He points out that there are cases often requiring immediate drastic action. This can result in taking measures to protect the child without having the opportunity to develop a therapeutic relationship with the family. He also pointed out that there are intrapersonal strains which the therapist feels within himself and interpersonal stresses between the therapist and the families and the other involved community agencies. The families may have a multitude of relations and problems in their work, court involvement, welfare agencies, etc. Unless there is some integration and communication, the various participants may work at cross-purposes and be played off against each other. In addition, clients bring into the therapy with the protective caseworker the feelings they have about previous experiences with social agencies. It is important to know about these because they could explain some of the negative reactions that are frequently encountered.

As was discussed earlier, the clients are not all the same. This discussion deals only with those clients whose neglect, abuse, etc, is based on psychological factors rather than mental retardation or physical illness such as temporal lobe epilepsy. Physical problems should be ruled out if there is any question of their relevance. Developmentally, not all the clients have reached the oedipal level and hence fall into two major categories. Galdston[11] and Kaufman[12] see abusing parents as suffering from a form of psychosis. Some parents who commit incest are also psychotic. I believe they have a schizophrenic core. The other, larger subcategory of clients who primarily neglect their children or who get involved in incestuous relationships are those with impulse-ridden character disorders. The clients in this very large group seen by protective agencies are suffering from an underlying depression. The kinds of difficulties they encounter in their lives and some of the treatment implications were discussed by Kaufman in "Persons Who Cannot Manage Their Lives."[13] There are people who cannot manage work, marriage, or child-rearing. None of the people in this group were psychoneurotic. They had not reached that level of development. These clients were either schizophrenic or depressive personalities using acting out to avoid facing their depression. Treatment of these people involves an active reaching out process and much of it is nonverbal. One of the countertransference issues this raises has to do with the feeling about imposing one's self on the client. The answer to the question of whether to take an authoritarian position is relatively easy if a child's life is in danger. However, if there is damage being done to a child or to a client, one does not have a right not to impose therapy. This is based on the assumption that the client's ego is so defective that it would be equivalent to allowing a 3-year-old to play with razor blades if one ignored the distress signals coming from the client. In order to feel that there is legitimacy to this approach, it is necessary to make certain that the evaluation of the ego defect and the danger is accurate. These clients may reject the therapist. Usually this is because the client's life experiences were those of rejection. So in a protective case it is necessary to see the client's behavior as a reenactment of the client's own experiences. In the long run the client will acknowledge his positive feelings at not having been able to do this rejection.

In one case there was a home investigation of reported neglect. When the caseworker got there, the mother was ironing, the TV was blasting, and the children were running around with soiled diapers. The house was cluttered and dirty, and a neighbor was there gossiping about the various romances in which they and their friends were currently involved. Attempts to engage this woman in a conversation were extremely difficult. However, by offering practical help with finances, health, school problems, the client began to respond. The importance of the therapist became evident when there was a missed appointment because of the therapist's illness. This illustrates how important it is not to take the behavior of the client at face value. It takes a great deal of determination and a thick hide to tolerate being ignored and treated as though the client wished you would leave. Countertransference feelings are often expressed by labeling these clients as "hard to reach," "multiproblem," etc. Another difficulty confronting the therapist is the fact that these clients are more action oriented than verbal, and they do not see cause and effect sequences. As a result, they behave impulsively and continue to get into the same jams without realizing that they are acting in ways that ensure the continuation and repetition of these problems. They act as though they are being persecuted because people expect them to pay their bills. All of this can be very discouraging to the therapist who comes from a background that includes logic, planning, and recognizing the consequences of his own actions. This communication gap produces a sense of alienation both for the client and the therapist. It is necessary to understand how the client functions and not be judgmental, but try to give the client the kinds of restitutional experiences that give them object constancy, a feeling of trust, and help them in their ego and superego growth.

Polansky et al[14] in their monograph on child neglect also describe the two kinds of personalities characterizing the parents who neglect and abuse their children. They also include a very interesting maternal characteristics scale, which could be an aid in diagnosis, and acknowledge that diagnosis is difficult.

The reason diagnosis has value is that it determines the treatment techniques and involves very different transference and countertransference issues. The following is a discussion of transference and countertransference in the (depressive) impulse-ridden character disorder and the schizophrenic patients who make up the majority of the cases seen in protective casework. This material is partly drawn from a paper presented by Kaufman [15] at a Simmons colloquium in 1980 and expanded by focusing on neglecting and abusing parents.

The expression of the transference depends on the developmental level, nature of the anxiety, object relations, and the structure of the ego. This composite of characteristics describes the various syndromes such as schizophrenia, depression, and psychoneurosis. In my experience none of the abusing, sexually molesting, or deserting-neglecting parents had reached the developmental level characteristic of the psychoneuroses. The people working in this field do not all agree with this conceptualization and believe that these types of parents fall into all diagnostic categories.

However, I will limit my discussion to the schizophrenic and depressed groups of patients. Schizophrenic patients are at the oral level of development, their object relations are symbiotic–monadic, and their anxiety is a fear of annihilation, destruction, or engulfment. Their ego mechanisms of defense are those characteristic of schizophrenia: isolation, denial of reality (eg, not being able to see their child as a child but as an adult who is supposed to take care of them and hating the child for not doing so), projection (particularly of their rage at not having received the care and nurturance they need and viewing the child as a destructive monster), and distorted thinking in their attitude toward the child (mother and father protecting each other rather than the child). Although at times they will momentarily interfere with the immediate abuse, in the long run they tend to support each other against the child and deny that they inflicted the injuries. There is a disturbance in superego development. They feel that their aggressive acts against the child are fully justified, and they give remarkably distorted rationalizations to justify it.

The parents exhibit the core problem found in schizophrenics — the wish for closeness and the fear that this closeness will result in destruction. One way to handle such fears is to become the aggressor and do the attacking.

For example, one mother described her reaction to her crying 2-year-old as a feeling that she would be eaten up. The child was demanding and defiant. No one cared about her or met her needs. Enraged by this situation she got up and pounded the child mercilessly with her fists. A marine sergeant described similar reactions to the crying of his 6-month-old son and kicked him in the genitals, screaming, "No brat will push me around."

Another mother placed her little child in the high chair and put the food in front of him. As children do, he dropped some of it on the newly washed floor. The mother described a feeling that she would fall apart, that her whole world was crumbling. She could not stand the anxiety. She picked the child up, flung him against the wall, and jumped on him when he hit the floor.

These are all parents who are struggling with their enormous wishes for parenting themselves and invest the child with great power to either give or withhold that love. Withholding or demanding parenting on the part of the child threatens the ego of the parent, who feels he will be swallowed up, engulfed, or destroyed. The reaction of attacking the child is viewed as life-saving for the parent. The parent is flooded by massive rage and then assaults the child.

This is the complex personality with which one has to deal when trying to treat the abusing parent. The transference reaction is one of wanting someone to understand the parents. Excessive sympathy and concern for the child is viewed as not caring by the parent. The therapist has to decide the degree of danger involved in leaving the child in the home. If the treatment does not involve removal of the child, then the work with parents involves establishing a relationship in the context of the above-described dynamic pattern and the associated transference reactions.

The countertransference feelings include horror at what the parents did or are doing to the child. For example, one case brought in for consultation involved a parent who was allegedly abusing her child. When the caseworker made a home visit and it was clear that immediate placement was necessary, the mother brought out her camera and said she wanted to take some pictures. The caseworker agreed. The mother undressed the child and then photographed the area on his body where she had produced wounds and scars by holding the child and putting a lit cigarette to these areas. The caseworker was horrified, bewildered, and almost paralyzed by such bizarre behavior. When the caseworker spontaneously expressed these feelings, the mother became enraged. If she had not been accompanied by the police, the caseworker would have correctly feared for her safety or her life.

Although extremely difficult, unless the need and helplessness of the parents can be seen, it is not possible to work with them. This does not mean that one condones the abusive behavior, but it does mean that if it is safe to leave the child in the home then the caseworker has to overcome the horror and anger at the parents.

These abusing families often are socially isolated, lack a network of community and social resources, and are suspicious of the interest of anyone working with them. These feelings also produce a reaction in the therapist. The need of the parents to shut out interaction with others because they are afraid of getting close also occurs in the treatment relationship. This feeling of being rejected, excluded, and having an iron curtain slam down is extremely frustrating to the therapist and can lead to wishes to take premature action to place the child, withdraw from the case and transfer it elsewhere, or retaliate. The important thing is to recognize these feelings and not act on them.

Conscious or unconscious awareness of the rage which is just below the surface in these parents is very frightening to the therapist. If this fear goes beyond a certain point, it creates more anxiety in the parents because it confirms their views that the world is a dangerous and destructive place. In some instances the therapist's fears are fully justified, and there are instances where therapists have been attacked, knifed, or thrown down stairs. However, if there is a sense that the aggression of the parent is relatively under control and the parents are amenable to treatment, then, to the extent that one can, it is important not to come across to these parents as afraid of them. This also means that not everyone should be working with this type of parent. Either extreme, a therapist who is excessively fearful or one who uses denial to the point of exposing himself to real danger, is no help to abusing parents.

Another somewhat paradoxical factor in cases of abusing parents is the fact that many of these parents can present an external appearance of relative normality interspersed with episodic outbursts of abusive rage. In many instances there is an intact family, a working father, and a mother who is a meticulous housekeeper. The child is fed, clothed, and receives adequate medical care. This apparent normality is disrupted by episodic outbursts. If the parents are seen in their relatively normal intervals then the therapist, not wanting to believe that the parents are a real danger to the child, may not offer adequate protection. Part of the countertransference of the therapist and often of the court officials is a need to view mother and father as "good" people and not want to see the pathology. One such case was that of a family where the child was brought to the hospital because he was in a coma. X-rays revealed a subdural hematoma and several old healed fractures of the extremities. The parents denied abusing the child even though the case had been referred by a neighbor who heard the child's frightened screams and saw the bruises on him. The parents said there was something wrong with the child and that he had a tendency to fall all the time. When the child recovered from the subdural hematoma and seemed well, there was the issue of placement. The case was brought to court and two well-dressed, coherent parents presented themselves. The father was steadily employed and earned a good living. The home was immaculate, and the mother described how she had given the child excellent care and how she always took care of his physical needs, including bringing him into the hospital as soon as the coma was detected. When asked if they ever struck the child, the parents answered by saying, "Doesn't everyone lose their temper once in a while?" The need to believe in the sacredness of motherhood, and the tendency to consider parental rights above those of children almost led the court to rule against placement. Fortunately, the judge had had considerable experience, including observing the deaths of several children who had been returned to such homes. The case was further strengthened by the therapist who, after overcoming feelings very much like those of the judges, carefully documented the facts by getting information from the school, where they reported the child coming to class with evident bruises on his body, and from neighbors and the medical evidence that the fractures were in all probability the result of assault upon the child and not caused by falls.

Another component of the countertransference feelings in cases like the above is the empathy with the healthy part of the parents who sincerely want to do the right thing by their child and give him the kind of parenting the child needs. In some ways the abusive episodes are dystonic to this healthier part of the parents, so that when they deny, rationalize, or distort the abuse they can be more convincing than one would anticipate.

The parents may, in part, identify with the abused child, which is why it is often the parent who will be the one to ask for help. In one such case the mother phoned the protective agency saying she had her child tied up in the basement and wanted someone to come over before she killed the child. This mother was a survivor in a family where her parents, siblings, and relatives had been killed because of racial persecution. She exhibited a mixture of feelings which included rage at the people who murdered her family, thus depriving her of the care and nurturance she needed. She also felt guilt because she was alive and they were dead. In addition, she identified with the aggressor as an attempt to cope with her feelings of helplessness and the need to view her child as the depriving parent. Then, like the persecutor, she directed her rage at the child, at the same time acting out the wish that someone had saved her family from murder by calling the agency for help.

The countertransference reactions to such a complex situation are often a mixture of anxiety, concern for the safety of the child, and compassion for the plight of the parent once the feelings of horror and fright are overcome. All of these feelings can complicate the important decision as to what is in the best interests of the child. Is placement indicated, or is this a case where treatment will be effective soon enough so that the parent–child interaction can be removed from the destructive experiences of the mother, or is the child in danger?

The above are some illustrations of the issues and the resulting transference and countertransference reactions encountered in working with the abusing parent whom I and others in the field view as exhibiting a form of schizophrenia which can be episodic in its manifestations.

The other numerically larger group of parents seen in protective therapy is made up of those who are grappling with depression. These parents are referred because they neglect their children. The depression is usually manifested by an impulse-ridden character disorder. These are people who have suffered the traumas of loss of parenting themselves but who do not have a sufficiently developed ego to overcome the depression by mourning and doing the necessary grieving to resolve this. The feel-ings of hurt over the loss become encapsulated, and because there is not sufficient ego development to face the pain of the loss, these people act out. Their acting out can take the form of antisocial behavior, stealing, promiscuity, vandalism, or reenacting the loss by deserting or abandon-ing their own children. Repetition compulsion and identification with the aggressor are two of the major ego defenses utilized to try to cope with their own losses in this maladaptive way.

The core anxiety in this disorder is fear of loss or abandonment. The object relations are dyadic, where people are viewed as need providers or need deprivers. The developmental level is a mixture of oral and anal traits. They have not reached the oedipal level of development. The ego mechanisms of defense are isolation, denial, projection, identification with the aggressor, and repetition compulsion. The superego is under-developed, operating at the shame rather than the guilt level. One of the objectives of treatment is to further the development of the superego. This complex of personality characteristics also produces the trans-ference reactions in these clients.

The following typical case illustrates the personality characteristics of the client and the reaction of the therapist to him. Mrs. J. was a 35-year-old woman who had had a series of children out of wedlock by different fathers. Somewhere along the way she married a man who was alcoholic, abusive, and who left her after impregnating her. She had not heard from him since. The mother came from a chaotic family where her father was alcoholic and deserted his wife and children. Her mother was promiscuous, did not give the children adequate care, and finally the children were placed in foster homes. The case was reported to the pro-tective agency because the children were not attending school. They were observed to be wandering around the neighborhood at night. The teen-age daughter was going with a much older group of adolescents who were constantly in difficulty with the authorities, drinking, using drugs, and engaging in antisocial activities. This girl referred to one of the gang members as her man, and at this time she was pregnant. Her older brother was arrested for taking a car without authority and was to ap-pear before the juvenile court. The mother, who had completed high school, was a cocktail waitress. She would frequently bring different men home, and it was believed she was prostituting. The children were not supervised adequately, nor were they fed or given the care that children need.

Pressure from the school and the court led to the referral. The mother was an attractive but overweight woman wearing excessive makeup. She worked until late at night, entertained her current boy-friend, and slept all morning. The children had to get their own breakfast, and school attendance was sporadic. It was felt that the mother did not encourage the children to go to school because she was lonely and needed their help to run the house. The home visit revealed a chaotic household which was dirty and lacked care. The caseworker offered to help the mother with the problem she had, as well as getting prenatal care for the pregnant daughter and helping to plan for the delinquent son. The mother talked about how she had been left as a child, that she never wanted that to happen to her children, but she could not help what was going on. She appeared frustrated, overwhelmed, and helpless. The next time the caseworker made a home visit the mother was not there. When she was finally contacted, she said she had to go to the store to buy some bread. During the course of treatment, the mother continued to be inconsistent in keeping appointments, but got extremely upset if the caseworker had a vacation or was ill and missed an appointment.

The transference reaction in this case is to reenact the desertion theme with everyone. The client saw no need to keep her word and keep her appointments. The countertransference reaction to this kind of behavior is to become frustrated, angry, and wonder if this case is worth the effort. It is essential to see the client's behavior as a reenactment of her own traumatic experiences and not take it as a personal rejection.

Some of the hopeless feelings which the therapist has are an empathic response to the depressive core in the patient. The patient had a series of life experiences which should have produced a depressive response. Instead, she takes flight from depression by her sexual promiscuity, seeing men as transient sources of sex and money, and by repeating the desertion she experienced by neglecting her children and getting involved with a husband who abandoned her.

Sometimes the therapist hopes that the repeated crises will somehow quiet down and then treatment can begin. This is a false hope. The client unconsciously needs these crises in order to avoid facing the depression, so the therapist has to deal with the client in her current situation. This can be extremely frustrating. Things seem to be a little better for a while; then the client regresses and the caseworker wonders if the treatment has any use or value. The countertransference feelings alternate between anger at and frustration with the client. The therapist needs a great deal of support and encouragement from the agency to be able to cope with these feelings.

These are clients who have multiple involvements. Many of them are on welfare. There may well be a pregnant daughter, so an agency dealing with unwed mothers may be in the picture, along with the courts and the schools. These clients are often called multiproblem families. In actuality they are multiagency problems. The therapist often gets caught up in the cross-fire of different agency approaches, and the result can be further frustration, because everyone assumes some responsibility and no one has sole responsibility for case management. Competitive feelings can be further stirred up by the client's need to play one authority figure against another. The origin of this need is related to the client's experience that parents and other authority figures in the client's life constantly let them down. The need to complain about the work of one agency to the therapist from another is a displacement of the anger at the authority figures in the client's life. The worker has to be careful not to become competitive or critical and must recognize what the patient is expressing.

In summary, the cases of neglect and abuse seen in various settings reflect different basic personality problems. Abusing parents are primarily schizophrenic in their defense systems. This can be confusing because they have an overlay of neurotic symptoms, particularly obsessive-compulsive patterns which include being overly fastidious about dirt. The transference is based on the cluster of personality traits described in this chapter. The clients want closeness but fear that it will lead to destruction. So they actively isolate themselves. The fear of destruction is projected onto the child, and with role reversal the child can be viewed as the destructive parent. The disturbance in reality testing is demonstrated by this process, especially where the client violently attacks the child believing he is saving his own life. The countertransference reaction to this behavior is often horror, fright, and anger. In order to work with these clients it is necessary to understand what is involved in the client's behavior, at the same time making a reality evaluation regarding the actual danger to the child. Case management is complex at best, but it is also influenced by the violent behavior of the client and the therapist's reaction to it.

The cases of neglect reflect a depressive pattern where the issues of loss and abandonment dominate. The client acts this out by neglecting the children, rejecting the therapist, and creating life situations filled with repeated losses and abandonments. Many of these children act out in antisocial ways, and this complicates the emotional reaction of the therapist. The countertransference feelings include picking up the depression in the client and becoming discouraged. There is enormous frustration, anger, and questioning of the worth of therapy when the client is actively rejecting. It is necessary to understand that the client is doing as he was done to and the caseworker must not personalize the process. This requires a certain kind of determination not to be rejected, a tough hide, and perhaps a touch of masochism. Understanding one's self and the associated reaction to abusing and neglecting clients is essential for the maximal use of the self in the treatment and management of these clients.

REFERENCES

1. Shengold LL: Child abuse and deprivation: Soul murder. *J Am Psychoanal Assoc* 1979;27(3):533-559.
2. Hill DA: Emotional reaction to child abuse within a hospital setting, in Ebeling NB, Hill DA (eds): *Child Abuse: Intervention and Treatment.* Acton, MA, Publishing Sciences Group, 1975, pp 37-40.
3. Flanzraich M, Steiner GL: Therapeutic interventions that foster ego development in abused/neglected children, in Williams GJ, Money J (eds): *Traumatic Abuse and Neglect of Children at Home.* Baltimore, The Johns Hopkins University Press, 1980, pp 569-574.
4. Freud S: *The Dynamics of Transference,* standard edition, London, Hogarth Press, vol 12, 1912, pp 99-108.
5. Kaufman I: The contribution of protective services. *Child Welfare* 1957; 36(2):8-15.
6. Serrano AC, Zuelzer MB, Howe DD, et al: Ecology of abusive and non-abusive families. *J Am Acad Child Psychiatry* 1979;18(1):67-75.
7. Kaufman I: Psychodynamics of protective casework, in Parad HJ, Miller RR (eds): *Ego Oriented Casework.* New York, Family Service Association of America, 1963, pp 191-205.
8. Ebeling NB: Preventing strains and stresses in protective services, in Ebeling NB, Hill DA (eds): *Child Abuse: Intervention and Treatment.* Acton, MA, Publishing Sciences Group, 1975, pp 47-51.
9. Lipner JD: Attitudes of professionals in the management and treatment of child abuse, in Ebeling NB, Hill DA (eds): *Child Abuse: Intervention and Treatment.* Acton, MA, Publishing Sciences Group, 1975, pp 31-35.
10. D'Agostino P: Strains and stresses in protective services, in Ebeling NB, Hill DA (eds): *Child Abuse: Intervention and Treatment.* Acton, MA, Publishing Sciences Group, 1975, pp 41-45.
11. Galdston R: Observations on children who have been physically abused and their parents. *Am J Psychiatry* 1965;122:440-444.
12. Kaufman I: The physically abused child, in Ebeling NB, Hill DA (eds): *Child Abuse: Intervention and Treatment.* Acton, MA, Publishing Sciences Group, 1975, pp 79-86.
13. Kaufman I: Helping people who cannot manage their own lives. *Children* 1966; 13(3):93-98.
14. Polansky NA, De Saix C, Sharin SA: *Child Neglect: Understanding and Reaching the Parent.* New York, Child Welfare League of America, 1972.
15. Kaufman I: Transference and countertransference. Unpublished paper presented at a colloquium at Simmons College School of Social Work, January 21, 1980.

4 The Initial Interview: Alliance Building and Assessment

Deborah A. Hill

The caseworker had visited the Allen home six times now and met with nothing but the empty sound of the doorbell ringing within, unanswered. Earlier in the day on her visit to the Stone household, the door was opened, Elizabeth walked abruptly away from her, and she was left to follow down the bleak hallway to hear the tale of a woman who had nearly killed her son and herself as well. On the visit to her next family she would be met with the steadfast assertion that the physical abuse inflicted was justifiable and if it had helped her, Mary, to learn right from wrong, why not her daughter, Dorothy?

Where does one begin when confronted with the enormity of the task presented? Can the time-tested "begin where the client is" possibly help us here? The starkness of these examples illustrates the challenges posed to workers in the protective service field in adapting proven casework technique to a group of clients who have generally not been able to ask for help themselves and often initially resist it.

The task of the assessing caseworker is to learn to see the world through the eyes of Mrs. Allen, Elizabeth, and Mary, to determine in what ways their children are suffering, and how a helping relationship can be established to enable them to grow and meet their children's basic needs.

The discussion will first center on the thinking and preparation which must precede the first contact with the family, then the initial interview and its opportunities for alliance building and, finally, a summation of the factors which form the caseworker's initial assessment.

PREPARATION FOR THE FIRST INTERVIEW

A most important part of preparation for the first interview is a psychological readiness to approach the task. This involves examining and dealing with one's feelings about the referral information, anticipating the family response to our involvement, and thinking through the feelings that response will arouse in us. The client's unconscious communications will need to be studied and responded to in a helpful way. Littner[1] and others have discussed the ways in which this unconscious material is revealed and the need for the caseworker to be attuned to her own feelings and responses. This kind of examination is basic to all effective helping relationships, but the kind and intensity of material presented in the child protective field, along with the involuntary nature of our involvement, evokes particularly strong and difficult transference and countertransference issues.

How the caseworker understands, accepts, and exercises the authority vested in her is crucial to the case process. Although the positive use of authority is part of treatment in all settings where protection is needed against serious self-destructive behavior or behaviors directed against others (eg, suicidal, homicidal, fire-setting behavior), in child protective work it is a constantly recurring rather than an occasional theme. Exercised as a therapeutic tool, the positive use of authority is designed to meet a specific need in an individual or family and, when communicated in a caring and clear way to an individual without sufficient inner controls to protect her child, this stance brings some degree of relief and sets the stage for the work that lies ahead.

Most, although not all, protective service referrals are involuntary. Clients have not been able to ask for help themselves, and problems have worsened to the point that an outside party has intervened. The vast majority have had little or no experience with helping people, have no notion of what a helping relationship is like or can offer, and feel hopeless, beyond help, or undeserving of it. Their experience includes unheard and unmet needs and authority figures who were perhaps absent, harsh, or inconsistent. These clients not only cannot ask for help, but may be terrified of intervention from any agency, particularly one which has child-placement functions. The client's fear and consequent resistance to the referral may take the form of flight and avoidance or angry defensiveness. That fear and resistance must be understood in light of the client's past experiences.

Despite the fact that the worker is dealing with an involuntary client with heightened defenses, the therapeutic framework from which she operates in establishing a helping relationship is rooted in solid casework theory. She utilizes the principles of good interviewing techniques basic to casework treatment. She listens, seeks to understand, conveys acceptance of the individual although perhaps not of his behavior, and begins "where the client is."

She uses great care in identifying and respecting the wide variety of defense mechanisms she encounters, knowing that the strength of the transference phenomenon in a more disturbed client will call for a clear focus on reality issues. She is alert to the absence of adequate defenses in the client who "spills" her problems and history indiscriminately.

"Where the client is" is generally a state of great fear about our intervention and its implications—in short—are we going to take the children away? Before discussing the content of the first interview, it is important to consider the worker's goals and the means of achieving them.

The purpose of the initial interview is to determine (1) whether and to what degree a child is at risk of abuse or neglect; (2) what seems to be contributing to or causing the problem; and (3) what services, if provided and accepted, can be of help to the family in dealing with the problems identified.

The vehicle to arriving at this assessment is the alliance with the parent. Although much is to be learned from observation, one's own and those of the referrer, it is the parent who in her own way provides the real information as to the source of trouble and the kind of help she needs.

It is through this alliance, or working relationship, that the goals of treatment will be identified and pursued. Without it, no positive, lasting effect will be achieved. Beginnings of important experiences stand out sharply in the mind, and the nature of the beginning of a therapeutic contact is not only long remembered but becomes a shaping force for what is to come. Perlman[2] and many others have provided a sound knowledge base upon which to draw in the art of alliance building. The worker must be well grounded in this knowledge as she seeks to engage those clients so fearful of our involvement and yet so urgently in need of help.

Before contacting the family, it is important to speak at length with the referrer. This provides clarification and elaboration of the facts and puts them in a clearer context. The feelings, concerns, and motives of the referrer can be more clearly understood, again contributing to one's understanding of the problem. One can obtain information about what efforts have been made to help the family and which ones have or have not proved useful. It is crucial to ascertain at this time whether the referrer was able to tell the family that he was making the referral and why. If this was not done and the caseworker can help the referrer to do so, this will prove useful to all. The referrer will be helped in this and future referrals to see that this material can be discussed in a constructive way once feelings are dealt with, that he can present the referral as helpful to the family, and that this will enhance his future working relationship with them. The family, in turn, will benefit in self-esteem from being treated with the respect they deserve, will be given an opportunity to respond to the material in the report and, even if they are angry and defensive, will have experienced the referrer as direct and honest, thus building a modicum of trust. It is particularly helpful if the referrer can cite a concrete need that he knows the family views as a problem and which has contributed to their stress, telling the family he has mentioned this problem to the protective worker. This conveys his concern and understanding to the family members and hopefully diminishes to some degree their apprehension about meeting the worker. Lastly, an explanation to the client by the referrer greatly aids the worker in getting on with addressing the real problems.

She can begin to build on the tenuous thread of trust established. It is hoped that all school, hospital, and agency personnel can be helped to deal directly and in an on-going manner with families in this way. Many neighbors and family members can also be successfully helped to explain a referral to a parent in a constructive way.

However, there remain those referrals, where for good reasons or not, anonymity of the referrer must be safeguarded. This can make the task of the interviewer much more difficult in that the energy spent guessing at and expressing anger toward a variety of people who might have wanted to hurt them, as they first see it, diverts the client from the task at hand, thus slowing the helping process when relief may be urgently needed. The worker, while allowing for the anger, must pursue the task of assessing the problems.

Except in emergency situations, it is useful for the caseworker to write to a family a few days in advance of her suggested home visit. A letter which states the fact of the referral, the worker's desire to be of help, and the suggestion of a first home visit time with an invitation to call if the time is not convenient, gives the client time to prepare for the worker's intervention. The tone set by the letter paves the way for the interview by conveying respect for the parent and the intent of being helpful. It gives the family some time to prepare for the interview, but not so much as to prolong anxiety, and it puts some control in their hands at a time when they may feel devoid of it.

Because so many families referred for protective services struggle with feelings of helplessness and mistrust, it is important that wherever possible the caseworker be prepared to continue to work with the family should on-going services be indicated. Constancy and continuity of care become necessary ingredients in a treatment relationship fashioned to deal with histories of profound loss and inconsistency.

INITIATING CONTACT

A range of possibilities awaits the worker making her first scheduled visit. She may find no one there (or no one answering the door), she may find only the children there, she may find a whole host of defenders gathered for the occasion, or she may find only the client(s) to whom she addressed her letter. Difficult as it may be to be prepared for any or all of the above, whatever one encounters begins to tell the worker something about her client and her problems and needs.

It is not at all uncommon for the client to express fear through avoidance and to not be home or not answer the door for what seem like interminable periods of time. The client is showing the worker one way she deals with stress, and she may think that eventually the worker will give up and disappear. Others in her life may have done this. It is important for the worker to maintain consistency, go back each week at the scheduled time and leave a note indicating she was there, disappointed not to see the client, and planning to come again the following week. Depending on the urgency of the presenting problem, it may be necessary to gradually strengthen the wording in the note to communicate "we must talk" rather than "would like to" talk. When finally the client and worker do meet, acknowledgment can be made of the degree of fear the client was experiencing and why. Workers are mistaken if they think nothing is happening during all of this "lost" time. In fact, much is happening and the process of treatment has begun.

The agency received a referral stating that Mrs. Allen was physically abusing her two sons, ages 4 and 6. Neighbors had called their public assistance worker on more than one occasion expressing concern about frightened crying from children and what sounded like physical fights between adults. The worker wrote Mrs. Allen a letter and followed it with five home visits, none of which were kept by the client. The worker's vacation time arrived and so as not to lose the consistency felt to be so important to the client, the worker's supervisor maintained the visit schedule in her absence. The original worker returned and resumed the visits. On the eighth try, suddenly the door was opened, Mrs. Allen unceremoniously said, "Oh, it's you," and proceeded to dive directly into the troublesome material at hand.

Clearly the worker's visits had been very much on Mrs. Allen's mind. The worker later heard about the brief involvement of a protective worker three years earlier whom Mrs. Allen had convinced that "everything was all right" when it was not. But when this worker kept coming, the client figured she really meant business and, after all, things really were out of hand with the children's father.

In some few instances, where one cannot gain entrance and the reported information puts the children at severe risk, one can seek court intervention to allow the assessment to proceed. However, this is not often necessary. The primary effort is to present the offer of help in a nonthreatening way.

Diagnostic is the mother's absence in the following case. The agency received a referral from the school stating that two siblings, ages 6 and 8, were physically neglected, poorly and inadequately clothed for the weather, hungry, and lacking medical care. The 8-year-old told her teacher about being left alone for long periods of time while mother worked. The 6-year-old boy was presenting increasingly rebellious behavior in the classroom. The worker wrote to the mother and scheduled a home visit. She was admitted by the children, who were simultaneously apprehensive and hungry for attention. They explained that their mother was at work. Mother's absence from the interview bore out the referral information and some time later as the worker addressed the mother's feelings about needing to work and the pressures of child care, she was able to acknowledge that the children's care was more than she could manage and she welcomed appropriate relief in providing for them.

Still another possibility is that of the worker being confronted with a seeming host of defenders ready to testify to a parent's good mothering. Here we have a frightened mother needing the support of others and showing evidence of her ability to enlist their services. The worker respects the client's need to defend herself in this way, listens carefully to what her friends say on her behalf, and notes the caring atmosphere surrounding the client as a strength. The worker divulges minimal information in the presence of others, if possible, and hopes that on an occasion in the near future the mother will be able to meet alone with the worker. Generally this happens very soon, the mother's initial fears having been alleviated by meeting the worker and seeing her intent to be open and helpful. Much work may go on in such a group setting. However, it may be useful at some point to inquire of the mother whether there is some place she and the worker may speak privately.

Whenever and however the initial contacts with the client arise, the worker has the opportunity to present herself in an open, direct, and caring manner. She must be explicit about the alleged facts in the referral and about why she is there. Sharing information with a family when it comes to us helps build trust and conveys that these are problems which can be talked about and dealt with. The worker listens carefully to the family's explanations, seeking to clarify from their point of view what has been happening. The worker allies herself with that part of the parent that wants to provide good care and safety for the child. She listens carefully for the stresses the parent is experiencing and openly acknowledges these. This conveys to the parent that the worker seeks to understand and help, rather than punish, as may be feared, and that the worker is seeking to define cause and effect relationships from what is happening. Because her attention is directed primarily to the parent, she asks to see the child in the first interview only if the situation warrants it.

The worker is listening carefully for the precipitants to the facts described in the referral as well as to evidence of chronic stress. The worker is wondering about a number of things: What recent changes have occurred in the family? Has there been a loss, a severed relationship, shifting alliances, change in concrete resources? Is the precipitant the very birth of the child itself? If so, how great an impact would then be expected when one is without significant others, without adequate financial resources, or as one so often sees, without a history of adequate parenting oneself?

Pearlin,[3] in seeking to understand why so many more women than men presented with psychological difficulties, found depression in women highly correlated with the severe demands upon parents raising young children. Stress was most evident when women were single, without supportive social relationships, and without a sense that life would improve for them. Makosky,[4] in "Stress and the Mental Health of Women," reviews the knowledge about the causal connection between a clustering of stressful events and worsening conditions in people's lives, but points to the need for studies which attend to the stressful conditions under which some people chronically live.

Certainly most protective service clients are women by virtue of their common single-parent caretaker roles and most suffer from chronically stressful situations. Such was the case of 17-year-old Jane, referred by relatives because of alleged poor care of 13-month-old Christopher. The referring source cited the presence of many teenagers in and out, with frequent drug use, allegations of feeding the baby alcohol, and presence of unsanitary conditions. It was with considerable difficulty (many unkept appointments) that the worker achieved a first interview with Jane, whose attachment to the baby, whom she seldom put down, was evident immediately. The house was cluttered, although not unsanitary and the worker suspected that Christopher's running around without diapers may have given rise to the latter concern. But the house was warm, and he was not chilled.

The worker met the boyfriend, who was initially challenging in his behavior. The client was a defensive adolescent, feeling rejection and criticism (current and chronic) from her family, and driven to repeatedly self-destructive behaviors with a street gang. Beneath the thin veneer of toughness, the worker saw a scared, lonely girl, needing help. The worker underscored the evidence of good parenting which she saw, but was explicit about the concerns raised. She elicited Jane's view of the problems, allied herself with her desires to see that Christopher got the care he needed, and offered a helping relationship. Christopher, while experiencing adequate, if overstimulated, care from his mother, most often was left in the hands of an ever-changing number of caretakers night and day as his mother found herself propelled through various activities, including frequent housing changes and evictions. Jane had dimly hoped that Christopher would change her life, that she would finally have someone to love her, approve of her, and make her feel valued. But she had had little preparation for the full-time demands of parenting. She could only sustain her parenting role for very limited periods of time and only when things were going well with her boyfriend. Jane was the unwitting victim of her repressed past, as Selma Fraiberg so eloquently describes in "Ghosts in the Nursery."[5]

Despite her tentative and periodic clinging to the casework relationship which helped her provide consistent mothering to Christopher, the normal adolescent need for freedom from responsibilities and her unconscious need to act out her self-hate in destructive ways proved the stronger forces. She ultimately elected to relinquish the baby's care. Outreach continued to her to try to engage her in help for herself.

It is customary for workers to hear parents deny both the facts in the referral and the presence of problems. This may happen out of their fear and/or be illustrative of their way of handling problems too big or painful to bear. Similarly, the worker may unwittingly collude with the parents' denial out of her wish to not see and confront difficult material. She may identify with the plight of the parent or feel intimidated by the parent and too quickly dismiss the referral as ungrounded or the incident as isolated and unlikely to recur. The crucial issue here is getting to know the family over time. A troubled family may be able to present as functioning fairly well in an interview or two, but then display signs of trouble. It is helpful to say to the family that adamantly denies problems and the need for your presence that you may indeed ultimately find that there is no need for your involvement, but that you can only determine that by meeting with them several times, at which point both of you will have a better idea of what is occurring and whether or not there are some ways you can be of help.

It is less useful and productive to focus on who might have done something to a child than whether simply something happened to a child to place him in danger. Sometimes well into a relationship parents can discuss their particular involvement in an incident and sometimes they never can. Distrust, fear, and guilt may be too great. Projection of blame onto others is a common defense in these situations. But what is important is that there be recognition that something serious happened or is amiss and whatever adults are involved are responsible for the care their children receive. The caseworker's goal is to help them meet that responsibility.

Mrs. C. was referred anonymously to protective services by a person who claimed frequent loud fights, beaten and frightened children, use of drugs, people coming and going at all hours of the day and night, and children playing unsupervised in unsafe places. There was no supporting documentation of any of the above, and Mrs. C. denied all of the concerns and with much anger speculated alternatively whether the referral had come from an obtrusive neighbor with whom she had had difficulty or her husband from whom she had just separated. Her thin, gaunt body radiated tension from every nerve. She had met the worker at the door together with her mother and sister whom she had clearly summoned for support. Her mother glared and spoke angrily to the worker, then sat in an adjoining room after a few moments of introduction, following which the worker had felt it reasonable to ask the client whether it might be possible for them to speak alone. The client presented good social skills, invited the worker into an immaculate kitchen, and offered tea. Between preparing tea and defensively producing children, ages 2 years and 9 months, to show how well cared for they were, she could only sit in her chair for a few minutes. Driven by anxiety, she was in nearly constant motion. She described herself as a nervous person and said that this unfounded report was going to make her even sicker. The worker gently picked up on this, asking for elaboration while also carefully listening to her explanations and the pressures she experienced from both ex-husband and neighbor.

By "beginning where the client was" and offering Mrs. C. help with a referral for her described physical complaints and by asserting both a need to be there and a desire to help, an alliance was begun. Typically, the client, in her own preconscious need to let it be known she needed help, cited a recent fall down the stairs sustained by her daughter which required hospitalization and during which she was questioned about how it happened. She had been afraid the baby would not be returned home. During the interview, she demonstrated throughout both her frustration with the normal behavior of her 2-year-old, large for his age, and her misperception of him as powerful and evil.

The worker could use mother's acknowledged frustration as an opening to wonder whether mother had thought of day care to give herself some respite. It was on the note of acknowledgment that, whether or not something had happened, mother was stressed and help would be useful in exploring day care and medical appointments that the second visit was planned.

Other times, parents may acknowledge the facts in the referral but defend their behavior as justifiable, as in the following case example.

Referral information from the school nurse revealed that 8-year-old Dorothy showed signs of a physical beating which was acknowledged by the child. Mother, a large, powerful-looking woman with an authoritative voice, acknowledged and defended her behavior with considerable feeling. She had told her daughter many times to come right home from school, and the child deliberately and repeatedly disobeyed.

She railed against the school nurse (who had not told her about the referral), "What will they get me for next?" The nurse had no right to "put child abuse on me. So many other mothers are leaving their kids out in the street, why don't they get child abuse on them?" Further, Dorothy's mother had herself been disciplined in this fashion, and it had taught her right from wrong. She shared her frustration in raising several children alone without any help from "the systems," including that represented by the worker. The worker conveyed acceptance of mother's anger, but said they really needed to find other ways to deal with Dorothy, because the beatings could not continue. As she listened carefully, conveying understanding and interest in the problems described, including that of gaining her children's respect and obedience, Dorothy's mother mentioned her fear that her daughter might be raped if allowed unsupervised in the streets, as a friend of mother's had at about the same age. She could allow herself to consider the possibility of a supervised play program. Identifying this need helped mother accept continued intervention. Still later she could share with sadness a history of childhood deprivation and violence, including her own adult episodes of far more serious losses of control than that described in the referral. Later yet, she could acknowledge she needed to find ways other than beatings to deal with her children. Four months after the initial referral, mother remarked at what a favor the nurse had done her—now she had someone to talk with about her problems.

The question "Are you going to take my child away?" is always felt and is asked either directly or indirectly. The thought may be experienced with indescribable anguish and terror by one parent and with a mixture of fear and desire by another.

To offer swift reassurance to a family the worker does not yet know well is not only premature, but conveys the perception that the worker, rather than making decisions in a thorough and thoughtful manner, acts indiscriminantly and impulsively (much as the client may do). Such a perception does not contribute to building an alliance based on trust and fails to present a useful and needed model of behavior.

Most helpful is the worker's conveying that she takes the question very seriously, that her solid conviction is that children's needs are best met by remaining with their families, except when a parent is unable to provide what they need, and that the intent of her services is to help the family do what is in the best interests of the children. Trust is further enhanced by her stating that she will always tell them what she is thinking and concerned about and that no contemplated move of such magnitude would happen without their knowing about it and having had every opportunity to demonstrate ability to provide care and protection to their child. (The exception to this is, of course, an event of such emergency nature that placement must occur immediately.)

ASSESSING DEGREE OF RISK

Among the areas which require careful thought and exploration in assessing the degree of risk involved are the following: What is the degree of the child's injury, neglect, or emotional distress? What are the parents' perceptions of the child? Is he endowed with positive as well as negative attributes? How inappropriate are their expectations? What is the age and vulnerability of the child? Is the child handicapped or viewed as defective? Is the event isolated or chronic? What symptoms does the child display? How do they interfere with his functioning? What is the parent's attitude toward what has happened and toward your involvement? What part do culturally shaped attitudes play?* What does the parental history contribute to our understanding? What symptoms do the parents display? How able is the parent to control impulses? What is the degree of parental depression? of family stress? What is the effect on the child of the conditions under which he is living?† What support systems exist? What environmental factors have contributed stress? What is the parent's capacity to use help?

In attempting to answer these questions we rely on information from family and others who know them (referrer, school, physician, agency), our observations, and our understanding of the psychosocial dynamics involved.

Sometimes it is not at all clear from the referral information what the nature of the problem is and whether it has protective dimensions. History may be crucial in helping us decide.

A physician referred 5-year-old Michael and his family for protective service evaluation. Mother had come to the emergency ward

---

*Corporal punishment in schools is allowed in 46 states in the United States and in many other countries.[6]
†Polansky et al[7] have devised scales for urban and rural settings which assess adequacy of child care in such areas as supervision, stimulation, housing safety, etc.

complaining of lethargy, nervousness, and inability to sleep. In the course of her discussion with the doctor, she mentioned she worried about her son Michael, who had sometime earlier been diagnosed with a minor heart problem. Since her move across country, nearly one year ago, she had not yet followed up on the medical evaluation recommended. Michael, being with mother, was examined and found to be a pleasant cooperative child and incidentally to have a bruise on the forehead described by his caring, if preoccupied mother, as sustained in a fall.

Mother was seen by a psychiatrist and also referred to protective services by the pediatrician who was concerned about the previous lack of medical care, although doubtful that the bruise was inflicted. Mother was highly receptive to the referral to protective services, responding to someone showing an interest in her and on her own kept the child's scheduled medical appointment (which showed the child to be fine now). She kept the follow-up psychiatric visits for herself where medication brought some initial relief. The protective worker saw no evidence, then or subsequently, that the bruise was other than accidental.

This case might well have been closed had the worker considered only the above. However, careful history-taking revealed a very long history of depression, a serious past alcohol problem, and consequent neglect of the three children.

The oldest child, a girl, had assumed the caretaking role of the younger siblings from an early age at considerable expense to herself and had not been protected from the sexual advances of her father. This child, now an adolescent, had flirted with running away and was now close to quitting school. Without intervention, the risk of her repeating her mother's history was high. Mother, although diligent in keeping the psychiatric appointments, was preoccupied with her own needs and felt helpless to effect change. She was alienated from many in her family and had few friends. Worker felt mother was unable to give emotionally to the children, to make good plans for them, and was vulnerable to slipping back into despair without active intervention. Thus, the worker continued her involvement focusing first on her feelings of depression and lethargy and later helping mother arrange for a therapist for the adolescent. Not for another nine months did she hear from mother quite incidentally, and as an aside, that nightly she put her 9-year-old to bed with diapers because of chronic bed-wetting, not yet medically evaluated. It was clear that this family would require help for some time to come, that until mother was sufficiently better she would not be able to meet all the children's needs, and that they would require strenuous intervention from healthy role models outside the home.

In contrast to the above case, the following is an example where serious presenting complaints did not result in the need for protective service intervention, but rather a referral for voluntary services.

A 4-year-old girl failed to be taken for follow-up medical visits for serious second-degree burns which could put her at high risk of infection and become life-threatening. The family failed to respond to outreach efforts. Contact by protective services found a large family of older children caring for the younger ones, no heat or electricity due to non-payment of bills, and mother in the hospital delivering a new baby. The older children, not understanding that just because the child was not experiencing pain she was not in medical difficulty, had not kept the appointment. They promptly cooperated. Mother, upon returning from the hospital, presented as an able and caring mother with a history of good parenting herself but one temporarily in distress following a move to an unfamiliar culture, abandonment by her husband, an inadvertent move into a drafty apartment she could not afford to heat, and ineligibility for certain public assistance services. She gladly accepted a referral to a voluntary agency in the town to which she moved in order to obtain better housing and be closer to reliable friends. This situation illustrated well the influence of poverty on the care of children.

In yet another case, referral to protective service was made when 14-year-old Tony was taken to the emergency ward by police with facial palsy following an alleged severe blow by his father. The family initially resisted evaluation. Once seen, Tony and his parents, who were separated, acknowledged the incident of inflicted injury. Exploration of dynamics yielded a picture of a family caught up in the crisis of father having left the home but who would be summoned by mother whenever Tony's behavior required more control than she could exert.

In this instance, Tony had deliberately and seriously hurt a younger sibling. A short period of intervention, taking note of the family's pain and ability to talk about their feelings, led to a referral for voluntary services, which they had been able to use successfully in the past. In this case, the event was serious, although isolated. The family was concerned about what had happened, could see that as a family unit they needed help, and each had evident strengths, including support systems. Both parents had responsible jobs and had arranged special schooling for the children in the past in accordance with their needs. The degree of family stress was mitigated by these factors, but without the focus brought by the referral and the seriousness paid the event, the family might well not have received the help they needed.

The following initial interview is striking in the degree of extensive pathology openly presented by the parent, as well as in the seriousness of the presenting complaint. Paul was taken by his mother to his neighborhood health center on a weekend. The nurse practitioner with whom his mother Margaret had a relationship was on vacation. Mother explained with considerable feeling of distress and frustration to the nurse on duty that she had struck 4-year-old Paul hard across the face causing him to fall against a radiator and strike his head. She was concerned about possible head injury. The nurse, who noted a history of like concerns in the medical record, conveyed to mother the importance of her making a referral to the local state child welfare agency. Mother responded with a mixture of fear and evident relief. She needed someone to help.

She felt she could manage over the weekend and was able to take Paul for an x-ray to a local hospital where again she was offered the relief that a hospital admission could afford, but she declined, wanting her son with her and not wanting to subject him to a frightening separation. She used telephone support from a hospital social worker over the remainder of the weekend, however, and when the protective worker arrived at her home, greeted her with a clear "I need help." With pressured speech and tense affect, Margaret, a thin, agile, articulate woman of 25 years spilled out her fears of loss of control in a torrent of words hard to hear. She described her love for Paul, his provocations, and her low tolerance for frustration. She acknowledged the event which led to the referral but said there had been many other times when she had suddenly lost control. She had given him a bloody nose from hitting his face against the floor, choked him until he was blue, and beat him frequently. "All I have to do is walk in the room and he is afraid of me — I'd like to change that . . . I'm afraid I might kill him . . . I'm capable of it."

She described mounting tension in her relationship with the father of her 9-month-old daughter, Betty. They had recently reunited upon his recent return home from prison. Bills were unpaid and father favored Betty. He kept talking of getting a job but none materialized. He was out a lot, and she was left to cope with the children. She had no one to turn to. She used to talk periodically to the nurse who was on vacation and who had understood the stress she was under. In response to inquiries from the social worker, Margaret explained the unavailability of her family.

Margaret grew up as the second child in a family of three children. With bitter resentment, she described her mother's drinking and leaving them alone for long periods of time. With a mixture of bewilderment and acceptance, she described how her father used to beat her frequently with a belt. She did not know why, but figured she had done something to deserve it. Besides, it made her respect and obey him. Once when her mother was drunk she told her that her father was not her biological father; Margaret stoutly denied she cared, although she knew she was darker skinned than her siblings. He had cared about her and that was all that mattered. He and she were inseparable. Her mother was jealous. Eventually when she was 12, her mother had abandoned them entirely, and they had all been placed in foster care. It had been terrible. She had felt like an outcast. She fought with her foster siblings because they had more privileges than she. As Margaret described her four years in placement, however, the worker did hear her speak with true affection of a female teacher and a friend who had cared about her and believed in her. At 16, she was sent home to her mother, with whom she fought physically, and soon thereafter she met and married Tom. She was attracted to him because he had had a rotten time of it, too, but like her was determined to change his life. Besides, he did not let her get away with things. He put her in line when she needed it.

During this initial home visit, the worker observed mother's impatience with both children. She seemed to have little awareness of normal child development. Rather than seeing Betty's exploring of her newfound world as healthy, her tentative crawling seemed only an annoyance and she plunked her roughly back in her playpen.

In response to Paul's whiney demands, she was at first angered, then felt increasingly helpless and frustrated as she was unable to satisfy his needs. She seemed to endow him with a power well beyond that of a 4-year-old and seemed in fact afraid of him in some subtle way. The tension between them was evident. Worker took note of his dark complected skin in contrast to his sister's towhead.

Worker acknowledged the evident stress mother was experiencing and let her know that temporary foster placement was an option while they proceeded to work together. Mother quickly protested but readily verbalized her desire to meet weekly with the worker and to pursue daycare planning.

Many things pointed to the conclusion that these children were at serious risk of continuing abuse: mother's own statement, her history of personal abuse and abandonment, which she was unwittingly repeating, her seeming identification with her abusive father whom she viewed as "all good" in contrast to her "all bad" mother, her identification with the darker skinned child as perhaps "bad," the age and vulnerability of the children, especially given Paul's provocative behavior and her perception of it as deliberate and powerful, her limited support system, and her history of serious difficulty controlling her impulses. Betty's father's return to the home and along with it their escalating tension and the crushed hopes of things being better, Paul's increasing skill at manipulating mother, and the absence of her seeming once supportive contact, the nurse practitioner, seemed to have contributed to an escalating of mother's loss of control.

On the positive side, the worker noted Margaret's eagerness for help, her capacity to talk, the fact that she related well with good eye contact and with appropriate affect. Also, she had never before had the opportunity of casework help, she wanted to be a good parent, she had had some positive figures in her life to whom she had been genuinely connected, and she was seeking to change her behavior.

The worker knew that weekly casework and full-time day care for both children must begin immediately, that mother would need to hear repeatedly that the children could stay at home only if they are clearly safe there, that mother would need to know how she could reach help 24 hours a day. The worker also knew that for Margaret the process of building a trusting relationship with a caseworker, from whom she would expect abandonment and punishment, would be a long one. Accustomed to acting out feelings, she would need help in recognizing when and why tension begins to build and learn new ways to deal with it. Only time would tell whether or not help had come too late or whether it would be enough to sustain her. Should it not be enough, the children would need to be placed outside the home, while work with mother continued.

In the following final case example, the anger borne of severe deprivation has been turned inward in the form of depression. The pathology is less explicitly conveyed by the parent, and behavioral observations and history cause the worker to conclude that the child is at serious risk of harm without intervention.

A nurse practitioner following 12-month-old Sara for routine care at a community health center referred her mother Elizabeth for protective service intervention. The nurse noted mother's frustration with the child and her depression. She knew of her past history of unsuccessful parenting of an older son who had been in placement outside the home for several years because of events which placed his life in danger. She knew that mother had serious medical problems which heavily weighed on her mind. She required renal surgery but her excess weight made the surgery too risky. She would need to lose considerable weight in order to be a candidate for this life-prolonging effort.

The worker knew that mother would understandably have some mixed feelings about seeing another social worker. However much a relief the placement of the first child represented for her, a new worker would bring back the memories of the problems causing the placement and the pain around the separation.

The worker soon learned that Elizabeth's manner of interacting with her was typical of her relationships in general. With features impassive and forbidding, she opened the door and walked away from the worker with no offer to follow or sit down. The next responses were loud, angry, and critical. The worker was experiencing the client's way of rejecting people before they rejected her. Because the worker persevered and because Elizabeth was so desperate for help, her story of abandonment spilled out in such a manner as to cause the worker to fear she would become increasingly depressed and unable to handle the affect; therefore she helped steer Elizabeth to more present-day concerns. On that and subsequent days she heard parts of a history of severe emotional abandonment and lack of protection by mother and physical and sexual abuse by father.

Running away from home, she clung in desperation to a man who abused her and fathered her first child, a son, whom she viewed with a mixture of desire and resentment. Her relationship with him was an intense one. She viewed his struggles for independence as rejections of her, and she saw in his behavior all the badness she despised in herself. Her behavior toward him was violent and uncontrollable, and he was placed at age 8 in a residential setting, too disturbed to tolerate the intimacy of a foster home. She thought of him with longing and visited occasionally. A woman of 34, she developed a relationship with Howie, a man of 55, and he fathered her second child, a girl. Living as a family unit, he assumed a major caretaking role for them both, tolerating with passivity Elizabeth's continual verbal abuse toward him. The needs of both were being met in this liaison. But as Sara grew older, Elizabeth's physical health was more taxed. Also, mother experienced as a threat the child's beginning separation and control over her environment. Baby-sitting services had already been put in place by the Visiting Nurse Association which visited regularly, but this relief was not enough.

The worker sensed that Elizabeth wanted desperately to succeed in parenting this child and was frightened at the possibility of repeating the past. Sara appeared to be a delightful alert child, obviously well nourished, well dressed, and cared for. The worker observed with grave concern, however, Elizabeth's need to keep Sara confined, either to her lap or playpen (ambulation and exploration were clearly not encouraged), and Elizabeth's ambivalence toward the child in the form of the merging of affection and aggression. For example, a kiss became a bite which left a small red mark and which hurt. As time went on, the worker saw the child responding inappropriately with laughter to this behavior. Love and hurt were becoming intertwined in her experience.

The worker knew that Elizabeth had turned her aggression against herself many times in the past and that her failure to take care of her health was another form of this. Having received from the client permission to return, "you can come back if you want to," she knew that her task was to ally herself with the part of Elizabeth's ambivalence that wanted to succeed at parenting and to begin the slow work of building trust and self-esteem, engaging Howie as an advocate and helping Elizabeth ready herself for surgery which, although risky in her situation, was critical to prolonging her life.

This case again illustrates a high-risk situation giving due consideration to the mother's personal history of deprivation and serious episodes of loss of control, her poor health, need to defend against abandonment by alienating others, and Sara's age. However, also present is a strong desire to parent successfully, a capacity to accept help, and the presence of a significant person in her life unlike her experience while raising her son. The prognosis would necessarily remain unclear for some time to come, but offering casework which respected the client's need for control and distance was the crucial first step.

Unhappily, not all clients can be engaged in a helping relationship. Sometimes because of this and the severity of symptoms presented, it is necessary to seek court intervention, and these circumstances will be discussed in a later chapter. However, the large majority of families that come to the attention of protective service agencies can indeed be reached if approached in a thoughtful way with care taken to build a helping alliance fashioned to meet a perceived parental need. Careful preparation for the interview coupled with conscious use of the relationship set the stage for an exchange where concerns are openly expressed, the client conveys needs, and goals are agreed upon. Judgments as to the degree of risk posed for a particular child must take into account a wide range of factors relating to the child, his parents, and the particular situation surrounding them. This judgment involves a process and must not be made with haste. Much is to be gained by careful reflection and much lost by premature decisions.

REFERENCES

1. Littner N: The impact of the client's unconscious on the caseworker's reactions, in Parad HJ (ed): *Ego Psychology and Dynamic Casework.* New York, Family Service Association of America, 1958, pp 73–82.
2. Perlman HH: *Relationship: The Heart of Helping People.* Chicago, University of Chicago Press, 1979.
3. Pearlin LI: Sex roles and depression, in Datan N, Ginsberg L (eds): *Life-Span Developmental Psychology: Normative Life Crises.* New York, Academic Press, 1975.
4. Makosky VP: Stress and the mental health of women: a discussion of research and issues, in Gittentag, M, Salasin S, Belle D (eds): *The Mental Health of Women.* New York, Academic Press, 1980, pp 111–112.
5. Fraiberg S, Adelson E, Shapiro V: Ghosts in the nursery: A psychoanalytical approach, in Fraiberg S (ed): *Clinical Studies in Infant Mental Health,* New York, Basic Books, 1980, pp 164–196.
6. Taylor L, Newberger E: Child abuse in the International Year of the Child. *N Engl J Med* 1979; 301(22):1208.
7. Polansky N, Chalmers M, Buttenwieser E, Williams D: Assessing adequacy of child caring: An urban scale, *Child Welfare* 1978;57(7):439–449.

5 The Art of Home Visiting

Elizabeth Reynolds Bishop

JOSE AND ROSIE

Arriving for an initial home visit in the assessment of a report of alleged abuse and neglect of a child, the caseworker and parent aide were let into the dark hallway by a tired, harried-looking Hispanic man. They were ushered into the dusky kitchen. Two broken chairs were ceremoniously placed in the middle of the kitchen by the man who said his name was Jose.

Having said his wife was "busy," Jose picked up a sponge and began to scrub small spots here and there on kitchen surfaces.

There was a tiny infant in an umbrella stroller by the stove. The workers had expected to see a second child, a 2-year-old girl. They peered into the kitchen corners, listening and waiting, and saw no one.

A huge German shepherd was tied to the porch post outside the kitchen window. He howled in distress because the rope by which he was tied was so short he could not sit down.

Jose announced that his wife, Rosie, was in the bathtub. The announcement seemed to be made to explain the splashing which could be heard from down the hall. He continued to busy himself with his odd scrubbing job. "I like to help," he said.

By now feeling very awkward and intrusive, the workers asked where the little girl was. (She was the child named in the report, and she had allegedly been beaten by Jose.) "Mary," he said, "she's with my mother."

Quiet again — the workers waited. One noticed a shadow drift across the ceiling. She decided that the sticky flypaper hanging from the kitchen light must have moved in the breeze. A second shadow, then a third, revealed it was a crow, no, two crows swooping around the room.

Jose explained that he and Rosie loved animals. "We take care of them," he said. They lived in the ceiling from which he had removed a tile to make them a home. He explained that he was helping Rosie by cleaning up after them with the sponge.

Jose obviously felt more at ease and, putting down his sponge, he crossed the kitchen to show the workers a large open wound in his wrist. He explained that he "felt bad" and had cut himself. The doctor had sutured it, but he had pulled out the stitches to show his bravery. He responded to the workers' warm, if somewhat alarmed, concern. He seemed pleased to be told to keep it clean and to take good care of it.

By this time there was a loud din coming from the bathroom. Rosie was yelling, "Give me a towel, you fool — how do you expect me to be out of here on time if I don't even have a towel?"

Jose took a towel to Rosie — the water splashed, the crows swooped, the baby cried, the dog barked, Jose resumed the sponging, and the workers waited.

Eventually, Rosie emerged — a beautiful, pink-cheeked, healthy-looking young woman in a flowered sun dress. There was something very appealing about her as she alternately stamped and shouted like a tantruming child.

The first home visit moved through its final half hour.

In those first moments, amidst colorful, wet, crow-filled confusion, the workers had gained knowledge and insight into this needy family's pathology which would have taken weeks to begin to piece together in a very inadequate manner in an office setting.

All levels of diagnostic knowledge and clinical skill were called out from the first moment of the assessment process. First and foremost, it was clear that two babies were, at that time, more than Jose and Rosie could care for. Rosie, a demanding, tempestuous "little girl" shouted her requests like a tyrant because of her rage, stemming from deprivation which was always ready to surface. The workers also learned she had a hearing impairment, explaining further her loudness.

Jose's very low self-esteem made him try desperate means to show his bravery. The young couple were really children themselves, desperately trying to have their dependency needs met by adopting animals for whom they could provide nothing. Nothing was working out. In the wake of Jose's and Rosie's deprivation, the little girls were at risk. So a report was filed and social workers were assigned to visit them at home.

It is important to examine the many issues raised and feelings evoked when social workers are assigned to do home visiting. In the home of an "at-risk" child, a worker can feel very vulnerable at times. The unfamiliarity of the surroundings, the seriousness of the problems, and the weight of responsibility can be overwhelming.

Historically, home visiting was the modus operandi of the social worker, but the status of this sort of reaching out lost ground as more emphasis was placed on a dynamic treatment approach. Much was said about working in homes being "unprofessional." Workers sought to avoid the labels of "Lady Bountiful" or "friendly visitor." In the 1960s there was a revival of commitment to reach out to the poor, and the home visit was more frequently used than before by the family-oriented therapist who was forging new treatment modalities.[1] In fact, a brief review of the literature on home visiting shows that much of it was written in the 1960s.

Those who enter the social work field have the opportunity to bring together their energy and deep commitment to people and the ever-growing body of clinical knowledge particular to the field of child abuse and neglect in order to design and define the art of home visiting. It is not only the best single way to work with families of children at risk, but also is a highly disciplined, sophisticated therapy.

Therapy done in an office where the setting itself is formal and constant, helps a worker maintain a professional role. When entering a home, he or she must "carry in" the professional role and the constancy necessary to prevent the visit from becoming merely a social one and so that clinical work may proceed.

Home visiting in protective services is an art which, if done well, requires sharp clinical thinking. As in all treatment modalities, countertransference reactions can impede its efficacy. Home visiting is hard work, and it requires tremendous energy. It can be frightening and often lonely work. All senses are stimulated as the worker enters a home. Sights, sounds, and activity can distract and make it very hard for the worker to attend to the client. The price of errors in judgment can be high, and decisions may have to be made on the spot and alone, which is an awesome responsibility. Because progress is often slow, home visiting can also seem less clinically interesting than other therapies unless the therapist continuously works to conceptualize the clinical issues.

There can be difficulties which appear at the outset as families whose children are at risk are identified. When children are being abused or neglected, their parents not only find it difficult to seek treatment, but frequently they hide from it. Visiting in the home is mandated in most states to reach out to frightened, resistant clients as well as to assess the degree to which children are at risk. When clients are frightened and resistant, workers may feel they are intruding into people's lives and invading their privacy.

If the difficulties and resistances can be overcome, the worker can develop his or her own art of home visiting which will have a therapeutic effect all its own. The act of reaching out to people where they live, of providing nurturance in their own homes symbolizes the workers' willingness to enter their world and share its pain while, during the whole course of therapy, the needs and degree of risk in the home are assessed and reassessed.[2]

As the prospective worker begins to explore some of the many facets of home visiting in the context of protective casework, he or she will do well to keep in mind the significance of homes in Western culture, the concept of privacy in the home, and the meaning of visits of any sort in the home.

WHAT IS A HOME?

A home is a person's or a family's sacred space. What it is like, why it is like it is, who lives there, and what the quality of life is which is lived within the walls reflects the personalities, the pains, and the joys of its occupants.

Within the walls of a home, people experience the intimate moments of their lives. They sleep, wake up, bathe, eat, drink, make love, raise children. They fight, scream, and rejoice; they cry, laugh, and sing. They may experience the warmth of positive object relationships, the anguish of negative ones, or isolation and loneliness.

Peoples' homes are a reflection of themselves. Their outer space reflects their inner space. The way the homes are decorated and furnished can reveal either the chosen life-style of the occupants or the economic position. It can also indicate depression, despair, and disorganization.

Early in training, a therapist learns that understanding a client's ego defense structure is of paramount importance. He or she must first learn what the structure is, study it, and try to empathize with the client. He must try to feel what it would be like to "live in the client's skin" and in his or her defensive structure. Primitive defenses evoke deep feelings in us. In the transference, we find out what kind of life the client is experiencing. Projection is one way clients show the therapist how they feel.

A home may be likened to the defensive structure of the ego. It is the means by which a client protects himself/herself from the world and the base from which interactions take place. When a therapist has assessed the level of a client's ego functioning, the task is to help the client maximize strengths and grow. Similarly when a professional enters a home, the task is to assess and to diagnose in a nonjudgmental manner.

WHAT ARE VISITS?

In a culture where privacy in the home is highly valued, whom a person allows to cross the threshold, whom he or she decides to keep out, and the way time is spent with visitors reveals much about strengths and weaknesses.

Strangers at the door may evoke fear. A friend or relative visiting at a time of need may provide nurturance and comfort. Significant relationships develop when people share affective experiences with others in the home.

Home visits made in the context of clinical work are conducted by bringing to bear all the clinical acuity that would be employed in the office interview.

The very fact that the interviews are conducted in the home can add to the therapeutic value by virtue of the power of outreach, by the varied opportunities to diagnose pathology and assess strengths as life is shared briefly in the family arena, and finally as corrective experiences of caring are offered to people who have suffered serious deprivations.

POVERTY AS A FACTOR

Child abuse is not a problem of the poor, it is a problem of the deprived. People who have been deprived of love and nurturance, who have not been fed in the areas of their narcissistic entitlement will grow to adult years still feeling like needy, empty children; empty vessels with nothing to give. Low self-esteem and feelings of helplessness and emptiness make it impossible to give, to meet the demands of children.

Depression overwhelms and that depression is perceived on a continuum between rage and helplessness. If rage surfaces when demands cannot be met, abuse will result; the child will be hit. If the depression rolls over like a tidal wave, leaving the parent helpless and inert, we will see patterns of neglect—the child will be left unattended in the crib or playing unsupervised. This kind of depression is the same for both rich and poor. It is just that the rich can hide it better and can buy services to substitute for and share parenting.

Many incidents of abuse may go undetected in the homes of people who use private professional services. Suburban doctors and hospitals are often unwilling to become involved in reporting abuse or are blind to it when the families they serve are prominent citizens. How sad it is that by denying the problem, they are denying help to a family which is in as great need for service as the poor family visiting the local clinic a few miles away.

It does remain that most reported child abuse and, therefore, most protective service home visiting is done among clients who are poor and depressed. Their homes may reflect their poverty, emptiness, depression, and disorganization. Countertransference issues erupt the moment we arrive at the home. The homes of families where children are at risk may evoke painful memories of hard times we have experienced, or they may be unlike any we have ever seen. We must admit the feelings which flow and monitor our reactions so that we can understand and accept our clients.

Upon entering a home, it is of the utmost importance that a worker remember that he or she is entering someone's sacred space — no matter what the condition of the building, the distance traveled to reach it, regardless of the number of dogs, the darkness of the halls, or the odors of the stairways; no matter how barren or cluttered or "hospital" clean; even no matter what signs of impulsivity, violence, or sexual acting out are encountered. As the threshold is crossed, the worker has entered the space where a person's most intimate moments take place. In a very real, deep way, it is a privilege to be there.

It is important to be aware of the fact that the home is the client's own space where he or she can feel comfortable. In some instances this may help the client feel more empowered to grow and set the pace of therapy.

The task at hand, having explored what homes mean and the significance of visits, is to devise ways in which psychotherapy can be conducted in the home while still respecting the family space, system, and style; the social worker looks for ways to carry on an interview in virtually any setting and still remain highly professional.

Sharing of the home space and observations made there are used to accomplish the therapeutic tasks of outreach and acceptance. Individual treatment can be done in the home across all diagnostic lines. Meeting the family and significant others in the home provides opportunities to become an informal family, community, and network therapist.

CLINICAL ISSUES

Outreach

When a family is referred for assessment of alleged abuse and neglect, most states and agencies require that the evaluation be conducted in the home. Most clients would never come voluntarily to the agency.

A letter is usually sent stating the purpose of the projected visit, the date, the time, and the worker's desire to help.

As we think dynamically of people whose histories of deprivation have left them empty and unable to fill the needs of their children, we realize that the abysmally low self-esteem and guilt imposed by internalized "bad" self-image has caused them to isolate themselves. The appointment letter may be perceived as a frightening intrusion. Often upon receiving the letter, the client will call the agency. Whether he or she is expressing anger or fear, the call gives the client a chance to hear the worker's voice. It is amazing how much can be resolved through this sort of telephone contact.

Bonnie Bonnie received a letter stating that a report had been filed which alleged that she had been observed in the street beating her 7-year-old daughter.

Immediately, she called the worker who had written the letter. She was panicked and raised her voice over the phone. "I'll have you lose your job for this. You can't just go around accusing people of being unfit. I've even been to my lawyer, and he'll take you to court. I have seven children. I've won these cases before. No one is going to take my kids away."

The threats continued, and it was a while before the worker could get in a word. Finally, she said, "The first visits will be for evaluation, and I'm going to be looking for ways in which I can help you." Bonnie threatened again, "You'll never get in my home—what do you know about kids anyway? I have a hard time with seven." Here was a gift for the worker. While striking out in fear and anger, Bonnie had allowed the worker to know that she was overwhelmed with the care of her large family, and the worker knew that with care and patience she could build a relationship upon her genuine desire to help.

The worker paused and said, "Seven *is* a large family, they must keep you very busy." Bonnie softened. "Busy is not the word for it. I have no time to think and no time to see you." The worker quietly stated that it was essential that the appointment be kept, "I'll be there on Wednesday at 2:00 PM, and we can talk then." The worker was, in this case, not surprised when she arrived to find Bonnie and her noisy brood were ready to begin to form a relationship.

Missed Appointments

There may be many unkept appointments in the early stages of a relationship in protective work. People who have had histories of deprivation and abuse have little capacity to trust and to form good object relationships. They will be afraid for many reasons. They will be afraid of the worker's intrusion, afraid of losing their children. They will both desire and fear becoming dependent upon the worker.

It is essential that the worker maintain clear professional distance. It must be remembered that the client may be reacting to the worker as to an unreliable figure in the past. The worker must believe firmly that the intervention can be a great gift, that the resistance is not for the most part due to the situation but rather due to the past.

Consistency and caring are shown by the worker who comes each week on time, knocks and, if no one answers the door, leaves a note saying, "Sorry to miss you. I'll be back next week — call me if you want in the meantime."

Even if several weeks pass before the visit is finally completed, therapy has been going on through the closed door. The client has learned that the worker will not give up on him or her. There has been a demonstration that the worker's expressed anger will not escalate in response to rejection by the client.

Susan   Susan's 7-year-old daughter Linda had been seen in the clinic with a burn whose etiology was unclear. Stories told were vague and contradictory. The doctor filed a report of suspected abuse. The worker, who had already known the family but had been on vacation when the event occurred, was having a hard time reaching out. Eleven scheduled visits were made to the home when noises of family activity could be heard, but the door was not opened. The children were occasionally seen in the community so the worker knew they were all right, but she was persistent in reaching out.

On the twelfth visit, the client opened the door and said with unconvincing surprise, "I did not know it was you, come in." She was ready to work. Trust had been built through outreach and persistence.

Acceptance

Early in clinical training, workers hear repeatedly the injunction to accept clients as they present themselves. They are taught to find strengths, to understand, to be compassionate. They are taught to be nonjudgmental and not bound by personal prejudice, as they discover deficits and weaknesses, so that they can help clients grow.[3]

On the one hand, it can be said that in a very real way, it is intrusive to enter a person's home when one has not been invited. Often clients are just plain ashamed and afraid of rejection or disapproval. On the other hand, when a worker enters a home and shares a few moments with the inhabitants in their own space and genuinely respects them for their part in the struggle, remembering that the pain is theirs, the acceptance itself can have a healing effect. The very fact that the worker has gone through the exercise of finding the home and waited at the door, and entered in a nonjudgmental, accepting way is a statement of desire to help.

Jane Rejected by her mother — literally thrown into the street at 9 years old — Jane lived with her elderly, very limited grandmother. Neither woman had the energy to care for herself, let alone to care for Jane's three children. They rarely left the home. Personal hygiene was poor, dirty dishes and laundry were piled everywhere. A child was eating from a dog dish; Jane raised a belt to hit him. The large dog snarled at the visiting worker.

In less than a minute, the worker had been able to see characteristics of abusive or neglectful parents. Immaturity, dependence, sense of personal incompletion, difficulty with experiencing pleasure, social isolation, misconception of the child, fear of spoiling children, belief in the value of punishment, unawareness of the child's "needs" are all factors alerting one to the possible presence of abuse or neglect.[4]

The worker as intruder into this painful scene had to form a relationship with Jane, who was an involuntary client to be sure. The task for the worker was to use clinical understanding to help her accept this family as they were. As it turned out, the work was done through displacement. As the worker was able first to befriend the hostile, but much beloved dog, the family felt her acceptance. In this instance, the children could not remain in the home because the deficits were too great, but the worker's acceptance enabled her to help the family grieve the loss and grow.

Transference and Countertransference

As a worker moves into clients' homes and encounters different lifestyles, defensive styles, relational styles, fears, hostility, and differences in race, intellectual functioning, sexual preference, he or she must recognize feelings and monitor reactions. The client must be helped to contain his/her unfulfilled needs and wishes. The worker's own needs and wishes should be contained as well.

Dependency needs may cause a worker to lose professional identity. Clients may have a counterdependent style, and their desire for acceptance and their need to care for people can lead them to be ready to feed us, the workers. If the worker is not careful, the cup of coffee which is taken as a sign of acceptance of the client may turn into one meal and then another and another. Reasons for the client's giving and the therapeutic purpose served by the worker accepting must be thought through before simply allowing the client to "feed." All behavior is purposeful. Just as the conversation which seems casual and friendly often contains carefully thought out clinical intervention, so the giving and receiving of a cup of coffee can be the vehicle through which therapy is facilitated.

Adrian   Adrian had emigrated from the Middle East. Her family of teenagers had struggled to gain social acceptance in a community where they had no peers of the same ethnic background. They had rejected their Old World family customs. At the time of the Moslem holidays, Adrian had cooked the lovely traditional food, but no one would share it with her. The worker shared a small Moslem holiday feast at 8:30 AM on a scheduled home visit. Adrian felt validated and fed by the worker's acceptance.

Countertransference reactions can be used as diagnostic tools. Sometimes a flow of positive feelings can signal client strength. It is important to explore the significance of nostalgic feelings, too. A worker who has either raised children or who has strong positive memories of childhood may, upon entering a home, be flooded with memories.

Sandra   Home visits were made to Sandra in the late afternoon when children were coming in from play and supper was being prepared. The children would wash up and gather in the kitchen. Their play "squabbling" and ability to converse all gave the worker a "familiar" feeling. She was reminded of her childhood and of her own children. She was able to use those feelings to realize that, although Sandra was having difficulty controlling her impulses due to her depression, she also had obvious strengths as a mother.

There can also be a tremendous sense of vulnerability felt on home visits. This sense comes from the great responsibility we bear for the safety of the children. It comes from the reality of the children's vulnerability. It can come from memories of our own vulnerability as children which can be useful in assessing the degree of risk in the home. However, the countertransference reaction to what a worker sees may lead to misinterpretation and a biased assessment of risk. Insights gained are not infallible. What is seen with our own eyes and heard with our own ears can be subject to misinterpretation due to countertransference.[5]

Workers who are not accustomed to being in homes where there are roaches or rats or body lice or to entering communities where they are in a racial or ethnic minority can feel seriously frustrated by the myriad barriers to the attainment of goals. Working conditions are uncomfortable. It is very scary to be with clients who hurt their children. "Burn-out" is a real danger if workers cannot learn to use countertransference reactions as diagnostic tools. What stresses one worker may not stress another as much.[6]

There is no question, however, that we will all experience stress and inner conflict. The hardest times, of course, are when our own conflicts match those of the client and when we feel needy in the same ways.

When the patient delivers into treatment a failure to form relationships which has been repeated over and over again, and which is repeated in the therapeutic relationship at a time when the therapist experiences rage at his own unmet needs, a crisis occurs. Paul Russell [7] calls this "the crunch." It must be turned into a therapeutic challenge.

Monitoring feelings of need, the worker assumes the "good mother" role. The client whose needs have gone unmet for so many years, whose sense of worthlessness and failure have long been reinforced, will be slow to accept the offering of genuine care.

Helen Alexander [8] describes how home visits provide an invaluable setting for a corrective experience of mothering. There is an offer, she says, of the "friendship and love of someone who is unreservedly on their side and who is pleased to see them grow and thrive." The home visit provides a chance to gain insight into the family life and struggle in a climate more relaxed than in an office. She states that parents' fear of spoiling their children can be remedied by allowing the parents dependency on the worker.

Most workers find it hard to reconcile the ambiguities of the role prescriptions. They are usually trained and accustomed to doing therapy in an office/agency setting with clients who refer themselves for service. However, if they can muster the energy to deal with the resistances clients exhibit and the countertransference problems, social workers have an opportunity, through developing a theoretical base for therapy in the home, to contribute to an emerging synthesis of a more truly psychosocial approach.[9]

Diagnosis

Jean and Tony   During an early assessment home visit to Jean and her 5-year-old son Tony, the worker was surprised to learn that Jean had an older son, 12, and a daughter, 6, who lived across the street with her mother. As Jean recounted the family story, she said, "Most naturally, I was young when the older ones were born and my mother raised them. Tony's father is black and my mother said two mistakes was enough so I have Tony."

Tony, a bright-eyed busy little boy with an adorable, impish smile, was playing with his trucks under the kitchen table at which the interview was being conducted.

Jean shared with the worker that Tony had been toilet trained from age 2 until age 4, but had been encopretic for about a year since she had left his father and returned from the South where she had been living. She was at her "wits' end" with his symptom and had resorted to beating him with a sneaker when he was soiled — the basis for the report of abuse.

During the course of the visit, Tony crossed the room and began to dial the phone. Jean commented, "He learned to dial my mother on the phone; he dials, waits for her to answer, and then hangs up."

Tony did this at least a dozen times, and the worker realized that the grandmother must be becoming very angry on the other end of the line and commented on that. Jean asked Tony to stop with a tone in her voice and a look on her face which Tony knew meant, "Keep it up, you're doing just fine." He, of course, complied with the latent, rather than the overt, spoken message. It was clear Tony was being used both to annoy grandmother and to make a connection to her.

Grandmother could not reach the house by phone so she sent Jean's older son over to spank Tony for her. Tony, terrified, tried in vain to hide under the bed. The older brother slapped and kicked him while Jean talked to her mother on the phone, "Now you see what *I* go through, Ma. He's impossible. He does it to aggravate. He won't mind me."

Tony had become the repository for everyone's anger, direct and indirect. His feeling of powerlessness and inability to make sense out of his environment revealed the reasons for his sympton. He was withholding his bowel movements as an unconscious means of demonstrating that there was one place where he could control his environment. The seepage around the impaction of the bowel caused the soiling, and Tony once again felt out of control.[10]

The entire interaction had taken place in only 10 minutes, yet the worker had had the opportunity to gain a depth of diagnostic understanding of this family which would have taken weeks to achieve in the office setting. For people with poor impulse control, who act out their anxiety and depression in behaviors which are completely ego syntonic, the home visit is an invaluable setting in which to observe what the client does not even feel is a conflict and would, therefore, not articulate in an office visit.

In this visit, Jean's lack of separation and individuation from her mother and the resultant symbiotic bind and hostile–dependent relationship were all observed through nonverbal behavior. Jean's nonverbal cues to Tony to continue the annoying phone calls were more powerful than her words to stop.

Coyle[11] described the great influence space has on family structure. The space in which the family lives is the place where the nuclear family is united. The home is the chief arena in which family members interact.

The life space of this family was divided by the street between the two buildings. Jean's mother was raising her two older children as her mother (Jean's grandmother) had raised Jean's older sister. Jean's use of the words "most naturally" (my mother is raising the two older ones) indicates that this pattern was ego syntonic for Jean. Disappointments in early relationships for Jean and her mother had set up in each a strong repetition compulsion. Since neither had achieved full psychic separation and individuation, the family was fully enmeshed. The worker was later to learn that there were far more primitive expressions of symbiotic ties between Jean and her mother, but this visit laid crucial groundwork.

As we imagine Jean alone coming to therapy in an office setting—if she would even come—it is safe to say it would have taken much, much longer to learn about the pathological relationships and enmeshed quality of this family. Jean perhaps would not have even thought of reporting the incident of Tony and the telephone, because her part in it was ego syntonic. In the home setting, seeing how Tony became the bearer of mother and grandmother's conflictual hostile–dependent bind and was then encouraged to act out "between" them, it was possible to set a goal to help Jean gain some awareness of her part in the interaction and to work toward making her maladaptive behaviors ego alien.

Jean's characterological style prevents her from feeling her depression. Anxiety was her briefly felt affect which impelled her to translate her pain into action. She would not have been able to verbalize exactly what goes on at home. She would never have described this or similar events because she could not experience them as painful or causing difficulty.

We could be with her in her pain, share it, help her identify it, and help her modify her actions and behaviors to reduce it.

Levine[12] suggests that the social worker bring along materials for creative projects or simple games which the family can play. These, she says, "can serve as media through which conflicts between members are revealed as they participate in activity and free-wheeling responses occur." She further states that in the home visit problems are revealed and diagnoses are more accurate as distortions are eliminated.

Stephanie   Stephanie was a depressed mother of five elementary-school-aged children. She had been alone with them since their father, whom she had never married, had left four years before. The barrenness of her home signaled her depression and lack of sense of being entitled to pleasure and joy. Her abysmally low self-esteem, which had its roots in her own childhood of deprivation, made it hard to meet her children's demands. She resorted to harsh punishments when they drained her energy too much. She rarely ventured out, and when she did, it was with all of her children "in tow."

The worker spent a series of home visits during the assessment phase playing games with Stephanie and her children around the kitchen table. Stephanie's harsh competitiveness with the children quickly revealed her neediness and symbolized the family competition for the meager supplies of love, energy, and money. During the sessions, as Stephanie was allowed to "win," she was also able to draw from the worker's modeling of appropriate behavior to learn possible new ways to interact with her children.

Poverty dictates much, but not all, of the substandard quality of the homes we visit. We have all known people whose economic position would allow for a better life-style, who because of depression or being unable to meet the myriad demands of children live either in stark, empty dwellings with cartons which have remained packed since a move, or with the clutter of family life piled all around. A person's level of self-esteem, creativity, and characterological style are revealed in the way the home is ordered. The literature contains much about the use of home visits for diagnostic work.

Behrens and Ackerman[13] warn that rigid adherence to classical psychoanalytic theory can lead to too much emphasis on the internal economy of the individual personality. Acknowledging that professionals often feel that home visits are an infraction of privacy (although it may be the only way to reach a troubled family), they feel that not seeing people in their homes dichotomizes person and environment to the detriment of the diagnostic process. In the home, one can focus on the interaction patterns, role behavior, physical environment, atmosphere of the home, daily activities and functioning, and reactive behavior of family members to one another.

Hollis[14] points out that a home reveals many personality characteristics of its inhabitants. The extent to which regressive or primitive oral or anal traits are prominent can be drawn from firsthand witnessing of client interaction with children.

Chaos and disorder can signal severe depression, intellectual limitation, or low self-esteem. By the same token, barrenness can signal the same assessment. Each detail is to be observed and weighed with other factors in the formation of a diagnosis.

Margarita Margarita, an Hispanic mother of four, suffered manic depressive illness. In the manic phase, she suffered religious delusions which caused her to discard all her possessions. As the cycles of her illness moved through the first year of treatment, the worker alternately saw a nice, but simple home occupied by an intelligent, well-functioning woman and her children whose brilliance and humor bore testimony to her parenting abilities and then later a barren home devoid of all furniture with her family sleeping on the floor. In periods of psychosis, Margarita's religious delusions "dictated" that she discard and destroy all household furnishings; auditory hallucinations caused her to shave her children's heads. Her unreliable, bizarre behavior greatly frightened the children. The worker took action through the court to remove the children from the home and to place them in foster care.

Because the worker had shared months of family events and interaction through home visits prior to the need to take action through the court, the family trusted the worker's genuine desire to protect. Margarita was hospitalized, and she received needed medication which she had been refusing and returned to the home to face the task of refurnishing the home and rebuilding life.

Home visits provided a chance for the worker to share the barrenness and unpredictability of the children's lives, for assessment to be made that the children felt that they were to blame for the disturbances they experienced, and that it was they who had to provide nurturance for their mother. Therapy in the home provided reassurance that they could rely upon caring adults for assistance when mother was unable to provide.

Extreme neatness and rigidly compulsive housekeeping may signal rage. Anger and dirt seem to be scrubbed away, bound, or sublimated by the harshly adhered to housekeeping rituals. As stated above, we must realize that such a home may be in fact an expression of a frail, defensive structure which may be holding a murderous rage. We must not be quick to encourage such a housekeeper to "let down" or "be good to herself" because in so doing, we might deprive her of her much-needed defensive pattern and may ourselves unleash the rage.

Helen   Helen's son had died tragically as a result of being hit by a car. She was referred for treatment because she could not bond with an infant daughter. She spent time rocking herself in a chair holding the baby and imagining it was her son in order to tolerate the holding. Her only release was to clean, clean, clean. Treatment was slow because to encourage her to grieve before she was ready would have been as risky as telling her to relax her cleaning rituals. The worker's weekly hour in Helen's home was at first tolerated coldly, but eventually and very slowly Helen's gradually growing ability to own her feelings enabled therapeutic progress. She briefly used group therapy to good advantage and, when treatment was terminated after three years, the little girl was a healthy child and, while not exuberant, she was allowed to play normally and even to mess up the house once in a while! Helen had learned to get in touch with sadness around her many losses and had gained new skills in self-expression.

It is important to note that our diagnostic observation in the home will also help us identify client strengths. A home which is neat but appears lived in, with artful decorations, however simple, tells us that the client has tried to design the space to express himself/herself. Positive countertransference reactions can be used diagnostically. If a well-functioning person enters a home and feels he or she is on "familiar ground," it is important to pay as much attention to this as to negative countertransference. We may be in the home of a person who is well defended and who has a good enough sense of self to feel entitled to beauty and pleasure.

Ongoing Treatment

Goals are to help parents replace abusive and neglectful patterns of child-rearing and methods of care. Parents are supported and rewarded as they learn ways of parenting which are conducive to a child's healthy development. To reopen channels for growth, we must build self-esteem, develop basic trust and confidence, and learn to make contacts with other people in their world, family, neighborhood, and community for supports. We must foster ability to enjoy life and have rewarding experiences.

The primary task is to aid the parents first so that they can care for their children. The parents' depleted reservoir must be filled so that they have something to give. Modeling behavior, stimulating the children, and bolstering sibling relationships are secondary to giving to the parents.

We must at all times remember that parents who present inaccurate information are not trying to outwit the worker, nor are they to be thought manipulative. They are, rather, like frightened children telling untrue stories to avoid being hurt. Home visits can afford the worker a chance to learn and see the truth and therefore be able to help.

Kempe and Helfer,[15] as they outline the dynamics of abuse, describe the parents as desperately needing gratification from their children, so they inflict severe punishments to ensure proper behavior. Abusive parents are highly vulnerable to criticism, so if spouse or a child gets mad, the parent must turn to the child for gratification.

People need others to validate themselves, to nurture them, to support them. They cannot live in isolation. They need support in the present and from the past. The isolation of the abusive parent is inflicted by guilt or humiliation of failure and by little ability to form good object relationships.

Alexander[16] states that the worker assumes the "good mother" role. It is difficult to reverse patterns long entrenched and stemming from the parent having had to gratify his/her parents' needs, where worthlessness and failure have for so many years been reinforced. Alexander goes on to say that in the relaxed climate of the home, the worker not only gains insight into the family life and struggle but can foster appropriate dependency. Parents who are allowed to be dependent can let their children be dependent. Their fear of "spoiling" their children can be remedied by this. Sometimes when the visits seem unfocused and too much like visiting, real therapy may be going on. The worker is offering to the parent "the friendship and love" of someone who is unreservedly on their side and who is pleased to see them grow and thrive.

A crisis of emotional deprivation can trigger the pattern of abuse stemming from the parents' having been raised in a similar system and criticized for failing to meet parents' needs. The worker has a chance to reverse this by giving sufficiently to the parents. A real goal of treatment is that the worker become a self object for the parent in accordance with Kohut's[17] concept of self object.

A self object may be defined as an individual or a group which performs a function or functions which are vital to the maintenance of the self and which, in later maturity, the self autonomously performs for itself, such as soothing, giving a sense of self-worth, narcissistic pleasure, and loving approval.

Elizabeth Elizabeth was a 30-year-old woman whose first daughter, now 10, had been in foster placement and residential treatment for four years since Elizabeth had seriously injured her while under the influence of drugs. The ambivalence in their relationship had never been sufficiently resolved, and although they had infrequent contact, which was sometimes positive, they could not live together.

At the time of referral, Elizabeth, who had had diabetes mellitus since her childhood, had recently delivered a son who was thought to be at risk. Elizabeth's illness prevented all but minimal functioning and a large group of paraprofessionals and professionals were needed to keep her going. The new strength in the situation was the relationship she had with the child's father, who provided her with loving support. Services by homemaker, visiting nurse, doctors, babysitters, and professionals involved with the 10-year-old in placement all had to be coordinated carefully.

Elizabeth had delegated a portion of her ego functioning to each provider, and keeping open communication between them was the first therapeutic task to help her function optimally and provide ego integrity. Elizabeth's history of abuse and deprivation had left her with no ability to trust. In fact, she was isolated in her home, even phone calls being perceived as an intrusion.

To this day, after five years of therapy, she still needs to begin each encounter with a gruff comment or a hostile "What do you want?" in the place of "Hello." She needs to do the rejecting first, always fearing rejection herself.

Years of home visits in which the worker did all in her power to give her a strong sense of identity and validation and to provide security to bolster that provided by the baby's father eventually fostered a sense of self-worth. She began to consider that she was worthy of better health. She began to lose weight and basked in the approval the therapist provided as she worked as she had never worked before to follow the medical regimen which could allow her to avoid diabetic reactions and insulin shock and render her more able to care for her child.

The fact that she had abused and refused to use prescribed medications at earlier times in her life was acknowledged and worked through.

In the context of the therapeutic relationship, she was able to use it as a mirror in which to view her present good functioning. With the diabetes now under good control, she and the worker together celebrated the new life and improved care of her child. She had been able, through treatment, to begin to neutralize her conflicts, change her life rhythms, and begin to confirm her own ego.

The process is long and slow because correcting maladaptive patterns established long ago takes time. It is important that workers doing therapy through home visits remain constantly interested in every household detail and in every statement and interaction and make full use of all observations in the therapy.

Pitfalls and Roadblocks

There are pitfalls and roadblocks to progress in every interview but, as in the office visit, these can be turned into "grist for the mill" of therapy.

Broken appointments are discouraging, and it is a strong worker indeed who can leave a fourth or fifth no-show visit without wondering what she/he may have "done wrong." But, as stated above in the case of Susan, much work can be accomplished through no-show visits and, as treatment goes on, they can be discussed as they would if a professional in analysis failed to keep an appointment with his/her analyst.

On entering a home where the television is blaring, one can, of course, ask the client to turn it down. This may help the client to value the hour and feel given to. On the other hand, the loud television can be considered as a resistance maneuver not, perhaps, very different from the weekly intellectualizing of the bright client in the therapist's office.

Television can be used in almost the same way we use play therapy with children or projective testing. Themes can be drawn out and identified by the worker and the client's reactions observed.

Elaine Elaine's youngest child, Susie, had severe cerebral palsy and was profoundly retarded. She repeatedly warded off any idea or suggestion that Susie's condition was irreversible. A soap opera, in which an adolescent was confined to a wheelchair, brought forth Elaine's tears, and through this displacement she began to mourn over Susie's condition and the loss of the perfect daughter she wanted.

Fraiberg [18] in her brilliant work on treatment of the baby as patient, recommends treatment of mother and infant together in the home, with therapy sometimes done through the baby, talking as the baby would talk to the mother.

> It is a therapy that moves from the mother's communications to the baby's, then back again from the baby to the mother. The method em-

ployed in this therapy is an adaptation of the method of psychoanalytic therapy, united with developmental guidance on behalf of the baby. The therapeutic work for the mother is one of listening, observing, and giving permission to feel and to remember that which can be remembered, examining the past in the present, undoing painful effects of the past, giving hope and the prospects of new solutions to old problems. The therapeutic work for the baby is one in which the mother is helped to recognize the baby as a symbol of her abandoned self, to find pathways to understanding the sorrows of early childhood (her own and the baby's), to find pathways of feeling which can unite the mother with her baby in hope instead of futility.

Peggy Visits with Peggy, age 16, were usually held in the bedroom. She was pregnant, depressed, alcoholic, and spending much time in bed. She was also rarely alone with her child at home. Usually, her house was a gathering place for several other adolescent mothers, so that going into Peggy's room afforded some degree of privacy for the interview. Peggy's borderline functioning and tendency to fuse made the worker intensely aware of the need to be just as clinically distant as she would have been in the office setting, while remaining at ease in the bedroom.

At times, the other young mothers would join Peggy and the worker in the bedroom. It was important to achieve a subtle balance between working with Peggy as a primary client and to give to the whole group for their own needs and as an informal network therapy for Peggy. This group was her support in the absence of a caring family and she, in turn, supported them. Theirs was a network which worked for them and one through which good psychotherapy could be done.

In the bedroom setting, a relationship was able to develop in which these young mothers were nurtured. Appropriate use of intimacy fostered their growth and increased their healthy expression of their emotional needs. As the worker reparented the parents, their ability to parent their children was fostered. The presence of the children enabled the worker to speak through them to their parents. While holding a crying child on her lap, the worker said for the child to his mother, "Mommie, I want a hug." The mother, with the worker's help, responded to the child's need. Later the mother could share with the worker her own needs for affection so long unmet.

In summary, although home visiting is demanding work, it is of great clinical value in therapy with families where abuse and neglect of children have been identified. The willingness to reach out to the families wherever they live is symbolized by the visit itself. Being in the home provides opportunities for initial and ongoing assessment of problems and strengths. Because the clients feel at ease in their own space, they may feel empowered to both set the pace of treatment and to modify behavior in accordance with new learning through therapy.

Finally, there is something deeply moving about being with a needy, deprived family, sharing for a moment their intimate space, helping them learn to acknowledge their own unmet needs through remembering their history, and helping them grow in ability to relate to one another in a healthy way.

REFERENCES

1. Turner FJ: *Psychosocial Therapy: A Social Work Perspective.* New York, Division of Macmillan, Free Press, Division of Macmillan, 1978, p 77.
2. Bloom ML: Usefulness of the home visit for diagnosis and treatment. Social Casework 1973;54:(2) p 67.
3. Hollis F: *Casework: A Psychosocial Therapy.* New York, Random House, 1964, pp 183–190.
4. Pollock C, Steele B: A therapeutic approach to the parents, in Kempe HC, Helfer R (eds): *Helping the Battered Child and His Family.* Philadelphia, Lippincott, 1972, p 11.
5. Hollis F: *Casework,* p 183.
6. Daley MR: Burnout: smoldering problem in protective services. *Social Work,* 1979;24(5):375–379.
7. Russell P: The theory of the crunch. Unpublished paper, 1976.
8. Alexander H: The social worker and the family, in Kempe CH, Helfer RE (eds): *Helping the Battered Child and His Family.* Philadelphia, JB Lippincott, 1972, pp 22–40.
9. Overton A: Aggressive casework. *Social Work,* 1952; 33(3):145–151.
10. Erikson E: *Childhood and Society.* New York, WW Norton, 1950, pp 50–58.
11. Coyle G: Concepts relevant to helping the family as a group. *Social Casework,* 1962;43:351.
12. Levine RA: Treatment in the home—an experiment with low income, multi-problem families. *Social Work,* 1964;9:19–21.
13. Behrens M, Ackerman N: The home visit as an aid in family diagnoses and therapy. *Social Casework,* 1956;37:11–19.
14. Hollis F: *Casework, p 174.*
15. Kempe CH, Helfer RE (eds): *Helping the Battered Child and His Family.* Philadelphia, JB Lippincott, 1972, pp 4–5.
16. Alexander H: In Kempe CH, Helfer RE: pp 28–29.
17. Kohut H: *The Analysis of the Self: A Systematic Approach to the Psychoanalytic Treatment of Narcissistic Personality Disorders.* New York, International Universities Press, 1971.
18. Fraiberg S: *Clinical Studies in Infant Mental Health: The First Year.* New York, Basic Books, 1980, p 551.

Where do I tie up all the ends?
Mine and hers
Are tangled
Like my old sewing box
With all the threads knotted together
because of neglect and love and
Anger — almost hate, and our needs
Into one big ball
of misunderstanding
I must untangle
To cope with the pain
And use any love that's remaining
to mend.

Written by a young mother
receiving child protective
services about her own mother.

6 Ego Assessment and Treatment Planning

Deborah A. Hill
Eleanor C. Knox

This chapter will focus on the development of a treatment plan arising out of a series of initial child protective assessment interviews in
which gross pathology, disorganization, and a state of crisis have been
identified. Discussion will include a review of the content of a
psychosocial assessment with emphasis on recognizing and utilizing ego
strengths which can form the basis of a treatment plan. This approach of
identifying and building on the client's own coping mechanisms is one of
supporting growth through ego enhancement and rechanneling of drives.
Case examples will illustrate the dynamics involved.

The protective worker must pay heed to the areas of a thorough
psychosocial assessment, outlined by Hollis[1] and others, while recognizing that there may be necessary gaps in information for a variety of
reasons. Essential areas include an understanding of the nature, extent,
and duration of the problem(s) as viewed by the caseworker, the parent,
and the referrer; an understanding of the precipitating event; the client's
social situation, including source of financial support, health and

employment status, and identification and description of significant others; the influences of the client's culture on the presenting problem; an historical understanding of the etiology of the problem(s), including personal and developmental histories; and a diagnostic picture of the client based on an appraisal of his ego functioning, including the areas of self-image, identifications, perception, reality testing, stress tolerance, judgment, nature of relationships, and choices of coping mechanisms. Some of these areas have been discussed in Chapter 4. This chapter will focus primarily on the two latter aspects of ego functioning: nature of relationships and choices of coping mechanisms.

Treatment planning evolves from sound diagnostic thinking, and the caseworker's treatment is continually enhanced by new knowledge and observations which contribute to that thinking and influence treatment planning accordingly.

The amount of information overtly shared by the client varies considerably. The caseworker's assessment must encompass her observations, and those of others who have worked with the family, as well as her thinking about those significant areas of history and present-day functioning which have not been shared. Information and history are best gathered by gentle elaboration in areas of the client's own focus, it being clearly explained to the client that the purpose of information gathering is to best understand the problems so that appropriate help can be planned. As discussed earlier, the development of a beginning working alliance is basic to obtaining meaningful information. In the vast majority of cases, this alliance can be established because of the existence of family needs. The client's natural fears and resistance to the caseworker's involvement are lessened by a number of factors, including her compelling need for a helping person in her life and for certain environmental supports or services. Further, the objective reality embodied in the reason for the caseworker's presence in the client's home is a concrete reminder that something important has occurred. Finally, the client's concern for the children lessens her resistance.

The following vignettes illustrate situations which are not uncommon in protective services:

As the caseworker entered the Smith household she met Mary, head bowed, intently scrutinizing the picture puzzle before her. On her earlier visit to the Jones household, Jimmy had proudly led her into the room and, his eyes ablaze with enthusiasm, showed off his new train set. On yet another visit to the Bennett household, Sara was soberly and painstakingly coloring within the lines in her new coloring book.

What, the reader may ask, is noteworthy about this? The noteworthiness lies in the fact that Mary, Jimmy, and Sara are not aged 9, 5, and 7, but rather parents of young children described as suffering from abuse and neglect.

The obvious gross pathology and enormity of problems in these families and in most protective service families can easily cause one to overlook or deemphasize individual and family strengths. Yet it is these strengths which hold the promise of growth toward better functioning and which can provide both client and worker with encouragement as they face the ups and downs inherent in the treatment process. In one sense it seems that the identification of strengths in some clients calls for arduous searching. From another viewpoint, given the overwhelming odds against which the client is struggling, one might marvel at the obvious strength called for to simply survive, much less to contain one's rage by racing trains or coloring within the lines. Were it possible to remove some environmental stresses from certain clients, one wonders what latent talents might spring forth. Most protective service clients have suffered from severe and chronic neglect and/or abuse as small children. Opportunities to experience fulfillment of basic nurturing needs were seriously curtailed. Combinations of external stresses and continual crises, along with internalized stress, have finally resulted in behavior toward their children which is described as abusive or neglectful. This represents a sad and unwitting repetition of their own experiences which they have tried desperately to avoid. The capacity to trust, to build self-esteem, to internalize controls, to learn, and to achieve had all been adversely affected causing ego deficits. It is these ego deficits which must be tempered ultimately as the casework treatment focuses on a support of the client's demonstrated strengths.

Winnicott [2] says that emotional development starts at the beginning of life, and stresses that it is essential to the growth of the child's healthy personality to have an environment of "good-enough mothering." It is important to remember that many of our clients have been deprived of this essential primary relationship. Instead they experienced a kind of parenting which led to unsuccessful completion of the developmental tasks of separation and a growing sense of self as an individual. Each of these adversely influenced future relationships and adaptation to later events. The first and primary relationship is fundamental to the development of all future relationships and to the growth of many individual characteristics. Other factors affect our personality. These are innate intelligence and talents, as well as the evolving components of memory, other identifications, cognition and, later, judgment, stress tolerance, impulse control, and reality testing. A composite of these factors is called forth to meet the growth tasks of life. Each new developmental stage allows for an opportunity to rework old issues and, given the proper environment, create new and improved ways of mastery, resulting in a sense of accomplishment and enhanced self-esteem. If mastery is less successful, there is a compounding of earlier failures and lowered self-esteem. All these combine to make up the self or ego, and the ego organizes and responds to life's stresses with a unique combination of coping mechanisms.

Perlman [3] states:

> Conscious intentional coping is probably the major process in which we engage the client with whom we plan short-term treatment. It is clearly central to crisis intervention; and even to long-term help, past the release of conflict-bound energies, past the necessary modifications of feeling and thought, there often remain to be learned and practiced the strategies by which action-in-task and person-to-person relationships can be carried out more efficiently.

In the treatment approach advocated here, we assume the client is in crisis at the time of the referral (although the situation may be chronic). Further it is assumed that family equilibrium has been disrupted. The caseworker seeks and selects specific ego strengths in the client and helps her utilize and reinforce these strengths to restore equilibrium. A casework relationship evolves out of the client's needs and worker's ability to partially fulfill some of the client's relationship deficits, thus improving the client's sense of well-being. This in turn enhances her capacity for relationships and alternative behavior.

The caseworker meets the client at a time of crisis when she has allegedly abused and/or neglected her child. The relationship starts at this moment of disequilibrium for the client whose normal state is tenuous at best. The factors which generally help maintain balance and control are: (1) one's current sense of well being, (2) one's resources and strength of recuperative power, and (3) the quality of the fundamental mothering one received. Given that the client has very likely had inadequate basic parenting, has little reserve, and is presently acutely overwhelmed, it is little wonder she is in a state of crisis. Feelings of past failures are evoked, and she struggles with a perceived sense of criticism of her mothering skills. Her child has made a demand on her which hits at the heart of her vulnerability and which has caused her to lose control.

While strengths are as myriad and unique as each individual, the following represent some of the characteristics commonly found or sought after among this group.

Of chief importance among these characteristics is the identification of some small amount of trust. A degree of trust sufficient to let the worker in the door is a significant strength and is crucial to the process which lies ahead. While some clients initially admit the worker primarily out of fear, and others with a clear plan of convincing the worker they have no serious problems, without this opening, no work can take place. The presence in the client's life of any present or past meaningful relationship shows the client's capacity to relate and provides a toehold for the worker in developing a relationship. The worker would want to listen for how that person had been meaningful to the client so as to obtain clues as to how she can be helpful. The client's ability to share information and feelings in whatever degree and of whatever kind is noted as an asset, as this gives the worker the opportunity to demonstrate that she can tolerate the patient's feelings, that they can be safely expressed.

One frequently encounters clients who are eager to please and who tell the worker just what they think she wants to hear. While one can recognize that it is the core need to be accepted that is manifested in this way, and while this posture on the client's part may currently ignore her own needs and those of her children, this need to please others may allow for the worker's continuing involvement toward the goal of the client eventually learning some ways to please herself.

The existence of maternal caring, despite neglectful or abusive behavior, is a significant asset. The caring may be laden with ambivalence, it may be overdetermined, it may represent an effort to make up for the client's own lack of care, but nonetheless, it represents a crucial strength to be bolstered. Caring may be distorted by poor judgment (letting the child go off with continually disappointing and potentially harmful father because the child yearns for the missing father, frequently keeping the child home from school out of some perceived need of the child, when in reality mother needs the child, or harsh beatings for misbehavior in order to teach child right from wrong), but nevertheless the caring represents a basic strength on which to build.

Other clients may be driven to helping or rescuing others, be they family, friends, neighbors, animals. Although this may signal the client's basic need to be rescued and given to, she is defending against this in a manner that brings her satisfaction and, possibly, the gratitude of others, raising her self-esteem. Also, these rescue impulses provide an available context for focus on the child's needs.

The client's sense of herself as a separate individual is a definite strength, as is the client's sense of pride in her children, and the ability to get some comfort from them is a positive finding. Although a mother's pattern of looking to her children to meet her own unmet needs is a problem, the fact that she feels deserving of someone's care is an important starting point for treatment.

Intelligence is an important strength, as is a sense of humor. The capacity to look with some small sense of objectivity at events or behavior and view them with humor is an invaluable asset.

A sense of the basic things children need is another critical strength; for example, an awareness that children need attention, limits, adequate food, clothing, supervision, and an opportunity to learn. Although parental expectations of the child may be too high, for example, that older children assume premature responsibility for younger ones or that a child excel in school, the fact that the expectation conveys a hope for the future in addition to a projection of the parent's need can be seen as a strength. Often poor judgment is involved when mothers go off to work, in an effort to provide more for their children, leaving them with inappropriate caretakers. The caseworker can, however, continually reinforce the mother's concern that her children receive certain things (often things she herself did not get as a child) while helping the parent assess priorities and act in a way that also protects the children.

Ability to manipulate the environment is an important asset. This may involve the cunning necessary to get what is needed to survive on a welfare budget, the ability to enlist the help of other people, to stand up for one's rights, or to display the qualities of resilience or "street knowledge" necessary for survival. While extreme manipulative behavior can have a negative impact, the client who can be helped to eventually be more moderate and discriminating in channeling her energies can do much to obtain needed services and feel empowered.

Fanatical housecleaning may serve a useful function for repressed feelings, for enhancing self-esteem, and for an outlet at times of stress. Hobbies and activities can help perform these functions as well.

An area of accomplishment or completion of a task in the client's life which can serve as a reminder that she can accomplish other things is very important. This may be continued attendance in school despite turmoil at home, working at a job for a period of time, learning a skill, or caring for younger siblings. Frequently clients view themselves as having no accomplishments, and identification of abilities by the caseworker can be extremely useful. This helps increase esteem and enables the risk-taking inherent in trying something new. As clients need to learn new skills in managing children and a household, every effort should be made to support evident skills. Some clients are adept at painting or wallpapering, others at ceramics, still others at puzzle or picture completion.

A client's ability to write about her feelings, such as in the form of poetry or diary keeping, helps to dissipate feelings in a productive way. This material may eventually be brought into the treatment sessions and put to further productive use.

Lastly, the failure to develop more regressed or self-destructive modes of functioning must be noted as a strength. The caseworker, in taking a detailed history of profound pathology, may wonder at the fact that the client is not psychotic or dependent on drugs or alcohol. She must assume that there were some positive influences somewhere in the client's life and must listen carefully for them in order to support and tap that well of strength which is enabling the client to cope with a multitude of stresses.

CASE ILLUSTRATIONS

The following case examples illustrate the development of treatment plans arising out of several evaluation interviews during which strengths are elicited and noted.

The Phillips Family

Mrs. Phillips was hurrying home after class. She had just taken her last test of the year. She had not finished it. She had flunked it for sure! There was only one more class this year. She would miss the classes. They were so peaceful and well organized. There was no confusion or yelling. And people talked to you. What on earth would she do all summer without school to keep her going? It was so different since her separation. She was anxious, she felt all jittery and scared. How could she manage the kids all summer? It seemed as if she were alone, even when her husband was there. She was alone except for the kids. The summer was going to be terrible.

She hurried into the house with something for supper, still thinking about her class and the long summer ahead. Suddenly she tripped. She had tripped over 10-year-old Donald's jacket and school books. He had strewn his things from the front door to the kitchen with his usual disregard for her. He always left his things around. He did it on purpose. He should know better than to play games with her, especially when she was so upset about school, her test, and summer coming.

This was it. She called to Donald upstairs, and he came to the kitchen reluctantly from the safety of his bedroom. She could feel it coming. She was edgy. She had had a terrible day. She did not want to yell at him, did not want to fight. She was tired of fighting. It was her house. He had seen his father fighting her when he didn't pick up his things, fighting about everything as a matter of fact. He just lay around and drank; never took responsibility, never helped her. They were just alike. Neither of them cared.

Mrs. Phillips and Donald started talking about the mess he had left. Dirty dishes all over the kitchen, too. How could she get supper? Before she knew it, she was yelling. At first Donald was sullen, quiet, protesting mildly that he had not done anything. A few moments later they were yelling, screaming at each other. It had happened before. Suddenly he came toward her with a knife. She fell.

She did not remember much after that until she "came to" in the hospital emergency room. She was sobbing and found herself talking with young Dr. Paul. A neighbor was with her. They told her she had not passed out. Her mind must have gone blank. Now she remembered the fight with Donald. They had been screaming when he picked up the knife. She had fallen in the tussle. Was she hurt? She seemed a bit shaky, but not seriously hurt. A few sore spots. What about Donald? Had he been hurt? She went to the waiting room and spent a few minutes with Donald and his elder sister, Jeannie. Donald was bruised up some too, but was okay. On returning to the examining room, she began to tell her story more calmly to Dr. Paul and nurse Miller. Although neither Mrs.

Phillips nor Donald had been seriously hurt, they were to return to the hospital frequently over the next four weeks. This was the first of a number of visits during which the hospital trauma team staff would help her unravel her tensions and begin to sort out her life.

Case material developed as follows: Mrs. Phillips was a 36-year-old separated mother of three children. Tom, the oldest, was 19 and lived across town with his girlfriend. Jeannie, 17 years old, and Donald, 10, were at home.

The family was supported partially by Mr. Phillips' support (payments erratic), supplemented by Mrs. Phillips' occasional earnings as a homemaker. Jeannie had an after-school job sometimes. Mrs. Phillips attended school part-time studying for her LPN certification. Jeannie was a high school junior, and Donald was in fourth grade.

Mrs. Phillips and the children's father had been married when she was in high school and became pregnant with Tom Jr. When Tom was 3½ years old and Jeannie a toddler, she left Mr. Phillips. They had a fight when he had been drinking heavily, and he knocked her across the room. She hit the table, was hurt, and had to be hospitalized. Mrs. Phillips had been pregnant and lost the baby. There were many other fights, but Mrs. Phillips reported this was the most serious. She could no longer take his drinking, fighting, lying around, and laziness. It was too much, and she had to do something. She would leave him. She would show him. When she was released from the hospital, Mrs. Phillips went back home to stay with her parents for a while.

Mrs. Phillips was the middle of three children of hard-working parents. Neither parent finished school, but father particularly valued education. He was self-taught, read a lot, and was good with his hands. He was a mill worker and brought home most of his money, but he never spent much time with the family. He was either out or in his workshop. She would go to his shop once in a while, but he ignored her. When she returned to her parents' home after her miscarriage, Mrs. Phillips suddenly realized how little she knew about her father and how much her parents fought.

Mrs. Phillips realized, too, how much she was like her father — angry, arguing, always doing something, but never really getting anything done. He knew people but was not close to anyone. She could not count on him. She did not know much else about him. When she was still with her parents during her separation, her father died of cardiac disease and alcoholism in his mid-forties. At that time Mrs. Phillips was 25 years old, Tom was 9, and Jeannie was 7½.

Mrs. Phillips' mother had not finished high school when she married. She stayed home and kept a clean house. She worked very hard but, like her husband, she had a terrible temper. They were always fighting. Mother was a seamstress and did sewing because money was short. While she had no medical problems, Mrs. Phillips said her mother always looked tired and appeared older than she was.

Mrs. Phillips could not remember ever being happy. Everything she dreamed about went wrong. She did not dream anymore. Her older and younger brothers always had more attention and got their way, while she was made to help with the housework. She was fearful of getting yelled at, hurt, or thrown out of the house if she did not do her chores.

Mrs. Phillips had few friends in school. She was too embarrassed to bring them home. She was not allowed to go out much because she had to do housework and watch her younger brother while mother did the sewing. Her first boyfriend was Tom. He was handsome and dashing like her father. Good with his hands, too, and a hard worker; she had liked him.

Their marriage was bad from the start. They had not gotten along. He never talked to her—just made her wait on him. He did not understand what it was like to have to spend all day running after first one baby, then another. He paid no attention to her and gradually spent more time away from home. She had less and less money for the house. They fought all the time. His drinking became more frequent, and the babies were bothering her, too. Then the night they fought and she had the miscarriage, she decided to leave him. During the next four years while at her parents' home, her mother looked after Tom and Jeannie. Mrs. Phillips worked part-time and took courses to get her graduate equivalent degree. It was a good time in her life. She was beginning to feel like someone, even though her father did not talk with her much, her parents continued to fight, and her mother was very critical of her still.

During this period she saw how difficult her mother's life was. Father was drinking more and more, and her mother had to take on even more family responsibility. Father would fight more openly on the job and with mother, too. He was sick often. He kept forgetting things and kept on drinking. Then after he died, Mrs. Phillips began to get very "nervous." She was no longer able to watch Tom and Jeannie after school, pick up after them, or watch them while she tried to do her homework. Mrs. Phillips reported that she could not remember much about this period when her father was so sick and after he died. It was all very confusing for her. When Tom asked her to come back to him, she did. Maybe he had changed; he said that he had and, after all, Tom and Jeannie needed their father. They were already 9 and 7 years old. Soon after they reconciled, Mrs. Phillips became pregnant with Donald. It started all over again, his drinking, the brutality, the blaming.

She remained with him until Donald was 9 years old; then they separated again. Even though they had been separated for nearly a year now, life was not much better. Had she done the right thing? She was so alone. She wanted to be a good mother, but how could she hold up under the strain? Everyone gave her trouble.

In response to questions about the children, Mrs. Phillips could give very little information. She did not know about their likes or dislikes, their friends, activities, what or how they were doing in school, or what they did at home after school before she returned. She knew only that the house was a mess, and it was Donald's fault, that while Jeannie used to help her around the house, mostly now she was very distant. She really did not know how she felt about that. She guessed it was all right.

Additional information obtained from the neighbor who brought Mrs. Phillips and the children to the hospital, from the children themselves, and from brief contact with teachers at school led to an understanding that information given by Mrs. Phillips herself was very understated. Attempts to contact Mr. Phillips were unsuccessful. Outside sources reported Mrs. Phillips had a terrible temper with frequent and unprovoked outbursts. She cleaned house incessantly and ran about in a frenzy much of the time. When the children were not home, she was in and out with different men who seemed to be drinking heavily, but she cared about the children and seemed pleased by some of their accomplishments. In recent months she was yelling at Donald a lot, and they had a number of physical fights. She lost her temper with him and had hit him several times.

The neighbors talked readily, and it was apparent that while they were critical of Mrs. Phillips, they liked her. They were concerned about her and the children. They went on to describe her as fluctuating between hot and cold—either friendly or ignoring them.

Contact with school revealed that Donald was at appropriate grade level, but his teacher was concerned because he was an underachiever and sporadic fighter. He was a bright enough youngster but was paying less attention in class and often his homework was incomplete. He was beginning to fail some of his subjects and skip school more. He seemed to be a very sad youngster and at times quite sullen. He had no friends and would do best when other children approached him. In the past few months he was fighting more and beating up the younger children and seemed to lose his temper very easily about small things. Jeannie was doing all right with her classwork and got passing grades. She was popular with the boys but resented group activities, particularly with girls. When she was encouraged by one of her teachers to participate in a group project, after-school activities, or a workshop on future careers, Jeannie remained aloof and was very insulting. This teacher was concerned about Jeannie and believed she was spending too much time with boys and feared her behavior would get out of hand.

The clinical impression of Mrs. Phillips was that of borderline personality with chronic depressive features and a question of alcohol dependency. The particular fight that brought the family to the emergency room seemed to arise from growing panic, loss of school contact and routines, while she was faced with spending more time with the children.

The more underlying threat appeared to be Mrs. Phillips' deterioration following her second separation from her husband and the unavailability of mother since father's death. Donald seemed age appropriate in many ways; however, there were beginning patterns of withdrawn and antisocial behavior. Jeannie was at risk of becoming increasingly isolated from and hostile toward adults in authority, and there was the possibility of sexual acting out. While this was in part typical teenage behavior, it appeared to be verging on the extreme.

Achieving a diagnosis is certainly a step toward determining treatment. We believe it is essential to go further by making an individual descriptive diagnosis looking at the ego strengths and the developmental phase of relationships. Then the treatment plan can be formulated in a contract with the client (whenever possible). Mrs. Phillips was depleted, openly depressed, terrified that she would lose control, or go crazy like her mother. She was angered that everyone else was messing up her life. What is there in this client and family that we can believe in to help her gain a beginning self-assurance? What will help her turn around the feelings imparted by a father who "ignored her" and a mother who was "too busy" to give her the encouragement she needed?

Defenses: Escape and flight; approach and avoidance   Mrs. Phillips ran herself ragged. She would try something and get sidetracked, start and stop. She was fearful of both the extra time on her hands (emptiness) with classes ending and the need to spend more time (closeness) with her children. She wanted to be with others, yet she needed to be alone. She needed Mr. Phillips and wanted to be with him, yet, how could she? She frantically avoided becoming like her mother yet had a need to be accepted by her. She was erratic with her adult relationships.

She needed to keep in mind that the children's father was a destructive man despite her pull toward him. The energy, ideas, and wish to achieve and have friends were there. Our work was to help her harness them so tasks could be finished and she could be pleased, so she could learn to behave with others in a way to avoid getting hurt or driving them away. Mr. Phillips had been a reasonably good provider and had a good work ethic. Later work might focus on these facts to help facilitate a stronger relationship between Mr. Phillips and Donald if it were possible.

Compulsivity   Mrs. Phillips' house was clean; she was easily upset by Donald's things being strewn about. She believed the house was a mess, although it did not seem so to visiting staff. She had been persistent, albeit haltingly, in pursuing further education and improving herself with part-time work. Introjection and identification were demonstrated by Mrs. Phillips' use of her father's emphasis on learning and her mother's emphasis on hard work.

Mrs. Phillips valued these things and equated them (unconsciously) with a good self. She hardly knew they made her feel good. She hardly knew she liked her father and mother for these qualities or that they liked her for them, the reason being Mrs. Phillips had also identified with the angry, fighting, rejecting side of her parents. She saw only that side of them. She knew them only as paying little attention to her and fighting with each other, and she had no awareness of the similarities between Mr. Phillips and her father and her marriage and that of her parents. Yet the fighting Mrs. Phillips did was very much like their fighting. It was one of the ways she had learned to behave.

Treatment work needed to be directed toward utilizing education, hard work, and learning, while aiding in the control of the anger, fighting, and physical outbursts. In a later phase of treatment, the absoluteness of her convictions (feelings) could be gradually tempered with more accurate information and more realistic perceptions.

Denial and projection   Mrs. Phillips was not significantly struck by the violence of her fighting with Donald which brought her to the emergency room. Had the neighbor not heard the row and been concerned, they would not have come. Mrs. Phillips regarded it as just another fight (even though Donald had the knife, had attempted to harm her, and both were out of control). She did not see herself as "frantically running about" — just tired now and then and sometimes not getting things done. She was unaware that she took on more than anyone could possibly do. She was unaware she did not know much about her children.

At the time of her first emergency room contact, Mrs. Phillips was just beginning to feel that things were out of control, when in fact her life had been out of her control since some time before her father died, perhaps beginning when he became seriously ill. From Mrs. Phillips' perspective, husband, children, mother, and father each were to blame in his turn. They made things go wrong, and because of them she could not finish things. Mrs. Phillips had little sense of self-responsibility or that she might be able to do things differently. The use of denial and projection were indeed helpful to Mrs. Phillips for if she saw the full reality of her situation, she would be overwhelmed. None of the children were living up to their potential, and they were starting to act out more. She and Donald were on a collision course where one of them could get badly hurt. Her marriage held no positive satisfaction, and she had no other meaningful relationships. Her mother was severely depressed, and mother as well as children needed her help.

For the present it was the worker's job to help Mrs. Phillips maintain her denial so that her tenuous adjustment would not be jeopardized. These defenses could and should remain in place as long as the protective service work can move forward (ie, she is willing to work with the agency) and as long as significant fighting with Donald does not continue. As

Mrs. Phillips becomes more in command of the situation and feels more accomplished, she will begin to take on more responsibility for her own behavior. The projection and denial must be challenged directly by the caseworker at times when the risk to the children heightens or Mrs. Phillips' resistance takes the form of blocking the protective service work.

Isolation   Mrs. Phillips retreats and runs from encounter to encounter. She has few friends and, when she does make contacts, she seems to get involved with men much like her husband and father — handsome and charming, but heavy fighters and drinkers. They end up yelling and fighting with each other. She has been hurt sometimes, although never seriously enough to require medical attention. When it gets too bad, she stops seeing her boyfriend and remains home alone for a long period of time. The women she meets all disappoint her. They do not seem to care about her, and they cannot be trusted, so why bother with them.

While this behavior is similar to the approach and avoidance defense discussed earlier, it extends it further by shutting off contact altogether. (If I keep my distance from people, they cannot hurt me vs I will fight with you when you get too close.) The themes of both isolation and approach and avoidance are of particular significance in the working relationship with Mrs. Phillips. Signs of anger at worker, "picking a fight," or backing away are signals that the client is experiencing a much needed closeness and simultaneously is becoming distrustful and frightened of that very closeness and caring she needs. Depending on what the specific issue is and what the contractual goals are, the caseworker could do at least one of three things: (1) allow Mrs. Phillips to back away a bit to remain in control; (2) utilize the relationship and take strong control to provide a supportive structure; or (3) point out the behavior, thus focusing on the relationship. This latter choice should be made only when working directly with transference issues.

Agitated depression   This should be handled cautiously, particularly when seen in combination with Mrs. Phillips' impulsivity. It can be a strength, however, when that energy helps her accomplish the many things needed to care for the children and the house, as well as to work part-time and go to school. Using up this energy also helps vent (in a disguised way) some of her anger.

In working with Mrs. Phillips, it is preferable to address the anger in its displaced and projected position, until she is in better control of herself and can tolerate introspection. The caseworker can focus on Mrs. Phillips' expressed anger toward men in the present and disappointment with women as examples occur. She also can work with complaints about the children's behavior as they emerge. Specific anger-provoking behavior can be cited by way of example and Mrs. Phillips helped to realize that it is all right for her to be angered or disappointed, but she may wish to consider other ways of approaching the children if she wants them to change the behavior.

For Mrs. Phillips, the heightened anxiety she experienced as her classes were ending, her tendency to "get into many things," her flight from family responsibility, combined with her compulsivity and pleasure in a clean and orderly house, led to an understanding of a woman who can feel better about herself and life the more she cleans and picks up and the harder she works. Conversely, she is threatened by the absence of a project with school out for the summer and the thought of more time with the children. A line of questioning which further explores her interests and tests out this hypothesis could lead her to consider a structured, readily accomplished activity, fulfilling her need for hard work and home improvement.

It is feasible also to help her evolve a plan that will give space for Donald's messiness and still keep her space neat and orderly. Mrs. Phillips might be encouraged to define limits and expectations for Donald and to carve out time for herself. One might also wish to explore activities that Mrs. Phillips could do with Donald and some friends: a trip to the zoo, a baseball game, or swimming. This would give time and attention to him but in a way that provides them both with a less intense relationship, thus honoring his ongoing need for more separation and her desire for isolation. Summer day camp might be a possibility also as Donald is at an age where physical mastery and expanding peer relationships are his developmental tasks.

In assessing strengths then, one looks to what makes the client less anxious, feel less harassed, and takes the side of the ambivalence in each of the operant defenses that can be turned toward a constructive plan. This provides maximum protection for the children and satisfaction to the parent.

The task is to defuse where possible the external, objective explosive situation for the protection of the children and to find an alternate pattern for a constructive relationship. Assessment of strengths, an approach familiar to most caseworkers, then becomes the tool for exploring with the client new ways to behave and avenues for further accomplishment.

Why do we say this? Why is it so essential to seek out, emphasize, and reinforce those positive strengths? Why indeed? Because we are "Pollyanna," prefer to "cop-out" on the fundamental pathology, or because we are inexperienced? In many ways it is far easier to be pleasant or avoid explosiveness. We take this approach quite deliberately, for every caretaker who is abusive and neglectful is under constant stress to contain feelings of primary rage, rejection, helplessness, and hopelessness, whether these feelings be disguised or open. During every moment with the child, there is a constant reminder, in one form or another, of the clients' own needs and deprivations. Their control is always tenuous and their defense system is in place for the purpose of maintaining optimal equilibrium. Our approach serves to reinforce the most helpful defenses while exploring ways to change those that are less helpful and to exchange shaky relationships for stronger ones.

Little successes help create new experiences. A change in perception follows and, ultimately, feelings begin to change. It is the sustained presence of the caseworker that emerges as the key to change, while the activities engaged in together become the tool of the relationship. It is the skill of the caseworker's selection of activities, pacing the intensity of the relationship, awareness of transference and countertransference issues and, ultimately, her behavior that permit and encourage the distressed client to move forward to a new developmental phase and further capitalize on her own inner resources.

The Roberts Family

Mrs. Roberts was referred anonymously to the state child protective agency. In identifying herself as a neighbor (but not willing to identify herself further) the referrer conveyed, with some degree of credibility, that she feared small children, ages 18 months and 3½ years, were being abused, that there were frequent sounds of loud fights heard coming from the Roberts apartment, and that adults came and went at all hours of the day and night. The referrer suspected drug use. She reported the children played unsupervised in a busy street and were often heard crying for long periods of time.

The protective worker regretted her inability to contact the referrer because of the opportunity that contact would have given to obtain additional information as well as assess the relationship between the referrer and Mrs. Roberts. However, knowing that the staff person who took the call sensed credibility and genuine concern in the referrer and knowing from experience that many anonymous calls, when explored, yield information even more serious than that originally conveyed, the worker knew she must see Mrs. Roberts without benefit of additional information. She knew, too, that having no documentation that the children were at risk, such as would come from a clinic or social agency, it would be more difficult to deal with the client's denial, should that be forthcoming.

The worker wrote to Mrs. Roberts, stating that the child welfare agency had received a report indicating that she might be having serious difficulty with her children and that the worker would like to meet with Mrs. Roberts at her home to learn whether there were some ways the agency could be helpful. She conveyed a proposed date and time for her visit, suggesting that Mrs. Roberts call if it should not be convenient and arrange another time.

The worker heard nothing in response to the letter, mailed several days in advance of the appointment. As she reached the building and climbed to the top floor at the hour of the appointment, she noted its general rundown condition, dark interior, typical of the only housing available in the area to those of low income. As the worker knocked, loud voices could be heard from within. The door was opened promptly, and in response to the worker's identifying herself, the client acknowledged she was Mrs. Roberts and her voice quickly rose as she said with some anger that, yes, she had received the letter and that she was having no problems whatsoever with her children. She demanded to know what this was all about. As she spoke, her mother and sister, clearly summoned for the occasion, appeared behind her, both attesting to Mrs. Roberts' good parenting. Maternal grandmother glared and spoke angrily to the worker, implying the agency was only out to cause trouble and should mind its own business. As the worker gently replied she would very much like to tell Mrs. Roberts why she was there and wondered whether they could talk together for a bit, the client begrudgingly demonstrated appropriate social skills, asking the worker to sit down at the nearby kitchen table. Her mother and sister promptly retired into an adjoining room. Worker sensed they were relieved to be able to depart. Mrs. Roberts, a tall, thin, young woman of 20 years, radiated tension from every nerve, reminding the worker of a taut wire about to snap. Her rage was palpable. She seemed in perpetual motion as with quick, abrupt movements, she moved about the kitchen readying coffee, pointed defensively to her clean kitchen and newly painted walls, and yelled to the two children to come meet the worker, as demonstration that they were clean and well cared for. She said she had been a nervous wreck ever since the letter arrived. Someone was obviously out to get her. Throughout the time she scarcely sat at the table for more than a few minutes, busying herself feeding an early lunch to the children and jumping up to loudly admonish Jeffrey, 3½ years old, to better supervise his sister, Kathleen, 18 months. The worker conveyed an understanding of how upsetting it must have been to get the letter and that she was glad of this opportunity for them to talk it over. She was glad to meet her family also, whose coming reflected their concern for her. She proceeded to explain her agency's function and to detail the contents of the report.

She explained the referral was anonymous and that she had regretted her inability to talk further with the referrer. She put the facts of the referral in the framework of concerns about the welfare of both the children and Mrs. Roberts and affirmed that she was there in order to learn from Mrs. Roberts how she saw things and to see how she might be of help. To Mrs. Roberts' frightened proclamation early in the interview "You're not going to take my children away!" the worker was able to state clearly that her agency's goal is the very opposite, that of helping families stay together, but that she and Mrs. Roberts needed to meet together for a while to try to understand how this referral came about and what she could do about it. Someone was evidently very worried, and the agency dealt seriously with such concerns. Mrs. Roberts hastened to assure the worker that she had already figured out who must have made this malicious call. It was probably her ex-husband with whom she had had a fight, and he must have called from out of state because she had no idea how to contact him. But the next time she saw him, he would really get a piece of her mind. She denied all the allegations in the report. She never let the children out alone to play; of course she was not on drugs — how could she care for her children if she were? Did she look like she was on drugs? As for people coming at all hours, only once had her brother been visiting late and when he had an argument with her boyfriend, also visiting, she asked him to leave. She did not hit her children. She might yell, but she did not hit. All of this was making her feel nervous. She felt sick.

Worker gently picked up on this and learned from client that she developed hives and eczema when she was upset; that she had a history of severe headaches, blackouts, difficulty eating, and weight loss; and that she had recently been having persistent stomach pains, but had not seen a doctor. She had no time, did not know when she could be seen locally, and had no one to mind the children. They were such a handful that no one wanted to mind them, and mother and sister, who lived at long distances, both had other responsibilities. They could not help. She had explored enrollment for them in day care, but could not afford the fees on her public assistance allowance. And of course, she said bitterly, she got no help from their father. He gets off scot-free, and she is left with all the work. She had tried so hard to make a good home for the kids, and all she has had is trouble. She no sooner gets one place fixed up when she has to move. She is in the process of moving now, even though she just repainted here. The landlord does not like children. Besides, the neighbors are difficult, always complaining. Suddenly it struck her that maybe it was her neighbor who had called the agency. She does not like Mrs. Roberts because of her children's noise.

At one point when Kathleen escaped from her brother and came to the kitchen requesting a cookie, Mrs. Roberts took her in her lap and hugged her. She commented that Kathleen had been a worry, she had recently had a minor head injury. She had fallen down the stairs while playing with her brother and had been briefly unconscious. Indignantly, she said the hospital had given her a hard time, they had insisted she see a social worker before she could take her home. What did they think, that she hit her or something? She had been afraid they would not let her go home.

Meanwhile, mother's sister wandered into the kitchen, in the guise of seeking a cigarette, sitting briefly but long enough to say she knew someone who had had a social worker who had been okay. Worker thought to herself that sister might also be in need of help, but knew this must await her alliance with Mrs. Roberts.

Kathleen, a somewhat fretful child, seemed content to sit on her mother's lap, but able to leave it as well. She looked to be a well-developed child with good motor development and some beginning speech. She was only mildly curious about the caseworker's presence. She was clean and well dressed. Worker saw no marks on the exposed parts of her body.

Jeffrey looked to be a large child for 3½ years old. His behavior toward his mother was noteworthy in that he responded to her requests or demands with an odd, fiercely challenging stare. Although he did his best to meet his mother's demands for supervising his sister or picking up after himself, she frequently yelled at him, it being her expectation that he would fail or deliberately disobey. He was noted to be aggressive with his sister. No obvious marks were observed on him, either.

As the interview was drawing to a close, the worker observed to mother that she could see how very much she cared about her children and was trying to provide the best possible home for them. (She had admired the paint job as mother, picking up on her interest, proudly showed her around the apartment, which like the kitchen, proved to be spotlessly clean and tidy.) It sounded as though mother was experiencing considerable tension and pressure, that she was worried about her stomach pains, and that finding day care for Jeffrey might give mother some respite.

She would like to return next week to continue the talk they had begun today and to meanwhile find out what openings the day care centers might have, should mother decide to send him, and what the walk-in hours of the local medical clinic are. Mother, her fear returning but less intensely, protested that these were not serious problems, but agreed to the appointment.

It was another three weeks before worker was able to sit down again with mother. Client called to cancel the next appointment, stating she was too busy packing and painting. The following week, worker arrived at the new address, willingly given, to find mother, who greeted her with surprise, saying she forgot the appointment and was on her way out to pick up her children. Worker did not press, acknowledged the importance of picking up the children on time, and scheduled a return appointment for the following week, which was kept. There followed additional kept interviews over five weeks. Although mother remained defensive about the report, the worker's sincere wish and demonstrated ability to understand and help gained her beginning confidence. She was desperately in need of help, and anger about the referral was slowly replaced by focus on Mrs. Roberts' problems and their history. It is noteworthy, however, that throughout this period, the worker's sense of connectedness with the client remained vague and tenuous. Anxiety remained her primary affect.

The worker learned much to help her understand both mother's resistance to intervention and her overall difficulty in coping. She elicited history in a way that made sense to mother whether it was inquiring as to whom she had available to her (which led to history of family relationships, peer relationships, and marital relationship) or what the children were like to care for (which led to their developmental history). However, history was given sketchily and without elaboration.

Worker learned that Mrs. Roberts was raised in a family where her father, whom she never knew, had abandoned them. Mrs. Roberts' mother had been a frightening figure who beat all the children, but Mrs. Roberts more than the others. She did not know why. When she was very young, she was sent to live with her alcoholic grandmother of whom she spoke somewhat longingly. Her two younger brothers and sisters remained with her mother. She did not know why her mother did not keep her. She returned home off and on; she and her mother fought bitterly and physically; and she would always return to grandmother's care. Worker listened for what grandmother had been like and heard that she listened and tried to understand, but that she did not let her granddaughter get away with things. She was strict about coming in early, insistent Mrs. Roberts attend school, and particular about things around the house. The client had friends who were important to her and had had one teacher who was strict, whose attention she sought, and who praised her drawing talent. She moved in with a girlfriend and remembers being able to eat better. She attended school regularly. She got involved with boys early and eventually met Arnold, who fathered her two children. Their relationship was a tempestuous one. He could never make a commitment to work or marriage. Later, to spite him, she married another man, David, whom she did not love, only to have that relationship terminate quickly. She had been attracted to Arnold because he was so good to her, bought her things, so she felt he really cared, but he was also good for her because he stood up to her and did not let her get away with things. David had been a passive man, a "mother's boy," and had no ambition. But he had given her children his name, and she was grateful for that.

Mother had been glad when she became pregnant with Jeffrey at 16. Jeffrey was born prematurely, had respiratory problems, and "nearly died on me." When his sister was born, he was jealous of her and treated her roughly. Jeffrey had always shared his mother's bed.

Worker found it noteworthy that on her third evaluation visit she heard client speak bitterly of both maternal grandmother and sister, whom she now perceived as rejecting and using her. As they had seemed her only sources of potential support, their perceived alienation would leave her quite bereft.

The worker learned that Mrs. Roberts' present boyfriend was Arnold, the father of the two children. Mrs. Roberts spoke of trying to effect a reconciliation and spoke optimistically of his intentions of getting a job. She cited his tolerance of going into debt to let her buy 16 nightgowns she craved. On the fourth visit, client's face was badly swollen, and she admitted that Arnold had beaten her during an argument in which she had struck him first. She blamed herself and acknowledged this was not an uncommon event. Since client could have canceled the visit, her need to let the worker know what was happening was evident. Worker wondered with her whether it would be helpful for the three of them to meet together, but Mrs. Roberts, as she had all along, needed to keep Arnold very much in the background for the present. That part of the work would need to await her readiness.

Also of great significance during this evaluation period was mother's searching explanation for feeling full of aches and pains one day—"they [referring to the children] probably beat me up in my sleep," she soberly speculated.

She also alluded to physical confrontations with a critical neighbor, enabling worker to better understand why the report which caused her involvement was anonymous. Mrs. Roberts also mentioned, as an aside, that maternal grandmother's health had been deteriorating, and she was now in a nursing home. This caused the worker to wonder whether it was her feared loss which had precipitated the increased tensions resulting in the anonymous referral.

Now having met with mother a sufficient number of times to gain a foothold of trust and to assess the dynamics involved, the worker was convinced that this was indeed a family at risk and that she better understood what mother needed and how the course of treatment was likely to unfold.

The worker perceived that Mrs. Roberts' sense of rejection by both parents had left her with vast unmet dependency needs and rage intolerable to bear, as reflected in her intense and perpetual anxiety. As a result of her mother's abuse and grandmother's neglectful parenting, basic needs were not met nor did she experience consistency or effective limit-setting. Not enough information was available to understand all the dynamics of Mrs. Roberts' relationship with her mother. We do know that Mrs. Roberts felt deeply unworthy and sought outwardly the controls she lacked within in becoming involved with Arnold, who was abusive. Her capacity to exercise control over her impulses was tenuous at best. She identified negatively with her son, projecting onto him her anger and "badness."

The worker experienced and observed her client's defense mechanisms — denial, projection, splitting, flight, reaction formation and compulsivity — and considered how to best work with these. She noted her pervasive anxiety and chronic somatization.

She felt her client's dynamics were best understood as characteristic of borderline personality functioning. The strengths, which were many, included Mrs. Roberts' bond to both children, her desire to feel more in control, her concern for their physical care and basic environmental needs, her undaunting search for approval, her organizational skills, punctuality, directness, and some constructive outlet for stress (housecleaning). These strengths would be emphasized and built upon in treatment.

Just as her mother and sister were seen by Mrs. Roberts as alternately supportive and rejecting, the worker expected Mrs. Roberts would continue to view her this way and that she should expect unkept appointments, distrust of her motivations, provocative testing behavior, perceived rejection, and demandingness. Mrs. Roberts would need to have the worker be clear and firm about their need to meet, yet allow her to set the pace of their work. She had seen no evidence that the mother was in any serious way resorting to alcohol to deal with stress, and the worker saw this as a significant strength, noting the positive identification with some of the more constructive coping mechanisms of maternal grandmother.

She would need much help with the cause-and-effect relationships in her behavior so that she could come to experience more control over her life.

The worker understood that maternal grandmother's worsening health represented a tremendous threat to Mrs. Roberts and that the perceived losses of esteem through criticism or threatened abandonment by the few significant others in her life would raise her vulnerability to the loss of self control which was already so tenuously held. These losses might also increase her physical symptomatology.

The worker and Mrs. Roberts negotiated a contract as Mrs. Roberts articulated her wish to feel less nervous, to feel calmer with Jeffrey, to have things go better in her relationship with Arnold, and to feel settled in her housing situation. She and the worker agreed to work toward these goals with the worker making weekly home visits.

Hopefully, a positive relationship with a worker who respected Mrs. Roberts' need for safe distance and focus on realities of daily functioning would enable her to eventually develop a network of relationships about her to which she could turn. This would occur as she discovered the caseworker could be trustworthy and reliable and that she could find things of value in that relationship. The opportunity to meet with a group of mothers at some point in the future would be helpful. This would offer support and a more diluted transference situation.

When mother could separate from him, Jeffrey would benefit from day care. When mother had some relief from his care, hopefully the times they spent together would be less intense.

It was unclear whether mother could tolerate the closeness of the relationship with Arnold, but should he continue to be a part of the family life, it would be helpful to offer treatment to him if and when mother could accept this.

This method, applied toward the goals of increasing Mrs. Roberts' self-esteem and the development of constructive outlets for her anger, would be expected to take a significant period of time. Consistency and continuity would be crucial.

The Brown Family

Evaluation in the following case leads to a decision for placement. Sarah Brown, 25 years old, was referred to the protective agency by her departing social worker who had worked with her for three years. The social worker's interventions had not been successful in lessening the neglect of the children which stemmed from Sarah's chronic depression. The worker's energies had been caring ones focused on Sarah and her needs. At the time of the referral, Susan was 2 years old and Mary was 4 months. The children, whose routine medical appointments were not kept, were not receiving necessary inoculations.

The worker wrote to mother expressing a desire to be helpful and referring to the departed worker's concern that she continue to receive services. She visited the home several times before she was admitted. That her presence was perceived as a threat was immediately evident. A large, chained dog barked and growled. Sarah admitted her after introductions and retreated from the door, leaving the worker to follow her into the dimly lit kitchen, uninvited. The degree of depression in Sarah was immediately evident from her physical appearance as well as her surroundings: she walked in a sluggish, stooped fashion; hair, body, and clothes were obviously dirty and neglected; and she was considerably overweight. The few times her eyes met those of the worker, they mirrored fear and despair. She retreated to a kitchen chair, and the worker did likewise. The kitchen reflected the same level of care she saw in the client — stacks of unwashed dishes, garbage not yet emptied, clothing and other items in disarray. Poverty was evident in the sparse furnishings and generally rundown condition of the apartment.

In response to the worker's low-keyed explanations of why she was there, the role of her agency as a helping one, and acknowledgment of her sense of loss over the departed worker, Sarah conveyed anger and helplessness. "The fact the children haven't had medical care is Ralph's fault. He said the children should see a private doctor. He knows best." Just to talk seemed a great effort. Her affect was bland and depressed, her mode of expression strikingly childlike. She had no money for carfare to get to the medical appointments, no one to help her manage the two children, and the long wait was more than she could manage. The worker acknowledged what a handful that would be with two young children and inquired who Sarah had available to help. "No one," was the reply. Limited information was painstakingly obtained, sufficient to make it clear to the worker that Sarah indeed had no one to turn to. Her mother was dismissed as never having been available, her father unknown, her three sisters and two brothers rarely seen, and her boyfriend, Ralph, around whom the only strong affect appeared, was repeatedly disappointing.

The worker indicated that she was there to help and that perhaps together they could find a way to get the essential medical care for them. She then focused solely on Sarah, gently reflecting on how hard it must be to lose the social worker she had known for so long and wondering how she had been helpful. The worker continued to focus on Sarah, although she felt apprehensive at not seeing either child — only a carriage from which no sound or movement arose. Picking up on the enormous job of child-rearing Sarah was attempting to handle alone and specifically her frustration in handling her 2-year-old, she offered the additional services of a parent aide who would visit regularly.

Sarah did not protest, and the worker felt this concrete attention to her acute loneliness and overwhelmed state was received with some relief. She left with a clear plan of returning the following week and bringing the parent aide to introduce her.

However, the worker could not gain access again for several weeks. Her knock on the door was met only by the barking dog within. When she did next talk with Sarah, she found things much as before. This time she met the children. Susan was quietly and intently trying to stick her finger into an electric outlet. She looked at the worker with only mild curiosity, eyes lacking the bright, alert luster of a healthy 2-year-old. She and her sister, sound asleep in her crib, were like mother, poorly clad and unwashed. A dirty bottle lay in the crib next to the infant.

The worker, having had to deal with a multitude of countertransference feelings from the start and struggling to combat the oppression she felt, knew that the tasks which lay ahead were enormous but could only be addressed one at a time. There was the issue of the belt lying handy across the washing machine and the belt mark on Susan. There were the broken phonograph records with which she was playing and the can of Drano in her hands, and there was Sarah's obliviousness to these things. There was dog feces on the floor, and Susan was eating out of the dog dish. Through all this, with the worker and parent aide dealing directly with the things which posed greatest danger to the children, a relationship was slowly being established with Sarah. The worker elicited her love of pretty things, and they talked about fashions together. The worker used Sarah's fondness for word puzzles to help her master some reading.

The worker used the displacement of the dog, whom Sarah adored and for whom she went out in a storm to buy food, to reflect on her caring for vulnerable creatures. Sarah acknowledged her loneliness, her sense of rejection by her mother, and her feelings of failure compared to a successful sister. Her desire to trust and use the help of the worker was strongly opposed, however, by her utter dependency on the approval of Ralph, who was distrustful of the agency involvement and strongly advised Sarah not to listen to the worker.

Thus the medical appointments arranged for the two children were not kept, despite plans for the parent aide to accompany Sarah and the children. She simply would not open the door. She protested that they did not need inoculations to protect against disease, that God would not want them to be sick. Patient explanation and concrete help could not offset her depression, intellectual limitations, and the threat of disappointing Ralph. Repeated efforts to engage Ralph through Sarah were not successful. In the meantime, no improvement in the home environment had taken place. Conditions continued to be as dangerous and unsanitary as originally noted. Sarah was unable to use the structure provided by the agency to provide essential basic care. The worker let mother know she would need to seek court intervention to order care if mother could not allow for it herself. Still, mother could not. The worker sought court intervention. Sarah appeared for the court hearing, knowing the worker was recommending the children remain with her but that Sarah comply with their medical care and safety needs and to keep weekly treatment appointments with the worker. The worker sensed that Sarah viewed this action in a dim way as a caring one, and she let the worker sit by her in the court waiting room and welcomed the amusement of drawing pictures, much as a small child would.

In the few sessions worker had managed to have with Sarah, she had seen the client's brief glimmers of a pleased response that someone was interested in her. She had heard enough snatches of history but particularly had seen in her observations that Sarah had been profoundly neglected, had received little formal education, and certainly had no help with child management issues. She had remarkably little sense of who she was as a person and what she felt or thought. Common responses to questions of what she thought about things were responded to by "My mother thought . . ." or "Ralph [boyfriend] says . . . ." Intelligence was limited. Judgment capacity was severely limited. Her desperate desire to be accepted by and cared for by Ralph, whom worker was never able to meet, ruled her behavior. She was torn between the two, continually disappointed by the unmet promises and frequent physical abuse levied against her, but looking to him to magically be the returned father who had abandoned her. The crisis which precipitated placement illustrated the subjugation of the children's needs to her own. In an argument with Ralph, Sarah held the baby out the window threatening to drop her if Ralph did not comply with her needs. She described the baby as favoring Ralph, conveying the criticism of her mothering skills she had projected onto the baby. She admitted that sometimes she felt like killing the baby and herself as well.

In this case, the prognosis for successful intervention was seriously impaired by the extent of pathology and the relative dearth of strengths upon which to build. The client was seriously impaired in her cognitive, social, and psychological functioning. There were no "lifelines" to help, and the desire to please and to reach out to the worker was countered by the client's need for the boyfriend, who promoted her distrust. Sarah's unmet dependency needs left her with little to give to her children. She had no effective channels for her aggression, which was turned inward in the form of depression and passivity. Feeling worthless and helpless, she looked to others to give her direction. Unfortunately, she had no consistently available people to whom to turn, nor had she ever had that crucial bond. She could not identify the children's needs as separate from her own or act on them. Her heavy reliance on denial and projection, while blunting intolerable inner pain, compromised her capacity to identify problems and deal with them. The worker was viewed primarily with distrust and as omnipotent. Sarah had little capacity to judge what behaviors led to what results. Diagnostically the worker viewed Sarah as suffering from an atypical personality disorder with significant depressive features. This, coupled with her intelligence deficits, caused the worker to recognize that expectations of sufficient change soon enough to care for and protect the children were unrealistic. In this family, it was the very existence of the children, rather than any particular precipitating event or stress, which taxed this mother so severely.

The worker felt the goal should be permanent placement of the children and ongoing treatment for Sarah, focusing first on issues of trust and identity.

COORDINATION OF RESOURCES

Most protective service treatment plans call for careful coordination of a variety of resources. Crucial and central to them all is the treatment relationship with the parent(s). Usually the worker can also serve as the coordinator of the other required services. These resources can only provide a useful function, however, if they are introduced in a timely way, if parents are involved in the planning, and if there are clearly stated goals to be achieved. Because it is not uncommon for clients to use the dynamic of "splitting," caretakers often find themselves at odds with one another, thus making close collaboration both difficult and extremely important. Chief among the resources often employed is day care. Day-care programs with qualified staff providing good care to children grants the child an accepting environment providing warmth, consistency, and help with a variety of developmental tasks. It can provide an anchor of security for a child whose life may lack this ingredient essential to growth. For mothers, the relief from 24-hour-a-day tensions that day care provides can sometimes enable a child, who otherwise would require placement, to remain at home. In order for day care to be productive, however, mothers need to perceive it as a constructive step rather than one which threatens their role as parents. Generalizing the benefits of day care for most children and particularly for the child in question can ease guilt and support good parenting for many.

Employment of homemaker services requires particularly careful planning. These services are generally sought when, for a variety of reasons, the parenting and caretaking capacities in the home are severely limited. Reasons may include the absence of the parent, illness of the parent, or the time-consuming needs of another family member because of illness, for example. In many cases the homemaker takes on the caretaking role. In those instances where the goal of the homemaker is to enable a parent to learn more useful homemaking or parenting skills, as is often the case in protective services, it is crucial that the parent be helped to see the service as supportive, not undermining, and that there be a clear program outlined in advance, including the goals to be achieved, the methods to be used, and the time period within which it is hoped the goals can be accomplished. In order to achieve the goals, there must be close coordination between the worker and the agency employing the homemaker.

Without careful planning, parents can easily feel undermined and criticized by well-meaning but overly directive homemakers, or they can passively allow others to take over for them, resulting in lowered self-esteem, regressed ability to care for their children, and puzzlement and anger when the service is terminated. If used appropriately, this service can be extremely useful and enhance the mastery of skills.

The utilization of parent aides is another important resource which is expanding and which, again, is a service provided in addition to and in collaboration with that of the protective worker. The role of the parent aide is an especially flexible one, both inside and outside the home. A parent aide is a paraprofessional, often a member of the community, who, through conscious use of a relationship, serves as a role model and as an advocate for obtaining a variety of needed resources. In this capacity, working under the close supervision of the protective worker, the parent aide establishes a working relationship with a parent (which is generally long-term in nature), offers emotional support, and provides a model for a wide range of behaviors. These include the care and management of children at all stages of development, and dealing with institutions and authority figures, such as welfare departments or landlords, in a constructive way. The parent aide meets identified individual needs. She accompanies the socially isolated or phobic client out of the house, teaches a client how to budget, use the telephone, plan nutritious meals, and to learn what to expect from and how to care for a new baby. She also accompanies the parent as an advocate to obtain necessary services, such as housing, legal, medical, or day care. She may transport children in foster care for visitations with natural parent and supervise these. She is an enabler, doing things with rather than for clients so as to help them develop lasting skills. In effect she lends ego to the parent in the context of the relationship, the quality of which is critical to the growth which occurs.

PARENT AIDE INTERVENTIONS: CASE EXAMPLES

Michelle, a 15-year-old adolescent, became involved with protective services when it was noted by medical staff that she did not have a secure plan for her soon-to-be-born baby. She herself had been in foster care, had run away, her whereabouts were unknown to her protective worker, and she had therefore become "lost" to the child welfare system. Her sole relationship was to the baby's father. After the protective worker developed an alliance with this initially frightened and resistant adolescent, the parent aide joined the treatment plan and worked with her on making plans for the baby, learning what to expect and, afterward, how to care for the baby. When unfairly evicted, the parent aide accompanied her to legal services and the housing authority. Michelle used these services exceedingly well, identifying with the parent aide's calm, assured motherly manner. She incorporated new skills, raising her esteem as an individual and a parent. Given her own impoverished background, she was able to use help well, hopefully to prevent a recurrence of her own family's difficulties. Her work was carefully coordinated with that of the caseworker who was helping her plan and make good decisions while reflecting on her history.

Denise was a 35-year-old phobic client who could not venture out of the house alone. She had markedly low self-esteem, was without meaningful relationships, and was involved with the protective agency because of physical abuse of her son. The parent aide took her out weekly for a carefully planned walk and some socialization and taught her a skill, knitting, which not only raised her self-esteem but helped occupy the long hours during which the tension built. Meanwhile the social worker was focusing on Denise's relationship issues with her mother which were the trigger for much of the child abuse.

Marilyn, a 23-year-old woman, was involved with the protective agency because of physical abuse of her small daughter. She suffered from depression, low self-esteem, and social isolation. The parent aide, after establishing a relationship in which the client could share her terror of using the telephone, helped with that, helped later by accompanying her to a school conference where she feared criticism, and much later with the fears and process of applying for a job. The client mastered all of the above and went on to further areas of growth. During all of this, weekly casework addressed the etiology of the problems and present management of the child.

Susan, 19, was a mildly mentally retarded mother of two young children. She came to the attention of the agency because of neglect. Having herself been neglected, undertaught, having low self-esteem, and significant depression, she was unable to reach out to others. The parent aide built on the strength of Susan's need and readiness for a relationship and her eagerness to please and to learn skills. The aide taught her, through modeling, sufficient child care skills and help with nutrition and budgeting that she could care satisfactorily for the children, make obvious gains in self-esteem, and feel pride as a mother.

Many other resources may be imaginatively and effectively employed — from substance abuse treatment programs to formal skill building programs to self-help groups like Parents Anonymous.

Sometimes the safety of the children requires the use of more extreme resources, such as those provided by foster care. Chapter 11 will deal with that in detail. Yet another resource less commonly available is that of residential treatment for the entire family. Whatever resources exist, they will be effective to the extent that they match the family need and are imaginatively and effectively employed and coordinated.

SUMMARY

In summary, this chapter has focused on the thinking involved in developing an effective treatment plan. Emphasis has been placed on the importance of sound diagnostic thinking, the identification of ego strengths which can be used and built upon in the treatment plan, and the importance of a coordinated approach to comprehensive resources in treatment planning. Case examples illustrating situations commonly found in protective service assessments served to illustrate this approach.

REFERENCES

1. Hollis F: Personality diagnosis in casework, in Parad HJ (ed): *Ego Psychology and Dynamic Casework.* New York, Family Service Association of America, 1958, pp 83–96.
2. Winnicott DW: *The Maturational Process and the Facilitating Environment.* New York, International Universities Press, 1965.
3. Perlman HH: In quest of coping. *Social Casework* 1975; 56(4):213.

7 Individual Treatment

Helen Vye Daley

Providing individual casework treatment to parents who abuse and neglect their children is critical to bringing about significant changes in behavior toward children. This chapter will discuss this conviction in relation to the observations gleaned from writers in the field of child abuse, an examination of the highly specialized process of relationship formation with these parents, a look at the educative dimension to the casework relationship, an understanding of the nature of the resistances encountered in engaging these clients in treatment, and a recognition of the highly collaborative role of the protective caseworker which is essential in supporting the process of treatment.

With the availability of a variety of treatment modalities today, ie, family therapy, group therapy, etc, practitioners are becoming increasingly concerned as to which treatment modality is best suited to the abusive parent with any given diagnosis. In the absence of scientific research data to serve as a guide on the issue, the contributions of authors in the field of child abuse may shed some light on the matter. Kaufman[1] stressed the importance of the individual treatment modality.

"Intensive casework focusing on the parents as prime clients is essential if work with these families is to be possible." Margaret Brenton,[2] in discussing the process of "resocialization" of the abusing parent, states that the reparenting aspect of this process requires a "slow, painstaking process involving a long-term commitment." Susan Wells[3] found two contraindications for family therapy with abusive parents: (1) extreme self-centeredness that inhibits participation in joint interviews and (2) an inability to act as parents. She suggests "additional individual support." In addition, Kaufman[4] sees individual treatment as the primary focus for the former group: "The narcissistic orientation of the abusive parent means it is necessary to focus the treatment on them." Clearly, their painful issues of being unloved, unprotected, and in some instances alienated, bespeaks such an orientation. A further rationale for individual treatment is expressed by Nancy Avery[5]: "We are not treating symptoms, we are treating total people who may be hurt children themselves." This approach to treating abusive and/or neglectful parents goes beyond crisis intervention or mere symptom elimination; it is geared to helping parents understand and cope with the underlying causes of their ego dysfunction. This type of client often requires a protracted period of intensive casework involvement before he/she can benefit from a substitute therapy or utilize a combination of treatment modalities, such as individual and family therapy.

What, then, are the unique elements of the protective casework relationship? It deals with the same issues of transference and countertransference as traditional casework in other settings. The term transference is used here to mean the client's unconscious responses to the caseworker as if he/she were a significant other of the client's earlier life. Countertransference is the caseworker's transference response to the client. However, the client's transference reaction to an authority figure is apt to surface earlier in the protective casework relationship due to the legal and societal right to intervene in the lives of clients on behalf of children reported to be at risk. The more benignly this authority is projected by the caseworker and perceived by the client, the less tension and/or potential destructiveness will be created in the relationship. It calls for the blending of the caseworker's skill in the use of authority and a high dosage of humanness. If authority is improperly used, early termination of treatment is a probability.

As a general statement of purpose of intervention with the client, protective casework seeks the following goals that are similar to traditional casework: (1) improved coping skills in the face of life stresses, (2) a more positive self-image, (3) a better attitude toward self and others, and (4) improved capacity to develop one's potential. The protective caseworker, however, has a more compelling goal: ensuring the safety of children at risk. It also seeks to assess the developmental needs of children and to ensure that they are met.

Halleck [6] suggests that all treatment relationships are ambivalent. In protective casework the client's ambivalence to the process of relationship-building tends to be more manifest, in part due to fear that the children may be removed from the parent's care and in part related to a variety of other factors. These may be identified as the client's ability to relate to others and the client's capacity to use help for self and family, particularly for a child who may be identified as symptomatic or damaged.

Many abusive parents are likely to suffer from low self-esteem or an unclear self-concept. They are generally insecure and respond to criticism, no matter how sensitively phrased, with hostility, denial, or rejection. Many of their spoken and unspoken cues signal such messages as, "Show me how to be a person," or "how to be a parent." Their low threshold of trust inhibits their ability to develop true intimacy—a necessary element in establishing mature, reciprocal relationships. This is often displayed in an ongoing competition for emotional supplies and attention between parents, a dynamic that undermines working directly with both parents. Part of the task involved here is to help them learn how to be mutually supportive.

Consistent with their deficiencies in interactional skills, many abusive parents are involved in fairly pathological ties with their extended families. Relationships with their own parents take myriad forms: overly dependent, symbiotic, hostile–dependent, or totally rejecting. Some parents are cognitively aware of the destructive impact of these types of relationships consciously seeking to avoid similar patterns, but unconsciously setting up an equally problematic situation. For instance, in reaction to an abusive grandparent's bid for controlling one mother, she developed a laissez-faire attitude in parenting her own children, who at an early age were not only uncontrollable but were exhibiting pseudomature behaviors such as independent decision-making and age-inappropriate self-care. These are often characteristic of emotionally abused or neglected children. Grandparents are particularly skilled at reaching out for help for their abusive "child-parent" while continuing their own deprecating relationship with the parent.

Initially family pathology can be difficult to assess, as most parents tend to be withholding out of fear of the protective worker's "power" to remove their children. This is not unrealistic, but once parents, even the more emotionally disturbed, perceive that the caseworker is interested in meeting their needs, the process of sharing information becomes less difficult. The absence of a supportive network of relatives or friends often contributes to a parent's readiness to use help. Where such information is not readily obtained, the course of the casework relationship can offer a good clue. Testing behavior, such as frequently missed appointments, failure to follow through on mutually defined tasks, or even extreme demandingness, are fairly reliable indices of the client's view and use of relationship. This may be inextricably linked to a deep sense of worthlessness or an unrealistic sense of self-sufficiency. The former may be an adaptive response to early repression of needs and feelings or an outgrowth of very negative experiences with other helping systems, such as an abrupt termination by another helping professional. The unrealistically self-sufficient client is often afraid to trust. In either case, these parents tend to be social isolates with limited or virtually no community affiliations. These are the parents that test the protective worker's maturity, resilience, and skill in building bridges of trust and caring.

Although the self-referring client usually rates highly in the self-awareness and motivational scales, this can be misleading due to a recognized tendency to manipulate. Their requests must be carefully assessed.

Mrs. S. once called the agency requesting help for her family because father had just slapped 3-year-old Sean 12 times. Further exploration of the situation revealed that Mrs. S. was equally impulse-ridden and had often provoked an abusive pattern between father and son.

The dynamic of parental aggression toward a child often includes one parent as the active aggressor, and the other as the passive assailant. Parents are usually unaware of the abnormality of this transaction. Thus it would be futile to expect that either parent would be an adequate protector for the child. The task of the protective worker becomes fourfold: (1) to interpret the process of interaction, (2) to clarify with parents their respective issues, (3) to support them in confronting each other with their frustrations and unmet needs, and (4) to seek alternative adaptive ways of coping and communicating. Implementation of this process can help to minimize and eventually eliminate the use of a child as a buffer/victim in their interactions.

A theory has been postulated by Kempe and Helfer[7] that one of the elements in the parent–child abuse problem is a "special" child—one that is targeted and ascribed certain attributes such as willfulness and stubbornness or one from whom the parent has unrealistic expectations. This certainly eliminates many of the cross-cultural families that we see whose sanctioned disciplinary approach to all children is simply abusive. It also does not account for the interesting but disturbing trend in shifting abuse to another child, once the primary target is placed outside the home. These latter instances suggest that child abuse may be more ego syntonic. When this is the case, such a parent needs help not only in understanding and managing intrapsychic forces but with practical creative approaches to dealing with the child.

In the area of child management, Arnold[8] has made some interesting suggestions which can be valuable to professionals. His notion of "making recommendations ego syntonic," ie, acceptable to the parent, has four steps worth mentioning:

(1) identification with the parents' situation and feelings;
(2) recognition of previous efforts at managing the problem;
(3) identification of the areas of parenting strength; and
(4) utilization of this area of parenting strength as the base for recommendations toward growth and change.

To put the last and probably most significant point in the process into operation, he made the following suggestions:

1. To the overprotective, overdirective, smothering parent, he suggests enlisting the parents' dedication and vigilance in ensuring adequate care for the child by introducing tasks that would promote the child's need for autonomy. A simple example would be the parent supervising, without assisting, the 5-year-old while he puts on his coat and buttons up.

2. To the harsh, angry, punitive parent, he suggests identifying with the serious sense of responsibility, the frustration with the ineffectiveness of the punishments, and allowing the child to "learn the hard way" by experiencing the consequences of behaviors. This approach seems more applicable to older teenagers.

3. To the perfectionist, overcoercive parent, he supports the parent's high investment in the child becoming a success, then linking the capacity to have fun with being successful and making the parents responsible for helping the child understand the relevance of fun to success.

Elsewhere Arnold[9] discusses two useful principles, especially for parents who are ambivalent and therefore inconsistent in their parenting role. He suggests the professional become "the heavy" for the parent when the child needs negative reinforcement. This involves stating the restriction in the presence of the child. The purpose is twofold:

(1) to support the parent in following through on a mutually acceptable restriction for which he would ordinarily have difficulty assuming full responsibility, and
(2) to shift the onus of negative reactions from the child onto the professional.

The second concept he discussed is the professional becoming "Santa's secret helper" which may be understood to mean teaching the parent a specific child management skill outside the purview of the child when the child needs positive reinforcement. He emphasizes that this should be done privately with the parent, so that the parent would be able to assume full credit for any positive outcome.

He cautions that this would not be useful for parents with problems in reality testing as the child would need the reality perceptions and judgment of the professional to reinforce his own sense of reality. Through the process of repetition and the power of the relationship with the caseworker, the parent could be helped to internalize and integrate the different roles of being a parent.

The above processes suggest that one of the primary tasks involved in treating abusive parents is education, since most parents lack knowledge in child development and child management. Margaret Brenton[2] emphasized this strongly: "Abusive parents must learn how to parent their children . . . how to nurture them . . . how to cope with stress without resorting to violence." This essential objective for parents can only be fully achieved when the parents' own patterns of unmet needs are corrected.

Clearly, there are situations that do not require such an in-depth approach, but many require a supportive relationship to work through an acute crisis situation to maximize the parent's coping potential, finding appropriate resources, and learning more effective responses to the child's behavior. Such situations may respond to short-term crisis intervention, as in the following case:

MRS. A.

Mrs. A. was referred to the agency by a neighbor in response to concern expressed by Mrs. A. that she feared losing control with her 4-year-old daughter. She had just separated from her alcoholic husband after he physically assaulted both her and the child.

Supported by the protective worker, Mrs. A. was able to work through her feelings of sadness, anger, and anxiety. She filed for a legal separation, accepted public assistance, found a job, and arranged day care for her daughter. She reached out to her friends at times when she needed emotional support and a temporary place to stay. Her extended family lived abroad but was concretely and emotionally supportive.

At one point during the above process Mrs. A. intimated that initially she was unaware of the full impact of the above changes on her daughter whom she perceived as becoming difficult to manage. As her own feelings of loss and anxiety began to disappear, she was able to respond in a more relaxed manner to her child and to accept her periods of irritability. With focus on management of reaction to the loss of her husband and strengthening her ego capacity for independent functioning, more effective parenting was accomplished within a year. This was due to her capacity for good object relationships and only a marginal amount of resistance encountered in the treatment process.

Perhaps one of the more natural yet difficult aspects of protective worker–client interaction is resistance. At the initial intervention phase the resistance may stem from the reality of intrusion and is seen as a misperceived assault on the client's life-style. This anger needs to be legitimized but followed by an expressed desire to be helpful. Usually most clients who are committed to resisting at this phase simply disappear or shut the worker out. Later in treatment, resistance may persist in a more difficult way, such as the client's unchanging pattern of projecting blame onto a child. While it is initially wise to work with the projections, it might be necessary to break through this defensive maneuver at a later time. This must be measured against the level of trust established in the relationship. One parent was able to begin dealing with her negative self-image after she was encouraged to identify similar positive and negative characteristics in herself and her daughter. A more difficult aspect of working with resistance is seen when both worker and client experience anger and frustration. Progress is impeded if the worker remains unaware and unresponsive to the transference and counter-transference issues.

Progress can be ensured when the protective caseworker assumes responsibility for the maintenance of collaborative contacts with other systems supporting the family. Due to the multiplicity of needs encountered in the chronic abusive/neglectful family, treatment also entails the cross-fertilization of different disciplines: medical, psychiatric, educational, and social work. These may require supportive ancillary services such as day care or homemaker services to achieve acceptable standards of child care. Sometimes this is not enough. It may be necessary that the therapeutic structure and authority of the court be brought to bear to motivate parents to utilize social services.

MR. AND MRS. O.

The following discussion will focus on the treatment processes and issues of an abusive client with very complex features; fear of closeness with paranoid tendencies.

Mrs. O. was specifically referred to the agency by a neighborhood health center aide due to an observed inability to set limits with her 3-year-old son and her expressed fear of losing control and harming him. Information about Mrs. O. suggested that she was disabled and potentially abusive. Later it was revealed that both parents were already physically and emotionally abusive of the youngster, an invariably preexisting reality when parents admit to "fear of losing control."

The background history indicated that Mr. O. was the last of eight children in his family with whom he maintained contact occasionally.

Physical deprivation was part of his developmental experience. Mr. O. had some capacity for warmth when not preoccupied with his illnesses. He did unskilled labor and was poorly educated. He suffered a back injury several years ago.

In contrast, Mrs. O. was from a smaller family and was the third of four children. Her parents lived close by and were constantly present. Mrs. O. was less talkative about her father although her perceptions of him which she shared indicated that he was quite rigid, very argumentative with her mother, and would often threaten to leave home. Her mother was depicted as being a depressed and limited woman and negatively reinforcing since her early childhood.

The initial stages of casework were geared to develop a positive working relationship with both parents. The objectives of our intervention were clearly stated, ie, to help parents cope with whatever problems they were facing and, hopefully, understand and reduce the impulse to strike out at their son. Mother soon made it abundantly clear that she was a bit wary of people telling her how to discipline her child. It was suggested to Mrs. O. that as parents they were responsible for the discipline of their child and were in an excellent position to share what measures worked and what did not. It seemed the wisest course was to be minimally directive with Mrs. O. and at least initially to stay focused on the first objective.

Assessment indicated no immediate environmental stress impacting the family. Difficulties seemed rooted in the intrapsychic and interpersonal areas of functioning. Mrs. O. was schizophrenic, Mr. O. an inadequate personality and alcoholic. Their marriage seemed sadomasochistic in quality with parents alternating roles. Mrs. O. took impulsive vacations. Their son seemed symptom-free, but exhibited a need for appropriate limit-setting and consistent nurturing. One feature of this was an emerging pattern of combined seduction and rejection in the mother-son relationship.

While the assessment procedure included both parents, the selected treatment of choice was individual therapy for parents due to the following considerations: (1) their narcissistic preoccupations; (2) the predominant defenses of projection, denial, and somatization (the hospital was a revolving door for each parent); and (3) lack of readiness to look at their respective contributions to their individual and collective distress. Mr. O. was referred to a male therapist.

Periodically worker would meet jointly with Mr. and Mrs. O. to discuss issues of joint concern but continued to work directly with Mrs. O. Play stimulus with the child was introduced by another social worker. Within a few months he began attending a nursery school for half a day, after Mrs. O. was able to share feelings of being overwhelmed and in need of some relief. Although ambivalent about the separation, normalizing the guilt brought her some alleviation of the anxiety experienced and made follow-through possible. There were days, however, when Mrs. O. kept her son at home under some slight pretext.

Treatment with Mrs. O. began on the first day of intervention when the worker acknowledged her intense struggle for survival and interpreted this as strength of character. Further comment was made about the enormous anxiety, interspersed with anger, that her struggles were generating, and hope was expressed that, with time, she would understand those feelings and be better able to cope.

From the sketches of family history obtained during the joint sessions with Mr. O., worker made a mental catalog of the necessary areas of work with Mrs. O. if improved adaptation were to be possible. They were as follows:

1. Self-concept: As a child and sometimes as an adult, her experience with her parents was "to be seen and not heard." Parents were abusive and emotionally rejecting. Among her peers, she felt like a "nobody," as other children laughed and jeered at her style of dress. This impaired her ability to socialize and have fun. As a student, teachers called her "stupid" and "dumb" and were physically abusive. She attended a special class and dropped out at age 16. As a wife, she was constantly reminded of her inadequacies and berated for her limitations. She saw mothering as a vital and important role for her, but was too threatened to discuss it. However there were indications of potentially pathogenic bonding issues (ie, role reversal).

2. Blurred Self-Identity: During periods of decompensation, she presented an undifferentiated sense of self. This level of ego impairment became apparent after a year of treatment. Mrs. O. called the day before the worker's vacation requesting that worker "do something" because Mr. O. had slapped their son several times for not finishing his lunch. Furthermore, she was fearful of entrusting him to the care of Mr. O., who was not at home then. Worker inquired about the severity of the incident. Mrs. O. assured worker that it was not serious at the time, but she did not want it to reoccur. Worker and Mrs. O. discussed the different options available to ensure protection for the child and settled on extending the nursery school to full time. With joint efforts, this was put in place for the next day. Upon worker's return from vacation, the incident was discussed with both parents; Mr. O. was not even aware of the occurrence and Mrs. O. was not aware that she made Mr. O. the perpetrator. Their son was adjusting well to full-time nursery school.

3. Reality Testing: Mrs. O. had recurrent fears of an ex-boyfriend returning to upset and persecute her.

In general, Mrs. O. at 25, was a woman of normal intelligence, although this was not readily apparent in her depressed state. She had an inquisitive mind and, at times, had a clear cognitive awareness of the problems she was facing and a less clear sense of the associated affective state. Her actions tended to be impulse-ridden. She had some ego capacity to organize, but was quite slow to integrate experiences and synthesize thoughts, feelings, and actions.

Treatment Steps

There were five noticeable stages during the course of our involvement: (1) dependence, (2) approach–avoidance, (3) intimacy, (4) approach–avoidance, and (5) independence. Above and beyond the potential difficulties inherent in the transference–countertransference aspects of the relationship, the fear of the worker's authority to remove the child took on enormous import during chaotic times in the family and impacted on the above stages to some degree.

Dependency   During the first year of treatment, the family experienced many medical crises, each member requiring hospitalization at some point. Also, marital difficulty occurred as exemplified by Mr. O's precipitous departure to visit an extended family member for a few days. The double desertion evoked in Mrs. O. a typical angry tirade with threats of retaliatory rejection. There was little surfacing of the hurt and pain involved. When asked how she was coping, she spoke of back aches, sleepless nights, and her son sharing her bed. This was discouraged on the basis that it only confused the child. An acknowledgment of the loneliness and sadness she must feel brought visible expression of sadness and near tears.

This led to her consideration of possible separation from Mr. O. An examination of the reality factors made her increasingly anxious, so worker decided not to pursue this, but concluded that in all relationships negative and positive feelings coexist and it was often helpful to share those feelings with one's spouse. Some of the feelings were identified, and she decided to discuss with Mr. O. how his sudden departures affected her. Subsequent trips were arranged, and Mrs. O. participated in the budgeting process to make these possible. She in turn was able to arrange a vacation trip for herself and son with extended family members as it was clear that separate vacations suited both of their needs.

There were times when the worker actively participated in bringing about needed changes, for example, procuring a restraining order against a relative who was causing much disruption to the household. As in most instances, Mrs. O. and worker had to work through her ambivalence regarding becoming assertive and establishing a sense of her own person and her right to preserve its integrity.

Approach–avoidance   One of the goals was to complete her high school education and become a dietitian. Initial steps were taken earlier but discouraged due to extreme anxiety and phobia regarding riding the bus. Management of this was done by arranging sightseeing trips and lunches with her outside her community. It also served a secondary purpose of exposing her to a variety of people in different settings. It was during one of these trips that Mrs. O. shared that "she learned to laugh" for the first time in her life. Actually, an untapped, latent sense of humor was helpful during some times of high tension. Simultaneously, she began to improve her personal grooming. High motivation replaced high anxiety to pursue her education, and she completed the process of application on her own. Her son began kindergarten the same year and continued in nursery school for part of the day. No adjustment difficulties were noted.

Inquiries regarding Mrs. O.'s progress at the educational center evoked hostility; she perceived worker's interest as "pushing her." Worker assured her that that was not the intent and some clarification of the misperception was needed. She later shared that this was her first experience of genuine interest in her welfare and that it frightened her. Worker accepted the fear and assured her of its normalcy in light of her experiences. She further elaborated on the negative expectations her family transmitted relative to her educational goals and on her struggle to overcome them.

Concurrently, it was learned that Mr. O. had dropped out of counseling and was drinking again. He was also placing more demands on Mrs. O.'s to stay home and take care of him. After several outreach efforts it became clear that Mr. O. needed a more authoritative stance regarding his resistance to therapy. His disruptions to the household were affecting Mrs. O.'s ability to concentrate. She was also becoming depressed and missing classes. Following a second episode of drinking, worker presented Mr. O. with the option of seeking counseling voluntarily or having the court order treatment for him. Mr. O. resumed counseling. Mrs. O. perceived the latter option as an "attack" and became quite hostile during subsequent sessions.

A period of temporary regression followed. The predominant symptom noted was paranoia. Mrs. O.'s ex-boyfriend was returning again, in her mind, with the intent to "snatch" her child. Worker interpreted her fears and tried to build in reassurances, but the anger and hostility continued for a prolonged period. Attempts to get behind the resistance were futile. She projected blame for all of her problems onto the worker and saw her as basically unhelpful. Worker declared an impasse in casework and suggested she could turn things around if only she could share who else was responsible for the anger. A surprising turn occurred.

Intimacy She acknowledged that she was angry with herself and was feeling quite frustrated. She had at times discontinued classes and kept that secret. This interference with her functioning revealed the extent of her depression. The educational center was quite responsive and had worked out a modified program, giving her credit for life skills and extending the time requirement. The onset of her depression was caused by her parents moving to another town, although they were still in contact. The move was devastating to her. Her parents were the only constant outside contacts she had prior to intervention. Several sessions followed in which she expressed rage at her mother for "desertion." The intensity of the affect and some loosely associated ideas indicated that earlier experiences and affects were being revived. Apparently the birth of a younger sibling, when she was 1½ years old occasioned her mother's psychological rejection of her and clearly interfered with the separation/individuation process. Worker tried to refocus Mrs. O. on the current reality—the parents' move, the reason for the move, and ways in which she could maintain contact. The worker's efforts were interspersed with transfer of the rage onto her with threats of harm. Worker suggested to Mrs. O. that she was not her mother and although Mrs. O. felt like hurting her, worker realized she really did not want to and in any event both for Mrs. O.'s protection and her own, she would not allow it. Worker repeatedly suggested that Mrs. O. was out of control and needed to calm down. Mrs. O. later explained that her brother, who was younger, had repeatedly caused disruptions in the parent's apartment and the landlord had asked them to leave. They then discussed the meaning of the change for her and also for her parents. Again, worker suggested that with loss came hurt, pain, and sadness. Mrs. O. then intimated that there was a "crazy side" to her personality, but she was afraid to touch it out of recognition of her own fragility.

In the interim, her son, who was now approximately age 6, became symptomatic, displaying hyperactivity which was interfering with his learning abilities. He was referred for a psychological evaluation as part of a special school evaluation process. The parents, school personnel, psychologist, and caseworker discussed the results of the evaluation. Recommendations included modification of his educational plan and incorporation of behavioral techniques to help manage his responses to the learning situation. He was referred to the local mental health center for therapy, and his parents were encouraged to participate to learn new ways of responding to him. Parents were responsive to this plan.

Approach-avoidance As treatment progressed, Mrs. O. completed her high school equivalency, graduated, and began job-hunting. Worker recognized the accomplishment and provided some concrete support for her graduation. Mr. O. terminated therapy and was holding his own. The family was heavily involved with the mental health center around parenting and some personal issues. The need to split off good parent/bad parent became self-evident. This is not an uncommon phenomenon in working with disturbed families. Some professionals understand the issue and avoid reinforcement of the family's need to see the protective worker as the "bad parent." Unfortunately, in one instance worker's own activity with Mrs. O. temporarily facilitated this split. She attempted to slap her son in the face for some inconsequential behavior during one of the caseworker's visits. Worker actively intervened by suggesting to mother that she would not permit it because of the danger involved. Mrs. O. was furious and challenged the worker's right to interfere with her interaction with her son. Worker accepted the anger, but insisted that they discuss the situation. Both discovered that the overreaction was a carryover from another misdemeanor for which he was not punished and which left Mrs. O. still angry. The issue of control became the next area of focus. Mrs. O. avoided a few sessions.

Independence   Mrs. O. secured a job and postponed her educational pursuits. The focus of treatment continued to be on anger, rage, and her control of both. One insight she had was that she had a "short fuse" and was developing ways of managing this. She acknowledged that as her son developed, he was also testing her ability to respond appropriately.The sessions at the mental health center dovetailed here. The psychologist who saw her son and occasionally Mrs. and Mr. O. (father less so) indicated that Mrs. O. had accomplished most of the basic work in psychotherapy with the worker but needed to synthesize and integrate more of her understanding of herself and others. Her son was making excellent academic and behavioral adjustment. Mr. O., whom worker saw periodically, particularly during periods of stress in the family, appeared more relaxed. He had had a couple of lapses in social drinking but they presented no significant consequences. He spent his time with his myriad hobbies and visiting friends. The family had earned its graduation from casework treatment.

Gains through treatment were impressive. The physically chaotic, disorganized, unkempt apartment of a few years ago was completely redecorated, and well kept. The tension-filled, crisis-oriented, multiproblem existence of the family had calmed down. The eruption into violent attacks between parents had disappeared. Both parents respected their need for space and mutual cooperation. Mr. O. had also developed a couple of friends in the neighborhood. Mrs. O. was functioning on a higher level. She recognized that she will probably be depressed occasionally but was not terrified by it. She indicated that when that occurred she would reach out for help.

In conclusion, the course of individual treatment is based on the diagnosed personality structure and needs of the parents as well as the other individual members of the family. Individual treatment remains the treatment of choice for these parents, but when diagnostically indicated, a combination of treatment modalities may be offered. These may include couple, group, or family therapy. Successful intervention

126

with the abusive and/or neglectful parent is often contingent on the worker's understanding and management of the difficult dimensions of the relationship-building process and an acceptance of the difficult manifest and latent issues that often characterize the parent's behavior. Skill in identifying the needs of the abused or neglected child and in eliciting the cooperation of the parents in meeting those needs is also essential. Identifying and managing resistance, a hallmark of the intervention process of treating these clients, is imperative in the caseworker's repertoire of skills. The length of treatment has some correlation to the chronicity of the problem. Successful outcomes depend on the client's motivation, spontaneous or elicited, and ability to use help. Protective casework can be painstakingly slow, but is essential if results are to be effective and of an enduring nature.

REFERENCES

1. Kaufman I: The physically abused child, in Ebeling NB, Hill DA (eds): *Child Abuse: Intervention and Treatment.* Acton, Massachusetts, Publishing Sciences Group, 1975 p 86.
2. Brenton M: Resocialization of abusive parents. *Social Work* 1981;26(2): 119–123.
3. Wells S: A model of therapy with abusive and neglectful families. *Social Work* 1981;26(2):13–118.
4. Kaufman I: The physically abused child, p 84.
5. Avery N: Viewing child abuse and neglect as symptoms of family dysfunction, in Ebeling NB, Hill DA (eds): *Child Abuse: Intervention and Treatment.* Acton, Massachusetts, Publishing Sciences Group, 1975 p 87.
6. Halleck S: *The Treatment of Emotional Disorders.* New York, Jason Aronson 1978, p 370.
7. Kempe CH, Helfer RE: *Helping the Battered Child.* Philadelphia, JB Lippincott, 1972, p 11.
8. Arnold LE: *Helping Parents Help Their Children.* New York. Brunner/Mazel Inc, 1978.
9. Arnold LE: *Helping Parents,* pp 12–13.

8 An Integration of Individual and Family Therapy

Marybeth Bronson

Parents who abuse their children live within a deeply troubled family web. Its pattern is not the design of mature adults carefully preparing an environment in which to raise their young. It is instead a net wrought, often in haste, by troubled, immature individuals in flight from a dispiriting entanglement with their own families of origin. It seems to matter little whether these parents leave their own families gradually or precipitously, in despondence or in defiance. They are unable to effect a true separation from troublesome family patterns of old. Illusion, distortion, and fantasy weave a gossamer bridge enabling their leave-taking. Then, as if by instinct, a new family web is spun in a pattern closely resembling the one thought to have been left behind.

It is a matrix not easily altered. There is little fuel within for initiative. Wariness greets outsiders. Change is met with distrust. Web filaments are pulled from the parent's internal reservoir of mistrust, insecurity, helplessness, anger, and despair.

It is within this internal reservoir that change must begin. Elements of trust, self-confidence, esteem, security, and hope must be added to the

128

parent's internal resources if the family environment is to become a nurturing one.

It is primarily the parents' characterological strengths and vulnerabilities which define family patterns and limit or enhance prospects for growth and change. Thus, intensive individual treatment of the parent must be the initial focus. Although a family systems model is indispensable in understanding the problems of child abuse, therapy with the whole family is rarely the most effective treatment modality during the beginning phase of work. The introduction of other family members should be carefully timed. Significant gains in individual or couples treatment are usually vital before inclusion of the other family members can work as a growth catalyst.

A brief review of the abusing parent's family heritage and consequent ego and superego impairments will clarify the need for initial emphasis on individual or couples therapy. Furthermore, due to the abusing parent's tendency to repeat the self-defeating patterns of the family of origin, this review will also be descriptive of the current nuclear family dynamics and, as such, will carry implications for later family therapy.

THE INTERGENERATIONAL CYCLE

Abusive or seriously neglectful parents psychologically are children who hunger for the nurturance their own parents were unable to provide. As young children, they were made by their parents to feel disappointing and inadequate. When one's first and most permeating intimate relationships etch out a sense of worthlessness, the template is set. This inflexible imprint then defines relationships to come. The child's unmet needs do not disappear but remain on to circumscribe future attachments. As Dana Ackley [1] so clearly articulates,

> Potential abusers both seek and shun intimate relationships. On the one hand, they seek intimacy in order to obtain what was missing in the earlier parental relationship. This need leads them to define a close relationship as one in which, like a child, they can 1) obtain emotional support and warmth without giving much in return and 2) depend on their partner to solve the problems of living that adults are called upon to solve. Alternatively, intimacy is shunned because the first childhood attempts were such failures. It is these failures that now lead them to believe that close relationships are dangerous and doomed to produce disappointment and threats to self-esteem because people cannot be trusted.

It is a scenario for failure and self-fulfilling prophecy. The sense of worthlessness leads to a liaison with an inadequate partner who cannot meet the emotional demands. The partner is equally needy. Then, still unsatisfied, the needs may give rise to the fantasy of being nurtured by one's own child. Consciously or unconsciously the fantasy is acted upon and a real child is born. The infant does not give. The infant needs. The child-parents are, in turn, disappointed, angry, depressed, helpless, and despairing. Just as the child was to be the source rather than the product of hope, projections and identifications may now lead the parent to view the child as the source rather that the product of despair.

It is a breeding ground for abuse and neglect. Other children may be born and primary relationships may change, but the parent's emotional desolation is not altered. It is here that treatment begins.

THE COUPLE

If the parent is coupled with another adult, couples sessions should work in tandem with individual treatment from the outset if an assessment shows the non-battering parent to be in some form of collusion with the abuse. As the parents' histories indicate and as the individual and family dynamics to be discussed will show, mutual deprivation and an inability to function autonomously are the basis for coupling. The result is an ill-conceived symbiosis with a paucity of sustaining nurturance. When a child is born, the meager supply of sustenance must be divided three ways. As Justice and Justice[2] summarize:

> The root of the problem is competition within the family system over which one will be taken care of by the other. The spouses fight over who will give to whom, who will wait on whom, who will do more for whom. The winner is taken care of and the loser turns to more extreme behavior to obtain care.

Thus, the parent who ultimately harms the child is sounding the alarm on behalf of the entire beleaguered family system.

The family systems theory of Bowen[3] identifies the triangle as "the smallest stable relationship system." A couple is seen as "an unstable system" which inevitably seeks a third element to achieve a kind of shifting balance. In the abusive family, the battering may represent a maladaptive quest by the couple for equilibrium. It can represent aggression displaced in order to preserve a desperately needed but tenuous dyadic tie. The nonbattering partner may be in unconscious collusion with the abusive parent or may simply feel powerless to effect any change without threatening disruption of the dependency-laden bond with the abusive partner. The fear of losing the partner by upsetting the equilibrium consistently shows itself to be more anxiety provoking than the familiar, albeit abysmal, reality of the relationship.

In any case, when child abuse is intertwined with couples issues, it is obviously advantageous to engage the pair in treatment. The goal may be to foster a less stressful equilibrium or to facilitate a separation in order to restore a measure of safety to the home and clear the way for individual growth and progress.

THE INDIVIDUAL PARENT

Toward a Cohesive Self and a Readiness for Family Therapy

Treatment intervention may offer an abusive parent the first enduring experience with another adult who comes unladen with dependency issues and free of exploitive demands. It is a relationship meant to focus on the parent's needs. The therapist will never undo the misdeeds of the unavailable, idealized, or vilified members of the family of origin. However, within the therapeutic relationship, the parent can be heard and understood. To be heard and understood for the first time can be revolutionary.

Heinz Kohut's[5] formulations of problems in early childhood development and consequent narcissistic deficits can be valuable concepts in understanding and working with abusive and neglectful parents and families. Kohut identifies soothing security, identity, narcissistic pleasure, and loving approval as building blocks in the development of "the cohesive self." The infant and young child rely upon a nurturing adult, a "self object," to perform these functions. Gradually, with sufficient nurturing, the child internalizes these capacities in the form of introjects and then, progressively through identifications, is able to perform the functions for herself/himself.

The abusive parent's early childhood experiences ruptured the development of these capacities and, thus, hold consequences for the ego development of successive generations. Individual treatment addresses key parental ego deficits and may move that parent toward readiness for positive shifts and changes within the family unit.

Capacity to self-soothe   The ability to soothe one's self is a prerequisite for nurturing others. Kohut sees this capacity deriving from the internalization of positive early introjects which later develop into identifications shaping one's character. The abusive parent's introjects and identifications are punitive, critical, and derisive. Their internal reservoir of ego strengths does not include the capacity to self-soothe. The therapist can serve as the source of a more benign image. An enhanced capacity to soothe one's self, in turn, frees one to nurture others.

Resilient identity   A positive solid identity is a source of self-confidence. In order to develop such an identity, the child relies on adults for validation of achievements. The abusive parent's childhood achievements were rejected, belittled, or unnoticed. Again, the parent in treatment can begin to internalize the therapist's active validation of real assets and achievements to form a more positive resilient identity. The strengthened self-confidence clears a path for more realistic expectations from one's partner and children and an augmented ability to appreciate and validate their accomplishments.

Capacity for narcissistic pleasure   The abusive parent seldom experiences feelings of pride. Only as qualities of the self are validated and experienced as part of the self can one begin to take pleasure in them. The expansion of a healthy capacity for narcissistic pleasure diminishes the formerly crippling effect of criticism by others. It frees one for the productive introspection, self-evaluation, and emotional risk-taking inherent in all growth and change.

Loving self-approval   The development of a cohesive self, founded on a combination of all of the above capacities, culminates in loving self-approval. The abusive parent is a foreigner in this realm.

Capacity for trust   The abusive parent's earliest intimate relationships have led him or her to believe that all close relationships will be denigrating or, at best, disappointing. The parent does not easily trust. Relationships become a self-fulfilling prophecy in which partners and children must ultimately fail them. Thus, for most, the outreach by a therapist offers a unique opportunity for a holding relationship free of the usual reciprocal demands and criticism. The trust fostered in treatment can then very gradually permeate other bonds.

Capacity for ego differentiation   Abusive parents have not developed the cohesive identity which would permit a healthy degree of autonomy within intimate relationships. They are dependent upon others to fill the voids. This results in the merging of ego boundaries and in a high degree of intensity. There is also a high potential for disappointment and conflict with their partners and children. Over time, a trusting bond with a therapist potentiates a more positive self-image and a concomitant degree of autonomy which may serve to shore up ego boundaries within the family unit.

The therapist serves as a self object in the treatment of an abusing parent. The process of change takes time. Trust and a true therapeutic alliance are won slowly. The parent's ego defenses, which help determine the shape of a family system, are firmly rooted.

Focal Ego Defenses and the Superego: Reverberations in the Family Unit Ego Defenses

The fragmented, rigid, and poorly differentiated ego of the abusing parent functions by dint of an array of primitive and maladaptive defense mechanisms. The defenses shape a constrictive web whose filaments will determine the patterns of family interaction and restrict the development and mobility of individuals confined within. An understanding of the defense mechanisms, the purpose they serve for the abusing parent, and the consequences for the family unit will be useful in beginning family therapy. Denial and repression are coupled with:

Splitting   The preponderance of negatives in the abusing parent's early object relationships causes the parent to protect the rarer positive aspects by unconsciously splitting them off from the negative. Good and bad internal object representations thereby remain separate and the tolerance for ambivalent feelings fails to develop adequately.[5] This unconscious maneuvering sets up a tendency in the family unit to label members as either good or bad. It becomes fertile ground for the creation of scapegoats and parentified children.

Projection and identification   The parent's inability to bear conscious internal conflict coupled with a pervasive early born sense of guilt may result in the need to project threatening impulses onto external objects. While this defense tenuously preserves the parent's fragile ego, perceptions of other family members become distorted. A new external arena for conflict is created. The children often become unwitting participants in the process of projective identification. Their still-malleable identities serve as receptacles for the parent's projections. By first projecting the unwanted impulse onto the child and then identifying with it, the parent manages to disown the behavior while vicariously experiencing it through the undifferentiated bond with the child.

Acting out   Acting out is yet another method by which the parent attempts to escape facing internal conflict or grief. The destructive behavior may be directed against the self or against other family members. The children, as either witnesses or targets of this destructive behavior, may react by identifying with the aggressor or with the victim.

Identification with the aggressor   In order to preserve an identity, indeed, in some cases in order to survive, the parent, in his or her childhood, may have internalized the aggressive traits of the powerful and threatening parent. The abusive parent's own children may be prone to this same coping attempt.

Identification with the victim   Identification with the parent as victim may also serve as a defense and may help clarify for us one source of maladaptive passive-dependent behavior so often adopted by at least one member in abusive families. In a family where one parent is the victim of physical or emotional abuse by others, a child's early bond with the victimized parent may preclude identification with the aggressor. If there are no alternative sources for a positive identification in a turbulent world, the child's only ballast preventing disintegration of the ego may be the internalization of the maladaptive, but at least clearly defined, role of the victim. The identification also harbors a secondary neurotic gain — alleviation of guilt feelings.

The Superego

The superego of the abusive parent is harsh. Its punitive quality, when coupled with the undifferentiated nature of the ties with the child, may lead to child abuse. Steele and Pollock [6] note, "When the parent misidentifies the infant as the embodiment of his own bad self, the full aggression of his punitive superego can be directed outward onto the child." They postulate further,

> Thinking of the infant as being the equivalent of the parent's bad self has been described as a misperception or projection. Projection seems unlikely, as it involves denial, the mechanism being, 'It is not I who am this way, it is he.' We feel the mechanism is, 'I am bad, he is bad just like me.' This is an identification process . . .

In other instances, the harsh superego is linked with projection. The previously discussed mechanism of projective identification is an example. The parent unconsciously projects his anxiety-provoking impulse onto the child who then acts it out. While experiencing vicarious satisfaction on one level, the parent's conscious superego moves swiftly to punish the child for the transgression.

THE FAMILY

Consequent Dysfunctional Family Patterns and Critical Developmental Stages

The product of the parent's narcissistic deficits, the rigid ego defenses, and harsh superego is an enmeshed family system. Fusion operates as the foundation of all family interactions. Ego boundaries are blurred. Having had little nurturance as fuel for their own ego development, the parents, in turn, have little to give. Lacking internal threads of cohesiveness, the underdeveloped individual egos mesh with each other in an effort to function as a whole. The result is dysfunction. Splitting of objects, projections, and maladaptive identifications give rise to tension, conflict, and abuse. There is a need for scapegoats. These may be selected by accident of ordinal birth order, gender, health, appearance, or disposition. Parentified children are chosen by similar means.

A child's developmental stages may be critical determinants in the timing and duration of a parent's crisis and loss of control. O'Connell [7] writes, "Stages in the psychosexual development of the child can serve as a stimulus for reactivating and re-working the conflicts from the parent's past . . ." Also, Scherz [8] has stated ". . . at each stage of family development there has to be a shift in object relations, identifications, and marital equilibrium."

Infancy potentiates serious problems for some parents who look to the child as a source of comfort and love. Kaufman[9] notes, "Parents who are extremely infantile and wish to be babied themselves resent the dependency and needs of their child and express this resentment in hostile ways."

The increasing strivings for autonomy of the toddler may trigger separation anxiety and harsh stirrings of the superego in the parent. The child's ambulation is experienced by the parent as abandonment. The child walks "away." The toddler's incipient verbal skills may replace some cherished tactile methods of connecting with the parents. The 2-year-old's favorite exclamation "no" may be experienced by the parent as recalcitrance or rejection.

The oedipal period may stir yet another set of parental concerns — sexuality and competitiveness. Zilboorg[10] writes, "The stronger the parent's 'conscience,' that is, the stronger their inhibitions, the greater will be their hostility against the child's freedom . . . To put it in technical terms: to the unconscious of the parents, the child plays the role of the id."

The turmoil of adolescence also provokes parental anxiety and conflict which may manifest itself as aggression toward the child. The child's heightened sexual urges form a receptive arena for a parent's projections. The adolescent's strivings for identity and conflicts about separation may in actuality threaten the parent with abandonment.

A child's age or stage of psychosocial development may also spark a repetition of emotional stress experienced by the parent a generation earlier. The dynamic at work seems to be more a process of identification than of repetition compulsion. When one's child reaches the age at which the parent experienced trauma as a child, the parent's identification with that child intensifies and the parent's unconscious links to the past trauma are revived. As the parent reexperiences the related feelings of loss, depression and grief, she or he may have less energy to nurture or tolerate frustration. The parent may need to decathect from the child who is triggering the revival of unresolved grief. As the parent withdraws, the child experiences loss. The intergenerational repetition of trauma thus comes full circle.

These family patterns and dynamics are instructive guides in the course of both individual and family therapy. They may help the therapist to fully understand the sources and nature of existing emotional stresses and to anticipate future conflicts. Jay Haley[11] states that the therapist must "choose the important variables most relevant to change" and act. The patterns discussed can serve as the therapist's blueprint for organizing and clarifying a seemingly chaotic array of individual and family symptoms and interactions. They serve as guides for therapeutic strategies for support or for change in maladaptive coalitions within the family.

Contraindications to Beginning Treatment
with a Family Forum

Certain countertransference feelings may mislead a therapist into starting treatment using a family forum. Identification with the targeted children
may result in a wish to include them as a central focus. Indeed, the children
may require close monitoring and intensive outreach and treatment. Particularly in the case of infants and young children, the most effective beginning format may, in fact, be time spent jointly with parent and child
modeling for and educating the parent. However, it is important that such
time not become a substitute for private sessions with the parent whose
separateness and individuality are ongoing key treatment concerns.

The therapist's frustration with a client's limited expressive verbal
skills is another pitfall which might result in a premature shift into family
therapy, where action can be met with action. However, the focal short-
coming here is not the client's poor command of language but, rather,
the therapist's limited patience and consequent leap toward a "cure"
which leaves the client behind. The only cure provided may be temporary
relief of the therapist's frustration. Poor expressive verbal skills are often
mistakenly interpreted to mean limited ability for introspection. In truth,
insight seems to be less a function of intelligence than of one's ability to
tolerate conscious internal conflict. The goal, then, is to enhance the
parent's tolerance for internal tension and dissonance. Again, the initial
treatment task is to help the parent feel understood. The therapeutic path
is to understand, to empathize, and to verbalize feelings for the parent. It
is the essence of good nurturing and, in the beginning, is best accomplished in private time with the parent.

To have the parent share treatment time with other family members
in the beginning creates pitfalls. It may dilute the intensity of the individual treatment relationship and inject elements of rivalry and conflict
which are best saved for a more advanced phase of treatment when the
parent's ability to trust, to bear anxiety and depression, and capacity for
conflict resolution have been heightened. Family therapy may set the
parent up to compete with or hide behind the children.

Having identified enmeshment and malfunctioning coalitions as
targets for change, the inexperienced therapist may be tempted to move in
quickly using the structural change techniques of family therapists such as
Salvador Minuchin[12] or Virginia Satir.[13] Premature use of these techniques, with their emphasis on the axiom that change in the family structure will then bring about changes in the behavior of individual family
members, does not place adequate emphasis on the rigidity and fragility of
the ego of parents in abusive families. The parent's ego forms the core of
the enmeshment and maladaptive alliances, and its deficits must first be
addressed before the family system can absorb significant changes.

From an Individual to a Family Treatment Forum

The fragile parental ego must first receive care before it can operate with a measure of autonomy. This is best achieved within a trusting tolerant individual treatment relationship. The individual growth may then usher in structural changes in the family. As the parent begins to feel understood, soothed, and validated, the rudiments of self-confidence and pride begin to faintly etch out a separate identity and the need to fuse with others is diminished.

Family therapy as a collateral to individual treatment can now begin. The parent's resistance to change within the family system has been diluted. The enhanced individual identity can tolerate more internal conflict, making room for changes in the family unit.

Once the parent is ready, the advantages of family therapy are numerous. Denial as a defense becomes more difficult to maintain in the face of live interaction. Patterns and coalitions are brought into high relief. One's position and role in the family become literally visible, if not immediately seen. If the introspection of individual therapy of the parent is failing to produce adequate insights or change, family therapy offers other approaches. The perceptions and misperceptions of one family member come up against differing perceptions of others in an open forum. Dialogue begins.

A striking characteristic of enmeshed families is the lack of verbal communication. Family treatment sessions offer a model for dialogue and, in this, an invaluable tool for clarification and conflict resolution. The therapist uses words to clarify individual feelings and family interactions. This labeling of feelings and the resulting clarity can dissipate anxiety and the potential for strife. Just as in individual treatment, the family may begin to identify with the therapist's perspective and methods. Words begin to replace impulsive action.

Lastly, and most significantly, family therapy heralds an end to the lowest common denominator in abusive families — emotional isolation. The seemingly simple act of gathering a distressed family unit together in the same room for the purpose of communicating one hour every week may, in itself, be the archetype of change.

CASE DISCUSSION

Twenty-nine-year-old Della is struggling to raise four children. She is a large, powerful woman who becomes a thoroughly imposing figure when her quick temper is unleashed. Only her humor rivals her temper in strength. Her boisterous manner can rally the children in glee but may all too quickly turn in the service of humiliation. Control of her children is of primary importance to Della. To this end, she loudly taunts, rants, threatens, and finally lets loose with heavy blows, using her fist or any object at hand.

The youngest children, 5-year-old Russ and 8-month-old Sarah, are generally spared the brunt of her rage which is directed most frequently at the oldest girl, Annie, age 12. The oldest child, Mannie, 14, was the target of Della's frustrations two years ago but has now discovered some immunity in his newfound role as "man of the house." Although Della appears content with Mannie in this role, his sister Annie experiences fury at his physically assaultive "bossing." On Della's movie night out, it can become the stuff of a furious fracas. On one occasion, the fracas climaxed in a knife wound to Mannie's leg, struck by Annie.

The absence of control of physical violence in this family forms a striking contrast to the tight regimentation employed by Della in daily household management. The house and children are well scrubbed and tidy. The two older children are assigned weekly chores and are expected to honor an early curfew. All but Mannie are forbidden to wander beyond the front stoop except to run brief errands.

When Della was told that a report alleging child abuse had been filed by the school headmaster on behalf of Annie, she was indignant and outraged. After all, her children were clean, well fed, and had proper shelter. She ran a tight ship and felt that her methods of discipline were her own business.

Annie displayed a large bruise received when she was hit by an iron hurled by Della during one of her frequent tirades. It had not been the first time Annie had sought recognition of her plight by school staff. Her transgression had been failure to meet the 5:00 PM curfew. As the primary target of her mother's punishing blows, Annie had become reticent, taciturn, and withdrawn. Says Della, "She hides out in a world of her own. I don't know what goes on in her head."

Della's rage at the abuse report led to threats to assault the reporting headmaster. She met with the social worker, she said, only out of her fear that her children would be removed from the home (an action never considered by the social worker). Della explained the need for the onslaughts against 12-year-old Annie, "My girl looks a lot older that she is. She's getting to be a woman and I need to watch her close or she will be getting into trouble with the boys."

The intergenerational pattern was emerging. Della had been the oldest of eight children and left home at the age of 15 to escape what she termed the "slavery" imposed by her own mother. With resentment, she explains, "I didn't have a mother. I *was* the mother." At an early age she had been responsible for the care of younger siblings and major household chores. As Della experienced it, there was not enough of anything to go around save rules, criticism, and harsh punishment dealt

138

by both her mother and father. Her one quite special source of love was her paternal grandmother who died some years ago. "I was her favorite. I think of her more like she was my real mother."

At age 15, Della deliberately became pregnant in order to escape the tyranny of her parents. Claiming no positive feelings for him, she later married the father of baby Mannie and gave birth to Annie before her turbulent relationship ended five years later after multiple separations, a miscarriage, and a serious suicide attempt.

Her bond with Allan, the father of her youngest two children, has been marked by a more rigid counterdependence and is somewhat less self-negating. However, it has, over seven years, been characterized by the same pattern of separations of increasing duration. Allan is now in the home only sporadically. Says Della, "Men have got it best. They make babies but come and go as they please without responsibility. Women are stuck at home. No freedom."

Della's escalating abuse of her pubescent daughter serves as a two-way mirror reflecting her own past and a view of her daughter's future. As her daughter approaches adolescence, Della experiences unconscious reverberations of forbidden urges and old conflicts of her own teenage years. She does not experience her daughter as an individual truly separate from herself and becomes convinced that Annie will repeat her own adolescent pattern. The blows of her fist may land on Annie but, on another level, are meant for the 15-year-old Della. The superego does not recognize generational boundaries. On an unconscious level, Annie's growing autonomy stirs fears of separation and abandonment in Della who redoubles her conscious efforts to control Annie. Unconsciously, her anticipation of loss and her sexual projections are seeing to it that her daughter replaces herself with a grandchild before departing. The self-fulfilling prophecy occurs when Annie, as the object of mother's projections and target of her anger, indeed begins to eye boys and to break curfew. The final irony lies in the potential for efforts meant to contain her daughter to become, instead, the catalyst for Annie's acting-out behavior and possible early pregnancy. Thus, Della's projections and identifications may serve as the germinal process in the creation of a third generation vulnerable to child abuse. The benefits of successful treatment intervention are accordingly far-reaching.

Treatment: Individual Phase

As noted earlier, Della initially greeted her social worker with righteous rage and denied having any use for weekly home visits or talk. Yet talk she did. Anger at the school headmaster shifted to ventilation of anger at Allan, her boyfriend of seven years. Allan enjoyed the comforts of her home but was equally happy to leave full responsibility for its maintenance to Della. It seems this role was one long familiar to Della, who had held the major responsibility of raising her younger siblings. Soon she began to flood the weekly treatment hours with resentment and anger at her parents, stored for three decades. The feelings which had previously been acted out were now being verbalized. By the fourth month of treatment, Della proclaimed without reservation, "I still don't think I abuse my children, but this is the first time in my life I've let this stuff inside of me out. That headmaster did me a favor. I wish I'd started sooner."

A year and a half of individual sessions began to nurture the seeds of a cohesive self sown many years before by Della's paternal grandmother who had favored this, her first grandchild. The treatment alliance apparently represented only her second enduring experience in a relationship not riddled with criticism, demands, and anger. Within this supportive, trusting, and reflective bond, the therapist served, in part, as a self object, emphasizing and reflecting for Della positive self-images and validating her strengths. As elements of confidence and pride expanded and her wobbly identity steadied, the therapy hour began to include questions and interpretations geared toward facilitating self-exploration and insight. Certainly, her angry avoidance of sad feelings, her undifferentiated tie to her daughter, and her negative identifications and projections lived on. However, her need for these defenses was waning.

Her individual sessions became increasingly filled with insightful speculations. "Maybe I have a hard time with Annie because she's the oldest girl, just like me. She looks like me and has a bad temper like me." Della was beginning to explore her identification with her daughter. Her motivation to understand and to probe signaled a significant tolerance for facing internalized conflict.

Treatment: Family Phase

The time was ripe for the introduction of family treatment as an adjunct to Della's individual sessions. Steadied by the anchors provided in her individual hour, she was now better prepared to withstand the buffeting brought on by changes in family patterns and alliances. Her fledgling sense of confidence led to a separation from Allan which endured the seasonal longings of holidays and anniversaries. Yet, she remained depressed. The conflict-producing family patterns and related stresses had been little altered in individual treatment. Symptoms included Annie stealing personal items from Della and from local stores. The only child free of school problems was Mannie. Five-year-old Russ was on the verge of expulsion from day care. Strife between Mannie and Annie escalated.

And on two separate occasions, Della reported seriously beating Annie for stealing and for ignoring curfew.

Now that Della was able to tolerate more internalized conflict, a family forum offered advantages over individual treatment alone. Her monologue regarding her daughter would turn into a dialogue in family sessions. With a social worker present to label, interpret, and clarify, the dialogue might serve as a wedge fostering more distinct ego boundaries and differentiation. Dysfunctional family patterns which had not previously been discerned by either Della or her social worker would come to life in family meetings. For instance, Mannie's role as "man of the house" could be labeled and dealt with by all parties affected. The related topic of absent fathers had, in Della's individual sessions, always been colored by the affect with which she was most comfortable—anger. Family sessions offered a forum for acknowledgment of 5-year-old Russ' sadness at the loss of his father, thereby diminishing his need to act out in day care. Once the youngest and least rigidly defended of the verbal family members introduced sad feelings into the arena, the path was paved for others to recognize their own ambivalent feelings about many issues. Thus, flexibility is introduced. In turn, the fuel for projection, splitting, displacement, and acting out is depleted, and the level of aggression, both manifest and latent, may subside. Finally, the weekly family sessions offered the social worker the opportunity to repeatedly point out the abundant individual strengths of each family member. As this self object function is modeled by mother, the rudiments of self-confidence, pride, and separate, more positive identities are nurtured. Portions of this process are illustrated by the following treatment highlights.

The Expression of Grief: Toward Ego Flexibility

Beginning with the first treatment encounter, Della's ventilation of long pent-up angry feelings created a swift current allowing her to bypass the more threatening underlying feelings of sadness. After all, there had been no one since grandma who could be trusted to listen and understand. Shortly before Christmas and not long after the start of family sessions, this changed. During an individual treatment hour, the deluge of invective aimed at all those who repeatedly failed her shifted abruptly to sobs of sorrow. Della wept about her inability to provide Christmas gifts for her children. This sadness displayed in the safety of the individual treatment hour then freed Della to do the same in a family session two weeks later. She began the family meeting with unusually impatient, controlling, and harsh behavior toward the children. She berated them with threats that the sum of their transgressions would add up to no Christmas presents. The anger turned briefly to humor. In the midst of a hearty laugh, tears of grief began to pour forth. The children sat in tense and bewildered silence. Their mother's subsequent words explained the sadness. She did not have money to buy them Christmas presents. The social worker's words clarified the confusing, rapid transition of emotions from anger to humor to grief. "Sometimes when your mother is feeling especially sad and she doesn't want to show it, she jokes or gets angry to cover it up. Her anger sometimes means she's really sad inside." This clarification planted seeds for later insights for Della. For her children, the explanation was less important than the powerful experience of seeing another family member risk a display of vulnerability in front of others and come out of it alive. Perhaps sadness would join ranks with anger and humor as permissible feelings in the household and would diminish the need for displaced aggression.

Unraveling Identification and Projection: Toward Individuation

The unraveling of Della's threads of projection and identification, which together formed an umbilical cord linking her to her daughter, was a key treatment goal very directly related to efforts to end her physical abuse of her daughter. Della's own identity formation, stunted by early negative introjects, was seeking completion through an undifferentiated bond with her daughter. Her conscious wish was for Annie to steer clear of the pitfall of early pregnancy into which Della, the adolescent, had fallen. However, the supremacy of the unconscious unfolded as Annie began to take on the identity of the 15-year-old Della and met with the adult Della's harsh superego in the form of physical abuse.

The first break in this cycle came in Della's individual treatment when her own stabilizing identity and nascent autonomy permitted exploration of her identifications with her daughter and entertainment of Annie as an individual separate from her. Her musings were usually tested out in individual hour and later replayed during family sessions.

At one point, she began to talk about having another baby and immediately said she would prefer another girl. She simply liked girls better. Della then experienced ambivalence. "Having a boy would be better because you don't have to worry about them growing up." She then reflected upon her relationships with men from her father to the present and burst into tears. "Men just make babies and leave. I'm tired of rejections and I don't want my girls to have to go through the same thing." Until this point, Della had seemed like a martinet whose limit-setting was devoid of caring. Now her growing ability to reveal vulnerabilities allowed for her well-defended tender feelings to come into play. Family sessions facilitated the gradual display of these feelings with the children present.

At pivotal times, special "couples" sessions were arranged for Della to interact with individual children. The first special hour was probably the first dialogue in years free of criticism between Della and her "distant" daughter. The taciturn Annie, whom mother had described as "in a world of her own" requested the special hour with the social worker and her mother to talk about sex and boys. During the time, Della regaled her daughter with humorous tales of her earlier years and grew more serious as she spoke of feeling closer in many ways to her daughters. She expressed her hope that Annie would not be hurt as she had been by men who made babies but rejected responsibility afterward.

This meeting was the first time Della's message seemed to be taken in by Annie. It was the first time it had been delivered without anger. Perhaps most significantly, the message contained the seeds of loving approval which would begin to enhance Annie's identity formation and dilute her need to prematurely fill the inner void with a baby she would soon resent.

REFERENCES

1. Ackley DC: A brief overview of child abuse. *Social Casework* 1977;58.
2. Blair J, Blair R: *The Abusing Family*. New York, Human Science Press, 1976.
3. Bowen M: Family therapy and family group therapy, in Kaplan H, Sadock B (eds): *Comprehensive Group Psychotherapy*. Baltimore, Williams and Wilkins, 1971, pp 384–421.
4. Kohut H: *The Restoration of the Self*. New York, International Universities Press, 1977.
5. Kernberg O: *Borderline Conditions and Pathological Narcissism*. New York, Aronson, 1975.
6. Steele BF, Pollock CB: A psychiatric study of parents who abuse infants and small children, in Helfer RE, Kempe CH (eds): *The Battered Child*. Chicago, University of Chicago Press, 1968, pp 103–145.
7. O'Connell P: Developmental tasks of the family. *Smith College Studies in Social Work* June 1972;42(3):203–210.
8. Scherz F: Unpublished lecture delivered at Smith College School for Social Work on August 12, 1970.
9. Kaufman I: Psychiatric implications of physical abuse of children, in *Protecting the Battered Child*. Denver Children's Division, American Humane Association, 1962, pp 17–22.
10. Zilboorg G: Sidelights on parent–child antagonism, *Am J Orthopsychiatry* 1932;2: pp 35–43.
11. Haley J: *Problem Solving Therapy*. San Francisco, Jossey–Bass, 1977.
12. Minuchin S: *Families and Family Therapy*. Cambridge, Harvard University Press, 1974.
13. Satir V: *Conjoint Family Therapy*. Palo Alto, Science and Behavior Books, 1967.

"I'm making a picture of a giant, a big giant. He's really big. His mouth is big, with lots of teeth. He is screaming. He's sad, too. See all the tears. No, they're not tears. It's blood. He's got blood coming out his eyes and his ears and his mouth, and he's got cuts on his face, and . . . ."

The child then quickly discarded the picture and compulsively wrote the numeral 8 over and over again on a fresh piece of paper. He wanted no part of the murderous rage displayed in the picture.

9 Treatment of the Child*

Barbara A. Holleman

INTRODUCTION

It is curious, but understandable, that there is relatively little in the literature about psychotherapeutic treatment of children who have been abused or neglected. Since 1962 when Kempe et al [1] first defined the term "battered child syndrome," attention was turned to where it could do the most good: on developing techniques of identifying the child, making contact with the parent, and offering services and treatment for the family because it is unthinkable to offer treatment to a battered child and to return him to a lethal environment. Programs and centers for assessing, treating, and preventing child abuse have been developed throughout the country. Because children are considered to be the product of their environment, except for instances of blatant pathology,

---

*For purposes of simplification, the sex of the primary caregiver and of the therapist will be given as feminine and the sex of the abused child will be masculine. Such usage does not ignore the fact that men abuse children, provide casework treatment, or that girls are the victims of abuse also.

145

treatment for the child was generally believed to be accomplished when services and therapy were offered to the parents or when the child was placed in foster care. However, often the child requires more than placement in day care or to have his parents in treatment, and in recent years abused and neglected children have been studied to gain a profile of their psychological deficits and needs. Often protective workers find themselves needing to treat the child, but unfortunately their caseloads are so large that they can only devote their energies to the family in order for any change to take place.

This chapter will discuss some of the indications for treatment, consider some of the psychological needs of the abused and neglected child, and illustrate some of the issues involved in child treatment within a protective framework. Casework treatment, with its reality orientation, emphasis on building ego strengths, goals, outreach, and complications in the protective setting, will be described and demonstrated by giving case illustrations. Countertransference issues will be discussed. Special attention will be given to the issues of loss, expression of aggression, and self-concept. Although only a small percentage of children are placed in foster care, considerable attention will be given to the loss of a parent because so few children placed in care are then referred for treatment. Emphasis will be on early development because evidence is clear that young children are more prone to being abused physically and because unresolved early trauma forebodes ominously for future mental health. Older children are apt to be abused sexually, but the impact of this experience is also influenced by the resolution of early developmental issues. The uncompleted treatment of a child in care and awaiting adoption will be presented to illustrate many of the issues discussed.

It may seem that the tone of the chapter is heavy and sad. Disruption in the development of basic trust, as Erikson[2] states, is heavy and sad:

> Some day, maybe there will exist a well-informed, well-considered, and yet fervent public conviction that the most deadly of all possible sins is the mutilation of a child's spirit; for such mutilation undercuts the life principle of trust, without which every human act, may it feel ever so good and seem ever so right, is prone to perversion by destructive forms of conscientiousness.

Being party to the separation of a parent and child is heavy and sad, particularly when neither understands the justification for such a drastic step. However, watching a child learn to forgive, form new attachments, and risk the rebirth of trust is not sad, and the offer of companionship in such a process is not heavy. To see a child develop the capacity to discover alternatives, choose the positive side of ambivalence, and modify behavior is hardly depressing. It may even be that a tendency to lightheartedness is essential to the work!

INDICATIONS FOR TREATMENT

It is always difficult, as Anna Freud[3] describes, to determine when psychotherapy is indicated for children because so much of their behavior is determined by the particular stage of development they have reached (with its concomitant anxieties and stresses) and because their personality structure is in constant flux and is thoroughly influenced by their environment until separation and individuation are achieved. It is also difficult to assess whether seeming weaknesses in accomplishment of developmental tasks will predict future symptom formation. Current symptoms which are syntonic to children, with the exception of extreme anxiety, do not cause them to complain, so their degree of suffering cannot be an indication for therapy. Impairment of functioning, although a signal for adult pathology, also may not indicate trouble because an alternation between progress and regression is normal. Freud[4] continues, ". . . there is only one factor in childhood the impairment of which can be considered of sufficient importance . . . namely, the child's capacity to move forward in progressive steps until maturation, development in all areas of the personality, and adaptation to the social community have been completed."

The determination for treatment is even more complicated within a protective framework because all the above elements are heightened in content, context, and affect. A child's development is seriously jeopardized when it is impinged upon by not good enough parenting or when his primary object has become his dreaded object through violence, abandonment, or indifference.

Treatment for abused children comprises, first of all, offering medical attention and extra caretaking services, such as therapeutic day care, after school care, or placement in foster home or residential setting. The family is offered a myriad of services, most important of which is psychotherapy. The question of whether or not to add therapy for the child to the intervention program becomes futher obscured as one tries to assess the degree of intrapsychic disturbance vis à vis an improved, or improving, life situation. The element of timing must be considered as one waits for change to occur and impact on the child because one wants to avoid disrupting the primary attachment, if possible.

Many studies have shown significant gains in IQ and reduction of symptoms by placement in foster care alone.[5-8] Indeed, many children, whether placed or continued at home, who have experienced abuse are survivors and have managed to separate and individuate, have a good sense of object constancy, and function at a high level of competency with amazing abilities and resiliencies, despite coming from an environment that seemingly precluded such achievements. Some children appear to be inherently more able to withstand abuse than others.[6] Good early bonding and care-giving seem to be the most obvious explanation. Another appears to be the child's ability to seek other need-fulfilling objects[7] and the parents' tolerance of the child's attachment to a surrogate figure.

It seems paradoxical that very little has been available in the literature about child psychotherapy in a protective setting until lately, although much consideration has been given to the intergenerational cycle between parents who abuse their children who were abused themselves[8] and whether or not violence breeds violence.[9] Furthermore, since World War II much attention has been focused on the consequences of maternal deprivation, separation, loss, and attachment mishaps as precursors of later emotional illness. These issues have been acknowledged as indications for treatment for children whose parents have died or divorced, for example, without the added dimension of having been "raised in the warmth of parental wrath"[10] before the disruption of the relationship. To broaden the context even more, a major task of early childhood is to sort out fantasy from reality at a time when oedipal wishes must be put to rest and amnesia and the mental apparatus is developing sufficiently to make use of identification to resolve the dilemma. As Anthony[11] puts it:

> ...the world the child constructs between the ages of 4 and 8 is dynamic, magical, menacing, animistic, and governed by an irrational causality. Inanimate things are not only alive and full of consciousness, but they are also motivated and able to punish.

It is complicated to evaluate for treatment the impact of violent punishment from a hostile, primary care-giver at a time when the egocentric child is sorting out so many emotional and cognitive tasks, and the degree of his differentiation from his early symbiotic relationship colors his understanding of what has happened to him.

Sound, dynamic formulations are not the only consideration, unfortunately, because a critical dimension of protective work is framed by social policy, economics, and politics. Research has suggested that the results of child abuse are less potent for a child's development than social class membership, deprivation, poverty, or race.[12] It is perhaps understandable, although hardly acceptable, that child welfare agencies are forced to focus on protection as the goal of their intervention, rather than on resolution of a child's psychological or developmental deficits, because of economic, social, and political policies. As the climate of political conservatism is felt, one has to question if we will be allowed to look beyond protecting the child and to consider helping him realize his fullest personality development. Our attention and energies will also need to address the social forces which mold his environment.

Historically, the mere fact of placement often has been considered a "cure" by workers who are untrained and overworked. Sometimes the situation in the foster home replicates the original pathology, and it is not uncommon for children to have had over 10 home changes in the first four years of life [13] or never to have been visited by their worker after placement to assess the efficacy of the situation. Frank[14] tested children placed in foster care and discovered 78–80% of the sample showed low-level, borderline traits. These he described as disturbances of affect, ego functions, object relations, peer relationships, self-concept, behavioral difficulties, expression of aggression, and unresolved mourning.

The children tested five years later were shown to have deteriorated in placement, without having received treatment, because, he suggested, most foster placements are geared to "normal" children. Nevertheless, referrals for treatment are rarely made unless blatant psychopathology is seen, despite almost common knowledge that separation and loss of a parent jeopardizes further development for a child. Simple environmental manipulation is not always sufficient to prevent occurrence of regressive phenomena which can produce a chronically disturbed and arrested character structure.[15] The irony is, as Martin[16] points out, ". . . in the child abuse case, since we are *prescribing* parent loss as a valuable treatment modality, we may not consider our helpful administrations as harmful." It is difficult within such a framework to consider offering therapy to resolve the "good" of what we have done.

In summary, the hazardous issues which beset normal development must be weighed carefully in relation to the child's strengths, resources, and capacity to move forward developmentally in order to understand the full significance of the trauma of abuse or subsequent parent loss. The interplay of internal and external forces must be carefully evaluated to determine the possibility of further normal development.

PROFILE OF THE ABUSED CHILD

In recent years attention has turned from identifying abused or neglected children in an emergency ward, general medical, or school setting to defining a constellation of psychological deficits which indicate a need for psychotherapy. A veritable laundry list of behavioral disturbances has been found in children who have been abused, excluding damages from neurological, nutritional, prenatal, or genetic insults. The disturbances, described elsewhere in the literature,[17–24] can be divided into basic categories of deficits in ego functions, object relations, self-concept, and expression of affect and aggression. The children have often been described as delayed in cognitive functions, to have flat or depressed affect, to be incapable of experiencing pleasure or establishing trust, to be indiscriminately friendly, to have oral or primitive patterns of relating, to have considerable shame and doubt and negative self-concept, to be hypervigilant, hyperactive, or perseverative, to tantrum, to be unpredictably destructive of property or assaultive, to be unable to express anger to adults, or to be self-destructive.

Difficulties in the expression of aggression, control of impulses, resolution of loss, depression, and self-concept require deeper exploration, both interpersonally and intrapsychically, because they are the central issues to be resolved. It is important to keep in mind that it is not the severity of the abuse or parental pathology which determines the degree of the child's psychopathology or developmental fixation but the adequacy of the parenting and the degree of the bonding which the child receives.

DISCUSSION

Aggression

Abused children develop a proclivity to violent behavior as a primary mode of relating to others. It is not so much they are more violent than others but, rather, that violence remains their dominant mode of relating to others because they lack the competence to express their needs or negotiate emotional needs in alternate ways.[25] The use of identification with the aggressor[26] to cope with the overwhelming fear and rage experienced during abusive episodes may explain this behavior. In an attempt to avoid being flooded by feelings of powerlessness experienced during potentially annihilating incidents, the child identifies with the aggression of the parent both in behavior and in attitude. Although he achieves some small measure of revenge on substitutes, he receives for his efforts to achieve mastery over terror only disapproval, the same disapproval he feels toward his primary object but which he cannot express because he still needs nurturance. However, the bind is further doubled because the animosity he arouses in others by his assaultive behavior gives him further reason to believe in his own innate badness, a belief which is the only way his egocentric logic can explain what has happened to him.

Anger turned inward, or "identification with the victim,"[27] is another key defense. In this instance, repressed, potentially overwhelming feelings of powerlessness cause the child to turn rage on himself. He sets up a series of interactions with his parent and all subsequent objects to recapture the highly intensified affect at the moment of battering which was both thrilling and terrifying. The situation was, ". . . though painful, nonetheless, how the child experienced attachment to the ambivalently cathected love objects." [28] The tendency to repeat this experience passively is also an attempt to discover what it was that he did that was bad enough to warrant such treatment. Scapegoating behavior, so exquisitely provocative, is an attempt to rework issues of trust and guilt by children fixated at a rudimentary superego which is turned against the self. [29]

Unexpressed aggression toward the parent must be felt as guilt, turned against the self in a pervasive deficiency of self-esteem and acted out repeatedly in ways to elicit punishment. Another displacement is seen in self-destructive behavior in which ". . . a transformation of the child's self-hatred into self-destructive behavior is catalyzed by ego deficits and impaired impulse control." [30] This is seen in various guises from a seemingly careless lack of concern for personal safety to overt accident proneness or to clear-cut self-mutilation, suicidal ideation, or attempts.

Although no studies familiar to this writer have investigated or corroborated this hypothesis, it is interesting to speculate if children who "select" this course of defense are the ones who had earliest bonding difficulties with their care-givers because of an incongruence of temperament or some other mishap of attachment. Never having experienced an ease of communication with the parent, and the parent's never having had an easy time coping with the "difficult baby," [31] a convoluted series of communication difficulties build up which convince the parent that the problem lies within the child.*[32] The child is therefore forced to incorporate this impression and begins to believe from his earliest experiences that he is at fault for everything that goes wrong, including the abuse.

Impulse Control

Unfortunately, identification with the aggressor, while preventing a breakdown of the ego as the child is enabled to move from a passive to an active stance by mimicking violence, also prevents the child from developing acceptable ways of controlling impulses. With no role model to copy how to suppress, delay, sublimate, or channel drives into self-enhancing assertiveness, the child is left with a pattern of unpredictable, assaultive behavior which is repeated endlessly in an attempt to resolve his trauma. He cannot introject or identify with representations which will help him form a superego as in healthy development.

Without the practicing experiences of learning to control impulses in

---

*While considering this formulation, it is important to keep in mind that the abusing parent is one without a support system, someone isolated, without resources to help care for the child, and often in a state of crisis where limited coping skills are severely taxed.

the presence of an external ego, the child cannot internalize precursors of superego formation because the process of changing the pleasure principle into the reality principle has not been consistently or predictably experienced. A pseudo-impulse control is formed which breaks down suddenly without internal warning signs, and the child is left with the only means of expressing his hostile feelings that he knows. Peer relationships are hampered by an unpredictable, blind violence which is seen in the grabbing of objects, destruction of materials, or in lightning-swift assaultiveness, as if to attack before being attacked. Again the unsuccessful interpersonal experiences feed the self-concept of being bad and unworthy.

Self-Esteem

The same defect in ego-building experiences to master drive control for effective self-expression, as seen in healthy identification with the aggressor, occurs in "identification with the victim."[33] However, in this case the superego is hypercathected with punishment and, unless the repetition compulsion is acted out in blatant pathology, it often goes unnoticed because the aggression is expressed passively. Identification with the victim does not create the turmoil that identification with the aggressor does, but the effect on the self-esteem is as damaging. The desperate necessity to maintain a lowly self-image is as rigid and difficult to change. The child develops a distorted lens through which to view reality and to misinterpret future experiences (such as placement in foster care) as further evidence and verification of his innate badness.

Shengold[34] elaborates the process whereby self-esteem is destroyed by the experience of abuse, which he dramatically calls "soul murder." He focuses on the terrifying "too muchness" and suggests that a "mind splitting" becomes a defense against the overload of affect. He believes the traumatic impingement of abuse threatens a child's sense of identity to a point where the overwhelming feeling must be blocked out, isolated, or denied, and the child is left with a confusion and a "hypnotic living deadness."[35]

Mastery of drive control in normal development is achieved by the mother's lending her ego to the child. In abuse the torment is given by the same person to whom the child must turn for containment and comfort of other distresses. Because there is no one else the child can turn to for the relief of the pain which the parent herself has caused, the ". . . child must break with what he has experienced and must . . . register the parent — *delusionally* — as good."[36] In order to survive, the contradictory images of the self and the parent must never be permitted to coalesce.

The child must ". . . idealize the tormentor, deny the torment."[37] Added to this perception is the delusive hope that all the terror and pain will eventually be transformed into love, which is a factor in the need to provoke parental wrath as the child seeks love instead of hate. This elusive search also explains the tenacity of the repetition compulsion, the need to maintain a low self-esteem, and the degree of resistance to the therapist's efforts to undo the delusion.

Loss

Resolution of the above concerns becomes further involved when the abused child is forced to lose his parent in order to resume development or to be protected. Much attention needs to be given to this issue in its various forms to understand and to ameliorate potentially overwhelming affects of sadness and rage.

Children placed in foster care have to undergo a process of mourning as they cope with temporary separation or work to relinquish permanently their bond to their primary object who still lives and may or may not visit them. To illustrate: "A nine-year-old in the process of being adopted said, 'But I don't know how to say goodbye to my parents.'"[38]

There is considerable disagreement about a young child's ability to mourn successfully. Furman[39] concludes that a child's ability to mourn depends on a variety of internal and external factors. Case illustrations of successful early mourning all show children who were sensitively prepared, consistently nurtured, and tenderly contained and supported in their grief by new care-givers who themselves were able to mourn and could tolerate the children's pain. The children were able to express their loss, decathect the lost object, form new libidinal ties, return to developmental tasks, and take pleasure in mastery.

The process whereby children are put in foster care hardly duplicates the life situations described in case illustrations of successful mourning. There is little disagreement about the impact of separation and maternal deprivation on a child or the influence of unresolved grief on later emotional health. A previous history of abuse increases the vulnerability to object loss which usually is affected by the stage at which the loss occurred and determines whether the child will regress, whether development will be arrested across the whole spectrum of personality, or whether there will be a retardation of physical, intellectual, or social functioning.

The child placed in foster care has already experienced some of the various stressors which abuse places on psychic development. The child's capacity to bear the stages of mourning that Bowlby[40] described of protest, despair (disorganization), and detachment (reorganization) depends on the degree of personality pathology before the separation and what resources the taxed, undeveloped, underdeveloped, or split ego has available. In short, it is the totality of the child's experiences prior to and during the process of separation as well as afterward in foster care which will affect his adjustment and resolution of object loss. On an intra-psychic level, will he develop coping styles which will enable him to adapt to the new environment or will they prevent him from working through loss? On an interpersonal level, will his new care-givers be able to help him work through the phases of grief or tolerate his displaced anger, irascible behavior, and yearning for reunion with the lost object?

Thomas[41] studied 35 latency children in foster care and added a preprotest stage to Bowlby's grief phases. Her assumption was that the disequilibrium of the first three stages could be resolved by successful grief work which would result in a stability and congruence of affect and behavior over time. The grief process was found to be sequential, but there was lack of stability in the middle phases of protest and despair as children moved back and forth between them before reaching detach-ment. Of significance was the finding that resolution of object loss and establishment of the new relationship, whether it involved permanent foster care or return to the parents, was associated with consensus about future plan of care.[42] Continued contact with the parents during place-ment did not seem to affect resolution of object loss as much as uncer-tainty about the future. A large factor in the child's successful resolution of loss was the foster parents' "sensitivity to children and ability to help them express feelings about loss . . . and their . . . spontaneous expres-sion of interest in increasing their knowledge and understanding of children in order to help them."[43] She concluded that 50% of the children continued to show some indications of interference in developmental tasks and impaired relationships indicative of unresolved grief work, but Walker[44] points out that some subjects, while appearing to have adjusted, may have been repressing and denying feelings of loss. Children who did not successfully reach detachment appeared to have more unrewarding relationships and constricted investment in tasks.

Walker[45] looked at the personalities of 20 foster mothers from the point of view of those who would be more able to provide the emotional atmosphere to help the child express feelings about loss, including yearn-ing and anger. He felt a "need-bestowing" mother, who created characteristics in a child for her narcissistic gratification, was less able to help a child express feelings of loss, yearning, and anger than a "need-appraising" mother, who perceived the real characteristics of the child and was able to facilitate grief work. He defined the following types of pathological mourning: overt, unresolved mourning as the absence of ex-pressions of yearning, anger, or a desire for reunion; and covert, unresolved mourning as the presence of fantasies which reflected disturbances in personal outlook, task mastery, or object relationships.

Walker's study of 26 Caucasian children concluded that those whose natural parents were living, were put in placement before the age of 6, had long-term foster care experience, with little or no parent contact, did not successfully resolve object loss. It was his unfortunate finding that most of these children were living with "need-bestowing" foster mothers and were not in emotional atmospheres which were conducive to resolution of grief or amelioration of ego deficits. It is equally important to remember that referral for psychotherapy would probably not come for children who "successfully" repressed and denied loss in various passive, compliant, depressive guises. It would only be the blatant acting out behavior to defend against the depression that signaled the need for psychotherapeutic help or a change to a new foster home, which compounded the problem even further.

Further consideration should be given to some defensive formations which impede expression of loss and grief in order to understand more fully the protest stage of children placed in foster care. Just as it was impossible for the child to express his anger and condemnation of his parent for having experienced abuse, he is equally unable to express his anger for having lost the parent.

Deutsch[46] described the "indifference" of children who have lost a parent as a defense against overwhelming anxiety. She went on to say that it ". . . is of great interest that observers of children note that the ego is rent asunder in those children who do not employ the usual defenses, and who mourn as an adult does." Wolfenstein[47] suggests that a child experiences parental loss as a panic of being unprovided for, a fear of annihilation, and a fear of "massive amounts of objectless libido of traumatic intensity" because he realizes he could not survive alone. Furthermore, the child not only does not have the capacity to control the dosage of emotional letting go that an adult has,* but he must also use developmentally immature reasoning to explain the loss.[49] Wolfenstein[50] believes the child therefore avoids protracted grief and the finality of death and remains intensely cathected to the lost parent, with fantasies that the parent will return and reunite with him. On the one hand the child acknowledges the loss of the parent, but the ego is split by denial and remains hypercathected to the lost object who is then idealized. The child both acknowledges and denies the reality of the parent's death. To illustrate: Freud[51] reported being shocked that a highly intelligent 10-year-old boy he was treating, whose father had been suddenly killed, said, "I know father's dead, but what I can't understand is why he doesn't come home to supper."

---

*At certain developmental stages he may even need to deny himself the catharsis of crying. Freud[48] notes that crying for latency children signifies a regressive loss of control and is therefore avoided because of the anxiety it generates.

Fantasies of reunion are so deeply imbedded in the unconscious and so hypercathected that they often cannot be acknowledged until the child is an adolescent and almost ready to give them up.[52] By maintaining denial of the reality of the loss, the child feels rage rather than grief which then becomes displaced onto other care-givers with narcissistic vindication. A repetitive cycle is established wherein the child, unable to renounce the lost object, becomes demanding to be taken care of and then turns the rage toward the world at large. The repetition of disappointments then substantiates a need for the lost parent because no one can help. This need for the lost parent then embellishes the idealized relationship with the lost parent,[53] which for an abused child is already a delusion. Thus one can see that the task of unraveling such fantasies in treatment is most difficult indeed.

Fraiberg[54] illustrated how defenses against affect toward the lost object prevented latency boys in residential placement from forming new relationships. She showed how children's behavior during the grief work phases (which occurred in the order of despair, protest, detachment), when interpreted by care-givers without clinical training, was reacted to in such a way that a working through of loss was prevented. Although the staff's responses produced a pseudo-adjustment in some children which was less taxing to the staff, it camouflaged an inability to form new object ties and various ego impairments.

The child's initial withdrawal was seen as a repudiation of the staff's willingness to help and desire to rescue. The child's mourning was seen as something to be gotten over quickly as the "need-bestowing" staff sought to make amends for the child's life. The protest stage, with its displaced anger and provocative behavior, was seen as a challenge of authority and need for the child to learn who was boss. Eventual compliance by some children was seen as successful adjustment with the "silent" inability to form attachments, although certain children had symptoms, such as enuresis or acting-out behavior.

In Fraiberg's study children were selected for treatment who showed a variety of behaviors from acting out hostile aggression, withdrawing depression, or a charming ingratiation that masked an impoverishment in ego and relationship capabilities. It was possible for the caseworkers to see how the variety of behaviors shown repeated earlier experiences and, by using transference reactions in treatment, to help the children gain insight into their behavior. Sometimes merely reliving the past in the presence of a benevolent figure helped resolve the old conflicts. Fraiberg demonstrated through case examples how casework treatment, by reviving rage and grief and by working through the experience of loss, enabled the children to become spontaneous and recover the ability to form new object ties.

TREATMENT: ISSUES FOR THE THERAPIST

Engaging the Patient

The differences between casework treatment in a protective setting and the traditional child guidance model of psychotherapy are easily apparent. Attitude, outreach, flexibility, and the press of reality are the dominant elements. Once the determination for treatment has been made, a difference in attitude is immediately seen in the degree of commitment on the part of the worker for it to be delivered to the child. Inherent in the concept of commitment is the sense of responsibility connected to all protective work because of the seriousness of the issues involved. We are not dealing with repressed fantasies and memories but with reality, as it is happening, when affect is high and defenses are being mobilized. The immediacy of the treatment to the trauma is what makes it so affective and effective.

Another dimension of responsibility is the power at the therapist's disposal. The interface of the reality that fears and wishes may be realized operates in treatment, just as it did in the traumatic experience of physical abuse, sexual exploitation, or placement in care. An appeal can be made to the court for treatment to be mandated, if necessary, or for the child to be removed from the home if new evidence is presented which requires this intervention. It may turn out that the parent or guardian simply does not have the choice to interrupt treatment.

While power can be a positive therapeutic tool in terms of reality testing and limit-setting, a kind of ultimate caring, it is also the breeding ground for a whole set of transference and countertransference resistances. The hairline difference between a police-state mentality and making the determination to protect a vulnerable child evokes all sorts of theoretical, ethical, and countertransference issues for the therapist. Judgments are made as value systems are compared and measured, as, for example, in determining how large or how deep in color a bruise must be to be called abuse rather than harsh punishment or when lackadaisical housekeeping or laissez-faire child rearing practices constitute neglect.

It is still a parent's inalienable right to make a child neurotic as children pass through developmental stages unresolved by their parents. However, can a parent be allowed to make a child psychotic? Do we have the right to intercede to stop the process, and if so, how much pathology is enough? The therapist's own feelings about authority and ethical beliefs and the flexibility or rigidity of her position are constantly being challenged. When to blow the whistle, to step in and intervene for the child in the grey areas of what is unacceptable is a constant concern and often must be weighed in the context of what is reasonable and functional. One has to consider seriously what price the child will pay for our interfering with the attachment to his parent, whether and how such a disruption will build or break treatment alliances which offer hope of future growth, and whether a better situation can be found in foster care. A further danger comes from getting caught up in the chaos of the child's situation so that issues become further obscured. Fortunately, such decisions are never made alone, and when they are finally made, however difficult and painful the process, they are made with conviction.

It may be that all parents want to be good parents (whatever that might mean to each of them). The enormous, narcissistic injury inflicted on parents when a referral is made to a child welfare agency questioning their child's safety under their own care is often felt as an "official" repudiation of their efforts and a validation of their worthlessness.

A parent's customary resistance to allowing a child to be treated is heightened by this blow to an already low self-esteem and a fantasy easily arises that the therapist is the perfect parent (just as the foster mother is believed to be above reproach). The positive transference feelings which facilitate a working alliance can easily be misconstrued as love for the therapist and engender a good deal of jealousy because the abusing parent easily believes the child could love anyone more than herself. The parent's need for the child to fulfill her own needs is also clearly threatened by the prospect of the child's forming an attachment to someone else or becoming differentiated to a degree that would change the equilibrium of the family.

Jealousy of attention given to the child is another danger, and play therapy may be seen as a more caring, more giving, more pleasurable therapy than that offered to the parent. The awareness of the social worker's power also presents the fear of the child's being taken away if he revealed the "worst truths," and certainly this could be a reality issue for any abuse in the future. It would be very hard to hide it from the worker.

This realization also works for the child, and he may be fearful of revealing current conflicts and abuse for fear of being sent away from his parent. The other side of this issue is the potential secondary gain for the child to displace expression of hostile, aggressive feelings toward the parent by baiting them with threats such as, "You can't make me do that or I'll tell so-and-so." The danger this poses for the scapegoating child, who provokes beating, is obvious, apart from its interference with the healthy demands and limit-setting a parent must make.

The therapist has to be very careful when confronted with new injuries not to overreact or say something to the child like, "There's a law to protect children from being beaten." This can be used as a feeble and futile protection against further abuse by the child and frighten or infuriate the parent to a point where treatment is sabotaged. It may even cause the parent to flee the area.

Countertransference

Countertransference rescue fantasies, always a danger in child therapy, are obviously whetted in child protective work. These are aroused by the seriousness of the child's plight and the therapist's desire to make restitution or to relieve pain. These apply to the evaluator for treatment as well as to the child's therapist because one's discomfort with the material might cause one to prescribe treatment when the innate strengths of the child might prevail in an altered situation. On a deeper level the therapist's attitude will be shaped by the degree of resolution and differentiation she has made with her own parents. If she has experienced deprivation or abuse herself, the stresses of the work may prove too difficult.

It is easy to align oneself with the child, to feel helpless and powerless in the hands of the seemingly indifferent parent, and to blame. The therapist's loss of differentiation with the child's plight may cause her to collude and to prevent therapeutic progress. The child will quickly perceive this stance of the therapist, may join her, and thus be prevented from achieving any acceptance of the reality of the deficits in his parent as he is concurrently experiencing them. He may also feel threatened to lose his attachment to his parents or feel he must give it up in order to engage in work with the therapist. The therapist's understanding of the parent, although the parent's behavior cannot be condoned, must be conveyed to the child at a deep level. True mastery, as McDermott[55] said, comes from not only being able to live with one's past but also with one's present:

> The ability to "forgive" the abusing parent through a psycho-therapeutic experience is a powerful factor in releasing the child from seeking constant repetition of the abusing experience in childhood, and from later reversing roles as a parent in a series of futile attempts to rid himself of its effects.

Just as the therapist must be able to tolerate and contain the child's pain of mourning a lost parent, so must she be able to help the child deal with the pain of ambivalence and with memories of the abusing parent. As long as these memories can be kept conscious and some of the affect can be tolerated, as Fraiberg[56] points out, the child can be helped to find an alternative to a later repetition of resolving overwhelming stress by striking out at her own child. The therapist's ability to be constantly aware of countertransference feelings toward the child's parents, to maintain a high regard for the part of the person that wants to be a good parent, and to convey this positive feeling to the child is probably the most important aspect of successful treatment. The therapist then becomes a model for the child as she demonstrates successful handling of ambivalent feelings toward the parent.

Working in a multidisciplinary setting which offers treatment for the whole family facilitates such a position and alleviates polarization. Frequent peer consultation with the mother's therapist, parent aide, or other providers to the family, including the child's teachers and significant figures at school, helps to keep the countertransference issues clear and provides support for the difficulty of protective work. The necessity of good supervision and consultation is also apparent to allow the therapist to ventilate and sort out the interface of protective, psychotherapeutic, and countertransference issues. It is the quality and quantity of this nourishment that prevents the therapist from becoming inured to the seriousness of the issues at hand as a defense against the strong feelings which not only must be aroused but also used empathetically in the treatment situation.

Another kind of countertransference, more subtle in its appearance, can occur in relation to the foster parent when the child is in placement because there is a danger of the therapist's displacing rescue fantasies onto them. While it may be easy for the therapist to help the foster parents recognize their need to "make it up to" the child for the abuse he has received, she may be blind to her own disappointment that the foster parents are not going to be perfect parents either. The child is going to have to work hard to adjust to the dynamics of the new home. This is especially difficult when the foster parent is of the "need-bestowing" type, when the parent's narcissistic manipulation of the child is obvious, or when the parent sabotages treatment for fear of losing control of the child. In these instances, a therapist assigned to work with the foster parent around child management issues is necessary and helpful.

A final issue for the therapist is seen in unrealistic, unconscious feelings of inadequacy. These are stirred up because of the enormity of the task, the immediacy of the work to the trauma, and the press of reality factors in the child's situation. The deprivation and orality of the children often make them appear as if they can never get enough, and the therapist, bombarded at many levels as the child expresses unmet needs, may feel depleted or unrealistically unable to give enough. "If only so-and-so were treating John, things would go better or faster," is a familiar feeling expressed. It is very important for the therapist to acknowledge these feelings to prevent burn out and to work them out in supervision or peer consultation in order to understand how universal they are. Accepting the limits of what one has to offer, in the face of all that needs to be done, can be a difficult position to maintain, but treatment for the child is usually the last intervention made to an abusing family. It helps to confer with the individual, family, or group therapists and parent aide to see that these feelings are shared. The single play therapy hour then becomes part of an integrated effort to help the troubled family and can be kept in perspective.

Outreach and Flexibility

Child treatment typically includes sharing enough of the child's treatment process with the parents to enable them to learn different ways of relating to their child. Helping to sort out communication miscarriages and teaching what are age-appropriate expectations for behavior, different ways of setting limits, and what a child's needs and feelings might be, when sensitively presented, make the child's therapist a resource person to the parent. Close work with the parent's therapist enables the timing of meetings and pacing of information and suggestions to be felt as supportive consultation. One must always be alert to the parent's low self-esteem, sensitivity to criticism, and self-defeating tendency to set up situations to be criticized.

Similar outreach is also very helpful to a foster parent if a child is in placement. The various phases of grief work should be explained to the foster parents and translated into current behavior symptoms. Mutual planning of coping strategies and support for the difficulty of the task can be very helpful to the foster parent who often feels neglected by child protective workers.

The commitment to treatment involves flexibility of approach and location. It may necessitate working with the child alone while outreach is being made to form an alliance with the parent, which may take months. Such a process requires special attention to resistance, transference, and countertransference issues. It may be necessary to treat the child in his school, and this may create all sorts of difficulties, depending on the school's willingness to have mental health services delivered on its premises. The teacher also has to be willing to accept the child back to her class after a session which may have aroused strong feelings or to accept the child's displaced anger because the session had to end.

Child treatment can be complicated because it operates on so many levels at once and can at times be embarrassing because it is noisy, disruptive, and potentially uncontrollable. The ease with which a therapist handles these issues often depends on the tolerance of the setting in which it takes place. Maintaining control of a child's impulses and behavior is a central issue for us all. We all fear what losing it might mean.* Since some regression is encouraged in the permissive play therapy atmosphere in order to rework resistances to effective control mechanisms, or to develop self-enhancing ego functions of drive mastery, there is always the danger that the child will regress too far or that our responses will not be sufficiently attuned or at the proper level of communication to prevent an escalation of loss of control. Often the therapeutic process appears like a loss of control to uninformed observers. Child treatment requires a therapist with considerable confidence to withstand its unpredictability and the disapproval of other adults who become threatened by the apparent disruption.

It is one thing for a therapist to sit comfortably in an office and wait for a recalcitrant child to join her from the waiting room when the clinic staff is aware and supportive of the issues at work. It is quite another to have borrowed a nurse's office in a school that is run by a rigid principal and have the child bolt out of the office at the end of the session and run throughout the building in hope the therapist will chase him! To illustrate:

> A beginning therapist's first treatment case in a neighborhood health clinic was a 5-year-old child who displaced his anger at having been neglected by his mother into making up tantalizing games of "catch me." Because his mother was uninvested in supporting his treatment, the therapist became responsible for his transportation to and from the clinic. An attempt to use her own car proved near disastrous as the child, resisting the end of the first session, undid his seat belt, opened the window and leaned out as far as he could en route to his school. She was afraid that he would have jumped out of the car and run off if she had stopped it. She as yet had no alliance to influence his behavior.
>
> The school personnel, who fortunately were also adaptable, worked out an arrangement whereby he was delivered to the clinic and returned to his home by school bus. However, there now was an unpredictable wait for the bus to come. Transitions were so anxiety-provoking for the child that he could not maintain control. With a devilish sparkle in his eye that was infuriating to her, he would manage to slip away from holding her hand and dart through the adult medical clinic (which had a large geriatric population) turning off lights in the examining rooms, racing up and down the hall a few feet ahead of the puffing therapist, and squirting mouthfuls of water from the drinking fountain. It was difficult for the worker to maintain an assured air and communicate to the child that she could help him stop losing control

---

*One has only to watch observers' reactions toward the hapless parent of a child tantruming in a supermarket to see how threatening this is. The child's loss of control tugs at our own defenses and arouses feelings of helplessness. Since it is our ego which must function for them at such a moment, we know we must intervene, but reasoning does not work. The degree of affect displayed before us has aroused our aggression, and it is not clear what will work to stop the child's behavior. We are further angered because we do not like to be watched when our efforts to bring the child under control may fail.

this way in the face of glaring physicians, shocked patients, and disapproving nurses!

Once the child ran away into the neighborhood and was gone several minutes. The therapist took as nonchalant a stance as she could master, turning her back to the direction in which he had run, waiting for him to return. He eventually appeared, worried, and questioned her seeming indifference:

"Why didn't you come after me?"

"I was waiting here, where we always do for the bus. Why should I have come after you?"

"I could have gotten lost. [Pause.] And I could have gotten hurt."

"Uhuh. But I was here."

He never ran away again. He also stopped running through the clinic, although he continued to run up the stairs faster than the therapist could and always had a sparkle in his eye, as if he remembered the fun of former chases. However, he now chose to walk independently, rather than having his hand held, and he was able to exercise control over his impulses.

He had learned about the constancy of the therapist in an additional context to the therapy session. Because she had been forced to become his care-giver for transitions to the clinic, he was able to experience how she reacted to provocation and anger (in a situation where he had quickly sensed she felt vulnerable) and to learn how she controlled her impulses and how she set limits on his behavior that did not retaliate.

TREATMENT: ISSUES FOR THE CHILD

Goals

Establishment of the relationship, as always, is the initial goal of casework treatment and will provide the medium in which all further work will be achieved. Whether the child presents as withdrawn, suspicious and fearful, or a whirlwind of aggressive, provocative behaviors, the basic issue of trust and mistrust will be worked and reworked as the child explores related issues of object constancy, differentiation, self-esteem, loss, aggression, and ambivalence. Acting out, denial, and avoidance will be addressed as attention is given to building ego functions, such as binding up strong affect, limiting impulses, organizing internal experience, structuralizing experience, and developing mastery of skills, rather than on helping the child to express explosive rage. We are not only dealing with repressed memories or fantasies but also with current reality. Therefore, emphasis will be less on achieving catharsis than on containment, on becoming aware of and learning to tolerate potentially overwhelming affect and ambivalence as these issues occur and recur in play and are clarified and interpreted. Labeling of feelings helps the child to understand the confusing affect, experience control, learn how to verbalize, and eventually choose different ways of relating. Positive regard, warmth, humor, and reflecting back the reality of the child's strengths are some of the other therapeutic tools used to achieve the goals.

Themes

The offer of a relationship immediately brings into focus issues of trust which may be disguised as an initial, superficial acceptance and pleasure at receiving the therapist's undivided attention and accepting mien. However, the apparent readiness to engage can also signal an inability to differentiate objects and can express an object hunger. One quickly notes a disparity between a seeming willingness to relate and a lack of eye contact and wariness of physical contact. Soon the therapist is challenged as limits are tested, often in a manner that provokes physical retaliation, as the child perceives the therapist's vulnerabilities and tests them. At the same time, on another level, there is a subtle reaching out to please the therapist, which is also startling to experience because it, too, is attuned to her emotional needs and vulnerabilities. The tenuous capacity for relating thus demonstrated becomes a focus of early work together and is a leitmotiv throughout the course of treatment.

Other themes and similarities of responses observed along the way of working and reworking issues of trust are clearly outlined by Martin[57] and McQuiston and Kempe.[58] They described a marked orality and need for nurturance as the contents of candy jars are devoured and candy is pocketed. The primitive quality of object relations is also seen in the little curiosity shown about the therapist as a person, and Martin cites one child who could not remember the therapist's name after six months of two-times-a-week therapy.[59]

Denial of loss during separation is an important defense. There is much resistance to acknowledging feelings of loss, and relief from these feelings is gained through efforts to control or a regression to testing of limits. Low self-concept is marked and seen in self-deprecating remarks, a resistance to trying something new, an inability to take pride in accomplishments, a quick frustration, low initiative, quick discouragement, and short attention span. The children are often described as having a joylessness, lack of spontaneity, inability to experience pleasure in age-appropriate activities, or even to know how to play. A rigidity of thinking, limited approach to problem solving, and primitive conscience is also seen. There is often an inability to connect cause and effect or to attempt to have any understanding of what is going on, which reflects the chaotic series of environmental crises which overload the child's ability to order, structure, or categorize and prohibits development of logical thinking. There can also be a thought disorder and an inability to distinguish fantasy from reality, self from others. Finally, there is often seen an inability to express feelings directly, whether they are aggressive, anxious, fearful, or affectionate.

It is as difficult for the child to express aggression directly as it is for him to trust. He goes through various stages as he learns coping skills to deal with aggressive impulses and feelings. Initially these are acted out in displacement, and once he has tested the safety of the working space (both in the office and in the relationship), by challenging limits, there is then a period in which he externalizes the feelings in the symbolism of play. Finally, an ability to recognize his anger, understand its source, and express it verbally is achieved.

Occasionally, with a child who has identified with the aggressor, the aggression is expressed physically toward the therapist and the child may need to be restrained physically to experience external controls over the impulse. Telling him that he is being held to be made safe, that he is being protected from losing control because no one gets hurt in this office is very important. The attack may have angered the therapist (a blow in the face generates instant fury), and it is very helpful for the child to see that when she is angry, she speaks in a firm, forceful tone and that, while clearly disapproving of the child's actions, she still approves of the child. Labeling that she has been made angry clarifies the child's perceptions and models a capacity to recognize anger and to express it without resorting to retaliatory violence. It may be easier for the therapist to cope with the physical show of aggression than with a devious expression as, when, for example, her favorite play materials are subtly destroyed.

A closer look at the stages of mastery of aggression may be helpful. Sometimes the testing begins with amusing questions, such as, "What would you do to a kid who broke your fire engine?" or, "What would happen if the paint spilled?" Sometimes the questions are even more guarded, such as, "How did that truck get broken?" Responses such as, "You need to know what I do when I'm angry," "You need to know what happened to the kid who broke the truck," followed by, "No one gets hurt in here," initially help the child to relax and may receive incredulous glances. Other times the testing is acted out and needs to be restrained by comments such as, "We don't paint when it can't be kept on the paper," or "You need to show me how messy you feel inside." If the impulse is acted upon and the paint has "accidentally" spilled, then the child can be shown how to clean up the spill. (Obviously, materials like paint that require some control would not be offered to an impulse-ridden child.)

Expression of aggression externalized in the symbolic content of play is a different matter. The therapist needs to spend much time interacting with the child at the symbolic level of the play materials before any attempt can be made to move to a higher level of ownership of the feelings. For example, clarification needs to begin with statements such as, "The car is out of control and is smashing into the house," before one moves to, "The driver is out of control," or later, "You are smashing the car." Comments that move too fast to link the feeling to the child may abort the interaction. To illustrate:

> After nine months of weekly therapy, Alex moved from displacement to externalization of anger in his play. Repeatedly, it was the fire that destroyed the house, not the boy doll that was "living" in the house, and certainly not Alex who was telling the story!
> One day he turned to puppet play, and after demonstrating an aggressive interaction between them, ordered the therapist to tell a story with them. She had the puppets act out an aggressive interplay wherein a "bully" bopped a small puppet and then was hit in return by a larger puppet who defended his little friend. Alex quickly put the puppets away and invented a game in which the therapist was told to pretend she was driving a car. Alex then became a policeman and delighted in arresting her for speeding, as he regained control. It seemed she had gone too fast!

Anger which occurs as a result of circumstances between the therapist and the child is very useful to explore but points out how very difficult it is for the child to express his feeling directly. To illustrate:

> A 5-year-old child, who lacked external supports for his impulsive rages because his depressed mother often withdrew emotional supplies from him, had recently been placed in a special educational class. His therapist transferred weekly sessions to his new school. In order to maintain some sense of constancy for him during his initial adjustment, she brought some of his favorite toys from her office for their use during their sessions. He had subsequently requested certain Matchbox cars, and she had forgotten them two weeks in a row.
> An attempt to suggest that he was disappointed and angry because she had forgotten them was totally denied. However, he could not contain his feelings, and he soon acted out frustration and anger in the content of play and made several comments about how he was sick of people "who tell lies." His anger mounted and eventually focused on a refusal to pick up the toys when the hour was up. He regressed to an old pattern of swearing roundly and threatened to punch the therapist or even to kill her if she insisted he help her pick up the toys.
> An attempt to clarify that he was angry at her because she had disappointed him made him even more upset. He had recently learned in an inpatient setting to gain some control over his aggressive impulses from having been physically restrained and having had the holding labeled as "being made safe." He screamed, "You're making me unsafe with all those wrong words!" When the therapist redirected that he was angry because he had to pick up the toys and that he did not want the

hour to end, he could relax with the displaced version of his anger and become calm. After 18 months of therapy, he still could not own the true source of his anger. Because he had so recently transferred to the new class from the inpatient setting and had to return to a classroom after their session, she was loathe to press the issue.

Experiences such as those illustrated show the amount of work that needs to be done before deeper working through can be reached. Good examples of deeper clarification and interpretation in linking the child's anger to the abusive or neglecting experiences with the parent can be found elsewhere in the literature. Throughout the course of therapy it is important for the child to recognize, acknowledge, and experience his anger while he uses the therapist's ego to contain it and to learn how to express it without violence.

The desire to please is another dominant theme that needs to be clarified and worked through to enable the child to differentiate his feelings from others. This can be confronted by showing that the therapist really wants to learn what the child wants to do and will not decide for him what color should be used or what game should be played. However, the efforts of the child to please can be very subtle. To illustrate:

A therapist, who believed herself in control of her need to rescue and to nurture children, was treating a child whose role with his mother had been to make her feel loved and lovable. The child had become very skillful at responding to another's emotional state. After six months of treatment, the therapist had a dream in which her own family had said it was all right for her to adopt the child. She subsequently learned that each of the child's nursery school teachers had had a similar dream of adopting him! Somehow the child had made each significant figure in his life feel loved in such a way that excited rescue fantasies and maternal drives.

By repeatedly helping the child to recognize and acknowledge his own wishes and to learn that finding a workable compromise for them with another person is the basis for a relationship, and not compliance with another's needs, he can be helped to challenge his own fantasies and to construct a realistic understanding of what he contributed, and needs to contribute, to a relationship. The immediacy of the treatment relationship to the trauma of his life allows him the opportunity to contrast the quality of this relationship with others and to learn that it can be duplicated elsewhere in his life. Just as the child learns that he is not responsible for another person's pleasure, he can learn that he was not responsible for another's rage or for the abuse he received.

Self-esteem can be enhanced by play materials that provide opportunities for building ego functions, sublimating impulses, and developing mastery of innate abilities. Initially the process of the activity may be all that can interest the child, and he needs mirroring experiences of positive regard, warmth, and reflection of the reality of his strengths before he can take pleasure in tasks. Sometimes it takes months before a child can experience pleasure or pride in the product of his efforts, before the positive self-regard that this entails has developed sufficiently. The child can learn not only that positive relationships can be built around his good skills but that responding to one's inner resources of feelings, thoughts, and abilities is the basis of what we all offer to a relationship.

CASE ILLUSTRATION

Five-year-old Eric was referred for play therapy by his mother's therapist, who had been working with his mother for eight months. Despite a willingness to work on her issues of dependency, abandonment, and impulsive rage in weekly home visits, and the offering of a homemaker and day care services, she had been unable to stop herself from abusing him. At the time therapy began, Eric had been in foster placement for two months with his younger brother, Roger, after a tumultuous separation from his mother. His mother and Jack, her boyfriend and Roger's father, had defied the court and gone into hiding, refusing to surrender the children. Eventually Eric's mother complied with the court order, the children were brought forth, and placed in three foster homes in ten days before they were settled.

Eric is an attractive child with deep-set dark eyes, touseled dark curls, and an impish smile. His upper four front teeth are missing, whose lack he blandly explains, "My father did it. He punched me in the mouth." He has excellent coordination and moves quickly and easily but with a suspicious recklessness and zest for dangerous situations. The day care staff was very attached to him, and his foster mother said he was one of the most appealing children she had ever had. She quickly indicated a desire to adopt him if he were eventually to be released.

A brief look at his early history and that of his mother revealed a troubled course. His mother, an identical twin, had been abused, abandoned, and placed in foster care, although she returned to her family as an adolescent. Her twin sister had been adopted at age 12. Eric was the product of her marriage at age 19 to a man of whom her family strongly disapproved because of his race and from whom she separated after a month because he tried to strangle her. Eric was born as she was working through the disappointment of that relationship and struggling to manage alone and to tolerate loneliness. She was both delighted by him, feeling that he was part of herself, and overwhelmed by the enormity of answering his needs. Unfortunately, he soon had a series of illnesses which appeared life-threatening to her and for which he was hospitalized three times between 8 and 14 months of age. He was evaluated for various serious conditions which underscored her fears of losing him and continued to have a number of illnesses until age 2. Although he had then achieved good health, his mother viewed his growing autonomy as rejection of her and described him as a very difficult baby.

During this stressful period, his mother became involved with Jack, who soon became unfaithful to her and openly rejected Eric because of his dark skin. When Eric was 3½, his brother Roger was born, and shortly thereafter, Jack left her for the first time. Eric seemed to become even more difficult to handle and was seen by his mother to be "headstrong," "overactive," and "uncontrollable." His mother, faced with loneliness again, and with the added burden of a baby (she had not really wanted) to care for, found herself locked in an unending control battle with Eric, who seemed to bait her to exasperation at every turn. She found she could not control her aggressive feelings for him, and when he was 4½, she asked for help. He was hospitalized with a 1-inch hematoma on his head, and she described incidents of throwing him across the room against a wall or smashing his face into the floor. She did not want to abuse him as she had been as a child, but there were times when she was powerless to stop herself.

Although initially fearful in his foster home, Eric's nocturnal enuresis and nightmares eventually stopped, and he seemed able to make a strong attachment to his foster parents. Their own children, 3 and 6 years older, respectively, accepted the new additions to their household positively. However, Roger, then 18 months old, could not make the adjustment. His behavior deteriorated as he had uncontrollable tantrums and developed sleep and eating disorders. The foster mother felt she simply could not handle him and asked to have him removed. Since he had never been the target of his mother's fury and was at a stage where object constancy was a developmental issue for him, a decision whether or not to return him to his mother or to find another foster home was being made as therapy began.

Eric was being referred for treatment now to help him sort out his ambivalent feelings and to rework issues of trust. He was unusually able to verbalize his sad feelings, but since his mother's anger at him had been experienced as a life and death matter, it was no surprise that he could only express anger by acting it out or displacing it subtly. He sought to control situations and people and could not cooperate. He had difficulties at day care separating from his foster mother, with transitions, with peer relations both individually and in group situations, and he was provocative of adults in a manner that invited physical retaliation as he challenged limits and was disruptive to materials. Occasionally he was unpredictably assaultive to his peers, but he could also respond empathically to their emotional needs. He was further noted to be intelligent, verbal, enthusiastic, and precociously perceptive to interpersonal cues and to details in his environment.

Two visits were made to the day care center to acquaint Eric with me and to alleviate his anxiety about transitions, because it was necessary for me to transport him to and from sessions. His capacity to relate and enthusiasm for good times were immediately apparent as he exclaimed repeatedly, "I love it here," while he explored the toys and limits of the office. Despite the apparent willingness to accept the offer of the relationship, there was noticeably fleeting eye contact as he expressed delight in the materials. He handled his anger when the hour was up by darting away.

As was typical of his relationship with his own mother, where he had often had to act the role of an adult, he had been asked to determine whether or not Roger should be returned to her. He was able to verbalize the bind he had been put in by his mother:

"I let them take Roger back."

"You said okay?"

"Yes."

"Why?"

"So they can get better and take me back too."

This was followed by a need to make a mess out of paints in the office, threatening to get it all over me as he explored what I would do to ". . . a kid who . . . ." Clarification of my position of not hurting when I am angered and how I would set limits on such behavior, plus verbalizing his need to show me how messy he felt inside, enabled this testing to stop and for him to express his sadness at not being home with Roger and his mother. A need to bring something home with him from the office began to surface.

Shortly thereafter, he shifted to a desire to fix "broken" toys and make things "to eat" out of playdough which we "shared." He acknowledged that he was still sad to have Roger back home but added, "I'll go back too. I know I will soon." He thrived on activities to develop manipulative mastery. He also made a series of homes for little things (ants, worms, etc) because, as he told me, "All need homes, you know." An example of a mixture of his inner strengths and resourcefulness and his inability to express anger occurred about this time. Through a breakdown in communication, he was delivered to the office one day when I was ill. The following week he asked me to write my last name on a piece of paper, "So the next time you're not here, we can find you!" Although he strongly denied feeling anger toward me, he was able to offer me some "poisoned food."

Another month saw him accepting the warmth of the relationship as seen by long periods of eye contact while he studied me openly, increased touching and directing me in play, and making plans for our future activities. He revealed central concerns through play: the boy is mad/bad and does not want anyone to see his face. We did, however, talk directly about his having gone to court, his wanting to be with his mother, the confusion in finding a suitable home ("We lived everywhere"), learning that his foster parents wanted "to make it up to me" by buying him things, and his discovering that he liked it there, "You should see my room!" His increased caring, ambivalence, and need to control the relationship was seen in the gift of a weed he had pulled, with the warning, "Watch out! It has sharp edges."

Changes occurred in his situation about this time. As he was digesting the assault to his self-esteem when Roger was returned to their mother, two more foster children arrived to share his bedroom and to compete for his foster parents' attention. Eric's suppressed anger began to surface in tantrums and unpredictable assaults. A further challenge to his equanimity occurred about the same time when family visits were moved to his mother's house because Jack had been injured. Roger had always been the favored child to Jack. This partiality continued in the family visits and seemed emphasized when visits were not held in a neutral setting.

Eric was able to verbalize sadness about not being able to stay at home with his family like Roger could, but he acted out anger by tantruming at his foster home and at school and by unpredictable, assaultive attacks on his peers. During the sessions, however, he could only displace anger by darting away at the end of the hour, or, if there were several people in the waiting room, by throwing himself on the floor and refusing to walk. His foster mother reacted to his sadness by taking it upon herself to allow extra unsupervised home visits, and he became caught up in the complicity of these until they were discovered. A general restlessness began to emerge in the sessions in which he could not decide whether the toys in my office or those from the closet which he used during family visits would be more satisfying. Indeed, he was dealing with two mothers, two fathers, four nurturing locations (home, foster home, day care center, clinic), additions to his foster home, and altered and secretive visits with his family which highlighted his apparent ostracism from them. My attempt to clarify this confusion for him with, "It's like you have two mothers," was responded to with, "And I have two fathers, too, you know!" Shortly thereafter, his mother and Jack separated in a violent quarrel during a family visit, and Eric lost contact with the man he was said to believe was his father. Eric's view of his mother as an assaultive rejecting woman was reinforced.

These events coincided with Eric's growing realization that he would not return home by Easter, a hope that had sustained him initially, and his growing confusion caused by his increasing affection for his foster parents. His play focused on damaging and then repairing games and communicating through objects, once bringing me up short with, "You're not listening to me," as I reflected incorrectly the latent content of his constructions. He was able to express his growing dependency and caring for me by acknowledging how he had cried when he was told I was ill and could not see him on one occasion.

Circumstances now allowed sessions to be transferred to a play room at the day care center. I had felt that the necessity of transporting him, while adding to his understanding of me in different contexts, diluted the transference aspect of our work together in the sessions. With all the confusing events in his life, it was necessary that our roles became more clear. Although he had been able to see how I verbalized anger at his provocations, in a firm manner that accepted him as a person and did not retaliate or resort to violence, the dual role of therapist–care-giver was allowing him to avoid deeper work on painful affect in the sessions.

The change to the new room revealed his need to deny loss, to control situations, and to rework object constancy in a new situation. After exploring whether the same limits held in the new room, he then asked to be traced on a large sheet of paper, ordered me to color him in, carefully duplicating his clothing, and insisted his portrait be hung on the bulletin board to await his return. Once this was accomplished, he was able to enjoy the toys which fostered mastery of visual motor skills. His anger at still another change was acted out vociferously as he rebelled at the hour's end by kicking everything in sight (except me) and running away to his classroom.

Eric began to focus on his growing affection for his foster parents as he made them cards for Mother's and Father's Day. He talked openly of his caring for them and his wanting to be like his foster father, Ken, when he grew up, although his desire to be a mechanic and fix cars was a mixture of Jack's taking cars apart in the junk yards and Ken's work as a plumber where he "fixes things." Often Eric would play out ambivalence as he made up games of being "rescued," which alternated with others in which he would be sent to jail. He would then take great pains to make his "cell" comfortable and would luxuriate in it, showing me how foster care felt to him.

Aggression was now externalized in the content of the play. The play house was destroyed by fire, by a strong wind, or by a furniture mover who stole not only all the furnishings but the windows and chimney as well. It was never Eric who wrecked the house. Any attempt to suggest that he wanted to wreck the house, hated nice houses, or needed a home badly, would abort the play.

When his lower deciduous teeth became loose, he fabricated a story that his mother had hit him during an unsupervised visit [in an attempt to express anger toward her]. His foster mother and teacher reacted strongly to this. I was summoned to talk to him. He was aghast to have me appear, seemed embarrassed, and was unable to tell me what had happened. The next few days saw a series of tantrums during which he tried to hurt himself as he turned guilt and anger on himself. Eventually he was able to tell his teacher the truth. We worked on how understandable it was that he was angry with his mother and how hard it was for a boy to be angry with his mother when he did not live with her and missed her so badly.

Outside the session, Eric was acting out anger in increasing severity. His teacher was able to maintain consistent limits and to contain his tantrums, but his foster mother was having great difficulty as she tried to cope with three disturbed foster children and with her disillusionment that Eric seemed to be getting "worse" under her care. His tantrums were very upsetting to her, but his assaults on his foster siblings and destruction of her own children's property were intolerable to her. He was reported to have tried to strangle one of them in a rage which replicated some of his mother's attacks on him. Other incidents involving neighborhood children showed an inability on Eric's part to moderate anger. He seemed to erupt into violent assaults without the slightest provocation. His foster mother became exhausted monitoring his play to protect the other children. The unpredictability and degree of violence that was so reminiscent of his mother's rages was very worrisome. Joint consultation was held with his teacher and foster mother to collaborate efforts to provide consistency of limit-setting, to define patterns of escalating rage, and to plan interventions before he became assaultive. Coping techniques were shared and adapted. Eric's behavior eventually subsided.

Toward the end of the first year of therapy Eric began to act out anger in the sessions. He demolished two punching bag clowns as he acted out an identification with "Rocky," a movie he had been taken to twice. He mimicked an angry adult throwing a rag doll around the room. He had puppets attack one another. He was still unable to own his actions as expressions of anger and would withdraw at any suggestion or clarification of the meaning of his play. Typically, after an expression of anger, he would compulsively turn to performing a task to build mastery or invent punishments for himself or for me for some other reason acted out in subsequent play.

His transition to a small, regular first-grade class in public school showed his progress in many areas. Notable was his increased ability to accept limits and to use his abilities to learn. Another big change was his increased capacity to tolerate the sadness of loss and separation. He was depressed for several weeks as the time drew near for him to leave the day care center. He became listless and would avoid eye contact with me or roll up in a ball in the huge pillow on the floor. We talked of sadness at leaving a place he cared about. On his last day, I verbalized how hard it was to say goodbye to his teachers and friends. He was then motivated to "fix" up clay that had hardened and made an awful mess as he reworked it with water. The slimy mixture was everywhere, and, as I waited, he decided to clean it up meticulously. As he did this, we talked about what he had liked about being there, and he responded, "Fun. Learning."

Our meetings returned to the clinic, and his transitions were handled by a parent aide. He was happy to return to familiar surroundings and reminisced fondly as he rediscovered old toys. He spoke of loving his new school and proudly showed off his burgeoning ability to read. He was able to talk of how he hated math and avoided it because he found it difficult. Games of mastery and competition, where he always cheated to ensure victory, occupied his attention. He also bound up objects and his hands with masking tape, saying, "I'm just like Rocky." He also said, "I miss my mother. I want to live with her." He glued pieces of wood together to make a house and insisted I build one for myself and place it beside his. He defended against jealousy that his teacher, of whom he was growing fond, made a birthday hat for a classmate by making one for himself. There were many positive resolutions to stress and conflict.

Meanwhile, tension mounted in the foster home as his natural mother wrestled with the decision whether or not to give him up permanently. His visits with her were now unsupervised in the home, and he began to spend weekends with her. His fantasies of reunion soared, and he talked of the joy of playing with Roger in bed in the morning and of being with his mother. However, she recognized that her identification with him was still so strong that she again felt uncontrollable anger mounting toward him when she perceived him as misbehaving. He, of course, needed to test her to see if she would still react violently to his provocations. After agonizing soul-searching, she decided to give him up to permanent foster care. Eric had been told that a meeting had been held to decide what would be best for him. Because his mother did not feel she could keep him safe and because of his foster parents' deep affection for him, they had asked for and had been given the role of being his parents. He would still see his mother from time to time, but he would not visit her overnight again. His home was to be with them forever. (However, the circumstances around his visits with his mother were never made clear to him because of his mother's struggle to work through the painful ambivalence of her decision. Having decided to give him up, she could not bear to see or speak to him for six weeks. It was an abrupt change and the longest separation from his mother since his placement 18 months previously.)

The foster parents reported that Eric responded to the news with what seemed like relief, and for a period of time he clung to his foster mother. They, however, were disappointed that the move to adoption seemed stalled and clearly expressed a need for a legal acknowledgment of their commitment to him and a need to have the power to make decisions for him. They dreaded the idea that they might find themselves in a position where they would care for Eric throughout his childhood and then his mother would appear during his adolescence and take him away. Having already waited a long time for a decision, they were anxious to have the matter settled, to claim Eric as their loving son, and found it difficult to tolerate emotionally the process of his adjustment to the realization that he would not return to his mother. An additional strain to the household was the uncertain status of Eric's foster brother and sister, who were also about to be released for adoption, in a very confusing and disruptive process. The foster parents had expressed a desire to adopt all three children. In their depleted state, they were hardly prepared to work through the protest stage of adjustment that followed.

Eric parroted that his parents were now Betty and Ken, but it was clear that he could not comprehend what the change meant to him. On one hand he reported that they were to be his parents forever, adding, "Betty loves me very much," and on the other he talked of expecting to stay overnight with his mother soon. He said, "I can't live with her, but I can see her." Although he could not bear to talk about not returning to her, he took pleasure in showing off how he knew the directions to her house as he ordered me one day to "Drive to where I tell you." (I had again become responsible for his transportation.) He showed me the little park where he loved to play with his brother. He talked of the fun of waking Roger up in the morning. It was hard to tell him that he would not do that any more and to talk of the difference between wanting and having. He immediately avoided the topic and me, too, as he turned away and refused to talk any more. When we got to the office, he consoled himself by doing a very difficult puzzle and took pleasure in his skill. The trip home was spent in silence. On other days defensive efforts to arrange objects neatly, fix broken toys, and to make order out of chaos occupied him. His affect was sad, and he looked peaked.

A series of illnesses caused a three-week break in treatment. Because there was no one available to help with his transportation and because of time constraints in my schedule, in order to provide as much constancy as possible during this adjustment period, sessions were held at the foster home for three months, when help with transportation returned. Play sessions in his bedroom, where he basked in the materialistic outpourings of his foster parents, who reacted to his sadness by giving him things, were very strained. His play had a forced, apathetic quality as he tried to take pleasure in the toys. There was little privacy as his foster siblings kept interrupting and his foster mother worked within earshot of us. She was interested to learn what it was we did in play therapy and began to offer agendas for our work together. We both tried to deal with the confusion of space and roles.

The honeymoon with Ken and Betty ended. Limit-testing escalated, temper tantrums appeared again with great vigor, and on occasion Eric became violently assaultive to his foster siblings. Less worrisome, but very troubling, was his destruction of their own children's favorite possessions. Again there seemed to be no warning to his mounting rage and its expression. He was also discovered playing sex games with his siblings. All members of the family became ill with a virus that lasted for several weeks, taxing his parents' coping skills even further. His school performance dropped, but when Ken met with Eric's teachers and conveyed how important he felt education was, Eric's behavior and performance improved. Eric told Betty from time to time that he hated her and did not want to live with her. After all the effort Betty and Ken had made to help him, his comments and actions were only seen as a rejection of their goodness, not as an attempt on his part to work through the rejection he felt from his mother. Betty felt she had lost the loving, understanding child she needed and was horrified by his violence and sexual activity.

Betty and Ken felt unsupported by me because of my identification with Eric and tendency to emphasize the positive aspects of his behavior, such as relabeling his looking at his sister's genitals as normal sexual curiosity and not latent perversion. Any suggestions I made or attempts to point out possible feelings behind his behavior were experienced as either blaming or not understanding the seriousness of the problem. A therapist was assigned to work with them and found it difficult to engage them because they insisted the problem lay in Eric's changed, disturbed behavior. They were so anxious that they were unable to be consistent with him and resisted any exploration into what his behavior meant to them. As their frustration mounted, Eric's attacks escalated. Life was described as a pitched battle, and his behavior was considered to be contaminating his siblings.

Everyone involved felt they were not doing enough and projected this feeling onto others. Therapy was increased to twice a week, and because I still remained responsible for some of the transportation to sessions, Betty began to greet me with a litany of his misdemeanors and ordered us to attend to her agendas to fix him up. Her frustration was so great that she once reported his misbehavior with an angry laugh and said, "Oh, he doesn't like for you to know he's been bad." It was hard to control my anger at the manipulation and feelings of inadequacy to get a handle on what was happening. It became obvious that the foster mother and I were involved in a competitive struggle and that she was feeling unsupported, not listened to, and powerless because she could not make decisions about where and by whom he would be treated. These feelings of helplessness were related to Eric's unresolved adoption status, their inability to make any long-term decisions for him or for him to bear their name, and the spectre that, after struggling so hard to help him, his mother would appear sometime in the future and take him back.

About this time Eric decided on his own to act out his part in making the decision about where he would live. After an angry argument with Betty when he resisted being punished for some misbehavior, he yelled that he hated her, hated her house, did not want to live with her anymore, and was going to go to his mother's house by himself. It had been a long, hard day, and she could not take any more from him. In exasperation she told him that he could go and she would not stop him. Furthermore, she would help him pack his clothes in a paper bag.

It was after supper and getting dark, but he left the house and began the five-mile walk to his mother's house. He did not know that Ken was following him a block behind. After a mile and a half, his bag, which was awkward to carry, ripped. He was tired; he stopped, scooped up his clothes, and began to cry as he decided to return to Betty and Ken. It was a moving reconciliation when Ken caught up to him, held him, and helped him return home. They talked of how they wanted one another but how his behavior had to improve. However one might feel about the way his threat to run away was handled, father and son made a commitment to one another. Ken arranged to take Eric to work with him on occasion on Saturdays, and the happiness of these excursions stayed with him for days.

Eric's feelings toward Betty were more consciously ambivalent. He inscribed the Valentine he made for her, "You are the best mother," which he explained to me was because she bought him so many beautiful clothes. Later, at Mother's Day, he painted a picture of a house, a sun, and flowers on a piece of wood and then painted over it until it was a mass of muddy colors. Again he started the happy scene and still again had to obliterate the forms. The second time, however, it looked like an abstract painting, and he happily gave it to her. The muddy picture was sheepishly discarded. The talk of hating subsided, and he told them of some of his memories of being hurt by his own mother.

In the sessions, a growing desire to please me, to impress me with his good skills and good behavior evolved, as if he were afraid I might see a bad side of him and cast him away too. He loved to clean up my office for me or to rearrange the furniture in an effort to regain control and to bring order out of chaos. He mimicked his teacher as he straightened up papers on my desk.

Betty's attempts to control the content of therapy had to be addressed, and I dealt with them by saying, "Betty really seemed upset by . . ." Clarification of what sort of behavior parents find acceptable and of the seriousness of hurting others was made. I recalled that that was why he had to stop living with his mother: because she could not control herself when she felt very angry. I reiterated that no one gets hurt in my office. However, Eric found a very satisfying passive aggressive stance to take and refused to talk about anything that Betty mentioned, such as his running away, or what his feelings were about it. Our space had been violated, and he needed to protect himself. He had the additional satisfaction of sensing that clamming up was upsetting to me and was a way of getting back at me for not protecting our boundaries better. Work together had to return to the content of the play without any hint of clarification or interpretation.

As his tantrums and assaultiveness subsided at home, he became accident prone and had a new bruise or scrape to show each week. He bound up toys with masking tape and painted them different colors to camouflage what was underneath. He bound his hands like "Rocky" and struggled to break them free. He "bandaged" imaginary injuries but rejected suggestions that he was sad underneath. Aggressive feelings modestly surfaced in rowdy games of rocket hockey in which he delighted in beating me or cheating to win. He enjoyed making a model car but had no interest in the finished product.

Spring came and we often went to local parks where he reveled in games of whiffle ball. He is well coordinated and hit the ball with great satisfaction. There was the pleasure of making contact with the ball and the fun of watching me run all over the place. The emphasis was on having fun, building skills, controlling impulses, and taking pleasure in growing mastery. Issues of safety were confronted directly. He was told firmly that I was angry when he jumped off a moving swing onto pavement after I had told him how dangerous that was, and he had promised not to do it again. Refusal to wear a seat belt in my car was also dealt with firmly as I insisted that sitting safely was what I expected. My driving him was the only way he could get to see me, and he needed to decide whether or not he could control himself. I was not going to drive anyone who might endanger himself.

Although our work is not completed at this writing, many changes have taken place, despite the various crises. Increased self-esteem is shown in his new interest in the finished product of his endeavors rather than just in the enjoyment of the process. Eric was also very proud to be promoted to the second grade, to a regular classroom, and loved to show off his ability to read fluently. He attended a behavior modification day camp that stressed "Stop, think, then act," and loved it. His behavior at home has improved enormously with an end to tantruming and assaults on his siblings. Visits in a neutral setting with his mother are about to begin on a regular, monthly basis.

His foster parents, their therapist, and I meet monthly to consult about changes and intervention strategies. Buoyed up by support and Eric's improvement as they became consistent in setting limits, they feel more confident in their parenting abilities and relate more spontaneously to him. Betty and Ken, their therapist, Eric's mother, her therapist, and I have also begun regular meetings to clarify communication between the parents as a better long-term arrangement for Eric than permanent foster care is made. If possible, a battle in court will be avoided, but Eric needs to know that he is allowed to "belong" to Betty and Ken in the years ahead, and they need to have official sanction for the degree of their commitment to him. A secure setting during his latency years, to which he can feel he belongs, needs to be achieved to prepare a solid background for his adolescence which may well be turbulent.

The goals of our further work together are to rework issues of trust, impulse control, deeper exploration of expression of aggression, tolerance of ambivalence, and loss. Sublimation of drives, building of skills, and pleasure in mastery will also be a focus. Attention will also turn to sorting out the reality of what he can have from what he might want and what contribution he could make to what there is for him, if he so wished.

SUMMARY

A brief survey of the literature of treatment for abused children has revealed that attention has generally stopped after the child was protected and has not been directed to helping the child achieve emotional health or full development of personality. A profile of the abused or neglected child revealed deficits in the areas of ego functions, affect, object relations, peer relationships, self-concept, impulse control, and expression of aggression. A discussion of the central issues of trust and mistrust and the difficulties in expression of aggression, development of impulse control, self-concept and self-esteem, and resolution of parental loss led to a description of how these themes appear in treatment. Issues for the therapist in terms of responsibility, use of authority, outreach, flexibility, and countertransference were explored. A case illustration of a child with severe difficulties in the expression of aggression, who used identification with the aggressor, had poor impulse control, low self-esteem, and was dealing with parental loss was given in detail to show the interplay of situational factors on the various themes which evolved in the course of treatment.

REFERENCES

1. Kempe CH, Silverman F, Steele B, et al: The battered child syndrome. *JAMA* 1962;181:17-24.
2. Erikson E: in Kempe CH, Helfer RE (eds): *The Battered Child,* 3rd ed. Chicago, University of Chicago Press, 1980, p 2.
3. Freud A: *The Writings of Anna Freud,* Vol. VI, *Normality and Pathology in Childhood: Assessment of Development.* New York, International Universities Press, 1965, pp 119-124.

4. Freud A: *The Writings,* Vol. VI, p 123.
5. Clarke ADB, Clarke AM: Some recent advances in the study of early deprivation. *J Child Psychol Psychiatry Allied Discip* 1960;1:26–36.
6. Martin HP: The consequences of being abused and neglected: How the child fares, in Kempe CH, Helfer RE (eds): *The Battered Child,* 3rd ed. Chicago, University of Chicago Press, 1980, p 356.
7. Martin HP (ed): *The Abused Child: A Multidisciplinary Approach to Developmental Issues and Treatment.* Cambridge, Massachusetts, Ballinger, 1976, p 147.
8. Steele BF, Pollock CB: A psychiatric study of parents who abuse infants and small children, in Kempe CH, Helfer RE (eds): *The Battered Child.* Chicago, University of Chicago Press, 1968, pp 103–145.
9. Curtis GE: Violence breeds violence — perhaps? *Am J Psychiatry* 1963;130: 386–387.
10. Galdston R: Disorders of early parenthood: Neglect, deprivation, exploitation and abuse of little children, in Noshpitz JD (ed): *Basic Handbook of Child Psychiatry,* Vol. II. *Disturbances in Development.* New York, Basic Books, 1979, p 589.
11. Anthony EJ: Communicating therapeutically with the child. *J Am Acad Child Psychiatry* 1964;3:108.
12. Elmer E: *Fragile Families, Troubled Children.* Pittsburgh, University of Pittsburgh Press, 1977, p 110.
13. Martin HP (ed): *The Abused Child,* p 157.
14. Frank G: Treatment needs of children in foster care. *Am J Orthopsychiatry* 1980;50:256–263.
15. McDermott JR: The treatment of child abuse. Play therapy with a 4-year-old child. *J Am Acad Child Psychiatry* 1976;15(3):438.
16. Martin HP (ed): *The Abused Child,* p 158.
17. Galdston R: Preventing the abuse of little children: The parent's center project for the study and prevention of child abuse. *Am J Orthopsychiatry* 1975; 45(3):374.
18. Reidy T: The aggressive characteristics of abused and neglected children. *J Clin Psychol* 1977;33:1140–1145.
19. Martin HP: The child and his development, in Kempe CH, Helfer RE (eds): *Helping the Battered Child and His Family.* Philadelphia, JB Lippincott, 1972, pp 104–108.
20. Malone CA: Safety first: Comments on the influence of external danger in the lives of children of disorganized families. *Am J Orthopsychiatry* 1966; 36:4.
21. Elmer E, Gregg CS: Developmental characteristics of abused children. *Pediatrics* 1967;40:596–602.
22. Beezley P, Martin HP, Kempe R: Psychotherapy, in Martin HP (ed): *The Abused Child: A Multidisciplinary Approach to Developmental Issues and Treatment.* Cambridge, Massachusetts, Ballinger, 1976, p 205.
23. Kinard EM: Emotional development in physically abused children. *Am J Orthopsychiatry* 1980;50(4):693.
24. Peterson KL: Contributions to an abused child's unlovability: Failure in the developmental tasks and in mastery of trauma. MSW thesis. *Smith College Studies in Social Work* 1973;44(1):24–25.
25. Galdston R: Disorders of early parenthood, p 598.
26. Freud A: *The Writings of Anna Freud,* Vol. II. *The Ego and the Mechanisms of Defense.* New York, International Universities Press, 1966, pp 109–121.

27. Silver LG, Dublin CC, Lourie RS: Does violence breed violence? Contributions from a study of the child abuse syndrome. *Am J Psychiatry* 1969; 126:404–407.
28. Pine F: The concept "borderline" in children. *PSA Child* 1974;29:355.
29. Bender B: Self-chosen victims: Scapegoating behavior sequential to battering. *Child Welfare* 1976;55(6):417–422.
30. Green AH: Self-destructive behavior in battered children. *Am J Psychiatry* 1978;135(5):579–582.
31. Milowe IE, Lourie RW: The child's role in the battered child syndrome. *J Pediatr* 1964;5:1079–1081.
32. Bronfenbrenner U: Toward the definition of "abuse provoking child." *Child Abuse Neglect* 1978;3:392.
33. Silver LG, et al: Does violence, pp 404–407.
34. Shengold LL: Child abuse and deprivation: Soul murder. *J Am Psychoanal Assoc* 1979;27:533–559.
35. Shengold LL: Child abuse, p 538.
36. Shengold LL: Child abuse, p 539.
37. Shengold LL: Child abuse, p 549.
38. Colon F: Family ties and child placement. *Family Process* 1978;17(3):306.
39. Furman E: *A Child's Parent Dies.* New Haven, Connecticut: Yale University Press, 1974, pp 233–270.
40. Bowlby J: Pathological mourning and childhood mourning. *J Am PSA Assoc* 1963;11:505, ff.
41. Thomas CB: An exploration of object loss and grief and mourning processes initiated by foster home placement. *Smith College Studies in Social Work* 1967;37:163–234.
42. Thomas CB: An exploration, p 231.
43. Thomas CB: An exploration, p 232.
44. Walker CW: Persistence of mourning in the foster child as related to the foster mother's level of maturity. *Smith College Studies in Social Work* 1971; 41:193.
45. Walker CW: Persistence of mourning, pp 196–197.
46. Deutsch H: Absence of grief. *Psychoanal Q* 1937;6:14.
47. Wolfenstein M: How is mourning possible? *PSA Child* 1966;21:109.
48. Freud A: The Writings, Vol. II, p 261.
49. Nagera U: Children's reactions to the death of important objects: A developmental approach. *PSA Child* 1970;25:360–400.
50. Wolfenstein M: The image of the lost parent. *PSA Child* 1973;28:433–456.
51. Freud S: in *The Interpretation of Dreams* (1900), *Standard Edition,* 4, London, Hogarth Press, 1953, footnote, p 254, 1909.
52. Wolfenstein M: How is mourning, p 105.
53. Nagera, U: Children's reactions, p 364.
54. Fraiberg S: A therapeutic approach to reactive ego disturbances in children in placement. *Am J Orthopsychiatry* 1962;32:18–31.
55. McDermott JR: The treatment, p 439.
56. Fraiberg S, Adelson E, Shapiro V: Ghosts in the nursery: A psychoanalytical approach, in Fraiberg S (ed): *Clinical Studies in Infant Mental Health.* New York. Basic Books, 1980, pp 164–196.
57. Martin HP (ed): *The Abused Child,* pp 205–209.
58. McQuiston M, Kempe RS: Treatment of the child, in Kempe CH, Helfer RE (eds): *The Battered Child,* 3rd ed. Chicago, University of Chicago Press, 1980, pp 379–390.
59. Martin HP (ed): *The Abused Child,* p 206.

10 Mother–Toddler Group Therapy

Elizabeth Reynolds Bishop

As a typical mother–toddler therapy group convenes for its weekly sessions, coffee is poured and offered to the mothers as they arrive and take their places around the table. Some members are quiet; others chat informally, reviewing the week's events.

In the next room the toddlers examine toys with the play therapists. Some have separated easily from their mothers; others are crying at being left. They are greeted and comforted by the play therapists. The mothers have usually turned over the care of the children fairly readily, relying on their hour as one time in the week when they do not have to meet their children's needs themselves. They come to regard therapy as a place where they receive nurturance, work through conflicts, and explore issues of parenting.

Group therapy with parents who abuse or neglect their children is a widely used treatment modality. It is widely used because it works. It works because it provides means by which the worker can provide nurturance and resocialization for abusive parents. Healthy dependence can be encouraged through nurturance. Independence can be encouraged through education as the worker adopts the necessary reparenting role with its many paradoxical facets.

It works for those clients who can endure the discomfort of early meetings and make a real connection to the group because it provides a supporting community, a surrogate "family" within which corrective experiences of interaction can be provided and attitudes of hope, self-respect, and feelings of competence can be kindled.

It has been the privilege of this writer to share life and witness growth for three years in a mother's and toddler's therapy group for parents and children in families where reports of alleged abuse and neglect have been filed. The group has provided an arena for growth in communication skills, self-esteem, and ability to form good object relationships.

Five women have formed the hard-working core of the group. We will review the literature and trace the development and progress of the group using their work as it illustrates the theoretical material.

Before members were invited to join the group, time was spent to develop a philosophical base and conceptual framework within which we would operate because, just as individual therapy with abusive parents has its own base of theory which encourages the fostering of dependence on the therapist, so does the practice of group therapy with the same population.

PHILOSOPHICAL BASE AND GROUP MEMBERS

A mother and her child are bound together through pregnancy in the closest of human relationships. Symbiotically tied, they function as one organism. When a healthy mother first greets her newborn, they bond anew as parent and child. At this moment the one is the giver and the other is totally dependent.

This child, any newborn child, can be thought of as an "empty vessel" which must be filled with food and love in an environment where appropriate limits can be lovingly imposed so that the child can develop a sense of self-esteem and flourish while moving from this primary object relationship to form new fulfilling ones.

Many children are not greeted at birth by parents who, from the start, are assessing what they have to give. From the moment of birth, abusive parents were raised in families where early needs for love and nurturance were unmet, in fact where their parents turned to them for these two essentials.[1]

If needs are not met, a child will grow to adulthood as an empty vessel. Having been abused or neglected in childhood, abusive parents have suffered untold deprivations which have left them scared and empty, with low self-esteem, and only minimal ability to trust or to form object relationships.

The anger engendered by such deprivation is going to be felt on a continuum of depression ranging on the one hand from inertia and self-loathing, and anger turned inward, with vegetative signs of depression which may lead to neglect, to rage and acting out of anger with hostility and aggression which may lead to abuse.

So the mother, who is herself an empty vessel because she was neglected and/or abused, will greet the new baby with an overwhelming tide of depression, hoping somehow the child can fill her emptiness. The progress and experience of the individual members of the mother–toddler group and of the group process itself could be plotted at any point along the continuum of anger turned inward or acted out, but depression is the common ground in which all child abuse and neglect problems grow. The task of individual and group therapy with abusive parents is to foster the kind of dependency which will allow the therapist to give to the client in the areas of narcissistic entitlement to fill the empty vessel so there will be something left over to give nurturance to the children.

Group therapy as an adjunct to individual therapy provides a chance for parents to learn about themselves in the past as it has an impact on the present and in the present as they plan for the future.[2]

Symbiotic ties which characterize hostile–dependent relationships with the family of origin and competitiveness with lover and spouse and parent looking to the child for care can be confronted and discussed in the caring group environment, and isolated people who lack basic trust can begin to grow. The opportunity to share provides growth in areas of weakness and allows discovery of strengths. Because, for those whose primary relationships are defined by symbiosis, all separations are experienced as abandonment,[3] the toddler component of group provides a model for working on separation issues.

A criterion for group selection, among others which will be mentioned below, was that each member should have an ongoing social worker who would provide monitoring of protective issues and individual psychotherapy. While in group therapy something may be lost which is provided in one-to-one therapy, there is also something gained which is unattainable in individual work. The two together provide the optimum service for abusive parents by allowing, when necessary, the regressive transference in individual therapy while the group situation invites the healthiest level of ego functioning. Healing can be accelerated in the group setting by group identification with each other and the leader, mutual support, dilution of transference, and the provision of a multiplicity of targets for aggression.

Recognition by each member that she is not alone and that others have problems similar to her own is the first step to reducing isolation. When group and individual therapists stay in close contact in the group setting, we can see in action what is speculated about in individual therapy.[4]

Reflection on individual work is welcomed in the group sessions, and members are also encouraged to discuss the group experience with individual workers. When individual workers are forced to take action through the court or to place children in foster care, members find the group a place to ventilate their anger and concern and an environment which provides both caring and comfort as well as understanding of the fact that the individual worker has acted out of concern to protect them and their children. Occasionally, a member comes to group having just learned from her individual worker that court intervention is planned for the protection of her and her children or having just been to court. Other members who have been through the experience and who feel that they have, after much pain, benefited from it provide comfort and explanation while inviting the anger and sadness as well.

It is a delicate matter to balance the needs of the group members to ventilate anger with their needs for the group therapist to monitor the flow of expression, thus providing a safe environment for all. Abusive parents need protection at times from the effects of their own rage. When anger directed at the group therapist, individual therapist, or other group members surfaces in group sessions, the therapist can adopt a protective stance which can help members monitor their expressions to a degree which allows them to own their feelings and to remain in group.

Of course, this stance has to be evaluated and reevaluated throughout the life of the group. It is our belief that care exercised here has been an agent of preventing further hostility. Rules and norms have been developed which have provided for reasonable peer control and have fostered growth in communication skills.

Before we go further into the process of the group, it is in order to introduce the five members of what we can refer to as the "nuclear family." Over the years there have been a dozen others who have been peripherally involved, have terminated precipitously, or joined recently and made unique contributions. Some of them will be mentioned as their interactions affect the group process. The "nuclear family" of five and their children will become well known. Because they have changed and grown so much, it is hard to remember them as they were. Doing so will give the reader a picture and a feeling of what courage it took for each of them to join the group. They will be described as they presented at the group screening interview.

Donna

Donna, a light-complected black woman was 24 when she joined group. Although she has a strong black identity, until she mentions it, because of her light skin and wavy brown hair, she is not thought to be black, a fact which has caused major problems throughout her life. She was rejected by her mother at birth, because she was "too white" and was going to be placed for adoption; however, her grandmother felt "sorry for her" because she was "so white" and decided to raise her.

Donna was heavy when she first joined group. Her appearance, long unkempt hair, old blue jeans and a loose-fitting green top, bare feet (sometimes even in cold weather), bore witness to her deep depression and abysmally low self-esteem which had made it impossible for her to care adequately for herself or her five daughters. She had been isolated for years; staying in the house, overwhelmed by the children, unable to keep up with her household chores. She had had an individual therapist for three years who had worked very arduously, making weekly home visits, to reach into her loneliness and to build up her self-esteem. A warm, caring parent aide had also visited her in her home weekly to help her with practical problems and provide modeling and instruction in child care and homemaking chores. By the time she entered group, she realized that she had definite and admirable strengths, chiefly her intelligence and knowledge of how the "system" works, how to work with welfare, school, and legal aid agencies, and a beginning sense of entitlement which mobilized her to seek service for herself and her children.

Struggling for acceptance and searching for a sense of self-worth, Donna filled early sessions with "tales of her accomplishments" to impress the group. She presented herself as the "best homemaker in the city," touting her ability to cook gourmet meals for holidays, artistically decorating her home, and sewing fashionable clothes for her children for Easter. The group listened silently and disbelievingly at first, but little by little through gentle confrontation helped her to accept herself and what she really could do which was, in fact, admirable.

Thinking back to the early days of group, this writer is aware that it took great courage for Donna to join. Deserted and rejected by her mother, raised by a grandmother whom she adored and feared, abandoned by the men who fathered her children, she had minimal ability to trust and little awareness of the strengths she did have to offer. How painful it was to see her need to present herself as unrealistically accomplished because her real strengths were evident to everyone but her. Group provided her with a place to find out who she really was and to genuinely admire herself.

Peggy

Peggy was 19 when she joined group. She had no bond with, and little feeling for, her oldest boy who was 5. With her younger child, a 3-year-old girl, she had a stronger bond. The different feelings she has had for these two children over time provide a window through which to look at her life history.

Peggy had been abandoned by her mother to live with an elderly aunt in early childhood. In the first five years, she received warm, loving care which imbued her with a caring for others and for the world which are rare to see in one whose life has, for the most part, been characterized by profound deprivation. At five, she was returned to her mother who had married by then. Her mother is alcoholic and was both abusive and neglectful of her four children.

Peggy recalls a childhood of uncertainty, learning to dodge the blows of her abusive mother, to find her own food, and to run away when she needed a good meal because, when she returned, her mother would feel remorse and give her "special" treatment for a few hours.

Her stepfather who had been abusive to her as a child committed suicide when Peggy was 10. Peggy herself had found him dead before she went off to school.

By the time she entered adolescence, Peggy was using drugs and alcohol and "hanging out" with a "rough, scared" crowd of teenagers. Like all her friends, Peggy's deep anxiety and sadness were intolerable and impelled her into action. She stole cars, broke windows, and defied police intervention and describes only feeling "real" while engaged in such impulsive behavior.

She married Peter one night on impulse, and they committed crimes together for a few months. By the time Peter went to jail, Peggy was seven months pregnant with little Peter. She did not want the child and recalls "feeling bad" for him right away because she did not feel related to him.

She left little Peter "here and there," stayed in bars calling up others on the phone to buy milk and diapers for him. When he was 3 months old, she called a local agency and asked them "to take him away," saying she could not care for him. She recalls crying in a bar that night. She distinctly remembers that she was not crying because she "felt bad" for giving her son away, but that she was crying because she did not "feel bad" and the very inability to feel, of which she was aware, made her feel empty.

The deep longing for caring and nurturance of the kind she probably had from her aunt in the early years had always helped Peggy form relationships with care-givers. Although her deep deprivation has prevented her from all but the most minimal incorporation of insight gained through therapy, she always evokes strong countertransference reactions from professionals who feel her need, her unfulfilled potential, and are struck with the desire to care for her. To some degree, this evoking of deep feelings comes from her use of projection, but it is also a sign of strength and potential.

Through a close relationship with the social worker for the agency which was providing care for Peter, she was persuaded to take him back when he was just under 2 years old.

This writer began working with Peggy shortly after she took Peter back. Her little girl was born a year later. She bonded well with the baby at first, but when the baby's father deserted her when Mary was 4 weeks old, she temporarily was emptied of feeling for the child and, overwhelmed by depression, she was unable to provide for her needs. Mary was hospitalized at 6 weeks, below birth weight with a diagnosis of failure to thrive.

It became necessary to file a care and protection petition on behalf of Peggy's children. The deep trust she had developed through the years of individual therapy enabled Peggy to acknowledge that the court intervention had been made to protect her children and to protect her from harming them.

Peggy was able over time to share with the group both her trust in the individual worker and her realization that it was necessary and beneficial that they were placed in foster care. Other members drew comfort from her when they were faced with court intervention.

When Peggy joined group, she looked older than her 19 years, but her youthful, athletic body and her engaging ability to express caring for everyone in a somewhat idealistic fashion still left one with the impression of a very young girl. Although her own functioning was often poor, she genuinely offered welcome, humor, and solace to all members.

Peggy's yearnings for the close family she had never had surfaced early in group life. She was the first to identify that the group had begun to "feel like a family." In one session when members were struggling for attention in an openly competitive manner, Peggy said reflectively, "we all sound like kids begging for the mother's attention."

Doreen

Doreen was a very depressed woman of 35. She had one little boy who had been badly bruised on both legs. Her characterological defensive style of avoiding her own problems and depression caused her to enter group each week begging the group's attention by telling "hundreds" of stories of tragedies, murders, accidents, and illnesses which had supposedly (or really) befallen others around her or been reported in the news. If this failed to draw from the group the caring she craved, she would impede group process, causing general avoidance of issues, by talking incessantly about recipes or "toy parties" or Avon sales. She was not welcomed by group, and it was a long time before she was incorporated into full group membership because other members felt overwhelmed by her neediness. Doreen had been born late in her parents' marriage and received poor care. She was massively obese when she entered the group, a fact which she attributes to an insatiable hunger she has always felt stemmed from the knowledge that she was hospitalized as a child for rickets resulting from malnutrition.

After a childhood of deprivation and an early adulthood characterized by flight and psychosis, she returned to her home area and married her husband, John, who is a depressed man who had lived at home with his mother until he was 38.

The birth of their child, Greg, who was 2½ years old at the time Doreen entered group, had placed burdens of responsibility on her and John which they could not bear. They desperately wanted him to be perfect so that "the world would think highly of them." When he was less than perfect, they would strike out at him in despair.

As time went on, through group process, Doreen learned to be more centered and to own her own real feelings to the extent that she could reduce her need to recount tragic stories and use group time to address her own issues. As her emptiness was filled, she began to be able to reach out for help with her problems of obesity.

Cathy

Cathy entered the group when she was 27. Her husband had been abusive to her and to her two daughters, and she had been too depressed to provide them or herself with adequate protection. Now, in the midst of divorce proceedings, her large family of origin was engaged in a "war" with that of her husband, resulting in frequent trips to court to settle suits, charges, countersuits, and countercharges. Cathy, at the time of group, presented as a depressed adolescent with little insight into her own behavior. She was in frequent scrapes with the law for her own impulsive actions which were totally ego syntonic.

Although Cathy presented her childhood as having been a happy time, she had in fact had an adolescence characterized by delinquency, similar to that experienced by Peggy. When Cathy entered the group, the two were in sharp competition. The therapist's task in the beginning was to help them work through whether they wanted to remain in the same group.

They wanted to resolve their conflicts, and work was done by group, over the first year they were in group together, to sort through their verbal and nonverbal messages and reactions to assess which remarks were springing from present interaction and which had their etiology in the past, during which each was in sharp competition.

Cathy brought to group a remarkable ability both to use individual treatment as a means toward growth and to verbalize how she felt that had worked for her. Her reactions to her individual therapists (she has had three during the time she has been in group) have provided a sounding board against which other group members have been able to examine what individual therapy has meant to them as well as the significance of all important object relationships in growth and development and ability to raise children.

Cathy's dramatic flair added life to the group from the start. She often jumped from her chair to act out or role play as a way of illustrating some event she wished to recount. Her anger flared easily, and she displayed her feelings affectively enabling other group members to own their feelings, too.

Susan

Susan, a legal secretary, was 30 years old when she joined group shortly after her second son was born. Her first child had died of leukemia, and she herself suffered severe cardiac problems resulting from rheumatic heart disease.

Susan presented an amazing kaleidoscope of both strengths and conflicts to the group from the start. She was well educated and sophisticated, in ways much admired by the group. She had had previous experience as a member of a therapy group for young professionals which she felt had helped her greatly.

On the other hand, her long-term relationship with her children's father, who was an alcoholic struggling for recovery, had been unstable and volatile. In the past, she had shown little ability to act on her evident knowledge that this relationship was destructive to her mental and physical health and undermined her strong desire to be a good mother.

The group was mystified at times by the contrast between Susan's obvious strengths and charm and her inability to separate from a man whom she so clearly presents as detrimental to her growth. However, through her knowledge of group therapy, she had been amazingly able to enable others to look at their own issues in the light of hers and vice versa. It has been a delicate task for the therapist to help Susan use group as a means to meet her own needs while recognizing that, at times, one way in which she does this is by almost filling the role of cotherapist in the group. The therapist, not wanting to reduce her ability to use the group for herself, made a decision not to verbalize the recognition that Susan was sometimes acting as cotherapist. The group expressed their realization of Susan's function as they were able.

So, these five women, Donna, Peggy, Doreen, Cathy, and Susan formed the nucleus of group. Each grew, and each enabled growth in the others. As they grew in different directions, they were able, in one way or another, to provide or allow for far better care for their children.

It will be useful now to trace the process by which growth took place. Transference and countertransference issues will be discussed through the stages of group life, beginning with the group's formation, decisions about group composition, rules and contracts, purpose and goals for both mothers' and toddlers' group, and the group process itself.

EARLY STAGES OF GROUP FORMATION

Agency recognition of the value of group therapy as an adjunct to individual therapy for parents who abuse and neglect their children was the springboard for the plan to form such a group.

Donna and Peggy were charter members, soon joined by Stephanie, who was involved with an abusive man and unable to protect herself and her children, and Helen, whose unresolved grief over the loss of her 6-year-old daughter had rendered her unable to care for her other children, including an infant boy.

The process in these early days is worth reviewing briefly in order to illustrate the various transference interactions. Donna was working hard to win acceptance from the therapist and Peggy by outlining her "achievements." It was clear that she had strengths, and it was painful to hear her distortions. Peggy was dealing with her intense feelings about her children being in foster care. Since neither had had sufficient mothering, sharing and competitive strivings were evoked in the transference relationship with the therapist. The therapist's task was to help Donna and Peggy begin to grieve the "good mother" they had both missed.

Both Donna and Peggy found that Helen's grief evoked unresolved griefs and losses of their own which they were able to share directly and enabled Helen to see her feelings as "normal," and all three mourned together.

It was amazing how, at first, mourning was enabled by group reaction to the death of Elvis Presley. All four were strongly identified with Elvis, mentioning his early life with poor parents, his music which for them expressed the pain and joy of life, and his death which resulted from dependence on drugs. Helen, who had the most tragic loss to mourn, was able to get the group to acknowledge that she had the closest, most important bond to Elvis Presley because she was a bit older and his music had become popular "in her years, when she was a teenager." She actually cried in the group session and was later able to cry over the loss of her daughter in individual treatment. Her tears were shared as others expressed their grief. When, after six months, Helen withdrew from the group, feeling that it was too costly to move as quickly as group seemed to be asking her to, she was able to explain those feelings and again all four shared experiences of loss.

Stephanie left group after eight months. Due to her masochistic tendencies, she found herself unable to separate from her abusive spouse, and the group confrontation about this challenged her passive stance more than she could tolerate.

Donna had begun to grow in ability to express her real feelings and benefited from the volatile manner in which the group members confronted Stephanie. She heard in their messages that people can mobilize their resources to change their lives.

Yalom's[5] work on transference and countertransference in group psychotherapy is helpful to the therapist in understanding the crises in early stages of group life. "There are some patients," he states, "whose therapy hinges on the resolution of transference distortions, there are others whose improvement will depend upon interpersonal learning stemming from work not with the therapist, but with another member." He further cautions both against the therapist ignoring the transference considerations in relationships with patients and thus misunderstanding transactions in the group and against seeing only the transference aspects of relationships with members, thereby doing violence to their autonomy.

Members were enabled to grow through real transactional experiences leading to the formation of object relationships in which each could learn to identify and manage feelings. Group sessions also provided an arena for members to share feelings about important figures in their past which created problems in present relationships. Of special importance was the responsibility to preserve and foster each member's relationship with individual therapists who had primary protective responsibility. Good work was done as members identified for one another the fact that appropriate limit-setting is a needed function of a good parent and that their individual workers were attempting to set limits in ways their parents had not when they were children.

REFERRAL PROCESS

Members were referred to group by their individual therapists who carried full protective responsibility. Whereas seeing an individual worker is mandatory, membership in group, although strongly encouraged, is voluntary. A commitment to regular attendance is asked, if a person chooses to join group, but the fact that the decision to join is voluntary gives each member a feeling of self-control.

The individual workers explain the group as a means toward individual growth in ability to name feelings and gain control in relationships.

It is further presented as a place to gain more adequate understanding of children's behavior and how to manage it.

At the time of referral, each member was invited to come to the office for an interview with the group therapist and given a choice about whether or not she wanted her individual therapist to be present. Each prospective member has chosen to have the individual therapist present; this affords a good opportunity to introduce the idea of a team approach to problems. It is explained that the team will be composed of the group member, group therapist, individual therapist, and parent aide who will provide transportation and lead the play therapy in the toddler group component of the program. From the start, it is agreed to by all that there will be open communication between all members of the team and that the individual worker will be apprised of all thoughts, events, and revelations made in the group.

In the pregroup interview, the group composition, the toddler component, and the group contract are discussed.

GROUP COMPOSITION

Prospective members are told that the group is composed of mothers, all of whom have had serious problems in taking care of their children, and that reports of their problems have been made to local authorities. The reports of alleged abuse or neglect of children form the common thread. Although it is hard to be thus grouped, members show immediate relief at not being alone with their pain—that others, too, have problems with parenting. It is a "giant step" to give up the isolation which has felt so protective, but it is one which feels good, too. Donna's words sum it up: "When you want so much to be a good mother, it's awful to admit you have problems. Joining the group makes you feel less alone."

Although the common issue shared by all is the report filed, members are also told that problems which everyone has in caring for children come from experiences which make it difficult to handle relationships and that group members will also share a desire to grow in ability to form good adult relationships with spouses, friends, and family of origin as they grow in understanding that the origin of their problems lies in their histories.

TODDLER COMPONENT

The play therapy group is first introduced as an opportunity for the children to be helped to grow while the mothers can enjoy "adult time" for themselves. As in all work with such needy parents, we must show the mothers from the outset that we see their needs first. If we were to say at the beginning that a purpose of the group was to help the process of appropriate separation and individuation of the toddlers, the mothers would be frightened indeed for they need the children to be part of them and the idea of separation would be perceived as a loss.

On the one hand, the symbiotic nature of the relationship between the needy, abusive, or neglectful mother and her child has them enmeshed in a tight bind; on the other, the mother's unmet needs make her unable to see her child as having any feelings of his/her own. This paradox is constantly played out and replayed as mothers differentially or alternately cling to their children, not allowing any separation, perceiving every separation as abandonment, or push them into the play room, ignoring howls of protest from the child at the abrupt abandonment by parent. In both instances, the child is expected to fill the parent's need first for closeness, then for distance and privacy.

It was often an issue for the therapist at first to concentrate on group process when the yells of a despairing child in the next room, unnoticed by the mother, evoked strong maternal feelings in the therapist. It was useful to reduce the therapist's anxiety as well as to provide some therapeutic didactic teaching to identify the child's feelings and to say that the play therapists would be helping the children deal with their feelings while the mothers' group was dealing with theirs. Later the group was able to use didactic teaching to learn that when a child cries expressing anger or sadness at abandonment, the feelings he or she is experiencing are essentially the same as those felt by an adult. Peggy said, "You mean when Peter and Mary cry when I put them in the play room they feel the way I do when Mary's father leaves me?" and, incredulously, "You mean they actually have feelings!"

Susan was an exception to the group norm as she had appropriate difficulty in separating from her child and acknowledged that it was hard for the child, too. Her process of working through this issue became a vehicle to work on growth in understanding bonding and separation.

Donna was able, through explaining her different feelings when she left one or the other of her children in the play room, to realize that the most serious problem she had was in her feeling toward one of her children, Jennifer, who was the hardest for her to manage. She recalled one day, when Jennifer was hitting the play therapist in anger, that at her birth she had felt bonded to her more closely than to any of her other children.

She had started breast-feeding her. A positive TB test caused the hospital to isolate her from her child, leaving her feeling "dirty and unworthy." Little explanation was given. Rejected and alone, she lost the warm feeling she had had toward the child. She then identified the tight hostile-dependent bind in which they were caught as having its roots in that early experience.

Thus, one of the group goals of reducing symbiosis between mother and child and that quality in other relationships and allowing appropriate separation is fostered by the toddler component.[6]

Further, the protected nurturing setting of the playroom provides an arena for growth in social skills, peer relationships, development of ability to accept appropriate limits, and development of gross and fine motor skills through directed play.

The parent aides, who provide both transportation to and from group and play therapy for the toddlers, offer a corrective experience of mothering and nurturance which is both therapeutic and practical in that it removes obstacles of need for baby-sitting and low motivation to go out alone which would otherwise greatly hinder group development.

Jennifer and Peter

Jennifer, Donna's daughter, and Peter, Peggy's son, were both angry and acting out. Their ability to accept limits was minimal, and they became sharp rivals in the playroom. For a while the play therapists had reason to fear that they would injure each other and damage property by their hostile acting out. A combination of labeling feelings and firm, but loving, actual holding began to help them contain their anger and express their sadness and neediness more appropriately.

Jennifer, using language she had learned in the street, yelled and threw a huge toy metal dumptruck at Peter. Fortunately, she missed, but Peter picked up a toy broomstick and brandished it first at Jennifer then at the play therapists. Each therapist instinctively went to the side of one angry child, speaking quietly and confidently, containing the violence, allowing the anger. Within a few minutes, each child was sitting quietly listening to a story and enjoying crackers and milk, secure with physical closeness and nurturance.

GROUP CONTRACT

The "rules" for our therapy group are few and strictly adhered to. They are reviewed with each member in pregroup interview.

1. Every member shall have an individual protective worker   This has been outlined above, and it provides group leader with freedom to explore all issues while not having responsibility to act on protective issues. It provides the mother with both therapeutic experiences, group and individual, which hasten growth.

2. Confidentiality shall be strictly observed   Members are informed about the group's deep concern about issues of confidentiality. Because all prospective members appear to have minimal ability to trust, in the pregroup interview each is given the opportunity to know the composition of the group and to raise concerns about confidentiality issues. Knowing whom to expect and coming to the realization that all members are invested in preserving personal privacy helps ensure maintenance of confidentiality.

3. Outside group contacts will be shared with group   It is impossible to prevent members having some moments of contact outside group, and they are encouraged to share these and to work through any tensions which emanate from them with the group. This is a good rule anyway, but it provides a chance in this group to address transference and reality conflicts openly as they are played out in real life.

4. Members will attend group every week and will notify leader if they will be absent   The issue of continuity in group discussion is raised, but far more helpful as a support to regular attendance is the metaphor of group being like a family in which each member is important and valued. This provides the first boost to self-esteem and feeling of acceptance and belonging.

5. Members will give the group at least a two-month trial period upon joining   The group therapist is open to helping prospective members reflect upon the fact that they will most likely be afraid and anxious at first. They are reassured that they will not be forced to talk or share anything until they are ready. Because it takes a while to feel at home, they are asked to give themselves and the group a fair chance by staying at least two months. In the context of helping prospective members anticipate what will be taxing about joining, it is helpful to tell them a bit more about what to expect. The universality of experience is again stressed. It is stated that everyone who has difficulty in parenting had some sort of serious deficits in childhood and that all share the feelings of anger over needs which were not met. Even though the new member probably will not acknowledge either the anger or the unmet needs, knowing they are there and understanding the feelings of emptiness and rage evoked when children's demands are expressed helps the person feel understood and not judged for the feelings they are experiencing.

Anger over unmet needs often has catapulted people into parenthood as a result of early pregnancy, usually in the context of destructive masochistic relationships. While sharing all this pain with group may seem scary, the natural tendency to thrust oneself into relationships common to deprived people can be turned into a group strength.[7]

While being honest that new experiences are hard and take time, group can be presented as a nurturing, caring place to work on problems.

On the very positive side, as encouragement, the group atmosphere is described as caring and informal. The new member is told that, after being brought to the agency by the parent aide, group gathers around the table with tea, coffee, and cocoa and that discussion usually begins with members sharing experiences of the past week. The presence of the coffee is important as symbolic of feeding and nurturance. If, for some reason, the water is not hot when the group arrives or the coffee supplies incomplete, the members vent their disappointments to therapeutic end, usually associating to early deprivations.

6. Members will be asked to give at least one month's notice and attend three termination interviews before leaving group   This rule is explained in the context of acknowledging that "good-byes" are very hard for everyone and that people need time to say good-bye to each other — that even when someone only belongs to a group for a short time, they become a real part of it and they and the group will grow through discussing any parts of their common experience.

As the pregroup interview ends, members are reminded that the purpose of the group is to help members grow in feeling good about themselves and in ability to care for their children as they learn to form good fulfilling relationships themselves.

It is heart-warming to tell the prospective member that group provides not only a chance and a place to work on problems, but also to discover strengths she did not even know she had as she hears others discuss their problems. She is gently reminded that she is not alone and that joining group will raise her self-esteem as she allows herself to be in contact with the wider community.[8] It is true that any mother who is striving for growth enough to make the plunge into group will find some area, whether food shopping, dealing with landlords, toilet training, bed time, plant growing, cooking, talking with friends or relatives, some area in which she feels more accomplished than some other member of group.

MIDDLE PHASE OF GROUP LIFE

By the end of the first year the group was solidly formed and functioning. There was a strong group identity. Mutual trust had developed to the point where affect-laden material was freely shared. Donna and Peggy had been joined by Cathy first and then Doreen and Susan and, although a few others had come and gone, those five had formed a working alliance which was enabling their growth. Donna was the first to identify the growth. She had been angry with Cathy over something which had happened between them outside of a group session, and she brought her feelings about it to the group, indicating a real change in the degree of her own approval of violence.[9]

"I was angry, but for the first time in my life, 'I did not talk with my fists.' I stopped and thought how can I let her know how I feel without losing my cool? I told her I did not like what she did and that I wanted to discuss with her that it hurt my feelings. I was amazed at myself, and I had new confidence in myself. I knew you [group leader] and the group would be proud of me. I've never been so aware of what I was doing."

In a real way, group had become, in Kohut's[10] terms, a self object for Donna providing security and self-soothing, identity and self-confidence, mirroring her ability to see herself. Furthermore the group, as a self object, gave her narcissistic pleasure as the idealized self object provided her with loving approval.

She went on to say how good and how different it felt and that she had gone home that evening feeling good about herself and had been able to spend a good time with her children. That weekend when her child was home from the foster home for the first time, she had been able to use the same skills of identifying and solving problems with him.

The next major step forward came in Peggy's efforts to help Doreen. Their interaction and communication is an illustration of Virginia Satir's[11] statement that "communication is the gauge by which two people measure one another's self-worth and it is the tool by which that level can be changed for them both."

Peggy, and all the other members for that matter, had always found it difficult to listen to Doreen's neediness expressed through her explosions of tragic stories and her resistance to discuss problems by filling group sessions with extraneous material. There had been a general conspiracy of silence, eye-rolling, and unexpressed anger. Peggy put the feelings into words.

"Doreen," she said, "I don't want to hurt your feelings, but there is something that I have to say. You come here every week and never have any problems of your own—then you talk so fast about everyone else's problems that we can't even understand you. I want to hear you, but you have to talk slower." Doreen heard the words, "I want to hear you" which seemed to raise her level of self-worth. She replied, "No one ever told me to talk slower."

Peggy went on, "You see, we all know that everyone here has problems, or we wouldn't be here. We want to help you but you have to tell us what's really happening just like we tell you."

Doreen tearfully thanked Peggy for what was obviously real concern, and both left the session feeling an increased sense of self-esteem. Peggy felt she had been caring and helpful, and Doreen felt valued and accepted by the group.[12]

Both Peggy and Doreen function at the borderline level. Group treatment is described by many therapists as effective in offering support and mutual control so desperately needed by these clients. As in Doreen and Peggy's interaction, group therapy helps clients learn to listen and understand each other's communications. They were able to confront ego centers and abrasive character traits in the safe environment of group.[13]

Cathy expressed her growth a few months later articulating how she had been helped by a combination of individual and group therapy. "I had a problem with my neighbor last night," she said, "and she wanted to hit me with a coat hanger. You're not going to believe this, but I thought about what Donna said when she was mad at me. At the time, I thought she was nuts to say it felt good not to use her fists because I wished then she would, but last night I said to myself you can be more grown up than your neighbor, and I asked her to come to my house and discuss the problem when we calmed down. Then I went upstairs and I was crying and I did not know why — then I realized it was because I had grown up and I wanted to tell my individual therapist how well I did. She will be proud of me." So the growth Donna had experienced in relationship with Cathy, Cathy now experienced, and the group had become a self object for her.

Susan's first real expression of growth came on a day when she and Donna were the only members present. Donna had experienced a death, and the absence of the other group members and the recent loss evoked Susan's grief for the good parenting she never had. The two women shared early experiences with death and abandonment. "I just realized something I never thought of before. Donna talked about her grandfather's death and it made me start to cry, only what I was thinking of was not a death but I was remembering what it was like to be alone in the house when I was little and to watch it become dark."

By that time both Donna and Susan were crying and both were able to be put in touch with their sadness over childhood deprivations and emptiness which had led to so many problems for them in adult life.

Susan went on to say "I got the same feeling recently when Bob (boyfriend) laughed at me because I was afraid I might not find my way back home by bus. I felt alone and lost even though he was there."

They were both helped to see that group absences and recent deaths were the catalysts for discussion of feelings of being alone and unnurtured in childhood and able, for the first time, to feel sadness in place of the rage to which they were both accustomed.

Growth in the Toddler Group in the Middle Phase

In the early phase of the toddler group, as mentioned above, Peggy and Donna's children were very difficult to manage. They appeared overly active and aggressive. As is common to children who have been abused, they were unhappy and unconforming. They had no idea how to accept limits, to trust that limits were imposed for their care and safety. Their self-esteem, like their mother's, was low. They had received no assistance in mastering the task of establishing a positive self-concept. Their extrapunitive aggressive behavior bore witness to the abuse they had witnessed and received.[14]

As the children began to know the play therapists as caring, nurturing, constant people, there began to be evidences of social and emotional growth.[15] The therapists had a hard job to set limits to keep the children safe as well as to enable growth in relationships by setting age-appropriate expectations.

As with their parents, the tasks were to help the children identify feelings of loneliness, anger, even tiredness and hunger. Peggy's son, Peter, was helped to say "I want my mommy" instead of hitting other children when left in the playroom.

Week after week the pattern was the same and group became a real part of the women's and children's lives. Susan had a birthday party one day for her daughter, Nancy. She said her family lived far away and because group was the one outside-of-home encounter Nancy had, she wanted the group to celebrate with her. Whereas the mothers were, at first, so self-engrossed and narcissistic that they would thrust their children in the playroom and then pour their coffee with no thought to the children's needs, they were now able to help the children to go to the playroom with promises to "be there" when the hour was over and "Mommy will have her time with her friends and you will play with your friends and then we'll see each other later."

REFLECTIONS ON THE THERAPIST'S ROLE

Group therapy with abusive parents requires much giving on the part of the therapist. As transferences develop, he or she may begin to feel the weight of the members' unmet needs and resultant rage.

Primary tasks tacitly set by group members include the expectation that discussions will be facilitated in a permissive atmosphere; that members will be helped to contribute to discussions, to clarify feelings; that development of insight will be enabled by finding meaning in remarks and interaction; and in the final analysis, that the therapist will mediate the discussion in such a way as to control uncreative hostility and prevent "things from getting out of hand."[16]

As stated above, it is a fine balance, difficult to achieve, between the group therapist stifling the expression of anger on the one hand, and being unprotective on the other. It is also very difficult to separate one's own personal hopes and aspirations for a group member from ones which she may have for herself or from ones related to one's own conflicts or needs.[17]

The problem of identifying personal hopes and aspirations for a group member and separating them from what may be a realistic expectation to set has been best illustrated by the sharp contrast in the directions of growth experienced by Donna and those by Peggy. Originally, this therapist had high hopes that both would grow in ability to care for themselves and their children. Both have grown, but in different directions.

At one point, Donna clearly and succinctly identified growth in her ability to care for and relate to her children. "I take more time with them because I feel better about myself. I have more energy for them. They listen to me because I listen to them. I try to give each one individual attention and I don't make 'crazy threats' which I hope I'd never carry out, like 'If you don't listen, I'll break your head.' Rather, I say 'Go to your room for a time-out until you can listen or we can talk reasonably about it.' "

Peggy's growth has been in her ability to recognize how very difficult it is for her to care for herself and how difficult, therefore, even to think about caring for children. She sadly acknowledges that she will not be able to raise these two children and is working toward releasing them for adoption. Over a very rough, painful road she has been able to grow toward this sad acceptance and the healing process begins. Throughout, she has remained caring and a constant interpreter of the process of protective service to the group and has made steady growth in her ability to tolerate her depression.

Winnicott[18] states that hardest to accept and own for any therapist are the negative feelings the group members induce. There is frequently an objective countertransference reaction which must be owned and monitored. Doreen's pressured ventilation of neediness was as hard for this therapist to endure as it was for the group, and it was important to acknowledge those feelings in order to manage them. However, when this therapist heard Peggy's nice, direct, caring confrontation, she was able to see Doreen's real need more clearly.

It was gratifying to see that after the group had been enabled to express the negative feelings, the positive ones flowed. One July as the group anticipated the therapist's vacation and all expressed a desire to "come along," Susan said, "Your car is too small to fit us all—we want to include Doreen [alluding to both her obesity and initial problems in gaining acceptance to the group]—you'll just have to rent a bigger car, you can't leave any of us behind."

Thus, the group provides a corrective experience of being in a "family" and openly expresses need to the therapist.

TERMINATIONS

For a long time the group had no real model for termination because those who had left were not "real members" of the "family," having been there only a short time. Doreen was the first to leave the group through formal termination, although others have chosen to stay in the group even after the protective case was closed. When her individual worker was ready to declare that her issues were no longer "protective" in nature, she announced that she was terminating. She handled her termination well, attending all termination sessions and genuinely trying to work through her loss and the group's progress. It was a very intense time for the group, and it took real energy to help them use the termination time creatively. They were both angry at Doreen for abandoning them, because they felt they had given her a lot, and jealous of her feeling of "no problems" expressed again.

The termination time provided a period of growth. They were able to articulate that group had in some way become a family and a substitute for supports absent in their own family group. They expressed newfound ability to acknowledge that the past deprivations were a source of their frustrations and to see their children as people with needs of their own. Their newly incorporated image of themselves as being worthy has enabled them to change their behavior toward their children and to make substantial changes in their patterns of behavior.[19]

The group said good-bye to Doreen, but in many ways still mourn her leaving with feelings which are as yet unresolved. They talk of her frequently, see her often in the street, and little by little they have been enabled to see ways in which they are talking about their own resistances as they talk about hers.

Donna's and Peggy's stories become a metaphor for discussing group progress. Recalling sessions in which they sipped coffee and got acquainted, the reader can remember Donna eased her tension by presenting as competent and confident.

Peggy's charactertistic generosity made her take on a caretaking role, interrupting the process of group discussion to serve coffee to the parent aides.

Donna, trying to seem in her glory, taught others 1001 ways to manipulate the welfare system. She described how she was redecorating her apartment and made it sound as if she were an accomplished interior decorator. She even said her children helped.

Peggy, who had made some not too successful attempts to do over apartments, remembered how she had made a "mess" and the children had spilled a gallon of paint, tried unsuccessfully to confront Donna.

It was clear to the therapist that Donna was massively depressed, "empty," and trying to fill herself with unfulfilled hopes and dreams. In the early stages of group life she had needed to impress the group with incredible tales of fantasied accomplishments. In one of her last sessions she graciously and meticulously taught a new member how to make a tuna casserole.

Peggy's ability to verbalize her need to release her children for adoption, while supporting protective interventions as helpful, are impressive. The fact that she stays in group both drawing and offering nurturance, is the anchor for her growing self-knowledge.

Susan has, of late, been able to set strong limits in her relationship with Nancy's father and shares the pain and joy of this with group, knowing they will accept whatever she says.

Cathy remains the articulate proponent for the combination of individual and group therapy and continues to put into words, as a gift to the group and to all the therapists involved, what treatment means to her.

The toddlers are growing up, and some have "graduated" from group to day care, kindergarten, and first grade.

In summary, it is clear that the population served by this mothers-toddlers therapy group has grown through expressions of real feelings, positive and negative, and that ways of handling confrontation have become part of group general knowledge and "laws" which are handed down through group history. "Generations" to come will add to that body of knowledge, and there is no doubt that the group will continue to serve its members well as a strong adjunct to their individual therapy. The corrective experience of nurturance provided by the therapist and group members as a surrogate family raises each mother's level of self-esteem. As they are fed in areas of narcissistic entitlement, they, in turn, are enabled to better fulfill the needs of the children. Over time, better quality care is given to the children by the mothers themselves. This care is enriched by the direct nurturance they receive in the play therapy group.

REFERENCES

1. Justice B, Justice R: One approach to the problem. *Public Welfare* 1978;36(4):13.
2. Justice B, Justice R: One approach to the problem. *Public Welfare* 1978;36(4):16–17.
3. Whiting L: Child abuse and neglect: A different perspective. *Public Welfare* 1978;36(4):24.
4. Redstone JF: Concurrent and individual and group psychotherapy: Theoretical considerations. Unpublished paper.
5. Yalom ID: *The Theory and Practice of Group Psychotherapy,* 2 Ed. New York, Basic Books, 1975, p 194.

6. Justice B, Justice R: Group therapy intervention strategies for abusing parents and evaluation of results, in Lauderdale ML, Anderson RN, Cramer S (eds): *Child Abuse and Neglect: Issues of Innovation and Implementation,* Vol. 2. Proceedings of Second National Conference of Child Abuse and Neglect, Houston, National Center for Child Abuse and Neglect, DHEW Pub #78-30148. April 1979, pp 349–359.
7. Bellucci M: Group treatment of mothers in child protection cases. *Child Welfare* 1972;51(2):114.
8. Steele BF: Working with abusive parents from a psychiatric point of view. Washington, DC, DHEW, 1975 (OHD 75-70) p 22.
9. Whiting L: Child abuse, p 24.
10. Kohut H: *The Analysis of the Self: A Systematic Approach to the Psychoanalytic Treatment of Narcissistic Personality Disorders.* New York, International Universities Press, 1971.
11. Satir V: *People Making.* Palo Alto, California, Science and Behavior Books, 1972, p 30.
12. Beezley P: Modern treatment options, in Schmitt BD (ed): *Child Protection Team Handbook: A Multi-Disciplinary Approach to Managing Child Abuse and Neglect.* Washington, DC, DHEW, 1975 (OHD 75-30075) p 270.
13. Horwitz, L: Group psychotherapy of the borderline patient, in Hartocollis P (ed): *Borderline Personality Disorders.* New York, International University Press, 1979, pp 399–422.
14. Kinard EM: Emotional development in physically abused children: A study in self concept and aggression. PhD Thesis, Brandeis University, Waltham, Massachusetts, 1978, pp 1–10.
15. Bean S: The parent's center project: A multi-service approach to the prevention of child abuse. *Child Welfare* 1971;50(5):281–282.
16. Hausman M: Parents groups: How members perceive curative factors. *Smith College Studies in Social Work,* 1973;44(1):179–199.
17. Hyman S: Failures in group psychotherapy, in Ruitenbeck H (ed): *Group Therapy Today: Styles, Methods and Techniques.* New York, Atherton Press, 1969, p 180.
18. Winnicott DW: Hate in the counter-transference, in Winnicott DW (ed): *Collected Papers.* New York, Basic Books, 1957, pp 194–203.
19. Wayne J, Avery N: Activities as a tool for group termination. *Social Work* 1979;24(1):58–59.

11 Separation and Placement

Richard A. Noonan

The decision to utilize foster placement in the context of providing protective casework intervention is an issue which evokes significant emotional turmoil in a parent–child relationship and also can be stressful to an agency or interagency network involved in working with a family. Use of separation as an intervention is intended to provide care and protection for a child at risk, yet it creates its own pain, in the experience of loss from one's family. Separation also requires the placed child to master the normal anxieties of living with strangers and to allow himself (herself) to be loved by these new, unfamiliar figures. Hence, before embarking upon the advantages of separation and placement, let us examine some critical implications of separation on the child and his family. It is the professional role of the social worker, through casework assessment and intervention, to facilitate maximum benefit and to minimize harm when separation is necessary for the protection of children.

It is well established that children require continuity of affection and consistency in structure in order to grow.[1] The mother of a newborn needs the opportunity of contact with her child as part of the bonding process, not withstanding any significant emotional or environmental stresses which do affect the quality of the mother's tie toward the newborn infant.[2] The young child, just out of infancy, needs constancy of affection in order to accomplish the very important tasks of that age, especially separation–individuation and establishment of object constancy.[1] Through continuity of appropriate attachment, the young toddler begins to experience self-determination and autonomy, and the parent–child dyad undergoes the stress of limit-testing, curiosity, mobility and wonderment, and limit-setting. The oedipal-aged child needs continuity of relationships to master the difficult intrapsychic tasks specific to his/her age and gender, so that the child's internal competition with parent of the same sex or the child's sense of desire for loving the opposite sexed parent in a new dimension can be relinquished through consolidation and incorporation of a new sense of identity, without significant recrimination and self-blame. The latency-aged child relies on continuity to foster a healthy, flexible superego, and to establish expanding peer relationships outside the family, knowing that one's sense of belonging to a family is unquestioned. The adolescent needs consistency of enduring parental relationships as he/she undergoes that difficult and trying process of gradually shifting from the dependencies of childhood to the independence of adult (autonomous) functioning, as sexual identity is explored and integrated, and as learning is achieved in order to pursue occupational ideals. At each and every developmental phase, continuity of the relationship with parents helps to serve the ego in its various developmental crises and tasks.

To introduce the experience of separation from familiar parents into the life of a child will cause an imbalance in the child's sense of equilibrium, and one may anticipate, to some extent, regressive responses in response to a separation. The above developmental tasks are characteristic of normal childhood. These must be taken into careful consideration by the decision-makers, when contemplating foster placement.

The worker has the professional knowledge and the responsibility to listen to a family in distress and to carefully assess the relative strengths and stresses within a family, involving the family to the greatest extent possible. The protective worker has a dual role as therapeutic agent to a distressed family and as protective agent on behalf of an abused/neglected child. When it is clear to the worker that there are clear and definite risks which are well understood and documented, then the worker uses his/her professional self to acknowledge that, concurrent with the feelings of love which the parent(s) have for the child, there exists a strong feeling of negative ambivalence which has erupted or is clearly about to erupt, causing potential harm or clear risk of harm to the growth and development of a child. (See below for full discussion of criteria for placement.)

The worker must carefully differentiate between voluntary and involuntary placements. In the case of a voluntary placement, the parent(s) possess sufficient strengths which enable them to participate in the assessment of the need for separation, and they appropriately follow through on a plan of voluntary separation in order to prevent foreseeable damage to the children. In the case of involuntary placement through court, there exists a documented risk of abuse and/or neglect which is causing or may reasonably be anticipated to cause substantial harm to the growth and development of a child, and the parent either lacks the capacity to acknowledge such a risk or refuses to utilize services necessary for the protection and care of the child.

Court intervention may involve supervision of services or may entail court-ordered placement. When to use voluntary and when to use involuntary placement is not always a clear-cut issue. The following case illustrates the complexity of differentiating between a voluntary and involuntary placement.

A 29-year-old schizophrenic mother, who was experiencing acute paranoid delusions, walked into an agency to inquire about foster placement for her only child, an 11-year-old boy. She had been moving from place to place and was currently living in abandoned housing. She was very fearful of being harmed and of harm coming to her son, so she kept him out of school. She was able to recognize that she was in acute distress which currently immobilized her capacity to provide appropriate care and shelter for her son. She went back and forth on the idea of placement. She had previously allowed her son to live with grandparents on both sides of the family during the past crises; however, she felt too embarrassed to approach them for help again, as she anticipated they would try to initiate legal action to remove her son from her.

It was clear that she was overwhelmed and in acute psychotic crisis; it was also evident that this mother felt unable to tolerate voluntary placement with the grandparents, however appropriate for her son, because of threats of legal action by extended family. After meeting with the parent and the extended family, separately and together, it was decided to pursue court intervention, in order to provide a stable placement, in an extended family home, to ensure psychiatric care of the mother, and to provide a time-limited period for realistic long-range planning for her son. The mother was greatly relieved that, during this time of stress, someone helped her formulate a plan that addressed both her needs and those of her son, without feeling overwhelmed by the pressures of the extended family. The mother was able to explain and prepare her son for the placement, which he readily accepted. The boy was glad that the judge would prevent "arguments" among the grandparents.

It has been our experience that voluntary separations are possible when there is sufficient ego strength in a parent to recognize that a temporarily stressful situation exists, which is harmful to his child(ren), and that there are no other appropriate alternatives except for voluntary placement to ensure the continued safety and/or well-being of the child. Throughout the decision-making process, the worker should have restoration of family unity as a short-term goal (when placement is indicated) unless the court makes a determination to the contrary. Every professional skill should be brought to bear to assist a family to help minimize the need for placement to the extent possible.

TRAUMATIC IMPACT OF SEPARATION

Littner[3] has elaborated some of the traumatic effects of separation on a child and has discussed some typical methods children utilize to survive. Littner notes that children experience (on either a conscious or unconscious level) "feelings of abandonment, which contain elements of loss, rejection, humiliation, complete insignificance, and worthlessness . . . and a feeling of complete helplessness." Such strong feelings evoke a painful sense of anger toward the parent (or a derivative figure) for the apparent desertion, and these feelings are often denied, as they are too overwhelming, and frequently redirected toward a more acceptable source, usually the child himself. Hence the child blames himself, and he searches for a specific "badness within himself" as the logical explanation for the separation and placement. Littner points out that many children tend to isolate whatever developmental crises they are currently experiencing in their lives concurrent to the separation experience. Children also experience a fear of punishment which is directly connected to their deep sense of anger and retaliation, as well as to an unconscious wish to get themselves hurt.

The worker needs to carefully differentiate the source of anxiety when fear of punishment is manifest in a placed child. This anxiety may be the result of a reaction to the separation and placement, or it may indicate that the child has identified with the "aggressor" as a defense.[4] For the children whose fear of punishment originates out of separation anxiety, the worker and caretaking family can help minimize this degree of anxiety by understanding the child's feelings around separation, arranging regular contact and visits with the parent, and providing realistic expectations of the child's ability to tolerate new caretakers. Bringing familiar objects from home can serve as transitional objects to alleviate separation anxiety. Contact with siblings and other significant others is also important and helpful to managing separation anxiety. The foster family selected to care for the child should ideally be suited to appropriate contact with the biological family. (See below for contact between parents and foster parents.)

For children whose fear of punishment is a manifestation of identification with the aggressor, the worker and caretaking family realize that the child has internalized a sense of identification with the aggressor in an attempt to master the anxieties previously associated with aggression directed toward himself. The source of the anxiety is not separation, rather it is fear of real injury and the accompanying feelings of helplessness and anger. Rather than accept responsibility for feeling angry, the child projects his own anger onto other adult figures in order to avoid feeling overwhelmed with his own anger, as such feelings evoke further anxiety of retaliation for perceived badness.

The above considerations are mentioned as prerequisite understandings to the decision to request separation and placement as an essential part of protective intervention, usually through court intervention. Whenever possible and appropriate, the protective worker should exhaust all avenues of retaining family unity because of the traumatic effects of separation on the child and the parents.[5]

CRITERIA FOR SEPARATION
AND PLACEMENT

There are legal requirements which must be adequately satisfied in order for a court to modify the parent–child relationship by temporary legal/physical custody being awarded to the appropriate state child welfare agency. A child must be exposed to a clear and present danger which has resulted in physical injury, which has contributed to "substantial neglect" of a child, or which can be reasonably expected to occur in the immediate future without such intervention. In making a determination of "clear and present danger," the worker must have made an assessment of the strengths and stresses within a family to the greatest extent possible (see Chapters 4, 5, and 6) and carefully evaluated the family's current capacity to utilize resources in the community to adequately cope with those dysfunctional areas within the family constellation which erupt in abusive or neglectful behavior toward the child(ren). When it can be established that failure to utilize needed community resources will eventuate in clear and present danger to the child, then the worker must be able to document said failure and document how said failure to utilize resources will result in risk of clear and present danger to the child.

Another important criterion to examine, in determining whether separation and placement are clinically indicated, is the current inability of the child to tolerate living with a parent or vice versa. It must be demonstrated that the current inability of the child to tolerate living with a parent is not only present, but also will lead to abusive or neglectful behavior in the form of a clear and present risk to the child's safety and growth.

In and of itself, a child's inability to tolerate living with parents is an insufficient basis to consider separation and placement, but such a situation needs to be diagnostically evaluated within the total context of the child's situation.[1] Such behavior may represent a lack of frustration tolerance and indicate an underlying ego disturbance in the child that merits extended diagnostic evaluation of the child within his family, without exposing the child unnecessarily to the traumatic effects of separation. Assessment of a child's apparent inability to live with a parent needs a comprehensive child-oriented facility to identify and understand the significance of such behavior within the context of the family dynamics and the developmental phase of the child. An evaluation will clarify whether intervention is needed to support parents in their management of a difficult child at home or whether separation is clinically indicated.

Another element which may indicate the need for separation and placement is threatened harm, ie, where the child is exposed to substantial risk of harm that can foreseeably create danger to a child's physical, mental, or emotional health and welfare. There is significant controversy about this position in that some experts believe that substantial physical harm or threat of substantial physical harm must be established, regardless of the degree of "mental or emotional harm" to a child, before placement against parental wishes is indicated.[6]

When it can be reasonably established that there are clear signs of significant deterioration in a parent–child relationship or level of functioning (eg, quality of care given to an infant) which constitute substantial risk of physical, or mental, or emotional harm that is likely to occur in the immediate future, there exist strong grounds to support use of separation and placement, in our opinion. Failure of an adolescent mother who is removed and isolated from family and significant others, to provide adequate and appropriate living quarters for her newborn child may constitute sufficient threat of harm to the child to warrant consideration of separation, given full examination of previous functioning, maturity of judgment, and absence of reliable, significant others. Repeated failure by parents to provide necessary supervision of a daughter who had been frequently sexually molested by siblings was sufficient to warrant separation, after considerable efforts to provide therapeutic intervention were rendered ineffective by parents' denial. We wish to underscore the importance of sound clinical judgment which incorporates as comprehensive an assessment as possible.

A reasonable alternative resource should be considered and explored by the worker before concluding that placement in foster care is the only recourse. There may be willing and able extended family members who are appropriate and familiar to the child and who are able to provide alternative caretaking for a child at risk. When extended family members are utilized, it is important for the worker to establish clear boundaries regarding discipline and visitation and to formulate an initial timetable of placement with built-in redeterminations of need for placement and clear expectations of parents.

Placement of a child within the extended family requires diligent consideration by the worker because the feelings and attitudes of the relative toward the parent(s) will need to be addressed in the treatment plan. Negative feelings or attitudes toward the biological family may often result in a strongly divided loyalty struggle which is, in itself, harmful to a child placed apart from the parent(s). Treatment efforts should concentrate on enabling caretaking relatives to have a realistic understanding of the child's need for a supportive, time-limited living environment, free from blame toward the child's family of origin, and to be able to endorse the goal of ultimate reunion with parents.

EXPERIENCE OF COURT INTERVENTION

Court intervention may be described as having three phases. The first involves the invocation of a petition, in which a probable cause hearing takes place, with notice to all parties, appointment of counsel, and presentation of the evidence by the petitioning agency. The second phase is the adjudicatory phase in which an investigation is conducted, and findings of fact presented, together with any legal determinations as to whether the allegation has sufficient merit to warrant an adjudication, in accord with the law. In the third phase the court makes its determination of the most appropriate plan for a child, with input from all concerned parties. The rules of evidence require direct testimony by the professionals involved in documenting the risk of abuse or neglect before the court. In order for agencies to be prepared for court intervention, their own legal counsel should review the worker's assessment in order to assure adequacy of the evidence, legal compliance with appropriate statutes, and due process considerations.

Court intervention into the life of a parent–child relationship evokes strong feelings of helplessness, perceived inadequacy, resentment, and fear of loss in the parent, with consequent feelings of hostility and anger toward the perceived precipitating agent. Court intervention also disrupts the autonomy of the parent–child relationship; however, it is our opinion that children who have known abusive or neglectful parenting are both fearful and relieved that an external authority has intervened to eliminate risks of abuse and neglect. Court intervention also brings about the entrance of legal counsel into the relationship between the family and the child welfare agency, which has its own demands on the worker.

The worker who petitions for court intervention continues to work with the family throughout the process of court intervention. It is important for the worker to utilize one's casework skills to help the family address and accept their feelings of hostility toward the worker or court intervention, without automatically giving in to the parent's frequently voiced request to have the worker transferred off their case. Ideally the therapeutic alliance can be strengthened enormously by working through the parent's hostilities with the worker and by a closer alliance of trust established between them; however, this is not always possible or realistic.

It is very important that the worker feel at ease with the use of authority which protective work entails, in addition to reaching out to understand a parent whose own emotional deprivation or need has interfered with his parenting capacities or to a parent whose ambivalence is sometimes overcome by impulses to strike out at a perceived threat, despite a loving attachment to a child.[7] It is essential that the worker have an unambiguous sense of a positive nonconflicted feeling about the use of authority in the protective intervention process, as this feeling (or its absence) is conveyed to the family consciously or otherwise.

A positive incorporation of the authoritative dimension will enable the worker to assist the family in addressing both their hostility and their fears of being judged as inadequate in their love for their child. A negative incorporation of the authoritative dimension will convey, consciously or otherwise, that the family's fear of being judged inadequate is confirmed in the subtleties of the worker's attitude toward authority, which the family sees as a response to their perceived inadequacy. Workers who have a negative incorporation of authority often attempt to conceal this through denial and reaction formation, with the result that they either collude in the parent's hostility toward court intervention (unknowingly) or disengage themselves from their clients, who, in turn, experience this emotional distance as rejection. Successful protective casework requires a worker to be free from these conflicts.

In some states, the court appoints an impartial investigator to assess the family situation and to submit a report. It is our opinion that court intervention merits a thorough, comprehensive assessment of family functioning in order to understand the interplay between family strengths and pathological issues which affect the emotional environment and parent–child interation. Frequently the protective service worker who needs to act in an emergency situation does not have the time to conduct a comprehensive assessment and needs to defer to the court investigator the opportunity for a more comprehensive study of the family.

To be helpful, investigators need to have an understanding of normal development as well as psychopathology, be skilled in interviewing parents and children, and be familiar with the statutory requirements of child welfare laws. The investigator may, in some instances of interviewing parents, be able to foster an improved understanding of the issues leading to court intervention through use of a nonjudgemental attitude and alertness to felt inadequacy on the part of the parents. A thorough assessment of the family, through the investigation, not only satisfies the statutory requirement of an impartial assessment, but also may be used as a vehicle to convey an understanding of the pertinent strengths and stresses within a family, in an unbiased atmosphere, so that they may further reflect on their needs as a family in stress.

The experience of court intervention as a therapeutic tool can be conceptualized on various levels: (1) containment of aggressive impulses in a parent–child relationship which is currently exposing a child to risks; (2) restructuring the treatment contract between family and protective service agency (and other agencies) when indicated; (3) containment of conflict among various agencies which are manifesting and/or reflecting conflicting elements of a troubled parent–child relationship; (4) mobilization of community resources to establish or develop resources in response to identified service needs; and (5) providing significantly disturbed families a time-limited opportunity to mobilize their capacity to utilize resources to address unmet family needs properly, before court makes a final disposition of an adjudicated child.

It is not uncommon for the family of an abused child to unconsciously invite various outside agents (agencies) to manifest various aspects of their ambivalence, with the result that the agencies may feel enjoined by the powerful dynamics of the family in a struggle with competing wishes. In such a situation, it is through an interagency conference that such struggles are appropriately identified and more effective means established to minimize misunderstanding through periodic communication. Court intervention is not necessary in order for such conferences to take place; however, it is frequently advisable that such interagency conferences be held in order to establish an agreed-upon diagnostic formulation and treatment plan to present to the court for an effective disposition.

PREPARATION OF THE CHILD
FOR PLACEMENT

Every child who is about to experience separation and placement with another caretaker needs to understand, on a realistic level commensurate with his age and capacity to understand, that such an action is necessary at this time in order for the parents to help themselves and the family. This is important to stress, as the child will naturally tend to see himself as the perceived source of badness. The social worker has the critical role of preparing the child for placement and, to the extent possible, enabling the parent(s) to help the child with the leave-taking process.

Parental involvement in helping the child with separation is of invaluable help to the child's understanding and acceptance of the separation; however, this task is frequently beyond the capacity of many parents in a situation involving involuntary separation. The worker serves as an auxiliary ego to the child in coping with the anxieties of separation and in meeting a new family. The worker personifies the child welfare agency which temporarily assumes the parenting function in conjunction with the foster family.[8] Many children who have already experienced discontinuity of attachment and nurturance in their biological family approach the caseworker with feelings of distrust and avoidance. However, the task of the worker is to establish as much trust and confidence as the child and situation will allow before placement, so that the worker can provide support to the child's adapting ego during placement.

If possible and appropriate, it is desirable to prepare a child for placement by visiting the foster family prior to placement. Even in crisis situations, it is preferred that the child visit with the foster family first and then, perhaps after a discussion with the worker in a nonthreatening atmosphere about the family, to return to the foster placement later in the day. Ideally, in a voluntary foster placement situation, the worker would prepare the child for meeting his foster family with pictures and information about who is in the family and then arrange for an introductory visit. The day of placement should be explained, in advance, to the child, and the parent(s) participate in saying good-bye and helping the child with leave-taking. The child may wish or need to bring along a transitional object (such as a favorite toy), conveying a sense of belonging and being loved in the face of anxieties to the contrary.

It is important for the worker to gather information about the child's likes and dislikes and to communicate this to the foster family so that these may be utilized in facilitating his transition to a strange environment. Child welfare procedures customarily require a physical examination of the child as close to the time of placement as possible. This can naturally evoke the child's sense of anxiety around fear of injury or punishment which the worker and medical personnel need to acknowledge in completing a physical examination.[9]

PLACEMENT OF THE NEGLECTED CHILD

For the neglected child, separation and placement ushers the child into a new, strange environment which the child frequently meets with blankness, indifference, and a lack of spontaneity. Galdston's[7] description of the neglected child provides diagnostic clues for management of placement with substitute caretakers: "The neglected child is a psychobiological robot . . . [for whom] existence is a matter of physiologic function . . . and no part or process of his body has been surcharged with emotion." Placement provides a slow, gradual opportunity for the neglected child to be exposed to increasing levels of stimulation, consistently, according to his capacity to tolerate or absorb.

In failure-to-thrive situations, feeding is the primary experience of caretaking. Initial rejection of food gives way to tentative then, later, voracious food-craving. Feeding of the young child becomes an important time for emotional feeding as well as nutrition. The foster mother will start with an inert, passive child and, suddenly, will be facing an intrusive, voracious, clinging child who frequently is unable to let her out of sight. Separation anxiety between the newly enlivened child and the foster mother will begin to assume significant importance and proportion. Such separation anxiety in the placed neglected child needs to be understood by the foster mother until the child is able to tolerate care by substitute figures.

Many neglected children have not been allowed to form ties with their parents because of parental needs to deny the existence of the child as a person, as manifest in parental refusal to accept the child's need for food, affection, etc. Parents of neglected children, especially failure-to-thrive children, are often significantly deprived themselves and need extensive psychotherapeutic intervention in order to master the troublesome events of the past which parenting has rekindled.[10]

Visitation between parent and child should be on a consistent basis, preferably in a neutral environment initially, until the child has established that the new, nurturing caretaker (or psychological mother) will not go away. There may be a temporary period when the child is unable to tolerate the separation anxiety evoked by visitation with the biological parent. This need in the child should be acknowledged and taken into consideration by the decision-makers in planning visitation between parent and child. Once a child who has experienced substantial neglect from biological parents begins to develop an attachment to the "psychological parent," then visitation will expose the child to the very insecurity which clashes with his need for emotional constancy. The following case of a seven-year-old child illustrates these points.

Charles, age 7, came to the attention of protective services when the mother was observed intoxicated in the welfare office while picking up her check. Following a report of suspected neglect by the welfare worker, the protective services team scheduled a home visit with the mother, which found her "completely intoxicated," along with four other drunken adults. Mrs. B. refused to acknowledge alcohol use, denied that she was drunk, and refused further contact with the protective service team. Collateral information requested from the school revealed that Charles was enrolled one year late and that he had missed 179 days of school in the two years he had been registered. Teachers reported that Charles frequently fell sound asleep in class, for up to two hours at a time. Within a month of the home visit, Mrs. B. brought Charles to the hospital, stating "he was hit by a car six days ago [and was] still limping" on the right leg. The next day, Charles was brought to the same hospital by a friend of his mother and was found to have a fractured right fibula, of undetermined origin. Charles' explanation was that he was "beaten up and robbed by neighbors."

Mother gave permission, over the phone, to admit Charles. During his two-week stay, Charles began sharing some bizarre stories of sexual play with adults, including graphic details of intercourse. Mrs. B. was observed intoxicated, smelling of alcohol, and speaking with slurred speech on many of her infrequent visits to Charles. The hospital held a trauma evaluation conference which concluded that mother's alcohol abuse and dependency rendered her currently unable to provide proper care and supervision and brought the matter to court, requesting foster placement.

Charles told the court investigator and the foster family that "my mother drinks too much . . . there's nobody to feed me, nobody to put me off to school, and nobody to spend time with me." Charles was not visited by his mother during the first two months in foster care. Charles began telling his foster mother he "didn't want to go back to her" [his mother].

Court ultimately granted permanent custody of Charles to the state child welfare agency, after noting that Mrs. B. made no effort to address her need for treatment of alcohol abuse which resulted in neglectful parenting. Court also noted that Mrs. B. made no effort to visit Charles and that Charles himself was fearful of being returned to his mother.

PLACEMENT OF THE ABUSED CHILD

For the abused child, the experience of placement with a substitute caretaker takes place in the context of a significant, ambivalent relationship, in which the child has known both affection and attachment as well as frightening rejection and aggression, manifested in discharge of aggressive impulses by a parent or parent figure. Hence, the child knows, in terms of actual experience, a loving parent and an angry, hurting parent. Given the age of a child, the degree of exposure to discharge of aggressive impulses from the parent, the degree of self-hatred in the parent, and other stressful factors, eg, environmental problems of inadequate or overcrowded housing, the experience of separation and placement from an acute stressful situation can be both a relief and a loss for an abused child.

The placed child will experience regression, in reaction to separation and loss of his family, and will experience, to varying degrees, fear of punishment and feelings of rejection. The child may attempt to defend against these feelings of loss with overcompensating behavior (eg, being overly compliant or too good) or pseudo-mature behavior. However, the worker and foster family need to recognize the underlying anxiety of separation, repressed anger, fear of further rejection, and the tendency of the child to blame himself for the "badness." Severely abused children may appear listless, apathetic, and unresponsive to all but painful stimuli, or they may take flight in fear upon any reproach.[7] Overt fear of adult figures is a derivative of repression and may constitute regression in service of the ego in reaction to a perceived threat.

The need to have the abusive experience repeated is often characteristic of abused children. Consistent nurturance with realistic expectations of the child by the foster family may, over time, enable the child to deal with his acute anxiety and to be able to tolerate the fears evoked by a strange caretaker who wishes to establish a relationship with him. However, this task is not always successful. Children need a patient, accepting response from their caretakers in order to manage this acute anxiety.

Abused children in placement will present testing behavior as part of their process of struggling to master their own fear of repetition of the abuse. Compounding the rugged limit-testing behavior, some children will use testing behavior to act out their anxieties around divided loyalty struggles, which can come from within themselves or may be their reflection of a custody battle drawn between biological parent and child welfare advocate. Children are sensitive to the nuances of the adult environment, and they will easily distort whether there is a real struggle or an imaginary struggle between parents and foster parents. At times children in placement will wish to secure a desired relationship by provoking damaging statements toward the less desired caretaker. The greatest testing behavior, however, is seen when, after the children have been reunited with the family, they test their parents to determine whether these newly acquired impulse controls will indeed be effective.

> Teresa, age 4, was admitted to a pediatric hospital for evaluation of "cold and congestion" at parent's request. Physical examination of Teresa revealed the presence of new and old rib fractures, which were reported to the child welfare agency and to the court. Teresa was allowed to remain with her parents, during the investigation period, with close supervision from the child welfare agency which was provided immediately. Teresa was subsequently reinjured by the father within a few days of the court hearing and was admitted to the hospital in serious condition with a ruptured spleen. Teresa's mother acknowledged that the father had been convicted of a criminal charge in connection with the death of her first child. Teresa was placed by the court in temporary foster care, pending court action.
>
> In the foster home, which consisted of foster parents and two sons, Teresa was described as "extremely fearful" of the foster father and

adolescent boys; however, she "warmed up" to the foster mother, not wanting to let her out of sight. Whenever any of the men in the foster family approached Teresa, she would cry, tremble, and become immobilized. For the first month Teresa was "a perfect child," complying with any wish of the foster mother. She gradually became more tolerant and comfortable with the foster father, after the first two weeks of placement.

In Teresa's case, the court ultimately removed her from her parents, noting that, despite mother's statements of belated recognition of her husband's emotional problems, mother's need to be dependent and close to husband prevented her from effectively protecting Teresa from the aggressive impulses which overcame father.

SERVICES DURING SEPARATION
AND PLACEMENT

During the period of involuntary placement of a child, the child welfare agency has the responsibility of developing a treatment plan which addresses the various needs of the family situation, including services for parents, services for the placed child(ren), visitation plans, diagnostic evaluation if needed, and ongoing casework with the parents. The expectations of a family by the worker are to be as clear as possible, and it is advisable that the entire service plan be formulated in writing, with a copy to the family.

For the abusing parent, there will be a strong pull toward the placed child. The parent may tend to overlook the underlying feelings of self-hatred and/or previous emotional threatening behavior and yearn only for the return of the absent child. In our opinion, it has been most helpful that psychiatric and psychological evaluations be considered by the court, during the investigatory phase of the court proceeding, in order to shed light on the identifiable strengths and stresses in the family unit and to facilitate sound dispositional planning.

The foster family needs clarity from the child welfare agency in the definition and elaboration of its role, so that role confusion is avoided.[10] The foster parents will strive to address the psychological tasks of parenting the placed child, through appropriate nurturance, consistent limit-setting, and an accepting, nonjudgmental approach to the child's conflicting feelings about the parents. The developmental tasks of the child are compounded by reactions to the separation experience, ie, regression, repression, and testing behavior within the child, and the underlying separation anxiety that time-limited foster care inherently entails. It is essential to the development of a cohesive foster care placement plan that the worker provide, to the best of his professional ability and judgment, clear goals within a realistic timetable. Visitation, in a protective service setting, is an important issue which requires the active participation of the worker in designing and developing an appropriate service plan geared to the needs and capacities of the child, parents, and foster family. Agencies should have appropriate facilities for visitation between placed children and their parents.

The child welfare agency assumes an important parenting function whenever a child is placed in foster care. Kline and Overstreet[8] have described the agency's role as parent in terms of acting in a reliably consistent way to provide for the various emotional, educational, medical, and other needs of a child in placement, in addition to sharing this responsibility with the biological family and the foster family. The worker ideally will epitomize reliability not only for the family, but also and especially for the child. To counter the child's sense of helplessness, it is advisable, given the age and capacity of the child, to introduce the child to members of the agency, such as the supervisor, so that the child begins to experience the reliability of the new authority figures in his life in a personal, rather than impersonal, manner. For older children who require placement over an extended period of time, it might be helpful to arrange a meeting for the child to talk with a representative of the court, eg, the probation officer, who can state, in a manner appropriate to the age and capacity of the child, the realities of the need for placement.

The purpose of such intervention would be to prevent distortion regarding the reason for placement and, hence, to improve the mental health outlook of the child. This can also be reinforced through the trusting relationship established with the worker. The worker's intervention into such areas as day care placement, school registration, clothing and medical needs is but a miniature demonstration of the agency's parenting function, carried out in a concrete way, so that the child begins to know the new authority in his life as a reliable and caring resource.

By the time-limited nature of their contact with children, foster families experience recurrent losses through termination of placement and should have supportive intervention to assist them in give and take of caring for placed children. Walker[11] has indicated, in his study of foster parenting, that successful foster parents have been able to master the pain and loss of separation adaptively, and therefore are in a better position to identify and acknowledge similar "grief" in the lives of the children placed in their temporary care. Unsuccessful resolution of loss issues by a foster family can result in a heightened sense of "divided loyalty" for the placed child, through unconscious messages from the foster family not to leave. Resources should be available, if necessary, to assist foster families in this area, eg, individual or family therapy and foster parent support groups.

CONTACT BETWEEN PARENTS AND
FOSTER PARENTS

The issue of contact between the parent and the foster parent can be, at times, a difficult and perplexing dilemma for the protective case-worker. At times, given the nature and severity of the risk to the children, it is clearly indicated that the identity and location of the foster family be withheld and kept strictly confidential in order for the protective placement to be a stable, nonthreatening environment, free from risk of perceived influence by the abusive parent. When such a need has been soundly established and documented, the child welfare agency needs the supportive assistance from the judicial authority to ensure the safety and confidentiality of the protective custody through court orders, including police protection. This is particularly true when a parent, with a documented history of poor impulse control and previous assaultive behavior, gives indication to the worker that he is "about to take matters into his own hands" by abducting the child from protective custody.

Contact between biological parent and foster parent may also be contraindicated when there exists strong evidence of a poor prognosis, with the likely possibility that the child, particularly an adolescent or hard-to-place latency child, may be permanently removed from the parents and suitably placed in the foster home on an extended basis, assuming that the foster parents would be appropriate candidates to adopt the child. In such instances, direct contact between parents and foster parents needs to be carefully considered for its short-term and long-term benefits and consequences. Lack of direct contact may facilitate neutrality of the foster family, in spite of the divided loyalty struggles the child may experience.

However, there are many situations in which direct contact between parents and foster parents is productive and beneficial, given a knowledgeable assessment of the strengths and areas of difficulty. Foster parents may serve as positive role models and, through their attitude of positive regard for the parents, they may attempt to minimize the parents' tendency to see themselves as inadequate and learn other ways of handling situations with their children. Sharing concerns about the care of the children can lead to reinforcement of good parenting skills. Contact between parent and foster parent is generally desirable in a voluntary placement, as long as the anxieties created by such contact can be appropriately managed by both sets of parents.

Adolescent parents often have limited capacities to tolerate success by another person in the parenting role where they themselves feel very vulnerable and pressured; they react accordingly with anxiety, hostility, and acting up behavior. Significantly emotionally disturbed parents and those who have demonstrated difficulties in accepting boundaries may be good candidates for very limited, structured contact with the foster parents, under the supervision of the caseworker, preferably at a neutral site other than the home of the foster family.

CRITERIA FOR RETURN OF
CHILDREN FROM PLACEMENT

It is advisable to recommend return of children when parents have clearly demonstrated that there is no active, clear and present danger of harm to a child and when it is considered that the child is appropriately prepared and ready to return home. Parents demonstrate this improvement through appropriate and indicated changes in their behavior as well as through a positive involvement in counseling. In the case of abuse, it is essential that the nonabusive parent demonstrate the willingness and the capacity to protect a child whenever exposed to a risk. The case illustration of Teresa is one in which the mother stated she would act to protect her daughter by keeping her husband out of contact with Teresa; however, her actions of maintaining close contact with her husband and her attempts to conceal this from the court and child welfare agency, together with her intense need for her husband to be close to her, made it unlikely that she would act to protect her daughter.

In the case of an abusing parent, it should be demonstrated by that parent that (1) there exists a growing self-knowledge of that impulse to discharge aggressive instincts onto a child which has resulted in substantial harm in the past and which may be repeated in the future, unless other preventive and protective measures are taken; and (2) alternate ways of managing potentially harmful situations have been discussed, learned, and acquired. The caseworker needs to know that the child's desire to test parents' limits will not be overwhelming to the parents. Gradual increase in visitations with the placed child will provide an opportunity for the parents and child to reestablish new boundaries in a monitored situation. Continued monitoring of parents' reintegration of a placed child in the family is necessary to ensure that improved ways of coping with stress or anxiety have been acquired by the parents and have resulted in a more effective parenting relationship.

It is not our experience that a court's finding of fact (adjudication) that abuse has occurred necessarily results in permanent removal of that child from parents, as many parents have been able to respond to the court intervention process by mobilizing their anxiety to begin to deal with issues by engagement in counseling and to ultimately make use of the opportunity which court intervention creates. We strongly concur with the suggestion that more longitudinal studies be done in order to broaden the data base to inform and modify public policy.[12] As clinical practitioners, we know that the process of court intervention may provide a family in distress with a temporary "auxiliary" ego and the time-limited opportunity to establish impulse control, reestablish appropriate sexual boundaries, and to frame a treatment contract which addresses the complex issues that erupt into child abuse.

For a parent to recognize that the child or children have been at risk of abusive behavior, and to proceed to learn more adequate ways of coping with those sources of anxiety which previously evoked abusive behavior, is indeed a strength worth noting and developing to the fullest extent possible. It has been suggested that intervention is harmful in that it disrupts a child's sense of parent as omniscient and all powerful. However, it is our experience that some children sense when their parents have been overstressed and that the children take refuge in knowing that someone has intervened to enable parents to reestablish healthy equilibrium and to eliminate what one child calls "the purple roses." [11]

CRITERIA FOR PERMANENT REMOVAL
OF CHILDREN FROM PARENTS

There are no clear and absolute criteria for permanent removal of children that can be applied universally, as each case must be thoroughly considered on its own merits. We can offer some guidelines for consideration which ought to be examined prior to making such a disposition (we are assuming here that court has already made an adjudication of abuse or neglect): (1) Have the parents pursued appropriate means to correct the dysfunctional parenting, eg, alcohol treatment, psychiatric evaluation, and demonstrated reliable follow-through,[7] (2) Has the treatment plan adopted by parents been effective, and has it been commensurate to the degree of pathology which gave rise to the dysfunctional behavior harmful to the child? (3) What is the age of the child, and how long must a child wait before a permanent relationship can be established? (4) Is there an appropriate, realistic alternative plan ready for the child? (5) As far as can be determined, what disposition is in the best interests of the child, and, similarly, what are the expressed interests of the child?

CONCLUSION

Separation and placement of a child for protective considerations is both painful and necessary. Separation for an abused child evokes both feelings of relief and an assurance of a healthy restoration of order in his or her life, but it also entails a strong theme of self blame, fear of punishment and injury, need to master these fears through reliving the situation with others, and, frequently, repression of hostility for loss of a loved one.

For the severely neglected child, separation and placement in a nurturing environment affords the opportunity to establish, perhaps for the first time, a bond with a nurturing, caretaking figure, and may enkindle joy and enthusiasm in an otherwise lifeless human being. During the placement process the protective caseworker prepares the child for placement, according to the degree of urgency, by explaining the need for placement in terms appropriate to the child's age and level of understanding. To the extent possible, parents should also be involved in the leave-taking and explain their needs in an appropriate manner, if possible. The caseworker demonstrates the role of a parent through reliable attention to the details of the child's needs, and, gradually, begins to establish reliable trustworthiness in the face of the child's expectations of mistrust and disappointment. Separation, for the parents, evokes deep feelings of inadequacy and fear of failure in loving their children, as well as hostility and resentment for the loss (temporary) of their child and for the disruption of their parental autonomy. Casework intervention during placement continues to address these deeply felt issues, through a clear identification in the authoritative role without conveyance to the parents' perception of being judged as inadequate persons; the worker reaches out to understand deprivation, ambivalence, loneliness, and the myriad feelings which preoccupy and impair the functioning of these parents. Visitation is conducted in a sensitive, consistent and supportive environment. Unless and until determined by a court, the eventual goal of placement is reunification with the parent.

There is considerable controversy around the criteria necessary for separation and placement to occur, with some recommending severe physical abuse risk being a prerequisite to placement. In our practical experience, a comprehensive assessment of the intrapsychic, the psychosocial, and the environmental factors, together with an assessment of the support network will establish (1) the existence of a clear and present danger, or (2) the severity of risk due to foreseeable, threatened harm, either of which are sufficient, in our judgment, to merit court intervention. In order to establish further knowledge, we strongly concur with the suggestion of longitudinal studies and other research studies to examine this area in detail.

Court intervention exists to insure the adequate care and protection of children at risk. The professional may also conceptualize that court intervention provides a time-limited opportunity to restructure a treatment contract with a family, when a family's stress has been manifest in abusive or neglectful parenting; it also may result in improved or increased interagency communication and coordination, and possible

226

mobilization of community resources when all other means have been exhausted. Court intervention itself often evokes helplessness, perceived inadequacy, resentment, fear of loss, and hostility in a parent. Increased parental awareness of the impulse to discharge aggressive instincts onto a child, development of alternate ways of coping with stressful situations, involvement in therapeutic intervention with improved parenting skills, all these are some of the factors suggested for consideration of return of a child.

Gradual re-integration of the child into a family through extended visits or overnights will provide a structured opportunity to re-establish new boundaries between parent and child. Even a court adjudication that a child has been abused or neglected, through a fact-finding hearing, does not, in and of itself, warrant permanent removal of a child, as parents have been able to successfully address their own needs in treatment programs under the supervision of a court. It is suggested that services continue with a family, following actual re-integration of a child to support both parent and child as they each test out these newly established boundaries within the family. Guidelines concerning permanent removal of children should include sufficient finding of fact, review of parental involvement in therapeutic intervention, capacity of the child to tolerate a divided loyalty situation (parents/foster parents) and the degree of harm sustained by the child as result of a prolonged delay in re-integration, documentation regarding the best interests of the child, existence of an appropriate alternative plan suited to the child's needs, and, when appropriate, the expressed interests of the child.

NOTES AND REFERENCES

1. Freud A: *The Writings of Anna Freud, Volume VI: Normality and Pathology in Childhood: Assessments of Development.* New York, International Universities Press, Inc, 1965, pp 62–92, 134–147. Also see Fraiberg S: *The Magic Years.* New York, Charles Scribner's Sons, 1959; Mahler M: On child psychosis and schizophrenia: Autistic and symbiotic infantile psychosis, in *The Psychoanalytic Study of the Child.* New York, International Universities Press, 1964;7:286–305.
2. Winnicott DW: *The Child, The Family, and the Outside World.* England, Penguin Books Ltd, 1964.
3. Littner N: Traumatic effects of separation and placement, in *Proceedings, National Conference in Social Work.* New York, Family Service Association of America, 1956, pp 1–7, 9–10.
4. Freud A: *The Writings of Anna Freud, Volume II: Ego and the Mechanisms of Defense,* revised ed. New York, International Universities Press, Inc, 1966, pp 109–121.
5. Mandlebaum A: Parent-child separation: Its significance to parents. *Social Work* 1962;October:10–62.

6. Goldstein J, Freud A, Solnit A: *Beyond the Best Interest of the Child.* New York. The Free Press, 1973. Also see Goldstein J, Freud A, Solnit A, *Before the Best Interest of the Child.* New York, The Free Press, 1979. In this latter work, the authors restrict the grounds for court intervention to four areas: (1) death or disappearance, (2) parental relinquishment of custody, (3) conviction of a sexual offense against one's child, and, (4) serious bodily injury inflicted by parents. However, the proposed Federal National Standards recommend intervention to protect children from *mental injury* (author's italics), ie, an injury to the intellectual or psychological capacity of a child as evidenced by observable and substantial impairment in his ability to function within a normal range of performance and behavior, with due regard to his culture. See National Center of Child Abuse and Neglect: Prevention and Treatment. US Department of Health, Education and Welfare, 1978. Also see Wald.

7. Galdston R: Dysfunctions of parenting: The battered child, the neglected child, the exploited child, in Howells J (ed): *Modern Perspectives of International Child Psychiatry.* Edinburgh, Scotland, Oliver and Boyd, 1968, pp 571–588.

8. Kline D, Furbush Overstreet H: *Foster Care of Children: Nurture and Treatment.* New York, Columbia University Press, 1972, pp 82–87.

9. Public Law 93-247. Federal Child Abuse and Treatment Act.

10. Fraiberg S: Ghosts in the nursery. *Am Acad Child Psychiatry* 1975; 14:387–421.

11. Walker W: Persistence of mourning in the foster child as related to the foster mother's level of maturity. *Smith College Studies in Social Work.* June 1971;41:173–246. Also see Thomas C: The resolution of object loss following foster home placement. *Smith College Studies in Social Work,* June, 1967;37.

12. Wald M: Thinking about public policy toward abuse and neglect of children: A review of *Before the Best Interest of the Child. Michigan Law Review,* 1980;78:645–693.

12 An Overview of the Legal System: Protecting Children from Abuse and Neglect

Sally T. Owen
Herbert H. Hershfang

Working with families troubled with problems of child abuse or neglect may be the most challenging and difficult task of a social work professional. In many, if not most, cases, the worker will not need to resort to court action to effect improvement in the family condition. In other cases, the mere availability of court action provides an adequate deterrent to child abuse or neglect. When court action is undertaken, it sometimes is intended solely or mainly as a means of alerting and enlisting community resources to the family's problems and needs.

The abuse and neglect of any child is a cause for concern; not only do children suffer at the time, but often they grow up to repeat the same parenting pattern with their children. The widespread prevalence of abuse and neglect is a national tragedy.

Often the protective service worker knows the family situation, its challenges and limits, and its successes and its pain, more intimately than anyone. When courts become involved, a foreign element is introduced with new and strange rules, at least from the worker's viewpoint. Moreover, the courts may not respond to the worker's recommendations, or even appear as concerned with protecting the child. Although the child may have a lawyer, parents' constitutional rights may be raised and argued forcefully. The hearing process is becoming more formal. Sometimes it takes on a life of its own, with concerns and delays that not only are not helpful to the child and the family involved, but actually harmful to them.

Obviously, whenever a new element, here the courts and law, is introduced into the family setting, complications may follow. But that is true whether a child is taken to a hospital for diagnosis or to a court for evaluation. Filing an abuse or neglect petition reflects a view that the prior family setting may not have been adequate. The new forum is threatening to the family. Parents, facing the risk of the loss of a child, or even only the humiliation of being considered wanting, and the child, whose future is being determined, have a right to have matters determined on reasonable bases, with due respect to the concerns of each.

In short, what may have started as an effort to help keep a family together, may, in the bringing of a court action, be viewed as an effort to do the opposite. The child's interest is not the only one involved. The parents, sometimes each parent, and the state, too, have a stake in the outcome.

Resolving the potential conflicts of these interests is at the heart of a court determination. Its process takes place in a society of ever-changing standards and values, and among people whose religion, backgrounds, notions of propriety, and styles vary a great deal. What is considered obvious and acceptable disciplining in one family or area, may be considered abuse in another. A case that is felt to warrant court intervention in one place at one time may be considered unworthy of such intervention elsewhere, or even in the same place at another time.

Because of the breadth and complexity of the subject, there are serious limits to what can be said about the law relating to child abuse and neglect in any one book, let alone any one chapter. Our purpose here is simply to provide the social work professional with a broad, basic understanding of the legal principles involved, an appreciation of the importance of the larger institutional framework within which individual state court proceedings are conducted, an awareness of the conflicting interests recognized by the legal system, and an understanding of how these conflicts are being resolved in legislation and court decisions. It is hoped that this knowledge will help permit the worker to use the system more effectively to protect abused and neglected children.

OUTLINE OF THE LEGAL STRUCTURE

The legal system for protecting abused and neglected children in the United States is characterized by complex interrelationships among governmental institutions at the federal and state levels. At the federal level, Congress has enacted legislation providing funds for certain protective services for states whose protective service programs conform to federal legislative requirements. Federal agencies are authorized to promulgate regulations with which states must comply in order to receive federal funds for protective programs. The federal courts interpret ambiguities in federal legislation, review federal agency regulations and actions for compliance with federal legislation, and determine whether federal and state child protective laws are constitutional.

At the state level, each state has its own civil and criminal laws[1] to protect children from abuse and neglect. State agencies, such as departments of public welfare or social services, also frequently promulgate regulations to flesh out each state's civil child protective laws. State courts, like their federal counterparts, resolve ambiguities in state legislation and determine whether state agencies directed to provide child protective services are in compliance with the authority vested in them by state legislation. State courts also review state child protective legislation to determine whether it conforms with the requirements of the state and federal constitutions. In addition, state courts resolve child protective disputes by applying common-law principles in situations not covered by state legislation.[2]

Within the context of this complex institutional structure, the legal system struggles to resolve disputes among conflicting interests. Thus, in some child protective cases, courts weigh the state's interest in protecting the child against the family's right to privacy and autonomy from state intervention. In others, the state's interest in protecting children in the most economical manner is pitted against procedural protections for the parent. Recently emerging interests include those of foster parents or other "psychological" parents which conflict with the interests of the state in the economical use of its resources or with the interests of the biological parent who wishes to have the abused or neglected child returned home.

This chapter will first examine the basic common-law principles of the parent as natural guardian and the doctrine of parens patriae, which are the foundation for understanding state legislation and court decisions. Next are reviewed certain US Supreme Court decisions which interpret the due process clause to restrict the state's ability to protect children. Federal legislation is then briefly outlined in order to understand its impact on state child protective legislation. Some current state laws and court decisions are then examined.

INFLUENCE OF COMMON LAW

At English common law, parents were the natural guardians of their children, entitled to their custody and responsible for their care and discipline. This concept was brought to the New World by the English colonists and incorporated into the American legal system.

Early American courts were extremely reluctant to intervene to protect children from abuse and neglect. Believing that parental discretion in disciplining children was necessary to maintain domestic harmony, the courts developed the general principle that minor children could not bring civil suits against their parents for abuse and neglect. Thus, in an 1895 Mississippi case, the court declared: "The state, through its criminal laws, will give the minor child protection from parental violence and wrongdoing, and this is all the child can be heard to demand." [3]

However, the early American criminal laws provided little protection for children. Socially acceptable standards for disciplining children were extremely severe. In order to obtain a conviction, the prosecutor would have to demonstrate that: (1) the punishment was grossly unreasonable in relation to the offense, (2) the punishment was "cruel and merciless," or (3) the punishment permanently injured the child. [4]

Beginning around 1825, states began enacting legislation authorizing state intervention to protect children from abuse and neglect by committing them to institutions called houses of refuge. Little distinction was made between delinquent children and those who had been abused and neglected. Commitment of both groups to institutions was viewed as necessary to inculcate sound morals and to prevent the children from later turning to a life of crime.

Since, at common law, parents were entitled to custody of their children, the courts had to find some justification for state intervention. Thus, to uphold legislation which removed children from their parents, courts adopted the doctrine of parens patriae from English chancery practice. This doctrine describes the power of the state to act in loco parentis to protect the property interests and the person of the child. [5]

The doctrine was explained by a Pennsylvania court in 1839 as follows:

> . . . may not the natural parents, when unequal to the task of education, or unworthy of it, be superseded by the parens patriae, or common guardian of the community? It is to be remembered that the public has a paramount interest in the virtue and knowledge of its members, and that of strict right, the business of education belongs to it. That parents are ordinarily intrusted with it is because it can seldom be put into better hands; but where they are incompetent or corrupt, what is there to prevent the public from withdrawing their faculties, held, as they obviously are, at its sufferance? The right of parental control is a natural, but not an unalienable one. It is not excepted by the declaration of rights out of the subjects of ordinary legislation . . . . [6]

The parens patriae doctrine was used by state courts extensively in the nineteenth century to uphold state legislation authorizing removal of children under extremely vague statutes. For example, an 1882 Massachusetts statute authorized removal of any child under 14 who "by reason of orphanage, or of the neglect, crime, drunkenness or other vice of his parents, is growing up without education or salutary control, and in circumstances exposing him to lead an idle and dissolute life, or is dependent upon public charity."[7] Poverty was another common ground for removal of children.[8]

In addition to vague standards, state legislation authorizing removal of children, whether for poverty, abuse, neglect, or delinquency, commonly provided extremely informal procedures. A justice of the peace or a magistrate frequently made determinations which could result in removal of a child until the age of 21. Parents were not always notified or provided with an opportunity for a hearing.[9] In most cases, these summary procedures were determined to be constitutional, with the courts using the doctrine of parens patriae to support their decisions.

PROCEDURAL DUE PROCESS

In the twentieth century, the US Supreme Court has been providing increasing procedural protections to families in cases involving state intervention designed to protect children. The state's interest in protecting children under the parens patriae doctrine is receiving serious scrutiny by the Supreme Court through its cases interpreting the due process clause of the Fourteenth Amendment to the US Constitution. State laws are being revised to conform to these evolving constitutional requirements.

The Fourteenth Amendment provides that: "No state shall . . . deprive any person of life, liberty or property without due process of law." The Supreme Court has interpreted "liberty" to include not only freedom from bodily restraint but also:

> . . . the right of the individual to . . . engage in any of the common occupations of life, . . . to marry, establish a home and bring up children . . . and, generally, to enjoy those privileges long recognized at common law as essential to the orderly pursuit of happiness by free men.[10]

Among the liberty interests protected by the Fourteenth Amendment, the interest in family autonomy has special importance. Thus, in 1972 in *Stanley vs Illinois,* the Supreme Court said:

> It is plain that the interest of a parent in the companionship, care, custody, and management of his or her children "comes to this Court with a momentum for respect lacking when appeal is made to liberties which derive merely from shifting economic arrangements."[11]

Stanley vs Illinois

In a still evolving body of law, the US Supreme Court has indicated that state legislation seeking to curtail parental liberty must provide certain procedural safeguards. One of the landmark cases in the area of procedural due process rights for parents is *Stanley vs Illinois.*[12] In *Stanley,* the court was asked to rule on the constitutionality of an Illinois statute which authorized removal of children from the care of their unwed father without providing him with a hearing regarding his fitness as a parent.

The court first indicated that Stanley's interest as the biological father of children that he had sired and raised was a "cognizable and substantial" one, despite the fact that the parental relationship had never been legitimized. The court also indicated that the children had an important interest. As such, any interference with that interest must be carefully scrutinized under the due process provisions of the Fourteenth Amendment. The court acknowledged that there are no hard and fast rules governing what procedures due process may require under a given set of circumstances, but those requirements must be determined by examining the precise nature of the governmental function involved and the private interest affected.

The court first examined Stanley's interest and indicated that such an interest "undeniably warrants deference and, absent a powerful countervailing interest, protection."

The court then examined the state's interest. It indicated that the state's interest in protecting children from neglectful parents was a legitimate and important one. However, the means utilized (removal of children from unwed fathers without a hearing) would prevent some fit fathers from caring for their children. While the state's interest in establishing prompt, efficacious procedures to achieve its goals was a proper state interest, state convenience in failing to provide Stanley with a hearing was held to violate the due process clause when important family rights were at issue.

Lassiter vs Department
of Social Services

The Supreme Court considered the due process clause of the Fourteenth Amendment again in 1981 in the context of a North Carolina court proceeding which terminated a mother's rights to her child. In *Lassiter vs Department of Social Services,* an indigent mother argued that the failure of the state to provide her with an attorney in these proceedings violated her due process rights. In reviewing the problem, the court indicated the ambiguity and the fluidity of the due process concept and, implicitly, the difficulty of predicting what due process will be required in various child protection proceedings in the future:

> For all its consequences, "due process" has never been, and perhaps can never be, precisely defined. "Unlike some legal rules," this Court has said, due process "is not a technical conception with a fixed content unrelated to time, place and circumstances."
>
> Rather, the phrase expresses the requirement of "fundamental fairness," a requirement whose meaning can be as opaque as its importance is lofty. Applying the Due Process Clause is therefore an uncertain enterprise which must discover what "fundamental fairness" consists of in a particular situation by first considering any relevant precedents and then by assessing the several interests that are at stake.[13] (citations omitted)

The court acknowledged that the mother's interest in parenting her child was a liberty interest constitutionally protected by the due process clause. However, in determining what process was due the mother before her parental rights were terminated, the court analyzed three factors: (1) the nature of the individual interest involved; (2) the risk of an erroneous deprivation of such interest through the procedures used and the probable value, if any, of additional or substitute procedural safeguards to that interest; and (3) the government's interest, including the function involved and the fiscal and administrative burdens that the additional or substitute procedural requirement would entail.

Acknowledging that this is the general formula for determining procedural due process rights when liberty interests are at stake, the court added an additional requirement in cases involving the right to appointed counsel for indigents. Because prior cases had established the principle that an indigent was entitled to appointed counsel only when the indigent would lose his personal freedom, the *Lassiter* court indicated that after the above three factors were weighed, their net weight would then be measured against the presumption that there was no right to appointed counsel unless the indigent might lose his or her personal freedom.

In applying this complex formula to the facts of the case, the court indicated that the mother's interest in the care and custody of her child was an important one and that this importance was heightened because at issue was not just an infringement of the interest but its termination.

Examining the state's interest, the court pointed out that the state's interest in the welfare of the child would lead it to share in the parent's interest in an accurate and just decision. However, the state also had an interest in economical administration. While appointment of counsel for the mother might increase the chances of a just result, the state would also incur additional expense for this service. However, the court concluded that the expense would be minimal relative to the importance of the parental interest at stake.

The court then examined the second factor—the risk of an erroneous decision if no counsel were appointed. The court acknowledged that the issues may be complex, pointing to the difficulties for many parents in understanding, much less refuting, expert medical and psychiatric testimony. The court also indicated that parents in many instances have little education, have difficulty in dealing with life and, at the hearings, are exposed to a distressing and disorienting situation.

Weighing all of these factors against the presumption against the right to appointed counsel, the court held that the determination regarding whether an indigent parent has a constitutional right to appointed counsel in termination proceedings must be decided on a case-by-case basis by the trial judge. In some instances where the risk of error is great, the parental interest strong, and the governmental interest weak, the presumption against appointment would be overcome.

Thus, the trial court in determining whether due process requires the appointment of counsel must in each case analyze such factors as whether expert witnesses would be called, the informality of the proceeding, whether there were particularly difficult points of law involved, whether the state has an attorney, whether criminal charges could be brought against the parent based on the allegations in the petition, the strength of the parental interest (termination vs temporary change in custody), and the capabilities of self-representation by individual parents.

Four judges dissented from the majority opinion. As Justice Blackmun noted in his dissent, the ad hoc review by the courts on a case-by-case basis of whether the presumption is overcome with respect to a particular parent is likely to be extremely burdensome and costly.[14]

Since 33 states and the District of Columbia already provide by statute for the appointment of counsel in parental termination proceedings,[15] the effect of this holding regarding appointed counsel is limited to those states without such statutory provisions.[16] However, the case also has significance beyond the issue of appointed counsel. There are many unresolved issues in abuse and neglect proceedings regarding what procedures are constitutionally mandated. For example, what notice must be given to parents prior to removal of children? May children be removed in emergencies without notice to parents? Is it constitutionally permissible to allow hearsay information in such proceedings?

Santosky vs Kramer

In 1982, the US Supreme Court again addressed procedural due process rights for parents in the context of examining New York's statutory scheme for permanent termination of parental rights.[17] The specific issue addressed was what "standard of proof" should apply in proceedings that would permanently sever parental rights.

The standard of proof concept relates to the degree of confidence the fact finder (the judge or jury, depending on the case) must have in the correctness of his or her factual conclusions. Thus, in criminal cases, because of the severity of the consequences to the defendant who is deprived of liberty if found guilty, constitutional due process requires that the judge or jury be extremely certain that the evidence offered shows the defendant's guilt is established "beyond a reasonable doubt."

In contrast, most civil proceedings impose the more lenient standard of requiring plaintiff to prove his or her case by a "preponderance of the evidence." Applying this standard, the fact finder must simply determine that it is more likely than not (greater than 50% probability) that plaintiff has proved his or her case, eg, that the child was abused. However, in some civil cases, because of the importance of the interest affected, an intermediate standard, that of clear and convincing evidence is applied.

Because New York's statute adopted the "preponderance of the evidence standard" in proceedings to terminate permanently parental rights, the parents in *Santosky vs Kramer* agreed that the statute was unconstitutional. The court agreed with the Santoskys that proceedings which would permanently terminate parental rights constitutionally required that the state prove their case in favor of termination by "clear and convincing" evidence.

While this standard will make it less likely that parents who are able to care properly for their children have their rights permanently terminated, this more stringent standard will also make more difficult the termination of parental rights in cases in which parents are unable to care for their children. As a practical matter, this Supreme Court decision is likely to increase the already lengthy period of time children remain in limbo in foster care.

The case leaves open the question of whether the "clear and convincing" evidence standard will also be required before children are temporarily removed from their parents. Because abuse and neglect commonly occur behind closed doors with only the child (who may be too young or too afraid to talk) and the abuser as witnesses and because these cases frequently involve psychological issues where expert opinions lack absolute certainty, application of the "clear and convincing" standard may provide less protection for the abused or neglected child than the preponderance standard.

Smith vs Organization of Foster Families for Equality and Reform

A 1977 US Supreme Court case raising procedural due process questions relevant for those concerned with child abuse and neglect addressed the issue of what, if any, due process rights foster parents have before children are removed from their care. In *Smith vs Organization of Foster Families for Equality and Reform*,[18] an organization of foster parents who had provided homes for one year or more for foster children sued New York State and New York City officials, alleging, among other things, that the procedures for removing children from foster homes violated the due process clause of the Fourteenth Amendment. In analyzing the matter, the court first asked whether the nature of the interest at stake was within the protection of the due process clause. The foster parents argued that when a child had been in a foster home for a year or more, a psychological tie was created between the child and the foster parents and that this psychological family had a liberty interest entitled to procedural protections under the due process clause.

Reviewing prior cases dealing with due process protection for families, the court stated that traditional biological families have a "liberty" interest worthy of protection under the due process clause. Significantly, however, the court acknowledged that the importance of the family relationship to the individual and to society is not based solely on blood relationship, but stems also "from the emotional attachments that derive from the intimacy of daily association, and from the role it plays in 'promot[ing] a way of life' through the instruction of children."[19] In what may be key language in predicting the court's rulings in future cases in which nonbiological family issues arise, the court acknowledged:

> No one would seriously dispute that a deeply loving and interdependent relationship between an adult and a child in his or her care may exist in the absence of blood relationship. At least where a child has been placed in foster care as an infant, has never known his natural parents, and has remained continuously for several years in the care of the same foster parents, it is natural that the foster family should hold the same place in the emotional life of the foster child, and fulfill the same socializing functions, as a natural family. For this reason, we cannot dismiss the foster family as a mere collection of unrelated individuals.[20] (citations omitted)

However, the court also pointed out legal distinctions between the foster "family" and the traditional biological family. The liberty interest of the traditional family is derived not from state law but "intrinsic human rights as understood by our history and tradition." In contrast, the foster family is a creature of state action in which foster parents and the state have a contractual relationship. Therefore, the court stated that, in determining what liberty interest should be accorded to foster families, it would look to state statutes and contractual arrangements which set forth the rights and responsibilities of the parties.

A second distinction the court made was between the liberty interests of foster families from arbitrary government intervention and those of traditional families. The court noted that procedural protection afforded to traditional families from state intervention does not detract from the substantive liberty of other individuals. However, in the New York statutory scheme, natural parents who voluntarily gave up their child to the state did so with the understanding that the child would be returned within 20 days of notice by the parent in the absence of a court order obtainable only upon compliance with rigorous substantive and procedural standards. The court determined that these parental rights would conflict with providing due process procedural rights to the foster family. Thus, when liberty interests deriving from blood relationship, state law sanction, and basic human right of the natural parents—interests reflected in contracts with foster parent from the outset—conflict with due process rights sought by the foster parent, the court found that the foster parents' liberty interest, to whatever extent it might otherwise exist, would be substantially diminished.

Using the principle of judicial restraint under which the court decides the case on the narrowest ground possible, the Supreme Court refused to rule on whether foster parents had a liberty interest. Assuming for argument's sake that the foster family did have some liberty interest that merited protection, the court examined New York City's and State's procedures for protecting the rights of the foster parents and indicated that the procedures protected whatever liberty rights the foster family had.[21] The court indicated that foster families' rights when children were returned to the natural parents were less than those available when children were transferred to other foster homes.

While the case was decided on very narrow grounds, the court's analysis is useful in indicating the direction in which the court may proceed in the future. For example, the court makes a clear distinction between foster parents whose relationship is formalized by contractual relations with the state and informal situations where a parent may transfer the care of a child to others indefinitely. In an analysis which emphasizes the expectations of the parties, it would appear that, in certain situations, the persons who had assumed responsibility for caring for a child for long periods of time "even in the absence of biological connection or state law recognition" would have liberty interests protected from arbitrary governmental interference in the "family-like associations into which they have freely entered."

The court's failure to reject outright foster parents' claim for liberty interests also indicates some sympathy with the concept of "psychological parents" which is an important issue in abuse and neglect cases in determining appropriate disposition.

SUBSTANTIVE DUE PROCESS

In addition to providing certain procedural safeguards to liberty interests, the Fourteenth Amendment's due process clause has also been interpreted by the courts to afford certain substantive protections to these liberty interests. Thus, in *Meyer vs Nebraska,* the court stated (in declaring unconstitutional legislation prohibiting teaching foreign language to children until they reach the ninth grade despite parental wishes to the contrary): "Liberty may not be interfered with, under the guise of protecting the public interest, by legislative action which is arbitrary or without reasonable relation to some purpose within the competency of the State to effect."[22] Thus, each piece of legislation must have some legitimate purpose and the means sought to achieve the purpose must bear some rational relationship to the end sought.

However, some liberty interests are so important that the courts scrutinize even more closely the constitutionality of the legislation. In these cases, the courts weigh the importance of the state interest against the importance of the liberty interest which is being invaded. Frequently, in such cases, the court requires that the legislation be narrowly drawn to express only the legitimate interest at stake. In addition, the law must serve a "compelling state interest" in order to be held constitutional.[23]

This more stringent test was applied when Ohio, through a city ordinance, sought to intervene to disrupt family life in the 1977 case of *Moore vs City of East Cleveland.*[24] In that case, the ordinance limited occupancy of a dwelling unit to members of a single family. "Family" was defined in such a way as to prevent Mrs. Moore from living in her home with her son and her two grandsons. While the purpose of the ordinance (to prevent overcrowding, minimize traffic and parking congestion, and avoid undue financial burden on the school system) was considered legitimate, the US Supreme Court found the legislation an unconstitutional violation of the family's liberty interest under the due process clause. Recognizing that the family is not beyond regulation, the court nevertheless stated: ". . . when the government intrudes on choices concerning family living arrangements, this Court must examine carefully the importance of the governmental interests advanced and the extent to which they are served by the challenged regulation."[25]

This case, by providing additional substantive due process protection not just to the nuclear family but to the extended family, may have important implications for the dispositional stage of abuse and neglect proceedings. Using a "best interests of the child" standard, state agencies, for various reasons, sometimes place abused and neglected children in foster homes with strangers when relatives are available to provide care. Among the reasons for such placements are that the foster family may have special training or experience in caring for emotionally disturbed children or, in some other way, may provide better care for the child than the "adequate" care available from the relative. The constitutionality of this procedure of placing children with strangers when "fit" relatives are available is an open question.

Although protecting children from abuse and neglect is clearly a "compelling state interest" justifying state invasion of the family's liberty interest, the *Moore* case, with its adoption of this higher constitutional standard in family matters, also leaves unanswered the question of whether state intervention is constitutional in cases in which abuse is "not serious," however severity is defined by current social standards.

Several other cases have also addressed the issue of substantive due process in the context of parental rights. Thus, the court in *Stanley vs Illinois,* in addition to analyzing the procedural due process rights of the father, also implied that Stanley's children could not be removed unless he was found to be an "unfit" father which involves application of substantive due process principles.

In contrast, the unwed father in *Quilloin vs Walcott* [26] was not protected by a substantive due process requirement that he be found "unfit" in order to allow his child to be adopted. In this 1978 case, the natural mother of an 11-year-old boy had consented to his adoption by her husband. The child had lived with the mother and her husband for seven years prior to the filing of the adoption petition. Although the child had occasionally visited his natural father, he had never received regular support from him nor had the natural father ever had, or sought, actual or legal custody of the child.

The Georgia statute whose constitutionality was tested in *Quilloin* provided that children may not be adopted without the consent of his/her legal parents unless the parents are found to be unfit. However, only the mother's consent was required in the case of illegitimate children.

The natural father argued that he should have veto rights over the adoption of his child as did fathers of legitimate children. Unlike *Stanley,* the father in *Quilloin* did receive a hearing on his petition for legitimization which he had filed after the adoption proceedings had been undertaken by the husband of the natural mother. The legitimization petition was denied on the ground that legitimization was not in the "best interests of the child."

The court ruled that applying the "best interest of the child" standard to deny the father the right to prevent his child from being adopted did not violate his substantive due process rights in this case. The court indicated that if a state tried to force the breakup of a natural family over the objections of parents and children without some showing of unfitness, the family's substantive due process rights would be violated, even if the state demonstrated that the breakup would be in the "best interests of the children."

However, applying the "best interest" test to the facts of the case did not violate the father's due process rights where the result would not be to break up the family unit but to give legal recognition to a family unit that had already existed for some time.

Quilloin clarifies substantive due process rights for two ends of the spectrum. (On the one end is the natural family living together where unfitness must be demonstrated to remove children, and on the other end is the unmarried parent who has never lived with the child whose natural mother and the child have long been part of a de facto family unit with another man.) The opinion leaves unclear what substantive rights exist in the natural parent who seeks to regain custody after having left a child for several years with another caretaker with whom the child had developed psychological bonding. Particularly difficult questions arise in those abuse and neglect cases in which the child has been removed from the parent for a long period of time, the parent has obtained therapy and would be capable of appropriately parenting, but the child has developed strong psychological ties to its foster family. Does the fitness standard still apply, or is it overridden by the "best interests of the child" test?

Although the family is protected from arbitrary government intervention by the concept of substantive due process, the family is not beyond regulation. Thus, courts have upheld as constitutional state legislation which prohibits or regulates child labor, even if such labor is in accord with the child's or parent's religious beliefs.[27] Similarly, laws have been upheld which require compulsory vaccinations or other medical treatment.[28] In contrast, state laws which require children to go to public schools (as opposed to private or parochial schools) have been found unconstitutional in violation of parental rights to choose the type of education the child will receive. Similarly, a state law which compelled school attendance for children beyond eighth grade was found unconstitutional as applied to Amish children because the Amish parents' interest in providing their children with informal vocational education was found by the court to be stronger than the state's interest in public education.[29]

Thus, the conflict between the state's interest in protecting the child under the doctrine of parens patriae and the family's right to protection from arbitrary intervention must be resolved on a case-by-case basis. In *Lassiter,* Justice Blackmun acknowledged: "Ours supposedly is a maturing society . . . and our notion of due process is, perhaps, the least frozen concept of our law."[30]

What process is due both substantively and procedurally to parents, children, psychological parents, extended family members, and others in the context of child abuse and neglect proceedings is an evolving and continuing concern in state and federal courts. The cases presented dramatize this struggle.

FEDERAL LEGISLATION: THE CHILD ABUSE
PREVENTION AND TREATMENT ACT

Enacted by Congress in 1974, the Child Abuse Prevention and Treatment Act [31] established the National Center for Child Abuse and Neglect which is now part of the US Department of Health and Human Services. The center is to serve as an information clearinghouse for programs for the prevention, identification, and treatment of child abuse and neglect. It is also required to publish and disseminate an annual summary of recent research on child abuse and neglect; to provide training materials and technical assistance for persons working in the area; to conduct research (or contract for such research) into the causes, prevention, identification, and treatment of child abuse and neglect; and to investigate the national incidence of the problem. The legislation also provides for demonstration programs.

Funds are also authorized to assist states in developing and implementing their child abuse and neglect prevention and treatment programs. In order for a state to qualify for this assistance, it must meet certain legislatively mandated requirements. These include:

1 • state laws to provide immunity from prosecution for persons reporting incidents of abuse or neglect;
2 • provision for reporting of known and suspected incidents of abuse and neglect;
3 • provision for prompt investigation by the state upon receipt of an abuse or neglect report and for taking immediate action to protect the health and welfare of the abused or neglected child and other children in the family when an incident of abuse or neglect is verified;
4 • a demonstration by the state that it has the necessary administrative procedures, trained personnel, training procedures, institutional and other facilities and multidisciplinary programs to deal effectively with child abuse and neglect cases;
5 • provision for methods to preserve the confidentiality of records to protect the rights of the child and his guardian; and
6 • provision for the appointment of a guardian ad litem to represent the child in judicial proceedings involving abuse or neglect.

For purposes of this legislation, the term "child abuse and neglect" is defined as:

> ... the physical or mental injury, sexual abuse or exploitation, negligent treatment, or maltreatment of a child under the age of eighteen,

or the age specified by the child protection law of the State in question, by a person who is responsible for the child's welfare [?] under circumstances which indicate that the child's health or welfare is harmed or threatened thereby, as determined in accordance with regulations prescribed by the Secretary.[32]

Many state laws have been influenced by this federal legislation and its implementing regulations. As of 1978, forty-two states had enacted or amended reporting laws which complied with federal requirements and made them eligible for federal funds for their protective service programs.[33]

STATE REPORTING LAWS

No one is able to assist families with child abuse and neglect problems unless there is an awareness that a problem exists. While some parents voluntarily seek help, many others will refuse to recognize their problems or request assistance.

Concerned with what was felt to be widespread underreporting of child abuse, the Children's Bureau [34] and the American Humane Association [35] in 1963 published model legislation and guidelines for use by the states in drafting statutes that would encourage physicians to report child abuse. Reasons given by physicians for failure to make reports included: fear of civil or criminal liability, concern that reporting would breach the confidential relationship between doctor and patient, reluctance to be perceived as an intermeddler, ignorance of where to report, and belief that, upon receiving reports, agencies would take no action that would benefit the child.[36] By 1966, forty-eight states had enacted some form of legislation to encourage reporting of child abuse.[37]

State reporting laws have gradually evolved to include more categories of mandated reporters, expand the definition of reportable conditions to include neglect as well as abuse, and provide for more comprehensive procedures.

While state laws vary considerably regarding who must file reports, teachers, health professionals, police, and child caseworkers are frequently among those required to report.[38] As of 1977, thirty-six states required social workers to make reports.[39] As of 1978, twenty states required "any person" to report known and suspected child abuse.[40] However, the majority of states authorize but do not require private citizens to file reports.

One of the most difficult problems in child protective law is formulating a definition of child abuse and neglect for purposes of reporting and for purposes of other forms of state intervention. As one commentator has noted:

Listing with precise specificity all those actions that constitute child abuse and neglect raises the possibility of inadvertently excluding dangerous situations that should be included. Generalized definitions risk overbroad applications that include behavior that should not be considered abusive or neglectful. Those who believe that most children and families generally benefit from the child protective process wish to expand the definition. Those less sanguine about the utility of child protective intervention naturally want to restrict the definition.[41]

Broad standards also permit arbitrary and discriminatory application. Thus, what one professional may consider a reportable condition, another may find acceptable child-rearing practice. Biases against lower social classes and minorities are less easily controlled with broader standards.[42]

Nevertheless, most states have adopted relatively broad definitions for reportable conditions, implying a greater concern for child protection (and faith in the effectiveness of state intervention) than for parental autonomy. In addition to the reporting of nonaccidental injuries required by early laws, 42 states require certain professionals to report child neglect, sexual abuse, and emotional abuse.[43] Massachusetts, for example, requires a mandated reporter who

shall have reasonable cause to believe that a child under the age of eighteen years is suffering serious physical or emotional injury resulting from abuse inflicted upon him, including sexual abuse, or from neglect, including malnutrition, or who is determined to be physically dependent upon an addictive drug at birth

to report the condition immediately to the Department of Social Services and to file a written report within 48 hours.[44]

Georgia's reporting laws require reports of any nonaccidental physical injury to the child, apparently without regard to the severity of the harm. However, only injuries inflicted by a parent or caretaker are reportable. Thus, the statute leaves the potential loophole of not protecting children from noncaretaking relatives such as the mother's boyfriend. Georgia also requires reports of children who have been neglected or exploited by a parent or caretaker or who have been sexually assaulted or exploited.[45]

Reporting laws generally require oral reports with subsequent written confirmation. Most states require reports to be made to social service agencies, although some require reports to be made to law enforcement agencies.[46] Some states permit reports to be made to more than one agency, increasing the likelihood of administrative confusion. State laws also vary regarding whether reports are to be made to local agencies or to a central agency.

Regardless of what agency is to receive initial reports, at least 47 states have established central registries for reports received. While these registries are potentially useful for improving diagnoses and case monitoring, measuring agency performance, and providing a data base for research, most registries are understaffed and unable to perform these functions.[47]

The reporting laws attempt to facilitate the reporting of child abuse by eliminating many of the concerns expressed by potential reporters before the enactment of legislation. Thus, all states grant immunity from civil and criminal prosecution to all mandated reporters who act in good faith.[48] This prevents accused parents from successfully suing reporters for libel, slander, defamation, and invasion of privacy. At least 40 states also provide immunity to voluntary reporters who act in good faith.[49] In a majority of states, immunity is expressly extended to permit the reporter to participate in judicial proceedings arising from the report.

The protection against having to disclose certain communications is expressly overridden in the reporting requirements of many state laws. While state laws differ, many establish privileges regarding certain communications (eg, between physician and patient, social worker and client, priest and penitent, psychologist and client, etc). Unless the protected person authorizes disclosure of the communication (ie, the client in cases involving social workers), persons subject to the privilege are prohibited from revealing the content of the communication. Some states provide exceptions in situations in which a crime has been or will be committed. Since many forms of child abuse and neglect are crimes in most states, this exception would facilitate reporting of child abuse. Although a legal mandate to report would take precedence over a previously enacted law creating a privilege, many state reporting laws specifically provide that communications involving child abuse or neglect are exempt from statutorily created privileges.[50]

In at least 39 states, mandated reporters are subject to penalties for failure to make reports.[51] Generally, the penalties are criminal in nature, providing for fines and/or imprisonment from $100 and/or five days in jail to $1000 and/or one year imprisonment. In reality, criminal prosecution is extremely unlikely and a survey of the literature by the authors has revealed no reported cases of prosecution. In a few instances, police have brought alleged violators before magistrates and verbal "warnings" have issued.[52]

Mandated reporters who fail to report have, however, been subject to civil lawsuits for damages arising from their failure to report, since the violation of a statutory duty (eg, mandated reporting) may constitute "negligence per se." Thus, in 1972, a lawsuit was brought in California on behalf of a child against the police, a hospital, and individual doctors for their failure to report suspicious injuries. Because no one reported the beatings, the child was further beaten by his parents and received permanent brain damage. The case was settled for over $500,000.[53]

In another case, in 1976, the California Supreme Court held that a physician's failure to diagnose and report a child abuse case which led to the child being returned home where she incurred permanent physical injury from further abuse constituted both common-law and statutory negligence.[54] If the facts alleged were later proved, the child would be entitled to recover damages from the physician for the injuries she sustained from the subsequent abuse.

While the number of reports has increased after the enactment of reporting laws, awareness of the problems revealed by these reports is only the first step in protecting children. Without trained personnel, funding, and an administrative structure to investigate reports received, reporting will be of little benefit. In fact, many reporting laws were initially enacted without the states' establishing a system for investigation and treatment when reports were received.[55] While some more recent legislation [56] provides for a very comprehensive scheme for investigation and treatment, the effectiveness of legislatively mandated programs will depend in large part on funding.

CIVIL PROCEEDINGS
IN STATE COURTS

Most state laws and administrative procedures provide for and encourage a family's voluntary use of protective services. Thus, protective services are often offered to parents after an investigation corroborates a report received.

However, in cases of serious abuse or neglect or when parents or caretakers fail to accept services voluntarily, court intervention is usually required. All states have both civil and criminal laws dealing with child abuse. The civil system, which is remedial rather than punitive in purpose, frequently uses the state's juvenile or family court as a forum.

Although juvenile courts were established initially to insulate child offenders from the more stringent standards and consequences of adult criminal courts, neglected and dependent children were also included within its jurisdiction. Hearings are generally closed to the public,[57] and the procedures are often more informal than in adult cases. However, recent court decisions regarding constitutional due process rights for parents and children are tending to produce proceedings that are more formal.

The court process is usually initiated by the filing of a petition alleging that the child has been neglected or abused within the meaning of the state law. Depending on the state, petitions may be filed by specified individuals (eg, county attorney, social worker, or probation officer) or in some states by "any person." The petition may be reviewed by the clerk for conformity with statutory requirements.

In order to protect the parents' constitutional rights, a summons is usually sent to them, notifying them of the date of the hearing and of their right to have an attorney present. In a majority of states, the law provides for a hearing regarding temporary custody of the child pending the more formal adjudicatory hearing.[58] In some states, such as Massachusetts,[59] after the petition has been filed, the court appoints a neutral party (frequently a social worker) to investigate the facts of the case and to make a report to the court. In others, the court may rely on its own staff to conduct an investigation, or it may proceed based on the report of the petitioning agency.[60]

The hearing may be divided into two stages. In the adjudicatory stage, evidence is introduced to demonstrate the court's jurisdiction and to determine whether the child has been neglected or abused within the statutory definition. If the petitioner's case is proved, the court will determine the appropriate disposition.

Adjudication

Procedures at child protective hearings vary broadly from state to state. As of 1975, twenty-five states provided for the right to appointed counsel both for the parents and for the child, six states for the parents only, and one state for the child only.[61] Historically, the petitioner, generally a child protective agency, was not represented by counsel. However, as procedures become more formalized and parents have counsel, representation for the petitioner is also becoming more common. In some states, the district attorney prosecutes these cases. In others, state social service agencies use their internal staff or retain private counsel. Jury trials are available in a limited number of states.[62] In some states, judges may appoint referees or masters to hear the case.[63]

As in the area of reporting, one of the most difficult issues in court proceedings to protect children is determining the definition of abuse and neglect for purposes of court intervention. States frequently have differing standards for reportable conditions and for court intervention. For example, Massachusetts, which mandates reports in cases of "serious physical abuse or emotional injury"[64] authorizes any person to file a petition with the court alleging that a child is without:

(a) necessary and proper physical or educational care and discipline or;
(b) is growing up under conditions or circumstances damaging to the child's sound character development or; (c) who lacks proper attention of parent, guardian with care or custody, or custodian or; (d) whose parents, guardian or custodian are unwilling, incompetent or unavailable to provide any such care, discipline or attention . . .[65]

Thus, cases which are not reportable may still be the subject of court action.

As with reporting laws, state laws dealing with court intervention to protect children in civil proceedings generally have opted for broader, less-specific standards in order to protect children rather than for narrowly drafted, detailed standards which would provide greater notice to parents of unacceptable child-rearing practices and which would also favor family autonomy at the expense of excluding some categories of children from protection.

These broad statutes have been attacked as unconstitutionally vague in violation of the due process clause of the Fourteenth Amendment. While courts have frequently narrowed the breadth of these laws through judicial interpretation, challenges to their constitutionality have been largely unsuccessful.[66] Thus, a California court [67] acknowledged that a parent in a dependency proceeding was entitled to due process of law which included notice through the statute of what parenting conduct was unacceptable. The statute in question was unusually vague and provided that a child may be adjudged dependent if he "is in need of proper and effective parental care or control . . . and has no parent or guardian willing to exercise or capable of exercising such care or control. . . ." [68] Nevertheless, the court determined that the statute did provide the parent with fair notice because there were cases which clarified the meaning of "effective parental care or control" to which the parent could have referred.

Faced with a similar attack on the constitutionality of a statute terminating parental rights as unconstitutionally "broad, uncertain and vague," an Oregon court [69] upheld the law's constitutionality, emphasizing the difference in cases which involve only the state and the individual, in contrast with protective cases where a third party, the child, also has an interest. The court stated:

> The procedure here is not the state against the parents. Three parties are involved: the state, the parents and the child. The welfare of the child is the primary consideration of the Juvenile Code of 1959 . . . . That the welfare of the child is the primary purpose does not lead to the conclusion that the rights of the parents are without constitutional protections. This emphasis upon the welfare of the child does imply, however, that . . . the constitutional issue must be examined with the interests of both the child and the parents. What might be unconstitutional if only the parents' rights were involved is constitutional if the statute adopts legitimate and necessary means to protect the child's interests.[70]

Another issue that frequently arose, before the *Santosky* case, in court proceedings involving state intervention to protect children concerned the standard of proof. As discussed in the section on procedural due process, the United States Supreme Court in *Santosky* held that a clear and convincing evidence standard is constitutionally required in cases terminating permanently parental rights. Whether such a standard must be applied in proceedings which fall short of permanent termination remains an open question.

Before the *Santosky* case, many states had specified the standard of proof by statute. One interesting resolution of conflicting interests of parent and child was adopted by the Massachusetts courts. Rejecting the "clear and convincing" evidence standard for fear that it might overly jeopardize the child's welfare and might preclude preventive intervention, the court adopted the preponderance standard but required that the judge prepare detailed findings of fact in child custody cases demonstrating a careful consideration of the evidence.[71]

Massachusetts and other states must now revise their statutes and update their case law to reflect the new *Santosky* mandate, at least with respect to that part of abuse and neglect proceedings that deal with permanent termination of parental rights.

Another perplexing question facing state courts concerns the severity of the harm to the child necessary to justify court intervention. While the vagueness of most state statutes could be interpreted to authorize intervention for relatively minor problems, courts concerned with the constitutional rights of the parents (see due process section) frequently narrow the basis for intervention through decisions. Others may achieve the same result by the court clerk's failure to accept petitions that do not meet certain standards of harm. It is not yet clear to what extent the courts will consider the purpose for intervention in determining the requisite showing of harm. For example, if the petitioner does not want to have a child removed but only wants the parent to agree to meet with a protective service worker once a week to discuss parenting issues, may state intervention be constitutionally justified with a showing of less serious harm to the child than if the petitioner was requesting that the child be removed? The US Supreme Court in *Lassiter* (see due process section) provided by implication some support for this position when it indicated that a higher degree of due process may be required under the Fourteenth Amendment when parental rights were to be terminated than when these rights were infringed in less serious ways. Although some commentators support differing standards of severity of harm depending on the goal of intervention,[72] and others would maintain a single standard,[73] the authors of this chapter are not aware of any court decision which has directly addressed this issue. However, several states have, by statute, adopted additional requirements that must be met before a child is removed from the home.[74] Louisiana, for example, does not authorize removal unless the child's "welfare or the safety and protection of the public cannot . . . be adequately safeguarded without such removal." [75]

Emergency Orders

In cases where the child is in immediate danger of harm or there is a serious likelihood that the parents will flee, there is not time to have a court hearing before removal. The police are authorized in all states to take children into custody on an emergency basis. At least 13 states also authorize child protective agencies to perform this function.[76] Recognizing the constitutional problems and the potential abuse of indiscriminate use of protective custody, states generally limit exercise of this authority to situations in which the child is in imminent danger and there is insufficient time to obtain a court order.

Some states have recently enacted legislation authorizing hospitals to take children into protective custody for 24 hours. The standard for exercising this power is generally not as stringent as that authorizing intervention by protective agencies. For example, New York authorizes the use of the "24-hour hold" when a hospital "believes the facts so warrant."[77]

Because parents have had no opportunity for a hearing before this serious invasion of their rights takes place, it is important, for constitutional reasons, that the exercise of any protective custody authority be subject to court review soon after its use. Many states set a time limit by statute.[78]

Disposition

After a child is adjudicated abused or neglected within the statutory definition of the state law, courts are authorized by statute to make dispositional orders generally using a "best interest of the child" standard.[79] These may include temporary or permanent orders. Children may be removed from the home and transferred to the custody of the state or another agency or individual. The child may be placed in foster care, a group home, residential treatment facility, or hospital. Frequently, children may be permitted to remain at home with a variety of conditions imposed, eg, parents must accept monitoring by protective service worker; attend therapy, parenting programs, or alcoholism counseling; allow a homemaker to provide services, take the child for medical treatment or evaluation; allow the child to attend day care, etc. Juvenile courts, in which many abuse and neglect petitions are heard, are courts of limited jurisdiction. As such, they may not have authority to make orders relative to parents. Thus, if a parent refuses to comply with conditions imposed by these courts, their only recourse may be to remove the child.

Cases frequently continue under the court's jurisdiction for long periods of time before a final decision is made to dismiss the case (because of improvements in the home) or to commit the children permanently to state agencies or other institutions. Once children are placed permanently in the custody of a state agency, the agency generally determines if and when the child will be returned home. Most states have no provision for periodic court review of children in state care.[80] Thus, children are frequently placed in foster care for long periods of time with no permanent planning for their future.

Termination of Parental Rights
for Purposes of Adoption

While children are in the custody of state agencies as a result of abuse or neglect hearings, parents generally continue to retain some rights with respect to their children. These usually include the right to consent to the child's marriage, to visit the child (although this right may be restricted by court or agency determination), and to make major nonemergency medical decisions. In contrast, through termination proceedings parents permanently and irrevocably lose all parental rights.

In at least 12 states, courts are authorized to sever permanently legal ties between parent and child in the dispositional stage of an abuse or neglect hearing.[81] In practice, this occurs rarely at the initial hearing since judges are usually inclined to offer parents an opportunity for rehabilitation.[82]

Many states have special laws dealing with terminating parental rights for purposes of allowing the child to be adopted in situations where the parent refuses to consent voluntarily to the adoption. As of 1975, twenty-three states required separate proceedings from the adjudicatory and dispositional hearings just discussed.[83] In some states, a different court handles termination proceedings. In Massachusetts, for example, abuse and neglect petitions are frequently heard in the juvenile courts, while termination proceedings are heard in the probate courts.[84]

Many of the same issues that arise in abuse and neglect hearings are also raised in termination proceedings: defining the severity of harm to the child justifying termination, procedural rights of the parents, etc. Many states have standards and procedures for terminating parental rights which are different from those established for abuse and neglect hearings.[85]

Appeals

Most states provide by statute for appeals from the adjudicatory and dispositional stages of an abuse or neglect hearing.[86] Decisions terminating parental rights may also be appealed. Generally, the appeals address only questions of law. Appeals courts will not allow attorneys to retry the case. Because the initial trial with frequent continuances may last many months, the whole court process, particularly in cases with appellate review, may leave a child's fate in limbo for several years.

CRIMINAL PROCEEDINGS
IN STATE COURTS

All states have a variety of laws under which adults may be prosecuted for child abuse or neglect. If the parent or other caretaker's action leads to the child's death, the perpetrator may be tried for murder or manslaughter. One of the difficulties in obtaining a murder conviction is the difficulty in proving the intent to kill.

Child abusers may also be prosecuted under a state's criminal laws dealing with assault and battery. However, parents have a right at common law to inflict punishment to discipline their children. Thus, some states authorize prosecution of parents only if the punishment results in permanent injury to the child or is inflicted with malice.[87] Other states permit prosecution for purposefully, negligently, or knowingly using excessive force to punish the child. What force is excessive depends on the facts and circumstances and is left to a jury to determine.[88]

Many states also have specific criminal statutes prohibiting cruelty to children. These include fines and/or imprisonment for sexual abuse, abandonment, torture, impairment of morals, contributing to the delinquency or dependency of a minor or other injuries to children.

Despite numerous criminal laws, parents and caretakers are rarely prosecuted except in cases of death or serious harm to the child.[89] From an evidentiary viewpoint criminal prosecutions are generally more difficult than civil suits because the case must be proved "beyond a reasonable doubt." There are also numerous evidentiary rules in criminal trials which tend to exclude evidence (eg, rules to deter police misconduct and to protect the privacy of communications between spouses). When these more stringent requirements are coupled with the inherent difficulty in many child abuse cases in obtaining witnesses who can testify about what happened to the child behind closed doors in its home, the reluctance of prosecutors to bring criminal actions is more easily understood.

More importantly, however, is the general ineffectiveness of the criminal system for improving the life of the abused or neglected child. Not only does the criminal system fail to provide rehabilitation for the family or services for the child, it frequently will aggravate the situation. Imprisonment of the parent will separate parent and child, while fines are likely to worsen the family's commonly already tenuous financial situation.

CONCLUSION

Court cases involving child abuse and neglect are among the most troubling and interesting. They reflect society's increasing efforts to be protective both of the child's welfare and of the parents' autonomy. Differing local standards and resources affect whether or not a case is brought to court and its disposition. Definitions of abuse and neglect are not easily agreed upon, nor are given facts necessarily interpreted the same way. Society's standards, values, and expectations are likewise not stable or clearly defined. Yet, when severe abuse exists, it is sometimes too late to act. Courts are or should be looked to and should be effective in reducing those instances.

NOTES AND REFERENCES

1. Not all state criminal laws specifically mention child abuse, but, nevertheless, authorize prosecution of persons who intentionally inflict serious physical injury on another.
2. The "common law" is a system of judge-made (as opposed to legislatively enacted) law that has its roots in early English history. It includes a body of legal principles that have evolved through judicial decisions made on a case-by-case basis in which a principle enunciated in a previously decided case serves as a precedent to be followed in later cases dealing with the same issue. The early English colonists brought this common law tradition over to America where it has continued to evolve in each state (except Louisiana which follows the French civil law tradition) as a body of law along with state legislation.
3. *Hewlett vs George,* 68 Miss. 703, 711, 9 So. 885, 887, 1891.
4. Thomas MP: Child abuse and neglect — Part I: Historical overview, legal matrix and social perspectives. *NC Law Rev* 1972;50:293, 304 (hereinafter cited as Thomas).
5. In re Gault, *US Rep* 1967;387:1, 16–18.
6. Ex parte Crouse, *Wharton (Pa State Rep)* 1939;4:9. While this was a delinquency case dealing with whether there should be a jury trial prior to the child's commitment, the language was also applicable to child abuse and neglect cases. See also In re Ferrier, *Ill Rep* 1882;103:367 (child committed to industrial school when parents unfit).
7. Ch. 181, §3 (1882) Mass. Acts and Res. 135, quoted in *Farnham vs Pierce,* Mass Rep 1886;141:203–204.
8. Ch. 325, §5 (1875), Wis. Laws. 633, quoted in *Milwaukee Industrial School vs Supervisors of Milwaukee County, Wis Rep* 1876;40:328, 334–335. See also Thomas, *supra* note 4.
9. Thomas, *supra* note 4 at 315.
10. *Meyer vs Nebraska, US Rep* 1923;262:390, 399.
11. *Stanley vs Illinois, US Rep* 1972;405:645, 650, quoting *Kovacs vs Cooper, US Rep* 1949;336:77, 95 (Frankfurter, J., concurring).

12. *Id.*
13. *Lassiter vs Department of Social Services, US Supreme Court Rep, Lawyers' Ed 2d* June 1, 1981;68:640, 648.
14. *Id.* at 665.
15. *Id.* at 654.
16. Even in states where there is no such provision, state courts may interpret state constitutions in such a way as to require appointed counsel.
17. *US Law Week* March 23, 1982;50:4333.
18. *US Rep* 1977;431:816.
19. *Id.* at 844.
20. *Id.*
21. Both the city and the state provided for notice and preremoval and postremoval administrative hearings for foster parents before a child was transferred to other foster parents except in emergencies. This procedure was not available if the child was to be returned to natural parents. However, if a child had been in foster care for 18 months, the foster parent could petition the court to review the status of the child, requesting that the court order that the child remain in foster care or be freed for adoption. This procedure provided a circuitous avenue for foster parents to attempt to predict in advance and prevent agency transfers of children to their natural parents.
22. *US Rep* 1923; 262:390, 399–400.
23. See *Roe vs Wade, US Rep* 1973; 410:113.
24. *US Rep* 1977; 431:494.
25. *Id.* at 499 (plurality opinion) referring to *Poe vs Ullman, US Rep* 1977; 367:497, 554 (Harlan, J., dissenting).
26. *US Rep* 1978; 434:246.
27. *Prince vs Massachusetts, US Rep* 1944; 321:158 (child prohibited from selling *Watchtower* magazines for Jehovah's Witnesses).
28. *Id.* citing *People vs Pierson, NY Rep* 1903; 176:201.
29. *Wisconsin vs Yoder, US Rep* 1972; 406:205.
30. Blackmun J: (dissenting opinion) in *Lassiter, supra* note 13 at 669, quoting *Trop vs Dulles, US Rep* 1958; 356:86, 101, and *Griffin vs Illinois, US Rep* 1956; 351:12, 20 (concurring opinion).
31. Pub L No. 93-247 (Jan. 31, 1974), *US Code* 42:5101 et seq.; Pub L 93-644 (Jan. 4, 1975); Pub L 95-266 (Apr 24, 1978).
32. US Code 42:5102.
33. Besharov DJ: The legal aspects of reporting known and suspected child abuse and neglect. *Villanova Law Rev* 1978; 23:458, 460 (hereinafter cited as Besharov).
34. US Children's Bureau, *The Abused Child—Principles and Suggested Language for Legislation on Reporting of the Physically Abused Child,* 1963.
35. American Humane Society, Children's Division: *Guidelines for Legislation to Protect the Battered Child,* 1963.
36. Paulsen MG: The legal framework for child protection. *Columbia Law Rev* 1966; 66:679, 710 (hereinafter cited as Paulsen). Many of these beliefs continued to result in underreporting even after reporting statutes were enacted. See Besharov, *supra* note 33 at 465.
37. See Paulsen, *supra* note 36 at 711.
38. Besharov, *supra* note 33 at 467–468.
39. Dahl G: Trends in Child Abuse and Neglect Reporting Statutes 5 (publication of Education Commission for the States, Rep No 95, 1977) cited in Besharov, *supra* note 33 at 468.

256

40. Besharov, *supra* note 33 at 469.
41. *Id.* at 474.
42. For criticisms of broad standards, see Mnookin RH: Child-custody adjudication: Judicial functions in the face of indeterminacy. *Law Contemp Prob* 1975; 39:226 (hereinafter cited as Mnookin) and Wald MS: State intervention on behalf of 'neglected' children. Standards for removal of children from their homes, monitoring the status of children in foster care and termination of parental rights. *Stanford Law Rev* 1976; 28:625 (hereinafter cited as Wald).
43. Besharov, *supra* note 33 at 472.
44. *Massachusetts General Laws* c. 119, §51A.
45. Code of Georgia Annotated §74–111.
46. Besharov, *supra* note 33 at 492.
47. *Id.* at 501–508.
48. *Id.* at 475.
49. *Id.*
50. *Id.* at 477.
51. *Id.* at 480.
52. *Id.* at 480–481.
53. *Time,* November 20, 1972, p 74, cited in Besharov, p 481.
54. *Landeros vs Flood, California Rep 3d* 1976; 17:399.
55. Besharov, *supra* note 33 at 496–497.
56. New York Society Service Law §424 (McKinney, 1976) cited in Besharov, *supra* note 33 at 497–498.
57. Katz SN, Howe RW, McGrath M: Child neglect laws in America, *Family Law Q* Spring 1975; 9:1, 60 (hereinafter cited as Katz).
58. *Id.* at 61.
59. *Massachusetts General Laws,* c. 119 §§21, 24.
60. Katz, *supra* note 57 at 59.
61. Wald, *supra* note 42 at 630.
62. See Katz, *supra* note 57 at 59.
63. *Id.* at 60.
64. See reference and text at note 44.
65. *Massachusetts General Laws* c. 119, §24.
66. In re J.T., *California App Rep 3d* 1974;40:633 (1st Dist. 1974); *State vs McMaster, Oregon Rep* 1971;259:291 (termination of parental rights case); Custody of a Minor, *Mass. Advance Sheets* 1979;2099. See also Barron A: 1975 (unpublished background papers) cited in Katz SN, Ambrosino L, McGrath M, et al: Legal research on child abuse and neglect: Past and future. *Family Law Q* 1977;11:151, 173, note 100 (hereinafter cited as Katz SN).
67. In re J.T., *supra* note 66.
68. *California Welfare and Institutions Code* §600(a).
69. *State vs McMaster, supra* note 66.
70. *Id.* at 296.
71. Custody of a Minor, *Mass. Advance Sheets* 1979;1117, 1127–1129.
72. Bourne R, Newberger E: Family autonomy or coercive intervention? Ambiguity and conflict in the proposed standards for child abuse and neglect, *Boston Univ Law Rev* 1977;57:707.
73. Wald, *supra* note 42.
74. Mnookin, *supra* note 42 at 244, note 84.
75. Louisiana Revised Statutes Annotated §13:1580 (3) (supp. 1975) cited in Mnookin, *supra* note 42 at 243, note 81.

76. Paulsen, *supra* note 36 at 686, note 54.
77. *Id.* at 687.
78. Katz SN, *supra* note 66 at 155, note 10.
79. Mnookin, *supra* note 42 at 244, note 84.
80. Wald, *supra* note 42 at 632–633.
81. *Id.* at 633–634.
82. *Id.* at 634.
83. Katz, *supra* note 57 at 67.
84. *Massachusetts General Laws* c. 119, §24; c. 210, §3.
85. Katz, *supra* note 57 at 58–63, 66–70.
86. Katz, *supra* note 57 at 10–11.
87. Besharov, *supra* note 33 at 485.
88. *New York Social Service Law* §417(2) (McKinney 1976).
89. Besharov, *supra* note 33 at 487, note 174.

13 The Social Worker as Researcher: Adding to the Knowledge Base of Protective Services

Lillian Pike Cain

In the 20 years since Kempe [1] coined the term "battered child syndrome," thousands of articles, books, and research projects have focused on every conceivable aspect of child abuse and neglect.* A majority of these published studies and funded projects are by physicians, lawyers, and other non-social-work professionals. Social work, however, is the profession most intimately involved with the abusing parents and at-risk children. A social worker is frequently the one who interviews the family when abuse is suspected, intervenes when removal of child is indicated, and works with the family when treatment is recommended.

While social workers in state and private protective service agencies have entire caseloads of abusing/neglecting parents, other social workers in hospitals, mental health clinics, and family agencies may have considerable contact with such parents and their at-risk children. Thus the

---

*Throughout this chapter the term "child abuse" will include physical and emotional abuse, physical and emotional neglect, and sexual abuse.

social worker is in a unique position to integrate clinical practice with carefully designed research studies. Despite the voluminous body of abuse literature, there is an ever-increasing need for social workers doing protective service work to document what they do, to relate theory to practice, and to test new methods of intervention.

In discussing the role of the social worker as researcher, this chapter will describe the types of research most commonly undertaken by social work clinicians and will highlight some of the most relevant published studies. It is hoped that once the seemingly awesome mystique of research has been attacked, the reader will realize the joy of combining research with clinical practice.

LITERATURE SOURCES

Prior to undertaking any research venture, one should first become acquainted with what others have already studied, written, and thought. Familiarity with the child abuse and neglect literature will enable potential researchers to compare their ideas with others, to replicate studies when indicated, and to examine results critically in light of their own clinical practice.

The best single source of information on identification, prevention, and treatment of child abuse is the National Center on Child Abuse and Neglect, created by the Child Abuse Prevention and Treatment Act of 1974 (P.L. 93-247). Its clearinghouse, which will remain after the national center has closed, has a computerized data base of about 10,000 documents, research projects, programs, audiovisual materials, and state laws concerning abuse and neglect. Libraries in major cities throughout the country have terminals capable of access to this data base; specific literature searches can usually be made for a fee.

The several editions of *Child Abuse and Neglect Research: Projects and Publications,* [2] which were produced by the national center between 1976 and 1979, are an excellent resource. The project listings briefly describe the purpose, methodology, research results, and ensuing publications, if any; the principal investigator's name and address enable researchers sharing common interests and concerns to communicate with each other. The publication abstracts, cross-indexed by author and topic, comprehensively cover a wide range of journals and books.

A number of annotated bibliographies dealing exclusively with abuse and neglect have been published. Kalisch[3] has summarized over 2000 abuse and neglect articles published largely in the 1960s and 1970s. Her topical grouping of articles, detailed subject and author indexes, comprehensive summaries, and complete citations make this an invaluable reference. A similar book by Wells[4] cites almost 2500 abuse and neglect publications published between 1962 and 1976. Her summaries are briefer and, in several instances, merely give the citation.

The most current social work literature source is *Social Work Research and Abstracts,* a professional quarterly that each year abstracts about a thousand articles on different topics published in social work and related fields. Each abstract briefly summarizes the article and cites the original source (author, title, journal issue), so that researchers can locate those that most relate to their own interests. The annual subject index quickly identifies those relating to child abuse. Under the earlier title *Abstracts for Social Workers,* this journal dates back to 1965, thus providing an extensive index to topics and journals especially relevant to social workers.

Social work journals publish a range of abuse articles dealing with practice, programs, research, and theory. A content analysis of four journals commonly read by social workers *(Child Welfare, Journal of Orthopsychiatry, Social Casework,* and *Social Work)* yielded a total of 27 child-abuse articles over a three-year period. While a heavy emphasis on practice and program issues reflected the profession's practice orientation, the paucity of research-oriented articles raised questions concerning the interrelationship of practice and research. It was noted that although social workers play a key role in evaluating and treating abusing parents and their children, observations made by social workers are seldom used as a base for research studies.[5]

IDENTIFICATION AND PREDICTION: WHO ARE THE ABUSERS?

Clinical research often starts with a question to be answered, a problem to be solved. How can potentially abusive parents be more readily identified? What works in treatment and what does not? How can a community program to help abused children be evaluated? What has happened to abusing parents and their children after services have been terminated?

A social worker in a busy emergency ward or prenatal clinic might especially be interested in identifying those factors that are associated with abuse in order to alert staff to be more aware of such families and to refer them to social service. Although all 50 states now have laws mandating certain professionals to report to the proper authorities suspected cases of child abuse or neglect, physicians have been especially reluctant to do so.[6] Past studies have not identified any consistent predictors of abuse. Alcoholism, poverty, adolescent parenthood, social class, prematurity, low birth weight, ordinal position, and personality of parent and child are but some of the factors that have been associated with abuse by some studies but not by others.

In studying the families of newborns admitted to a regional intensive care nursery, Hunter et al[7] identified social isolation, a generational cycle of abuse and neglect, marital problems, inadequate child care arrangements, and congenital defects as being associated with later reported abuse. Earlier, Helfer,[8] in discussing the etiology of child abuse, has suggested three possible causes: (1) parent's potential for abuse, resulting from poor mothering in parent's own childhood, isolation from those who could offer help, marital problems, and unrealistic expectations of the child; (2) unusual child who provokes the parent to abuse; and (3) family crises that upset interfamilial relationships and thereby cause the potential abuser to lose control.

In looking at those factors associated with abuse within an AFDC-recipient population, Wolock and Horowitz[9] identified large family size; material, social, and physical deprivation in parent's own childhood; and more difficult material circumstances and more social isolation than other welfare families. In what is probably the largest epidemiological study of child abuse ever attempted, Gil[10] examined a nationwide survey of almost 13,000 incidents of child abuse reported to central registries in 1967 and 1968 and a more comprehensive sample of 1380 of these children. He concluded, as he has in several subsequent writings, that violence against children is culturally determined and that society is responsible for the most serious forms of abuse.

Noting that environmental stress, poverty, and certain parental personality characteristics are among the causes of abuse, Egeland and Brunnquell[11] asked why some parents abuse their children while other parents, who display the same personality characteristics and are under equal stress, do not. In a critical analysis of the psychopathological theory of child abuse, Gelles[12] noted that most of the studies are inconsistent and contradictory, fail to test any hypothesis, lack a truly representative sample of abusers, and fail to pinpoint the personality traits that characterize the pathology. He stated that among the 19 traits identified by investigators as typical of abusive parents, there was agreement by two or more authors on only four traits.

Claiming that relatively few studies have attempted to predict families at high risk for parenting disorders, Altemeier et al[13] interviewed 1400 expectant mothers concerning attitudes, experiences, and knowledge of child-rearing; the authors concluded that their own instrument needed refinement since the great majority of mothers identified as high risk had not demonstrated evidence of parenting disorders at the end of the first year. They quite wisely cautioned against reacting negatively to parents identified as high risk since such responses might actually increase the risk through diminished self-esteem and increased stress.

Social service departments seldom have the luxury of interviewing every family that utilizes an emergency ward or pediatric clinic. Thus, a department might wish to develop some method of identifying those families at risk for abuse and neglect. The social work researcher might begin by examining the records of all families referred for protective work within a three- or six-month period. Utilizing a checklist based upon those predictors cited in some of the studies, the worker might note which characteristics are found in the referred families. Since medical records serve multiple purposes, the data will not be uniform for all families; completeness and accuracy of the records will vary. One record might note that the parent is a 16-year-old adolescent, for example, whereas another might fail to give the mother's age. The researcher has no way of knowing whether the second record did not record the mother's age because she was not an adolescent, she refused to give her age, or the person recording the information felt that age was unimportant. Examining the records will, however, give the researcher an idea of which variables to include in the proposed project and thus will be a valuable, preliminary step to a more controlled study.

In doing a study, the social worker must ask one researchable question. For example, what are the factors associated with child abuse? The question as posed is too broad and thus has to be narrowed down to a manageable undertaking. The worker should decide whether to focus on socioeconomic factors, family dynamics, personality of parents, or any other selected aspects. From the chosen perspective, the social worker might decide to develop a checklist of various factors associated with abuse and see to what extent those factors are present in families referred to social service as potentially[14] abusive. In undertaking such a study, the worker must first define the population. Would everyone coming into the emergency ward be screened? Or would only those parents bringing in a child under age 6? Would such a study be limited to families referred for protective services, or would it include all families so that the at-risk and not-at-risk families might be compared? The design of the study, and thus the results, are greatly influenced by the manner in which the population is defined.

A clearly defined time limit should be placed upon any study. For example, the worker might decide to collect data on all cases seen within a one-month period. If a study continues for too long a period, it is more difficult to maintain the enthusiasm and cooperation of others. Also, in a clearly defined time framework it is easier to survey all designated cases and be certain that some do not "fall between the cracks."

When undertaking a study, it is imperative to secure the cooperation of those in other disciplines who might be involved with the designated population. The worker should take the time to explain the purpose of the study, to discuss any necessary time commitments from others, and to clarify how the referrals will be made. If others agree with the purpose and importance of the proposed study, it is much more likely that the data will be collected.

The most important aspect of any study has to do with the subjects. Any parent who will be participating in the research must be told the purpose of the study, give informed consent, and have the right to refuse to participate without jeopardizing his or her ongoing care by the hospital or agency. Most hospitals and agencies have a human studies committee that reviews all proposed studies and sees that the patient's rights are protected. Committees may differ, however, on how they interpret a patient's rights; record searches, for example, may or may not require a patient's permission.

TREATMENT OF PARENT AND CHILD: WHAT WORKS?

Social workers in hospital, agency, and clinic settings who offer casework and group work services to abusing parents and their children should begin to ask: what works? what types of intervention modify behavior and prevent future abuse? In reviewing various treatment modalities, Shorkey[14] noted that individual and group psychotherapy, family therapy, transactional analysis, behavior therapy, and humanistic–behavioral group therapy can all be used in treating abusing parents. Although the theoretical concepts and the techniques differed in the reviewed reports, each program of intervention combined therapy with other supportive social services to reduce stress and improve clients' daily life satisfaction, required vigorous activity by worker to maintain clients in treatment, and reported positive changes in most of the clients. None of the studies, however, utilized a control group or a single-subject design to evaluate the effectiveness of the treatment; most reported on small numbers of clients served. Shorkey noted that empirical research on the relative effectiveness of promising treatment procedures is almost nonexistent because few communities have systematic or extensive treatment programs.

The social work literature relating to the treatment of abusive families is more apt to offer practice-oriented rather than a research-based analysis of outcome. In recognizing the amount of stress generated by abusive families, Elkind et al[15] recommended a team approach with administrative decisions being handled by a clinician who does not have direct service responsibilities. Holmes et al[16] suggested that social workers often feel outrage toward abusive parents and thus resist treating them; the authors' vignettes illustrated such casework issues as developing a treatment relationship with the parents, understanding parental rage, modifying parents' behavior, and evaluating the necessity for placement. Moore,[17] in agreeing that social workers are often resistant to working with abusing parents, felt that the worker must be persistent and assume the role of the caring, but firm, parent. Ebeling[18] suggested that by developing greater sensitivity to transference and countertransference issues, the worker will be better able to cope with the many strains of protective work. Hill[19] noted that a medical staff may react with anger and a sense of helplessness to a permanently injured child and pressure the social worker to try to make everything right immediately.

In discussing the initial interview with an abusive parent, Goldberg[20] offered concrete advice, such as where to place the chair, how much eye contact is appropriate, how to elicit information, and when to remain silent. Anderson[21] noted that such listening skills as empathy, self-awareness, nonjudgmental listening, and feedback are a crucial aspect of therapeutic intervention with abusive parents. Roth[22] gave step-by-step suggestions on how to differentiate three kinds of abuse (situational, behavior-patterned, and chronic) and then identified what he believed were four typical characteristics of abusing parents (low self-esteem, fear of rejection, isolation, and low frustration tolerance). He noted that the abused child is often in need of treatment, a finding that Cohn,[23] Kinard,[24,25] and others have likewise discussed.

Much can be learned from descriptions of treatment cases. A social worker who feels confident enough of his or her own clinical skills to be able to write up treatment failure as well as success can, by relating case material to theory and relevant literature, make a significant contribution to the field. Social workers who daily must cope with resistant, often hostile, clients will be comforted to know what others have tried, what has both worked and not worked.

The single-subject design, a quasiexperimental procedure in which a single case serves as its own control, is one way in which changes in a client's behavior can be assessed and evaluated.[26] The social worker notes which aspect of a client's behavior is to be changed, decides on some appropriate treatment intervention, and then later again measures the behavior and plots the change on a graph. Although this method has been criticized as having too narrow a focus for most social workers,[27] the careful delineation of treatment goals and interventions can both enhance practice and help generate research findings.[28]

Relatively little has appeared in the literature on what works in treating abusing parents. A modification of Kiresuk and Sherman's[29] goal attainment scale might be used by the social work clinician interested in evaluating treatment. Under an adaptation of this scale, the worker and client together would set two or three easily measured treatment goals that might be realistically achieved within an agreed-on time period. For example, possible treatment goals in working with abusive parents might be getting them to keep regularly scheduled clinic appointments, encouraging a mother to send a child to school each day, and helping a father to stop severe spankings. At the end of the time period the worker and the mother or father together would assess whether the parent had achieved the desired goals and then would set new ones.

In order to quantify the treatment outcome, the researcher would develop a numerically weighted scale. A score of 3 would be given each goal that was completely attained, a score of 2 for partial attainment, a score of 1 for nonattainment, and a score of 0 for behavior that had deteriorated. Thus if all clinic appointments within the time period had been kept, the parent would be scored a 3 on this one goal. If most appointments had been kept, a score of 2 would be recorded, and if most appointments had been canceled, a score of 1 would be recorded. If the parent had formerly called to cancel appointments but during this time period had neither called nor kept any appointments, then the behavior would have actually deteriorated and a 0 would be recorded.

By keeping a record over several months of treatment, the worker will be able to note what progress, if any, has been made; by noting what types of intervention were primarily used with a client, the worker may begin to discover what works best. The worker may notice, for example, that scores improve when support is used with the mother but that the father's scores improve when confrontation is used. Since the goals are individually set, based upon a psychosocial diagnostic assessment, treatment outcome can be evaluated on a case-by-case basis.

A social work researcher might also, over a period of time, decide to do a comparison study of treatment outcome of abusive families and families referred for other reasons, such as marital problems. By utilizing the modified goal attainment scale for all of the families in treatment, the worker can begin to determine whether abusive families make more or less progress. The set goals, however, should be easily measured and scored. While one of the objectives of treatment, for example, may be to help a mother become less depressed, there is no simple way to measure the internal experience of depression. The goal, therefore, should be stated in behavioral terms. If the mother's depression is manifested by her staying in bed most of the day, a goal might be for her to get out of bed and dressed each morning. For another mother whose depression is expressed through long periods of crying, the goal might be to go through an entire day without weeping.

In doing a comparison study and in using this goal scale with all clients, the worker might assign a score of 0 for "deterioration," a 1 for "stayed the same," a 2 for "some improvement," and a score of 3 for "much improvement." Because each client is measured from a baseline of individual current functioning, a mother who has to work on controlling violent physical outbursts against her child will have as much chance of showing improvement as a mother who has to concentrate on not having so many arguments with her husband.

The modified goal attainment scale allows the researcher to measure an individual client's progress over a period of time and to compare different groups of clients. It not only begins to answer the question of what works in treatment, but it encourages the clinician to think through with a client what the treatment is all about.

EVALUATING NEW PROGRAMS

The social caseworker who develops innovative programs to treat abusing parents should also plan ways to evaluate the effectiveness of these programs. A systematic data collection system should be built into a program from the beginning. The program's goals should be clearly understood and some means developed to evaluate the extent to which these goals have been achieved, perhaps through well-designed instruments that will collect uniform information from both staff and client participants.

Many agencies have introduced innovative treatment programs as an adjunct to their traditional casework services. Several programs utilize volunteers to increase community awareness or to work directly with clients as mentors.[30,31] One Massachusetts private protective agency, in a departure from its former reliance just on casework, developed a variety of groups, including a mothers' discussion group that focused on intrapsychic dynamics; an adolescent group for clients' children that used both activities and discussion; and a task-oriented group where therapy was linked to successful completion of a task.[32]

A Nebraska family service agency developed a positive parenting program for abusing parents that met two hours weekly for socialization, education, and small group discussion.[33] The goals included attitudinal changes, social support, and increased knowledge about parenting. Utilizing a quasiexperimental design, the researchers tested the participants and a comparable nonparticipating group at the beginning and then four months later. Significant change was noted in the participants but not in the control group. Burch and Mohr[33] concluded that there is a need for more careful evaluation of the trend toward short-term, problem-solving therapy since longer-term treatment may be needed to consolidate treatment gains. Although questions might be raised about the research methodology, the article is significant because it gives a more complete description of the research procedure than many social work publications.

The Boston-based Parents' Center Project for the Study and Prevention of Child Abuse nicely combined service, training, and research with therapeutic day care for preschool children and a weekly discussion group for their parents.[34] While gains in ego functioning and age-appropriate development were noted among the children, there was no correlation between the progress made by a child and the parents. Even when parental progress was negligible, however, the concurrent treatment of the parents probably kept children in the project.

Because the problems of child abuse are often firmly entrenched and of long standing, several interesting residential programs have been developed for entire families. The Park Hospital for Children in Oxford, England, through a multidisciplinary approach, provided short-term residential services for parents and children in order to establish basic trust in all family members, protect the children from further abuse, and prevent the parents from committing a crime.[35] A similar residential program in Missouri offered a supervised, supportive environment with each family having a two-room apartment with private bath but sharing communal kitchen, dining, and recreational areas. Day care was offered the children while adults participated in counseling, life skills, and educational classes.[36]

A family service agency in California developed a therapeutic weekend camp program for abusive parents, with child care for the children. During a series of weekends, totaling more than 120 hours, traditional psychotherapy and family life education were offered along with music, art, recreation, and practical classes in nutrition and budgeting. A blend of social casework, behavior modification, humanistic psychology, and education was used in emphasizing self-esteem, self-gratification, mutual sharing, and empowerment or taking responsibility for one's own life.[37]

In offering any new program, it is most important to evaluate what has gone well and in which areas improvements might be made. An essential ingredient of any group or residential services for abusive parents would be a systematic program evaluation, with parents having an opportunity to express what has been most helpful and in which areas improvements need to be made.

The social work clinician who undertakes groups for at-risk families might prepare a brief questionnaire that could be used with successive groups. Sociodemographic data, such as parents' educational level, family income, and number of children, will provide a description of the group as a whole and some basis on which to interpret the results. If sensitive questions, such as income, are categorized (under $5000, $5000–8000, over $8000), parents will be more likely to check off the appropriate response than if they are asked outright, "What is your income?"

A simple rating scale might be developed in which participants rated from excellent to poor a number of items pertaining to the group's activities and desired goals. If several groups were offered throughout the year, the clinician might decide to offer one group for mothers only, one for fathers only, and one for mothers and fathers together. Comparing the ratings from the different groups may reveal that one type of group works better than another. The social worker should be most cautious, however, in considering the rating scale results as definitive without taking into account the fact that the individual groups might differ in ways that would bias the results. (If the mothers, for example, were attending the group voluntarily while the fathers were sentenced to attend by a judge, the extent of group satisfaction obviously might vary considerably.)

In evaluating treatment outcome, the clinical researcher may decide to offer only some abusive parents an opportunity to participate in a therapy group; those not offered a group could serve as a control. Similar data, such as sociodemographic, attitudes toward child-rearing, and extent of abuse toward the child, might be collected from both participants and nonparticipants at the beginning and conclusion of the group. Comparing the before and after results of the two groups will give some indication of treatment outcome. Again, however, the clinician cannot assume that differences are attributable to group therapy. Were the two groups the same at the beginning? What other experiences did individual members have during the group's time period that might have changed the outcome? (Appearing in court on an abuse issue, having one's child placed in foster care, or severe illness, for example, might have a far greater impact than therapy upon the parent's functioning.)

Social work research is often criticized for lack of a control group. Ethical concerns, however, may prevent an agency or hospital from denying patients treatment simply because of a research design. If lack of staff creates a waiting list, those parents awaiting a group may serve as a control if their characteristics are similar to group participants. The researcher will want to assess, however, to what extent feelings generated from being on a waiting list have affected the responses.

FOLLOW-UP STUDIES:
WHAT HAPPENS TO ABUSIVE FAMILIES?

A hospital or agency that has treated abusive families may wonder what has happened following termination. Have treatment gains been maintained? Were families generally satisfied with the services? Is there a need to reach out to these families at some later date?

Most of the follow-up studies with at-risk parents and children are medically oriented and look at the extent to which children are rehospitalized or more seriously injured. Thus in a five-year follow-up of

54 children treated for injuries at the University of Rochester Medical Center, Friedman and Morse[38] found that children suspected of originally being abused or neglected were more apt to suffer subsequent high-risk injuries than did children from the suspected accident group. In contrast, in a follow-up study of 17 abused children and a similar group of accident victims, Elmer[39] found little difference between the two groups; both sets of families displayed violent behavior and were equally disorganized and drug dependent.

Follow-up studies of therapy with abusive parents present several problems. Abuse and neglect are sensitive issues, often shrouded in secrecy. Parents may experience more guilt and shame and be less inclined to discuss intervention than would a parent being seen for depression or marital problems. The family's right to privacy may mean that the parents could be contacted for a follow-up interview a month after treatment ended but not a year later.

At the time of termination the social worker might ask abusive parents how they would feel about being contacted at some time in the future. A release might be signed indicating whether the parents are willing to be seen again, under what circumstances, and by whom. Many families might welcome a follow-up phone call from the therapist whom they had seen for several months but would resent a similar call from a stranger. Even though the parents sign a release, any subsequent refusal to participate must be respected.

Even when parents initially agree to being contacted later, the rate of attrition is apt to be high. Abusive families may move frequently and thus be lost to follow-up. Medical care may be fragmented and scattered among a dozen different hospitals, clinics, and agencies and thus make impossible any research into subsequent treatment. If a child has been removed from the home, the parent may continue to feel angry and refuse to have anything further to do with an agency or social worker.

Because a follow-up study does present so many problems, record reviews are a common way of ascertaining what has happened to at-risk families. By examining the medical record for a period of several months or years, a worker will be able to determine the extent of a family's continued contact with the hospital. As previously noted, however, ordinary medical records are apt to be incomplete; the abused child's record may have greater gaps and inconsistencies because of the family's tendency to seek out several caretakers in many different settings.

The social work clinician may also do follow-up studies through mailed questionnaires, phone contacts, in-person interviews, or even a combination of all three. Each method presents certain problems.

Mailed questionnaires often yield the poorest response. Families move, and the post office no longer forwards letters beyond a certain time limit. Unless subsequent mailings are sent, the researcher often has no way of knowing whether a follow-up survey that is not returned was ever received, was misplaced, or whether the parent refused to participate. Mailed questionnaires should be brief, easily understood, and preferably precoded; if a parent only has to check boxes, the chances of completion are greater than if long, involved responses must be written out.

Telephone interviews are biased against those with no phones or unlisted numbers. Parents who are contacted, however, are often likely to participate since they have a certain amount of anonymity and can either answer the questions then or arrange for a later time. If a follow-up is conducted by phone, as much thought should be given to the type of data collected and the phrasing of the questions as is done in a structured in-person interview.

In undertaking any study, but especially when conducting in-person follow-up interviews, great care should be taken to collect only data that relates to the basic research question. Gathering extra information "in case it is needed in the future" will result in long interviews that confuse and possibly frighten the parents. The questionnaire should be carefully constructed in clear, simple language; the wording of the questions, the order in which they are asked, and the lead-ins or brief explanations as to why a particular question is being asked are all important and affect the responses.

A follow-up study has great potential to help social workers better understand the process of treatment and how families really felt about their contacts with the agency or hospital. Once some distance has been placed between the therapist and family, parents may be more able to evaluate their experiences objectively and to share in a research interview some of their feelings about the therapeutic intervention.

CONCLUSIONS

The merging of research and clinical practice, once successfully undertaken, will become a life-long adventure, adding a deeper dimension to the social worker's efforts to treat abusive families. After the first research project has been completed, the worker may wish to undertake more complicated studies. A number of excellent research sources are available.

Wechsler et al,[40] in a clearly written text, discuss how to choose a research problem, design a study, select a sample, gather data, and analyze the results. Over a dozen articles, largely by social workers, nicely complement the text and illustrate the relevance of research to social work practice.

Two texts used in many schools of social work, Selltiz et al,[41] and

Bailey,[42] are comprehensive references; despite a certain amount of overlapping, they are both invaluable to the novice researcher. Weiss's[43] succinct text and Struening and Guttentag's[44] more exhaustive anthology are helpful for those interested in program evaluations.

Much social work research today is computerized. Although numerous computer languages and programs exist, the Statistical Package for the Social Sciences (SPSS) is one of the most relevant for social workers. Although programming the data requires specialized training and is best left to an expert, the SPSS primer by Nie et al[45] is essential for an understanding of the computer printouts; the exhaustive complexity of the text, unfortunately, makes it difficult for the social worker who has no basic computer background.

Before undertaking a research project, an agency or hospital may wish to hire a social work research consultant to advise on the study design and sample selection; the consultant will later be invaluable in suggesting how to analyze the data and in helping to interpret the findings. Local schools of social work are often excellent resources for such consultants.

The social work clinician who has intimate knowledge of how to identify and treat abusive parents and who initiates innovative programs for at-risk families is the ideal person to undertake research that will add to the knowledge base of protective services. Unless the clinician, either alone or in collaboration with a social work researcher, investigates the causes of abuse and outcomes of treatment, the practice of social work will never attain its full professional potential to help abusing parents and their children.

REFERENCES

1. Kempe CH, Silverman FN, Steele BF, et al: The battered child syndrome. *JAMA* 1962;181:17–24.
2. US Department of Health, Education and Welfare: *Child Abuse and Neglect Research: Projects and Publications.* DHEW Publication (OHDS) 79-30248, Washington, DC, 1979.
3. Kalisch BJ: *Child Abuse and Neglect: An Annotated Bibliography.* Westport, Greenwood Press, 1978.
4. Wells DP: *Child Abuse: An Annotated Bibliography.* Metuchen, NJ, The Scarecrow Press, 1980.
5. Cain LP, Klerman LV: What do social workers read about child abuse? *Child Welfare* 1979;58:13–24.
6. Cain LP: Child abuse: Historical precedent and legal ramifications. *Health Social Work* 1980;5:61–67.
7. Hunter RS, Kilstrom N, Kraybill, EN, et al: Antecedents of child abuse and neglect in premature infants: A prospective study in a newborn intensive care unit. *Pediatrics* 1978;61:629–635.
8. Helfer RD: The etiology of child abuse. *Pediatrics* 1973;51:777–779.

9. Wolock I, Horowitz B: Child maltreatment and material deprivation among AFDC-recipient families. *Social Serv Rev* 1979;53:175–194.
10. Gil DG: *Violence Against Children.* Cambridge, Harvard University Press, 1970.
11. Egeland B, Brunnquell D: An at-risk approach to the study of child abuse: Some preliminary findings. *J Am Acad Child Psychiatry* 1979;18:219–235.
12. Gelles RJ: Child abuse as psychopathology: A sociological critique and reformulation. *Am J Orthopsychiatry* 1973;43:611–621.
13. Altemeier WA, Vietze PM, Sherrod K, et al: Prediction of child maltreatment during pregnancy. *J Am Acad Child Psychiatry* 1979;18:205–218.
14. Shorkey CT: A review of methods used in the treatment of abusing parents. *Social Casework* 1979;60:360–367.
15. Elkind JS, Berson A, Edwin D: Current realities haunting advocates of abused children. *Social Casework* 1977;58:527–531.
16. Holmes SA, Barnhart C, Cantoni L, et al: Working with the parent in child abuse cases. *Social Casework* 1975;56:3–12.
17. Moore JG: Yo-yo children — victims of matrimonial violence. *Child Welfare* 1975;54:557–566.
18. Ebeling NB: Preventing strains and stresses in protective services, in Ebeling NB, Hill DA (eds): *Child Abuse: Intervention and Treatment.* Acton, Massachusetts, Publishing Sciences Group, 1975, pp 47–51.
19. Hill DA: Emotional reactions to child abuse within a hospital setting, in Ebeling NB, Hill DA (eds): *Child Abuse: Intervention and Treatment.* Acton, Massachusetts, Publishing Sciences Group, 1975, pp 37–40.
20. Goldberg G: Breaking the communication barrier: The initial interview with an abusing parent. *Child Welfare* 1975;54:274–282.
21. Anderson G: Enhancing listening skills for work with abusing parents. *Social Casework* 1979;60:602–608.
22. Roth F: A practice regimen for diagnosis and treatment of child abuse. *Child Welfare* April 1975;54:268–273.
23. Cohn AH: An evaluation of three demonstration child abuse and neglect treatment programs. *J Am Acad Child Psychiatry* 1979;18:283–291.
24. Kinard EM: Emotional development in physically abused children. *Am J Orthopsychiatry* 1980;50:686–696.
25. Kinard EM: Mental health needs of abused children. *Child Welfare* 1980;59:451–462.
26. Hersen M, Barlow DH: *Single Case Experimental Designs: Strategies for Studying Behavior Change.* New York, Pergamon Press, 1976.
27. Ruckdeschel RA, Farris BE: Assessing practice: A critical look at the single-case design. *Social Casework* 1981;62:413–419.
28. Nelsen JC: Issues in single-subject research for nonbehaviorists. *Social Work Res Abstr* 1981;17:31–37.
29. Kiresuk TJ, Sherman RE: Goal attainment scaling: A general method for evaluating comprehensive community mental health programs. *Community Mental Health J* 1968;4:443–453.
30. Rosenstein PJ: Family outreach: A program for the prevention of child neglect and abuse. *Child Welfare* 1978;57:519–525.
31. Withey V, Anderson R, Lauderdale M: Volunteers as mentors for abusing parents: A natural helping relationship. *Child Welfare* 1980;59:637–644.
32. Wayne J, Ebeling NB, Avery NC: Differential groupwork in a protective agency. *Child Welfare* 1976;55:581–591.
33. Burch G, Mohr V: Evaluating a child abuse intervention program. *Social Casework* 1980;61:90–99.

34. Galdston R: Preventing the abuse of children: The Parents' Center Project for the study and prevention of child abuse. *Am J Orthopsychiatry* 1975;45: 372–381.
35. Roberts J, Lynch M: The treatment of abused children and their families. *Social Work Today* 1977;8:10–12.
36. Wood PE: Residential treatment for families of maltreated children. *Child Welfare* 1981;60:105–108.
37. Oppenheimer A: Triumph over trauma in the treatment of child abuse. *Social Casework* 1978;59:352–358.
38. Friedman SB, Morse CW: Child abuse: A five-year follow-up of early case finding in the emergency department. *Pediatrics* 1974;54:404–410.
39. Elmer E: A follow-up study of traumatized children. *Pediatrics* 1977;59: 273–279.
40. Wechsler H, Reinherz HZ, Dobbin DD: *Social Work Research in the Human Services,* ed. 2. New York, Human Sciences Press, 1981.
41. Selltiz C, Wrightsman LS, Cook SW: *Research Methods in Social Relations,* 3rd Ed. New York, Holt, Rinehart and Winston, 1976.
42. Bailey KD: *Methods of Social Research.* New York, The Free Press, 1978.
43. Weiss CH: *Evaluation Research Methods for Assessing Program Effectiveness.* Englewood Cliffs, NJ, Prentice-Hall Inc, 1972.
44. Struening EL, Guttentag M: *Handbook of Evaluation Research.* Beverly Hills, Sage Publications, 1975.
45. Nie NH, Hull C, Jenkins JG, et al: *SPSS: Statistical Package for the Social Sciences,* 2nd Ed. New York, McGraw-Hill, 1975.

14 Preventing Child Abuse and Neglect: Issues and Problems

Stephen Antler

During the past two decades, professionals and the public have been repeatedly informed of the extent to which child abuse and neglect are serious social problems.[1,2] During this period, the National Center on Child Abuse and Neglect was established, new legislation was passed in every state to improve legal procedures, reporting systems were developed, and child protective services were expanded dramatically. Nonetheless, the floodtide of abuse reports continued unabated. While our knowledge of the conditions which foster abuse and neglect have increased, few preventive measures have emerged which are designed to encourage an improved family life or to alter the social conditions or institutions that provide a fertile environment for the neglect and abuse of children.[3]

The reason for this inability to seriously address the issue of prevention is, in part, a result of our national failure to develop programs which direct their attention toward changing the conditions under which children are likely to be harmed or to recognize the intimate relationship between contemporary economic and social conditions affecting families and the problem of maltreatment.[4] There is sufficient evidence available to conclude that a significant and continuing link exists between child abuse and neglect and low income.[5] While not all low-income families engage in neglectful or abusive behavior, the severe stress that poverty creates reduces the quality of family life and makes it more likely that families will be unable to provide a reasonable environment for their children by reason of the extreme financial and environmental insults which they must endure.[6,7]

During the past few years researchers have established that approximately 750,000 children are reported to child protective agencies annually for abuse or neglect.[8] Child abuse reports, although significantly smaller in number than those for neglect, are clearly more dramatic and receive greater public attention. Indeed, although in the public's perception abuse appears to be a significant cause of child mortality, in fact only about 700–1500 children are known to die annually; a much larger number are severely injured. In comparison, some 50,000 children are killed annually in automobile-related accidents. Despite the continuing rise in child abuse reports, several studies have concluded that the incidence of abuse and neglect is many times larger than the reported incidence.[9,10] Indeed, as new problems such as sexual exploitation and institutional abuse are investigated, it is likely that the total of maltreated children will rise to levels many times the reported number.[11]

Despite the attention directed toward research, publicity, and reporting, rarely have the personnel and service resources been available to adequately treat growing caseloads.[3] As a consequence, marginal or less serious cases are often unserved or referred while scarce resources are targeted to potentially serious situations. Prevention, or even intensive service to help children remain within their own families, is effectively limited by a critical shortage of resources. Indeed, where service is available, it tends to emphasize provision of substitute care since federal funding formulas in the past placed few limits on foster care services.

In a similar vein, changes in the structure of the family (eg, the growth of single-parent families resulting from divorce or out-of-wedlock births, increases in teen-age parenthood, and the rise in two-worker families) suggest the extent to which families with children are under greater stress than in previous generations. Despite dramatic changes in family structure and composition, no new public programs have been developed to provide supports for family life. By simply addressing the dramatic and politically popular issue of direct intervention in cases of child abuse and neglect, the larger question of the appropriate mix of public social welfare programs and social services for families in transition is disregarded.

The perspective taken in this paper assumes that improvements in the prevention of abuse and neglect cannot be realized without simultaneously addressing, in some measure, more general social conditions affecting modern families. These conditions include poverty, unemployment, and poor health, and they also encompass a variety of new problems affecting contemporary families arising out of changed values and altered family forms. While the promotion of a reasonable material environment for families is an important component of a preventive program, prevention in child welfare must also involve the elaboration of a system of services that responds to the new problems that changed family styles create for family life. These services, which are commonly available in other advanced societies, include options for child care for working and single parents, educational and counseling services, as well as outreach programs that assist families in finding their way through the maze of public or private social programs.[12]

It shall be argued in this chapter that a program offering such comprehensive services, one that goes beyond the treatment of families with histories of abuse or neglect or of families deemed most prone to maltreat their children, must be recognized as the cornerstone of a realistic preventive approach. In the first section of the chapter, I will analyze some of the historical, ideological, political, and cultural factors which inform present-day policies regarding prevention; in the second section I will suggest that this amalgam of diverse elements, most of them following a public health concept of prevention, forms an inadequate basis for formulating social welfare policy. An alternative model for conceptualizing the problem of deterrence and prevention will be outlined.

CULTURAL BAGGAGE OF PREVENTION: HISTORICAL BACKGROUND

The concept of prevention in social services derives from models that, not surprisingly, evolved from the field of public health. Indeed, it was early public health advocates who provided the first and most durable outlines of governmental responsibility for public health as their investigations frequently led to the determination that large-scale sanitary programs, achievable only through governmental action, were necessary for protection against disease.

The establishment of preventive health programs is by no means a modern development. The ancient Hebrews developed elaborate codes to discriminate between what should be eaten and what should be avoided. Although often of ritual significance, the rules frequently had a sound basis in health. Ancient Romans recognized the relationship between pure water, cleanliness, and health and built an expensive and elaborate system of aqueducts designed to bring water from mountains 60 miles away. However, modern concerns with public health are most directly traceable to the appalling, crowded, unhealthy tenement conditions of the 19th century into which the poor of industrial England were increasingly crowded.

It was apparent even to the most ardent laissez-faire ideologue of the 19th century that commerce could not continue in a virulent environment in which reasonable health could not be maintained. As early as 1834, Edwin Chadwick, in a report entitled an "Inquiry into the Sanitary Condition of the Laboring Population of Great Britain," documented that filth and overcrowding were directly related to poor health.[13]

Chadwick was not only important in the development of public health. He was subsequently secretary to the Poor Law Commission which led to the reforms of poor law procedure and ultimately became an outspoken advocate for environmental measures designed to improve health among the poor and the working class. His use of data to support reform made him an effective and innovative advocate whose methods were to influence generations of reformers.

In the United States, less industrialized than England and with a smaller population of aged and dependent poor people, the issue of prevention in public health did not become salient until serious epidemics, attributable primarily to environmental causes, began to afflict overgrown and underserviced American cities on a regular basis.[14] New York, for example, assaulted by devastating cholera epidemics on three occasions between 1832 and 1867, finally overcame its ignorance of the disease, prejudices against the poor, and social darwinist ideology to recognize the importance of developing political institutions and the engineering capability to guarantee a supply of pure water and effective garbage collection and sewage disposal, the basic elements of maintaining public health and avoiding large-scale plagues.[14]

Indeed it was largely social darwinism in concert with poor law ideology and practice imported from England, with its Elizabethan emphasis on the deterrence of dependency rather than promotion of human welfare, that impeded early programs to protect public health.[15] Supported by a strong calvinist tradition and galvanized by the quasiscientific ideas of social darwinism, American public institutions designed to improve health seemed to contradict the notion of "survival of the fittest" and were vigorously questioned by early social service theorists.[16] Josephine Shaw Lowell, for example, a founder of the Charity Organization Society (COS) and a dedicated social darwinist, saw the society's mission as the prevention of indiscriminate giving and the application of scientific methods to determine need.[16] Above all Lowell and the COS vehemently opposed publicly supported action on behalf of the poor on the grounds that public action had a corrosive effect on individuals and would create a new class of paupers.

By the late 19th century, however, American cities were confronting a new problem: the management of large numbers of immigrant children whose parents had either died or abandoned them as well as a growing problem of family dependency aggravated by the frequent boom-and-bust cycles of an undisciplined economy. Many of the conditions confronting contemporary social welfare were first defined by the 19th century: unemployment, ignorance, poverty, bastardy, abandonment, alcoholism, and illness were rife among the immigrant and poorer classes but were again largely seen as a problem of individuals. Through the efforts of progressive reformers such as Jane Addams, Florence Kelly, Jacob Riis, Sophinisba Breckinridge, Julia Lathrop, and others, social welfare objectives were broadened to include social reform as well as individual rehabilitation. Basing their program on enlightened self-interest as well as a passion for social justice, they were, consciously or not, framing a preventive social program that emphasized the social components of individual problems.

The ideas of progressive reformers were the foundation of subsequent social welfare developments that placed increasing responsibility upon the federal government for the elaboration of a variety of social programs that, although without a comprehensive plan, ultimately provided the outlines of the modern welfare state after 1932.

The passage of the Social Security Act in 1935 and its subsequent amendments through many administrations expanded on an implicit, largely unacknowledged commitment to provide for basic material needs for all. Furthermore, the founders of the program sought to improve human welfare by building a modest but significant redistributive effort into the benefits program.

Continuing in the tradition of poor law, however, most public social programs of the postwar period were directed at the material conditions of individuals while families remained a peripheral concern of the public sector. In the 1950s and thereafter new interest in families emerged as a result of the increasing incidence of divorce and teen-age pregnancy as well as rises in the rate of juvenile delinquency — all problems associated with what some called a decline in the family.

Moreover, the growing suspicion that at least some programs, such as aid for dependent children, contributed to family break-up by limiting eligibility to single women with children led to a reassessment of the role of public programs directed toward families of the poor. With the passage of amendments to the Social Security Act in 1957, 1963, and 1968, a transition was made whereby federal aid to the states for the provision of social services to individuals and families was to become a permanent feature of American social welfare. Additional social legislation directed at runaway youth, family planning, and child abuse and other forms of domestic violence further redefined the federal role in relation to families and created an increasingly close relationship between the judicial and social service systems.

Ideological and Political Issues

Further development of social programs and social services directed at families has been constrained for several reasons. First, modern American government has viewed family life as essentially outside its scope, competence, or interest. Indeed, the first, albeit reluctant and inconclusive White House Conference on Families was not held until 1980, although a White House Conference on Children, which affirmed the importance of family life, was held as early as 1909 and regularly thereafter. Public-sector assistance has been limited to occasions when family deviance or disorder spill over into the community and become a matter of social concern; in practice this means that the poor are most often the subjects of public intervention.[4,5] Second, even when family private matters such as child maltreatment develop into social problems for the community, government ordinarily acts through provision of cosmetic, underfunded programs with numerous roadblocks to hinder and limit social service intervention.[3] Third, aside from the crisis episodes that tend to trigger intervention from the public sector, most so-called preventive services and programs are focused on deterring future antisocial behaviors. When eligibility for a day care program, for example, is conditioned by the existence of neglect, it is a leap of the imagination to describe this as prevention.

Nineteenth century ideas about the role of the state in relation to families have little bearing on 20th century conditions. Productive and commercial arrangements have contributed to changes in values that have altered the contours of individual and family relationships with the larger world and have shifted the texture of family and neighborly intercourse. If families and communities were ever as self-sufficient as many nostalgic analyses would have us believe, there is certainly a convincing body of contemporary evidence that they no longer have the same personal, familial, and social resources available when problems occur. Laslett,[17] Keniston,[18] Lasch,[19] Featherstone,[20] and others have documented with dismaying detail the extent to which changes in contemporary families create greater and more complex internal and external pressures which require extensive community amenities to assist families in fulfilling their responsibilities.

Families as Private Matters—The Role of Government

In law and custom families occupy a special status in regard to the state. The early English concept that a "man's home is his castle" has been an important guiding principle in the evolution of policies toward families. Once viewed as "a little commonwealth," independent family government has traditionally been a primary vehicle for moral education and social control.[21] Thus government intervention has been restricted only to those situations where families are unable to carry out their primary responsibilities for child care, economic support, and moral development. Indeed, the primary, explicit role that the state has occupied in relationship to families until relatively recently has been to register and regulate marriage and divorce and to act as a referee in situations where economic or parenting relationships between family members require adjustment due to the dissolution of marital arrangements through death, divorce, or desertion.

In recent years, as new family styles and family structures have emerged and as the incidence of divorce has risen, the courts have played an increasingly significant role in disciplining families, requiring them to participate in social services, and in regulating new family arrangements.[22] Thus, child custody has increasingly become a subject for negotiation as judges have permitted joint custody arrangements and recognized the importance of fathering as well as mothering.[20] Increasingly, the courts have been called upon to regulate the child-rearing arrangements of homosexuals, disabled persons, interracial couples, and unmarried parents or parents-to-be (eg, a lower court recently ruled on the rights of unmarried mothers to abort the fetus in the face of opposition by the alleged father).

In addition, the public sector has, of late, provided increased support for intervention through social welfare institutions in situations where families engage in family violence: child abuse and neglect, institutional abuse, spouse maltreatment, and elder abuse are all growing problems for the courts. Perhaps the most recent, critical arena of family intervention concerns the regulation and control of reproduction outside of marriage. Over a million teen-age girls become pregnant annually and many require material assistance as well as counseling and legal protection.

Recent legislative and judicial developments portend increasingly severe limitations upon abortion, particularly for teen-agers unable to obtain parental approval. While the ostensible purpose of this new policy to require parental concurrence with teen-age abortion is to involve the family more directly in the decisions of minor children, it seems clear that a secondary objective is to discourage abortion where possible. Teen-age mothers have thus been unwittingly and cruelly drawn into larger ideological and political debates in which, ironically, conservatives are demanding more governmental restrictions on private decisions while espousing an ideology that stresses a reduction in government regulation.

Nonetheless, as one consequence of the ideological limitations placed upon family interventions, the public as well as the private sector tends to target limited resources for the deployment of services designed to offer therapy and advice rather than for basic family income and social supports.[23] The residual approach, often described as the safety-net or life-line model thus dominates American social welfare, limiting public services primarily to the poor.

Prevention and the Politics of Social Services

American inability to construct policies designed to provide a coherent framework for family supports has encouraged and sustained the development of numerous limited-purpose programs designed to intervene in a variety of social problems or to support a network of services such as those in the child welfare area. A secondary consequence of the incremental proliferation of programs and services has been to split professional and lay constituencies and to pit them against one another as they compete for resources and power. Often, as in the case of child abuse and neglect, the political influence of the individuals or groups that "discover" the problem is also identified with specific types of intervention.[1]

Thus, in the protective field, these characteristics of the legislative process have led to several curious anomalies, many of which are supported and nurtured by the helping professions. For example, although most observers have concluded that serious mental illness is not usually associated with child neglect, mental health interventions are most often the most available form of service.[24] Conversely, while individual and family stress associated with economic deprivation, family break-up, or other environmental factors are frequently associated with abuse and neglect, these problems have received little programmatic attention.[5] The literature and practice of the protective field continue to emphasize individual case treatment strategies, neglecting the provision of broader social programs that provide positive approaches to family development.[23]

It would be shortsighted, however, to claim that social services for families and children are limited in their development simply as a result of legislative and professional shortcomings. American attitudes about the role of the state play a significant role in shaping social services and in constraining their purposes. The notion of limited state responsibility and power spills over into social welfare programming, effectively limiting consideration of more comprehensive policies for families designed to support family life. Indeed, it is fair to say that, although we have begun to take note of the more general changes occurring in families, we have not yet begun to provide services designed to minimize the stress these changes usually produce.

DETERRENCE AND PREVENTION: ALTERNATIVE MODELS

Prevention of child abuse and neglect focuses on intervention within families presenting a history of family problems and should properly be classified as secondary prevention. Since child protection is associated with the possibility of court involvement and the risk of separating children from the family, what is described as prevention within the field may be experienced as coercion by the client. In this sense, the dictionary definition of deterrence provides a guide: "to keep a person from doing something through fear, anxiety, or doubt." That elements of fear and coercion exist in relationships between agencies and clients requires little documentation. While explicit coercion is not always a part of the relationship between a client and a worker, the family is continually aware that court action and removal of a child is a possibility and that the worker has the power to influence the decision.[3] Moreover, it is not in the client's power to terminate the relationship; that power remains with the agency. Coercive interventions need not be heavy-handed, nor are they necessarily unhelpful. However, such intervention can only apply to families already in serious trouble. Therefore, they cannot be construed as preventive, except in the most limited sense. To provide preventive programs, services must be developed that have more universal applicability and are offered prior to determination of family problems. It is to this issue that we now turn.

Prevention and Family Policies: Contemporary Dilemmas

While the public health model of prevention is ordinarily thought to be synonymous with prevention in social services and child welfare, its misapplication, as previously shown, may often cloud rather than illuminate the child welfare services question. The public health model of primary prevention defines health as the absence of disease, although there are strong currents within public health which embrace a broader and more comprehensive definition. The World Health Organization, for example, has defined health as "not merely the absence of disease or infirmity, but as a state of complete physical, mental and social well-being."[13.]

Social welfare formulations seem to demand concepts which are more global than the essentially clinical concerns of public health. Public health interests center around limiting contagion by controlling the passage of disease-bearing entities from one susceptible organism to another or, secondarily, to altering individual life-styles or environmental factors known to contribute to disease. Reliance on these models in resolving child welfare problems often leads to "victim blaming": placing the emphasis of intervention on changes in individuals rather than alterations in the social environment.

A more useful framework for preventive social service and social welfare planning may be elucidated through an analysis of social services focusing on the values underlying service provision, the conditions under which services are delivered, and the population factors determining eligibility. The prevailing ideology of social services in the United States, which has been restated by the Reagan administration, holds that most social services are essentially residual in nature; that is, they are operated under the assumption that the forces of the normal marketplace provide for the needs of most individuals and families and that the public sector should only come into play temporarily as a "safety net" at the point of personal or familial breakdown. Normally functioning families are viewed as largely self-sufficient and capable of selecting, purchasing, and utilizing services through their own personal and economic resources.

An alternative framework, described as the institutional concept, is more accepted in other advanced nations than in the United States and emanates from a radically different perception: that within the context of the problems of normative family life social services are required which should be available to all as a matter of public interest and responsibility.[23]

In the United States, public opinion accepts the necessity for certain services as institutional features of social life. For example, libraries, public sanitation measures, elementary and secondary schools and, in some areas of the country, community colleges and universities are seen as continuing public responsibilities available to all residents regardless of ability to pay. Similarly the Social Security program recognizes the special needs of the elderly, disabled, and certain widows with young children. In other advanced Western nations, national health insurance, family allowances, and child development services are seen as normal features of government provision. The universal availability of services and benefits under the institutional model, as well as its emphasis on the development of supportive–facilitative programs, contrasts with the bias which heavily emphasizes case services provided to those exhibiting aberrant social behavior.

Although an institutional framework for the delivery of services to families allows wider latitude for innovation than the residual approach, which carries with it the opprobrium of the state as "night watchman," the more regularized and freely available services of an institutional system are still, to some extent, reactive to society as it is evolving rather than as it can be.[25] The universal and nonstigmatizing features of institutional services or social utilities, as Kahn[23] has described them, encourage the elaboration of supportive and supplemental family services such as day care, national health insurance, and other ordinary services normally utilized by families. However, some analysts have suggested that these services focus on reacting to social changes through service provisions rather than promoting new or more just behaviors within the context of a changing society.

Certainly in the United States, there is great hostility to the idea of using government programs or laws to promote social changes. Yet that is precisely what the Voting Rights Act of 1965 sought to accomplish in the area of racial relations and what the Economic Opportunity Act of 1963 sought to do for the poor. It is hardly accidental that, subsequent to passage of these landmark acts, there was a rapid reduction in commitment to them. Nonetheless they stand as examples of the kinds of actions available to government under appropriate conditions.

Some other nations have fewer problems with the notion of an activist government seeking to promote new behavior through social legislation. Sweden, for example, has sought to abolish corporal punishment of children (see Appendix). All Swedish programs for families have, as their goal, reduction in sexual inequality and the promotion of shared marital roles.[26] By law, paid child care leaves are available to all families. Perinatal health care is available to all through the national health program in order to ensure family health, and family income programs provide generous assistance.

Can policies such as these be described as preventive? Or is prevention merely an outgrowth of a larger, more conscious, and far-reaching policy that seeks to shape the direction of society by promoting specific social values through family programs? In this sense, the Swedes have forsworn "accidental" policy, and, with the tools and knowledge presently available, seek to promote policies having known and agreed upon purposes that will shape the future of the nation.[26]

To speculate about prevention in the American context is both challenging and disillusioning precisely because our political institutions and government policy are moving away from a comprehensive, institutionally based preventive system and in the direction of a 19th century view of more limited public responsibility and a social darwinist conception of the poor.

The family policy model Sweden has adopted is undoubtedly more far-reaching than is immediately practicable in the United States. Our more heterogeneous, complex society has markedly different political traditions, a larger and more diverse population, and radically different values and ideologies. Nonetheless the changes that are occurring within American families, as well as the increasing stresses experienced by many in their child-rearing activities, require an altered perspective on the relationship between families and government. It is through a new commitment which promotes helping families as a legitimate and important core of public activity that prevention of child maltreatment can be considered.

The current administration has, in a few months' time, engineered a massive redistribution of federal budget priorities, thereby placing a moratorium on the consideration of new ideas for expansion and development of social welfare in America. More importantly for the longer term, a new and more private-sector-oriented ideology, traveling under the labels of supply-side economics and neoconservatism, has sufficient credence to slow if not to reverse the flow of liberal and progressive ideas that have endorsed the expansion of public responsibility for families.

Although the liberal perspective in government rarely ventured beyond support for deterrent programs targeted to specific social problems, it at least provided an environment and a philosophical context for consideration of creative alternatives for providing help. The new ideological conservatism, however, while not necessarily inhumane, seeks to narrow the focus of governmental responsibility and to target government priorities toward defense and the economy. In defining government responsibility for social welfare as a minimum program for the truly needy (a group as yet undefined), the new ideologues have reduced contemporary policy debates to sloganizing by right and left, even as budgetary priorities develop that are at variance with the commitment to maintain a "safety net." Until these ideas of government responsibility have been assessed by the public, there seems little opportunity for discussion of alternatives that are more responsive to changes in contemporary family life.

CONCLUSION

The prevention of child abuse and neglect will remain an illusory and distant goal without a thorough reconsideration of the social policies that guide societal priorities. A decade ago, Daniel Patrick Moynihan,[27] in criticizing the headlong rush to create new programs during the 1960s, observed that the pressure to generate programs without agreement and understanding of larger policy objectives was inherently wasteful. Moynihan's perception can be applied to contemporary child protective efforts with disturbing ease. New, often experimental programs have been created, yet there has been no public discussion of comprehensive policies toward children and families. Although the need for child welfare service seems to be increasing at a rapid rate, there has been little discussion of the underlying causes that may contribute to family problems.

Child welfare programs, indeed virtually all social service programs, are thus trapped in a continuing cycle of crisis intervention. Limited social welfare interventions have been dominated by poor law concepts of personal fault and social darwinist ideas of the role of the state. Social services and social welfare professionals in defining their own tasks have tended to rely too heavily on public health concepts of prevention and have been unable to win approval for a broader model of social service. Nevertheless, there are numerous frameworks developed over the past two decades which provide models of the types of policies and programs that can offer the potential to frame a preventive approach whose components touch upon the central needs of all families for support in their child-rearing activities.

A Program for Prevention

In this chapter, it has been argued that prevention of child abuse must involve a shift in basic approaches to the welfare of children as well as in priorities of the child welfare system. First among these is a national policy providing opportunities for poor families to attain a reasonable standard of living. Poor families are subject to far more stress than those of higher income, a self-evident proposition that hardly bears discussion. Many of the poor are single mothers, a group sometimes dubbed the "new poor" since these women are disproportionately represented among the destitute. Without money and without the relief that can be afforded by a second caretaking person, these mothers are especially disadvantaged. However, improvement of the economic circumstances of poor families does not suggest simple improvements in public assistance benefits. Rather, it does reflect a need for synchronizing family income, employment, and child care policies that make work feasible for those willing and able to accept jobs or education but also provides reasonable income for those unable to work. Similarly, family allowance schemes such as those in France, Sweden, Canada, New Zealand, and other nations recognize the economic hardships which many families experience, particularly in the earlier years of the family child-rearing cycle when income needs are increased and earnings tend to be at their lowest. These policies in which social benefits are linked to family size have not been demonstrated to decrease the work ethic or to provide incentives for excessively large families.

In addition, a basic component of a preventive program requires attention to the needs of families for relief from child care as well as the needs of young children for social and educational experiences well before entry into grade school. A variety of flexible options for children and their families should be available on a sliding fee basis. Child care programs, however, need to adapt to the unique needs of two-worker and single-parent families as well as those of "traditional" families with one working partner. Moreover, not all families needing day care programs are interested in congregate care; many would prefer family care either with relatives or neighbors. Segregation of abused, neglected, or special children should be avoided for the same reasons that now guide the policy of mainstreaming in public education—in order to avoid the problem of stigma and lowered expectations placed upon these children and their families.

A national program offering child care to all families needing or wanting such care would enable mothers to pursue employment or training or simply obtain needed time off while providing a wholesome, developmentally sound, program for children. A system of community-based programs and facilities could provide opportunities for assisting parents who needed help in fulfilling their parental obligations as well as providing an early warning system for children and their families requiring more intensive or specialized help. If such a program sounds unrealistic and visionary, let us recall that the nation was on the verge of providing the beginnings of such a program in the early 1970s through the Child and Family Services Act sponsored by Senator Mondale and others. Unfortunately, the program, which embodied a broad national commitment to child welfare, was vetoed by then President Nixon on the grounds that it would promote "communal styles of child-rearing."

The third component of a preventive policy involves the implementation of a national health care program that at a minimum is designed to provide a full range of perinatal health services. The optimum program, which is probably further in the future than more limited versions, would involve a health program designed to provide universal access for all to the health system. However, more limited programs designed to provide care through pregnancy and early childhood could not only reduce stress among families, but would also have significant impact upon the incidence of birth defects, maternal and infant mortality, and retardation.

While these three programmatic components would have a significant impact on family life, there is still another issue that seems more elusive than the problems which can be addressed through direct program intervention: the general incidence of violence in American society. David Gil[9] has described the use of violence as endemic in the United States and has claimed that domestic violence will not be reduced until we have a clearer understanding of its relationship to the violent character of American society. Gil claims that radical economic and political changes are required, involving changes in both government and the economic system if violence is to be reduced.

Other researchers have concluded, after extensive surveys, that violence is commonplace in families, affecting perhaps 10% of all families per year.[28] Thus, societal aggression frames the child abuse question as well as the causes of other forms of domestic violence. If we are unable to address questions surrounding the more general acceptance of violence in American life, significant reductions in child abuse may prove more elusive than we now suspect and will hinder the movement toward prevention.

Strategic Questions for the 1980s

Within the political context of the 1980s, it is well to ask how new programs for families might receive political support. Are there any new constituencies concerned about family issues that can swing the tide away from its conservative direction and encourage new initiatives? Without constituencies which see their immediate interests linked to broader government programs despite the higher taxes these may well entail, there seems little likelihood that the ideological currents of the past decade will be reversed.

The answer to this, I believe, may develop from an understanding of the changes in families that have taken place over the past two decades as well as with new ideological movements among women which represent a nascent political force of great power. In combination with other constituencies that have benefited from government social welfare programs, a new force might emerge that sees family life and social welfare as inextricably intertwined.

The women's movement, for example, while currently lacking a forceful voice in the political process, is rapidly growing in size, sophistication, and credibility. New currents within the women's movement are concerned about the possibilities of family life within the context of feminist concerns about equality, independence, and career. Recent public service cutbacks have caused many feminists to become more self-consciously political about the relationships between social programs and new possibilities for women. The seemingly powerful impact of the Moral Majority in shaping the dialogue on family issues has similarly alerted feminists to the importance of greater organization and intervention within the political process on questions relating to women and families. Feminists now realize that new life-styles which merge work and family life will be impossible to achieve without significant public support for child care and other social services. A *New York Times Magazine* article by Betty Friedan [29], a leading voice of the feminist movement since the early 1960s, emphasizes that feminism cannot afford to leave the family issue to the right wing: the feminist agenda for the 1980s, she insists, must embrace support for issues involving families.

Two other demographic factors also bear consideration as sources of support for family-oriented programs — the trend toward increasing numbers of single mothers and working mothers from two-parent families. While there are currently only one million single-parent households nationally, their problems are increasingly familiar to a wider public. Working women with children, however, are a significantly broader group, encompassing more than 50% of women with young children. While not every family either requires or will use outside assistance in their child-rearing, this growing army of two-worker families is encountering considerable economic and social stress as it attempts to synchronize child-rearing with work. With the advent of high levels of inflation, many of these families cannot retain a middle-class life-style unless both adult members are employed. Thus, it is not a matter of choice or ideology that causes these families to seek two incomes; it is a question of necessity.

Minorities, too, have the potential to become an increasingly significant political force. Black and Hispanic leaders have been quick to criticize the current administration for policies that will lead to reduced benefits for minorities. Black and Hispanic families, in particular, stand to benefit from increased public concern about family life.

These constituencies, while currently unable to express their political choices to very great effect, are an undercurrent in the political drama likely to emerge during the next few years. Should they become involved in selecting the social policy choices in the 1980s, new alternatives for families are likely to emerge.

Indeed, within a few years it is quite likely that the political pendulum will again swing away from the far right toward somewhere near the center. Under these conditions, a broader discussion of the strategies for dealing with child maltreatment will be possible. Easy solutions, emphasizing minor program improvements offered without regard to the larger problem of the welfare of all children and their families, will have only passing relevance to a discussion of prevention as this political change occurs. An assessment of child maltreatment indicates that fundamental shifts in social policy and an emphasis on family security should be the cornerstones of a serious preventive program.

REFERENCES

1. Antler S: The rediscovery of child abuse, in Pelton L (ed): *The Social Context of Child Abuse and Neglect*. New York, Human Sciences Press, 1981, pp 39–54.
2. Pfohl S: The discovery of child abuse. *Social Probl* 1977;24(3):310–323.
3. Antler S: *Child Protection: Readings in Policy and Practice*. Washington, DC, NASW, 1982, pp 6–18.
4. Zigler E: Controlling child abuse in America: An effort doomed to failure? Proceedings of the First National Conference on Child Abuse and Neglect, Washington, DC, Dept. of Health, Education and Welfare, 1976.
5. Pelton L: *Am J Orthopsychiatry*, 1978;48:608–617.
6. Woloch I, Horowitz B: Child maltreatment and material deprivation among AFDC-recipient families. *Social Serv Rev* 1979;53:175–194.

7. Horowitz B, Woloch I: Material deprivation, child maltreatment and agency intervention among poor families, in Pelton L (ed): *The Social Context of Child Abuse and Neglect.* New York, Human Sciences Press, 1981, pp 137–184.

8. American Humane Association: National Analysis of Official Child Neglect and Abuse Reporting, Denver, Colorado, 1978.

9. Gil DG: *Violence Against Children: Physical Child Abuse in the United States.* Cambridge, Massachusetts, Harvard University Press, 1970.

10. Light RJ: Abused and neglected children in America: A study of alternative policies, in *The Rights of Children.* Cambridge, Harvard Educational Review, 1974, pp 198–240.

11. Finkelhor D: *Sexually Victimized Children.* New York, Free Press, 1979.

12. Kahn AJ, Kamerman SB: *Not For the Poor Alone. European Social Services.* Philadelphia, Temple University Press, 1975.

13. Bloom M: *Primary Prevention: The Possible Science.* Englewood Cliffs, New Jersey, Prentice-Hall, 1981, pp 29–48.

14. Rosenberg CE: *The Cholera Years.* Chicago, University of Chicago Press, 1962.

15. Trattner WI: *From Poor Law to Welfare State.* New York, Macmillan, 1974, pp 116–135.

16. Fleming D: 1963. Social darwinism, in Schlesinger AM Jr, White M (eds): *Paths of American Thought.* Boston, Houghton Mifflin Sentry Edition, 1970, pp 123–146.

17. Laslett P: *The World We Have Lost.* New York, Scribner, 1965.

18. Keniston K: *All Our Children: The American Family Under Pressure.* New York, Harcourt, Brace, Jovanovitch, 1972.

19. Lasch C: *Haven in a Heartless World: The Family Besieged.* New York, Basic Books, 1977.

20. Featherstone J: Family matters. *Harvard Educ Rev* 1979;49(1):20–52.

21. Demos J: *A Little Commonwealth: Family Life in Plymouth Colony.* New York, Oxford University Press, 1970.

22. Halem L: *Divorce Reform: Changing Legal and Social Perspectives.* New York, Free Press, 1980.

23. Kahn AJ: *Social Policy and Social Services,* 2nd Ed. New York, Random House, 1979.

24. Nagi SZ: *Child Maltreatment in the United States.* New York, Columbia University Press, 1977.

25. Titmuss RM: *Social Policy: An Introduction.* New York, Pantheon, 1974, p 26.

26. Kamerman S, Kahn AJ: *Family Policy: Government and Families in Fourteen Countries.* New York, Columbia University Press, 1978.

27. Moynihan DP: 1970.

28. Gelles R: The social construction of child abuse. *Am J Orthopsychiatry* 1975;45(3):363–374.

29. Friedan B: *New York Times Magazine.* Nov. 18, 1979, p 1940.

PART V
International Perspectives

15 Aspects of Child Abuse in Britain

Alan J. Bedford

AN OVERVIEW

In the past decade child abuse has become Britain's most news-worthy social work issue, a fact having a considerable impact on casework practice and attitudes. Creating public awareness of the "battered-baby syndrome," as it was then known, was at first a slow but then rapidly accelerating process. As Parton[1] notes, "the discovery of child abuse in Britain, its definition as a social problem and the sociolegal reaction against it required the coalition of a certain organised interest in the 1960's and early 1970's."

Following the crucial article of Kempe et al[2] in 1962, early attempts to create awareness were from the medical profession, first in ortho-pedics, then most notably in forensic pathology and paediatrics. It was not until the late 1960s that the subject was aired more widely when the establishment of a Battered Child Research Department (BCRD) by the National Society for the Prevention of Cruelty to Children (NSPCC) in 1968 generated considerable impetus to the dissemination of knowlege. The NSPCC had taken note of the work of Kempe in Denver, Colorado, and set up the BCRD to create a comprehensive program of study and treatment of families where a child had been battered and to help build up an informed body of opinion on the battered-child syndrome.

The general philosophy in the numerous journal articles emanating from the BCRD followed the line of Helfer and Kempe and colleagues in *The Battered Child*.[3] Parents assaulting children were seen as grossly immature, deprived of the essentials of childhood themselves, and unable to cope with the dependency of young children. Treatment was seen as a slow process whereby the adults would be "reparented" by supportive casework, available on demand. The approach would be essentially nonpunitive and nonintrusive. The importance of prompt intervention was stressed, particularly not missing the early warning signs.

The BCRD's first publication by Skinner and Castle[4] suggested that 60% of battered children would be reinjured if there was no professional intervention and that siblings of injured children were highly at risk. Among other themes promulgated were the views that the worker having to take legal action should not also be primarily responsible for the therapy[5] and that multidisciplinary assessment and treatment coordination, especially through the case conference, were of crucial importance. At this time treatment was still very much focused on the parents. Indeed with the more predominant child focus of the 1980s, it is strange now to read that "direct interest in the infant should be avoided and the focus of the visit must be the parent, otherwise she will begin to feel frozen out by both the worker and the child."[6]

The BCRD papers certainly produced interest in the professional world and in relevant government departments. By 1972 Castle and Kerr[7] were reporting an increased number of diagnosed injuries and recommending that central registers be set up to pool scattered information on children at risk. Parton, in his paper "Natural History of Child Abuse,"[8] argues that a combination of developments at this time produced the breakthrough in establishing battered babies as a major issue. He points out that the then minister of social services, Sir Keith Joseph, was propounding the theory of the "cycle of deprivation," in which social problems were passed from generation to generation through the family, a theory which fitted neatly with the conventional view of the etiology of child abuse. Concurrently an ad hoc group of interested professsionals met at Tunbridge Wells to pool information on treatment and management which had been developing in a rather piecemeal fashion.[9] Sir Keith attended this conference, and a few days later the government announced an enquiry into a case where a 7-year-old child, Maria Colwell, had died at the hands of her stepfather, despite a multitude of agencies being involved. The Tunbridge Wells group chairman, Dr. Alfred White Franklin, told Parton, "While the timing of Maria Colwell and Tunbridge Wells was coincidental, the combination was explosive."

The public inquiry [10] produced massive media headlines and the catalog of low-level awareness, poor interagency communication, inconsistent professional practice, and the sheer unhappiness of Maria's life produced a demand for action. The professionals involved in the case were exposed as never before and, although Stevenson's minority report [11] tried to highlight the complexity of a social worker's task in cases like this and refused to apportion degrees of blame, an era of social work began where the pressure from the fear of making a "mistake" at times exceeded the stress caused by working with difficult, damaged families. The case of Maria Colwell reemphasized the necessity of multidisciplinary coordination, and the government urged the setting up of area review committees. [12] These consisted of senior personnel from all the professions involved in child abuse in each area. The committees' tasks were to approve written procedures for detailed case management, review the work of case conferences, provide education and training, monitor the quality of work in the area, and publicize the referral processes. The committees were to be responsible for a register which would coordinate information on children and allow concerned professionals to check quickly if a child was already known to be at risk. One of the constituent agencies, usually the local government social services department or an NSPCC special unit, would run the register on behalf of the committee.

The government also continued to promote the case conference and by 1976 was urging police involvement and a total sharing of information in the best interests of the child. [13] It is important to note that although the social services departments, the NSPCC, and the police have legal powers and duties in respect of abused children, there are no statutory reporting laws in Britain and the whole management system is based on voluntary cooperation that is recommended strongly by government.

By the late 1970s a general system of managing these cases had been established. Most areas published procedures which bind each agency to a strict sequence of action following a referral of "nonaccidental injury" (NAI), a term which had superseded the more emotive "battered baby." The procedures include holding a multidisciplinary case conference on each case. Although constituent agencies retain the right to independent action, the moral pressure to consensus is great. The conference looks at the diagnosis, whether statutory action need be taken, and at the coordination of a treatment plan. The children where NAI is proven or highly suspected have their names placed on the register.

Many reports on fatal cases show that lessons about early warning signs, the need to communicate with other agencies, poor case recording, and so on are still being ignored. On the other hand many people have been concerned about the dangers of hindsight judgment on professional decisions, the destructive impact on the workers involved in the cases who are subject to trial by the media, and the continued lack of any real consideration of the resource limitations on training and manpower. The British Association of Social Workers published a code of practice for social workers and supervisors in 1975 [14] setting very high professional standards, but this too was criticized by some social workers whose organizations did not have the resources to implement such ideals.

Regardless of one's view of inquiries, the impact was to harden the resolve of government and area review committees to produce ever tighter procedures and a more all-embracing register system. This led to "advice, guidance and instruction to professionals on an unprecedented scale." [15] Inevitably criticism followed that management issues were superseding treatment, prevention, and an understanding of abuse itself. Sutton [16] argues that "labyrinthine sets of procedures" have been developed to ensure social service departments are never held culpable, while the resources and will to come to grips with the problem, especially in the preventive sense, have been lacking. He describes the procedures as ends in themselves in which work on child abuse revolves around conforming to the rules rather than a sensitive examination of personal and societal causation.

Closely linked with this view is another which sees Britain's response to child abuse as defensive, safety-first social work, concentrating on registration or removing children from home to protect the agency rather than considering the rights of the family members. Some have looked at the haphazard development of registers and the moral stigma they argue is attached to registration and claim that the whole child abuse treatment system is a considerable threat to parents' civil liberties. [17] Criticism of the system, which has often come from a segment of the social work profession, has left fieldworkers feeling more ambivalent about their right to use that system to protect children. Dealing with abused children needs a high level of confidence, something which seems to be challenged with each new development in thinking.

The NSPCC would argue that a well-run case conference system, together with a carefully controlled register on which cases are monitored by child abuse specialists, produce a lowering of reinjury rates. [18] The NSPCC special units, which provide this service and readily available consultation, have been a successful development and a model for governmental guidelines.

An important change through the 1970s has been the extension of treatment techniques. The BCRD noted that the reparenting model reduced reinjuries and improved the general family situation, but the parent–child relationships and the children's emotional development remained distorted. Emphasis has therefore been laid on direct work with children[19] including play therapy or psychotherapy and the use of family centers where parents and children can spend time together in a therapeutic environment, perhaps as an alternative to separation. There has also been a recognition of the value of more short-term work, of a behavioral or task-centered nature, to complement or as an alternative to more traditional long-term work.

A key development through the 1970s has been the broadening of the criteria of child abuse. The early research of the BCRD and the first formulation of procedures concerned physical injury to babies and toddlers. The first registers run by the NSPCC contained only the names of children under 5 years old. It was soon realized that the problem of NAI to children affected all ages, and Maria Colwell's death at 7 highlighted this. Thirty-eight percent of children notified to NSPCC registers in 1976 were between 5 and 16 years old.[20] Together with the extension of ages, the criteria for abuse also expanded to take in emotional abuse. This development was inevitable given the anomaly of a comprehensive management system being brought in to deal with even small incidents of physical injury while complex and more permanently damaging emotional trauma were overlooked.

Currently there is an upsurge of interest in neglect, and the recently formed British Association for the Study and Prevention of Child Abuse and Neglect (BASPCAN) has been highlighting the professionals' "neglect of neglect." Once again a well-publicized inquiry on a fatal case of child neglect has helped to stimulate interest.[21]

The government's Department of Health and Social Security has recommended that registers include children suffering from physical injury, neglect, failure to thrive, and emotional abuse, and it offers definitions in an attempt at standardization.[22] Their suggestion for failure to thrive and emotional abuse lays emphasis on the outcome for the child rather than the type of abuse itself: "children who have been medically diagnosed as suffering from severe non-organic failure to thrive; or whose behaviour and emotional development has been severely affected; where medical and social assessments find evidence of either persistent or severe neglect or rejection." Sexual abuse was not included as a separate category although many area review committess have unilaterally decided that this form of abuse needs the same procedural response. BASPCAN has circulated a discussion document[23] to ensure sexual abuse is not overlooked.

Child abuse is now firmly established as an unprecedented major issue of professional and public concern with tremendous demands on time and energy. This is despite the fact that there is no clear evidence of increasing violence to children. Indeed, in areas where there are NSPCC registers, Creighton[24] suggests serious injuries are in decline. She estimates the number of deaths for England and Wales in 1976 as 65 in contrast to the "two-a-day" claim which attended the burst of publicity in the early 1970s. The scale of emotional and sexual abuse is unknown, with problems of definition and reporting rendering quantification almost impossible.

For practitioners the result of the explosion of interest in child abuse has been that they face far more dilemmas than that of relating to the damaged families with both care and control. The media pressure is such that the social worker is constantly in a situation where he can rarely be seen to be right. If a child is allowed to stay at home or is rehabilitated quickly after an injury and later dies, the public reaction is merciless. On the other hand the media are quick to highlight alleged breaches of civil liberties and supposedly callous separation of children from their parents. Social workers are accused of being self-protective if they take what they see as preventive action to safeguard children, yet are labeled as lacking even in common sense if they fail to act. This type of pressure makes casework planning even more stressful. Another dilemma is how to provide effective treatment. A large majority of this work is done by social services departments whose staff carry a generic case load. The same departments have also been affected in recent years by cutbacks or limits in expansion. Considerable problems are faced in allocating enough time to each family in face of competing demands from many varying client groups, and the workers face the frustration of contrasting public and professional expectation of intense involvement with their own day-to-day experience. The fact that much of the imaginative casework is done in specialist centers with a restricted case load only emphasizes the point.

Now that the wider concept of "child abuse" rather than "battered babies" is the focus, professionals are forced to consider not only the more discrete issue of physical injury but the complex area of what is an acceptable quality of family life. Social workers in the field are now having to make their own assessments. Although the courts are still the ultimate test of the right to intervene, social workers have to work without any real consensus of what is acceptable given the variety of classes and cultures in Britain.

In drawing attention to the dilemmas facing social workers, it should not be thought that preventing and treating child abuse is an impossible task. There has been great progress. Awareness of the significance of minor injuries and failure to thrive has grown tremendously in all professional groups. Well-run registers and case conference systems are reducing reinjuries and attempting to ensure that adequate attention is given to each case. The emotional impact of all forms of abuse on children is recognized, and an awareness of the long-lasting effects of sexual abuse is being spread. It is to the great credit of dedicated professionals, often working in less than ideal conditions, that this progress is being made despite the complex philosophical and moral issues which daily challenge each child abuse worker.

NATIONAL SOCIETY FOR THE PREVENTION OF CRUELTY TO CHILDREN

The significant part played by the NSPCC in establishing the battered-baby syndrome as a major issue is referred to in the previous section. However, it was a new conceptualization rather than a new problem that was put forward, for the NSPCC had been dealing with child cruelty of all types since 1884.

The work of the New York Society for the Prevention of Cruelty to Children had been noted by a traveling businessman who returned to England to form the Liverpool society in 1883. The London Society for the Prevention of Cruelty to Children began in 1884, and in 1889 it amalgamated with 31 groups from all over the country to become the National Society for the Prevention of Cruelty to Children.

It was largely through the NSPCC that the first acts for the prevention of cruelty to children in 1889, 1894, and 1908 were placed on the statutes. Many subsequent acts have borne the mark of the society's work.[25] In 1895 the society was granted a royal charter empowering it to "prevent the public and private wrongs of children and the corruption of their morals." The society's officers, its inspectors, are authorized by the secretary of state to take children before the juvenile court if they are in need of care or protection. No other bodies except the local government social services departments and the police are so empowered. The society is also able to prosecute parents for cruelty in the adult courts.

As a voluntary body, the society has been almost entirely funded by public subscription, a mark of the popular esteem in which it is held. The voluntary status has also enabled an independence of thought and action to pioneer new attitudes, something especially crucial in its early days when there was a level of child poverty and cruelty almost impossible to believe for a supposedly civilized society. An autobiographical account by an NSPCC inspector published in 1912[26] shows as almost commonplace a level of neglect and injury a current social worker might see only a few times in his career.

The NSPCC has gained a reputation for prompt and meticulous investigation of any allegation that a child is at risk. Should the situation so dictate, action will be taken through the juvenile court to protect children. In its early days the society widely used the tool of prosecuting parents for neglect or cruelty when that seemed to be in the best interests of the child. Despite the fact that in many cases there was a positive response from parents to this step, it was realized that cruelty was not simply a moral failing to be punished but a multicausal problem that needed careful and concentrated social work help. In 1980 the NSPCC annual report noted only eight prosecutions (compared to 2884 in 1901) and even the 166 cases where a juvenile court action was taken comprised little over 1% of the NSPCCs new cases that year.

The society's annual casework statistics (Table 15-1) testify to the quantity of work undertaken and the NSPCCs important role in the 1980s despite the extensive developments of the welfare state. Table 15-1 shows the surprisingly high proportion of self-referrals, a further mark of the society's reputation as a caring as well as controlling agency. Whether investigating an allegation or responding to a self-referral, the aim is to prevent ill treatment by appropriate social work support and intervention. The 87,542 home visits in 1980 point to the outreach of the NSPCCs 250 officers who offer a 24-hour service.

Table 15-1
NSPCC Casework Statistics
October 1, 1979–September 30, 1980
(England, Wales, and Northern Ireland)

Referral source		Referred problems	
General public	6651 (41.5%)	Children left alone	3547 (22.2%)
Parents in charge	4380 (27.4%)	Neglect	3172 (19.8%)
Other agencies	3229 (20.2%)	At risk of injury	1731 (10.8%)
Other relatives	1740 (10.9%)	Nonaccidental injury	1383 (8.6%)
Total new cases 16,000 (100%)		Others*	6167 (38.6%)

Statutory action		Client contacts	
Prosecution	8 (0.05%)	Home visits	87,542
Juvenile court	166 (1.0%)	Other casework visits	38,747
		Office interviews	7512

*Includes housing, financial, matrimonial, and other emotional problems.

In addition to supportive casework for parents and children, the NSPCC has established a number of play groups to serve either deprived communities or the needs of specific referred children. The society also has two family centers and a parentcraft center where parental involvement can offer new opportunities for improved parenting on both emotional and practical levels.

The NSPCCs School of Social Work, in addition to training staff for the society, provides many courses for all professional groups, thus extending the agency's influence on attitudes and skills in child abuse in Britain.

Through the Battered Child Research Department, the society was at the fore in pioneering the new work on battering and, in addition to its research, began, from 1973, to set up special units in several parts of the country.[27] These run parallel with the inspectorate and aim to provide a specialist focus for the growing multidisciplinary management of child abuse. They are staffed by social workers and honorary paediatric and psychiatric consultants from the community. In addition to a controlled case load of serious abuse cases worked with intensively, the units have several other functions. Usually they manage the register of children at risk for the area and monitor the work done on the families concerned by regular contact with the main social and health workers, ensuring that professionals are communicating with each other and encouraging regular assessments. The NSPCC believes this monitoring to be a task for skilled child abuse teams rather than a purely administrative exercise. The unit also has an important role in multidisciplinary case conferences, either as consultant or chairman, often producing the minutes which are an important aid to practice. The child abuse area review committees' educational role will usually be delegated to the unit and sessions are arranged for health, social work, and teaching staff.

The combination of casework, consultation, and education has been rewarding, both for the areas concerned and the unit staff. However, as extensive systems for managing child abuse already exist in many areas, more recent requests to the NSPCC for special units have centered on the treatment role, as this is felt to have been, perhaps, the most neglected aspect of child abuse. One of the NSPCCs special units is in the London Borough of Haringey. The author, unit leader since 1978, describes some aspects of the team's work in the following section.

AN ASPECT OF THE NSPCC, AN INTERDISCIPLINARY CHILD ABUSE TEAM

The NSPCC Haringey Special Unit is the direct descendant of the NSPCC's Battered Child Research Department. In 1974, following the completion of its treatment research, the department moved to North London and enlarged to become the National Advisory Centre on the Battered Child. The functions were to continue treatment research and to become a national resource for information, education, and advice about child abuse. With many special units developing in the rest of the country, the national functions, including the library, were underused and the team became more involved in local casework and consultation. Eventually, with funding from the London Borough of Haringey, the center became the NSPCC Haringey Special Unit, while the library and the NSPCCs child abuse consultant moved to the NSPCC headquarters to become more available nationally.

The unit has three main responsibilities: a treatment service to the local borough; a consultation service, particularly at case conferences in the borough; and a teaching service on the management and understanding of child abuse for professionals in the London area. Although the number of staff has varied, the maximum team has consisted of a unit leader, four social workers (empowered to take statutory action), and a play therapist. This has been supplemented by four part-time specialist staff members: a child psychotherapist, a clinical psychologist, a child psychiatrist, and a second child psychiatrist used as a staff consultant.

The design of the team followed directly from the BCRD findings which have been evaluated by Baher et al[28] and Jones.[29] In particular it was felt there should be facilities for the accurate assessment and individual treatment of children since the reparenting style of casework, aimed at meeting the parents' dependency needs and fostering long-term emotional development, had not substantially altered the parent–child relationship or the child's emotional position. Specific child therapy was recommended in addition to the therapeutic day care which was widely used.

Combining staff from five separate professions to meet this task has been inevitably difficult and can only be developed over time. Bourne and Newburger,[30] Schmitt,[31] and Steele[32] have looked at the advantages and disadvantages of a multidisciplinary team approach to child abuse. Special problems occur when the whole team is employed by a social work agency which has statutory powers in respect of children, assumes responsibility for their protection, and insists on a consistent laid down procedure for responses to suspicions of child abuse. In addition the NSPCC, as a voluntary agency, particularly depends on public support and finance and must maintain a high level of public credibility, a fact only sustained by consistent and reliable responses. Within this context there can be conflict between the team's view of a therapeutic ideal and agency demands.

Interdisciplinary Child Abuse Team Management

Referrals are discussed by the whole team and agreement reached on the suitability both for the client and the agency. Treatment planning is done in the same way, with significant changes in direction brought back to the group. Requests for consultation by other agencies are similarly allocated with written reports supervised by the unit leader. Casework supervision of the social workers is by the unit leader; psychotherapist and psychologist by the staff consultant (a child psychiatrist), and the play therapist by the psychotherapist. Supervision of joint work does not find an obvious channel and various ad hoc arrangements are made.

The unit leader has management responsibility for all members of staff, regardless of supervisory position and, in turn, he is accountable to the NSPCC hierarchy. The issue of how the unit leader (a social worker) can be responsible, for example, for a consultant psychiatrist is worked out by a simple rule of thumb. The unit leader determines what other tasks professionals in the team do, but how they do it is left to professional discretion so long as that does not offend agency policy.

Authority

There is always pressure from within an interdisciplinary team for members to be accepted as equal and decisions only taken by consensus. This occurs where many casework decisions are deliberately made in a group setting because of the advantages various perspectives can bring to those decisions. Indeed Schmitt and Grosz[33] argue that there should be consensus decision-making in treatment planning. However, from time to time there are exceptions to this and the unit leader may overrule the group decision for reasons of agency policy or because it might have an unacceptable impact on other agencies. This issue is complicated by having in the team individuals who, in other work situations, occupy a different role or status. The author believes that the unit leader must resist any pressure for total group control and maintain the right to make a unilateral decision. This is particularly crucial in child abuse work where the agency has a policy to act in a particular way and where public and professional credibility is important to the agency's survival. In this team the different disciplines work for one agency and therefore do not retain a right to unilateral action, as they might in a multidisciplinary case conference in the community.

A related issue concerns to whom the case "belongs" when two or three workers combine to take various roles for the same family. The author's view is that the wholly employed team member, the social worker with statutory powers, must have the coordinative authority to run the case and to pull together the work done by colleagues within the team and with other agencies. This should apply if the social worker is doing co-therapy with the high status consultant psychiatrist or even if the nonsocial worker is doing most of the work. Without this authority the social worker may be placed in an unnecessary dilemma should there be a need to act quickly and may not have the confidence to make decisions, a crucial commodity in child abuse work. The previous point should not be taken to indicate any disrespect for the part-time specialists. Their skills, perspective, and friendship are crucial to the efficiency of the team and its stressful task. The key lies in keeping a role identity in doing what one is trained to do. Therapists treat while social workers treat and also manage cases. Although the team members inevitably and healthily begin to accommodate toward one another's styles, if the process goes too far one loses the value of specialism.

Confidentiality

Britain has no mandatory child abuse reporting laws, and so issues about what to retain inside a therapeutic relationship are quite complex. In most settings doctors and therapists adhere to strict rules of confidentiality stemming from the code of ethics of their profession. Work for a child abuse agency must modify these standards if the multidisciplinary team is to survive as a cohesive unit. Such modification is not easy, and a child psychotherapist may feel reluctant to inform his social work colleagues when a child confides that he has been hit by his parents. The child may not be speaking the literal truth, but rather trying to achieve something in his relationship with the therapist. Alternatively, there may be a real issue to investigate. If the therapist tells the social worker who then calls to discuss the incident with the parents, what does this do to the child's faith in the therapist, or the parents' confidence to bring the child for therapy? If there is no response to the child's comment, he may feel abandoned in his moment of need. If there are obvious injuries, there is not such a dilemma, but in less clear cases the conflicts for the workers are great. A similar dilemma may face one of our psychiatrists who assesses a parent and is told, "I hit Bill much harder than people think, but don't tell anyone."

The author's view is that, especially where different professionals are working for one agency, information given to one member of the team should be processed as given to the agency. As that agency has child protective functions, it must act accordingly. Thus in clarifying therapeutic contracts with parents or children, no member of the team must give an unrealistic commitment to limitless confidentiality.

Working together in this situation requires a great deal of confidence in each other which can only be achieved by regular meetings and discussions. Fears by therapists that a social worker is being unnecessarily pedantic about agency procedure or by social workers that therapists are being "precious" about their relationship with clients must be discussed and worked through.

Our experience has been that the position of mutual trust has been reached, but from time to time details of bruising are not passed to the social worker responsible for the case. This was not because of any point of principle but in the context of the therapeutic session the bruising did not assume the significance a statutory social worker would have attached to it. In the context of a child finally being able to communicate a desperate sense of inner hopelessness to his therapist, a small bruise on the cheek could well appear a minor matter.

Intrateam Relationships

A social worker dealing with child abuse frequently feels overwhelmed. "The danger of being caught up in a client's chaos is ever present. He may begin to feel angry, frustrated and sometimes at wits' end."[34] There may then be a tendency for a social worker to look to the part-time specialists in the team for the solution, feeling that this is being withheld. When the specialists reflect the problem back to the social worker for further consideration, the worker may feel even more hopeless, rather than appreciate the consultation being offered. The part-time team members, who have less control over the unit's work flow, may feel undervalued if the social workers prefer to work with the family themselves or choose another member of staff for cotherapy. These feelings must be explored together and an atmosphere created whereby each team member is valued as equal but different. No one is the fount of all knowledge, and no views are discounted. This may appear elementary, but when a team begins to reflect the dynamics of the families it works with, it is far from easy. Some agreement also needs to be reached on fundamental issues of philosphy, and Gustaffson et al[35] describe some of the problem in doing this.

The tool the unit has used for many years to look at these feelings has been a weekly "work discussion group" for all professional staff. Judith Trowell[36] has described the process of this group during a difficult period in the unit's history and her role as consultant to the group. She describes how, following a period when the meetings seemed destructive and fruitless and her own role was challenged, the group eventually began "to look at the workers' feelings of uselessness and hopelessness in relation to the tasks set them by the institution and ultimately by society. The difficulty of combining the role of care giver and authority figure could be acknowledged and staff began to make attempts to evolve ways of dealing with this conflict . . . [which led to] . . . an increase in the interest and enthusiasm in the institution's work and an eagerness to work coupled with an awareness and acceptance of conflicts and limitations." She concluded that "if the pain and discomfort of the work discussion group can be tolerated, it can lead to an increased understanding of clients as their unconscious processes are replicated in the group, become available and then can be used for work."

Staff Consultant

The value of a consultant (one with no management responsibilities) to child abuse workers must not be underestimated. Trowell[37] describes the difficulty of being both the consultant and psychiatrist in the team. By seeing families herself and being part of the thinking about specific cases, it was hard for her to maintain a boundary between the two roles. Similarly, it was hard for the team to accept in a positive way the consultancy of someone working on cases with them. Subsequently a second psychiatrist has been employed to do clinical work and participate in case discussion, while Dr. Trowell takes a staff consultancy role only and chairs the work discussion group. On an individual basis the unit also believes that a worker and supervisor may need to consult a neutral outsider, recognizing the possibility that from time to time a supervisor, because of his own contact with this case, may not be able to retain objectivity.

Supervision

The emotional entanglements of working with abusing families requires regular supervision which must include a managerial element. In an interdisciplinary team the channels of supervision may be unclear. The unit leader is only qualified to supervise social workers. It was arranged that the child psychiatrist, experienced in therapy, supervise the psychologist and the psychotherapist who in turn supervises the play therapist. This situation works well in terms of enhancing the quality of work but leads to some difficulties when supervisors without management responsibility are in conflict over what information should be retained within the supervisory relationship and what ought to be shared with the unit leader as manager. Unless the boundaries of each role are clear to all concerned, there is a danger of either a supervisee feeling his confidence is betrayed when information is shared, or of collusive subgroups being formed.

Supervision of joint work is important but difficult to arrange. For example, when a social worker and psychologist are doing co-therapy or doing individual work with different family members, it is essential that these workers are seen together as well as in individual supervision as the quality of their relationship with each other will be a large factor in determining the successful outcome of therapy. The boundaries between individual supervision issues and team decisions must also be respected. For example, the team may feel a case is best allocated to a certain worker. The unit leader must have the right to veto this without being obliged to reveal his reason, which may be related to a confidential issue currently being worked on in supervision.

The previous points may be elementary in casework supervision but assume great importance in child abuse because of the extreme emotional impact of the client upon the workers.

Relationship with Other Agencies

The unit comprises one interdisciplinary team but is part of another, the network of community resources. The relationship a specialist child abuse team has with this group is a delicate one. Some social or health workers may rightly look to the unit for expertise but in doing so deny their own competence or skill. The unit worker must help others see what they can or cannot do themselves, but in doing so may be accused of not being interested enough to really help by taking over the case. This mirrors the social worker–consultant relationship within the unit.

A second issue is the resentment by other social workers with large generic case loads of the time and resources available to a specialist team. It is hard for them to appreciate that a small case load of abuse cases brings pressure of its own, with more time to think and absorb the awfulness of the child's life or the complexity of decision-making. Within the unit it is only by regular meetings that mutual understanding can develop. Another problem will be the high standard the unit staff will set themselves on working with other agencies. They feel under pressure to justify their specialism by always being "right" and conforming strictly with management procedures and professional codes of practice. It is difficult when holding these standards to accept lower ones in others and easy to overlook the constraints others have in their own work situation. Unless these constraints are acknowledged, our consultancy will not be accepted meaningfully, particularly if an uncomfortable issue is being discussed.

Advantages of an Interprofessional Team

The great strengths of an interprofessional team working in one center are its flexibility and range of resources. The variety of staff and different specialties provide a very detailed analysis of any casework problem and offer a fuller range of treatment facilities. There is less chance of clients splitting professionals than when the same group of workers combine in a looser network involving different agencies. Perhaps most important is the opportunity to combine those with and without statutory authority and establish a balance between care and control that must be clear in our own minds if clients are to benefit from our work.

CASEWORK

Our view is that regardless of the presenting injury or incident, it is the atmosphere of living in an abusing family which causes the significant damage to children. The work is aimed at change in that area, not simply the prevention of violence. Unless this is clarified with families, it can be hard to maintain them in treatment after the initial crisis is over. The goal is to help families change attitudes and feelings so that the child can continue to grow in a nurturing environment. The means will be both traditional psychotherapeutic techniques and also methods aimed at behavioral change. One, to the exclusion of the other, may not be enough to effect permanent movement.

Motivation is a question that a child protective agency may consider with some ambivalence. The unit seeks an indication of motivation in parents and insists that other agencies get consent from them before referral. This varies from the NSPCC inspectorate who will attempt to engage a family regardless of parental motivation if it seems in the child's interests. However, should a child appear to be seriously at risk during treatment, the unit may have to dispense with consent and insist on contact regardless of what the parents feel. Similarly no guarantee can be made to a self-referral that the NSPCCs legal powers will not be used. Twenty percent of the unit's case load have been subject to statutory order at some time, and in half of those the legal process began after the unit commenced work with the family. Thus motivation and mutual agreement on therapeutic contracts have to be regarded with some skepticism on both sides, not an easy way to build up trusting relationships. However, if our clients are to be able to combine care and control in a warm way, then professionals must be able to deal with this dilemma themselves.

Referrals

In order to maintain a balanced case load and to be involved in preventive and curative roles, the unit has broad criteria for referrals, taking any aspect of abuse from a variety of sources (Table 15-2). Children can be up to 16 years old, but two thirds are of preschool age on referral.

Assessment

Following the NSPCCs earlier research, the aim is to offer the child and his family a thorough assessment, taking advantage of the child

Table 15-2
Cases Assessed or Held by the
Special Unit August 1978–July 1981

Referral source			Referred problems		
Social workers	37	(49%)	Fear of abuse,		
Hospitals	14	(18%)	emotional abuse	41	(54%)
Parents	13	(17%)	Nonaccidental		
Health visitors	8	(11%)	injury	34	(45%)
Others	4	(5%)	Sexual abuse	1	(1%)
	76	(100%)		76	(100%)

specialist team. Psychiatric assessments are used to screen for any gross disturbance and to assess the need for and the viability of therapy for the child. Usually the child will be seen with his parents as well as separately. This allows the psychiatrist to see how the parent and child cope with each other and with separation and also to assess the child's ability to relate to another in his own right. Trowell and Castle,[38] reporting on 66 children psychiatrically assessed at the unit, said that it was "alarming that almost all the abused children were emotionally disturbed and in need of some form of help, so that even if abuse does not recur they remain with visible problems." They also assessed nearly half the identified children's siblings as in need of therapy. Assessments can also assist major decisions such as whether to rehabilitate. The following conclusion on a 5-year-old boy helped to confirm that a rehabilitation was appropriate despite a nonaccidental injury:

> John is coping surprisingly well with the upheaval and uncertainty. He has ego strength and has had "good enough" mothering . . . , his anxiety level is not unexpectedly high and he has obsessional patterns but not sufficient to cause concern in view of his situation. His behaviour seems appropriate. He could return home when the parents have worked through a little more of their difficulties.

Psychiatric assessments of the parents consistently show a level of deprivation, depression, and egocentricity which makes it difficult for the parents to understand their children's need for therapy.

Assessments by the psychologist are used in two ways. First, assessments are used to gain a measure of developmental progress. Children living in abusive families demonstrate speech delay, coordination and communication problems, and difficulties in expression.[39] Second, projective tests such as the Bene-Anthony Family Relations Test or the Children's Apperception Test (CAT) can highlight the child's preoccupations and his view of himself in the family and in social situations.

Six-year-old Robert described one picture in the CAT as follows: "The rabbit is in bed and it is raining. He is sitting up and dreaming about a ghost, a bad ghost, which will scare him, a man under a cover, who came from where scarey things come from. It is a 'he' ghost, a man ghost, Dracula. He is nice because he hurts other people when they are naughty. The rabbit is not naughty." This combination of impotent fear and ability to enjoy violence reflected his home life where Robert was very afraid of his mother's violence but could express his own anger only in a way which provoked her to more. He was beginning to take pleasure in her responses and the need for therapy for child and parent was clear.

In addition to any psychiatric or psychological assessment, the social worker will also have been assessing the family, observing the family dynamics in a wider variety of settings, and obtaining a social history. The contrasting perspectives are pooled in the case discussion group and plans made for ongoing work. Some parents are unwilling to bring their children or themselves for psychiatric assessment, and in some cases the social workers feel their own preliminary assessments are adequate. In all, 60% of treatment cases over a three-year period received a psychiatric assessment; a third received psychological assessments. If medical examination is necessary, paediatric resources from the community are used.

Treatment

The intention here is to look at how the psychology of an abusing family affects the way in which an interdisciplinary team can provide therapy. It is our view that the vast majority of parents who are now abusing their children experienced a childhood lacking warmth, consistency, and joy. Although by now this is regarded as a truism, its confirmation provides a consistent reminder that one must consider the needs of all family members.

Despite the much greater focus on the children in recent years, it is still the first task in beginning treatment to make a relationship with the parents. Without this no work with any part of the family will be very successful. Whatever form of therapy is eventually offered to individuals or whole families, the social workers will probably spend the majority of their time with the mother or father or both. Unless the parents feel understood, supported, encouraged, and have confidence in the social worker's ability to contain their anxiety or anger, any therapeutic work with the child will have minimal impact. It is therefore important that there be an ongoing relationship with the social worker who will remain the family's focal point of contact with the unit, regardless of whatever else the interdisciplinary team is providing. The nature of this social work with abusing parents has been well documented,[40,41] especially the need for consistency, a nonjudgmental attitude, and a capacity to deal with testing out without a subjective response.

However, to have created a relationship with the parents is not enough. Even a massive investment in mothering by professionals left the children with problems in their own right and "did not enable the parents to function effectively as parents of emotionally disturbed children."[42] It is therefore hoped that the range of skills available in the inter-disciplinary team can help the family members both as individuals and in their relationship with each other. In order to achieve this, a variety of techniques with individuals, couples, or whole families may be used, but little success is likely unless the timing is appropriate.

Our experience over a number of years, confirming that of Martin and Beezley,[43] is that unless the parents feel their own needs are being met, they will sabotage anything aimed at helping the child. The parent may not be able to tolerate the presence of the child in a room during an interview yet refuse to accept a separate treatment provision for him. The resistance to the child's needs being met may come in several ways, such as simply not bringing the child for therapy or asking him many critical questions and so intruding on the child's private relationship with his therapist. Often a social worker will have to develop a relationship with a parent over many months before a child can enter therapy. Children have the ability to sense unspoken parental ambivalence about treatment and may be unable to commit themselves emotionally to a therapeutic rela-tionship. Urgent as the child's needs for individual help may be, there is little point in commencing play therapy or psychotherapy until the parent is able to give some level of commitment and support to it. A closed door in the unit or in the child's own home is no barrier to the emotional intrusiveness of a parent, and so individual interviews with children must be carefully planned. One should be sure that the parent can cope emo-tionally with the child receiving attention.

Mr. Santini superficially approved of play therapy for his son, Carlos, aged 4, but the therapist wrote, "I felt as if I was unable to make any rela-tionship with this boy who treated me merely as another object in the room and the session felt thoroughly chaotic. I began to sense a hostility from the parent before and after sessions." When the author discussed this with Mr. Santini, he described how he had adjusted Carlos's clothing to test if it was moved during sessions. Mr. Santini had always found it hard to see Carlos as a separate person, and the father clearly found the play therapy for his son personally intrusive. However, openly acknowledging these feelings and discussing them with the father made a positive impact on his attitude to the therapy. After the next session the therapist noted, "Carlos seemed like a changed child. He began to treat me as a person and would often use my name, talking directly to me and inviting me to join in his games." She went on to describe a fan-tasy game Carlos played about a bad snake in the dark outside the therapy room which could not come into the room while the "nice and friendly" frog and fish could play in the light, thus symbolizing the meaningful time he and the therapist could have now father no longer tried to intrude.

Similar problems arise when one or both parents need interviews separate from their children. The children, who by nature of the case feel deprived, may resent the attention given to their parents or fear that the private discussion is about punishing or removing them. This feature is especially noticeable in the more deprived, chaotic families.

In one such case the author was trying to conduct a marital interview not long after the father had been convicted of sexual assault on a daughter. The case notes read that "the parents had got the children upstairs so that I could have a private time with the adults. Mrs. Browning had bribed them with sweets; however, for the next hour the children waged guerilla warfare with us . . . Susan 6, Brian 7, and Sheila 11, came down at different times to split on the others or to ask for something, only minutes later to say they didn't want it. They also banged on the door and ran upstairs without saying anything. It was really quite infuriating." At a later family interview it emerged that the children were frightened that one of the parents would disappear.

Wherever possible we try to conduct interviews with subgroups of the family at a separate venue (like the therapy room at the unit) where the cooler emotional atmosphere and physical distance enable a greater concentration on the task in hand. If it is viable for the whole family to use the unit for family therapy sessions, this is encouraged. This is not to underestimate the value of home visits where the majority of our work is done. Indeed, home visiting may be the only way to maintain contact with a family. Plans to see individuals or subgroups of the family must take into account the feelings of the remainder with something extra being considered for them. It is only at a later stage in treatment that a very deprived family will allow a member to receive something without compensation for the others.

Although much individual work is done at the unit, most sessions involve parents and children together, either informally in nonfocused supportive work at home, or more formally in family therapy or play sessions. Martin and Beezley[44] point out that although parents may well make personal gains from individual therapy, "to ensure that the parents' attitude and behaviour towards the abused child changes the distorted parent-child relationship needs direct intervention." With joint work the same principle of being aware of the needs of all present needs to be followed. The temptation to communicate with the adults at the expense of engaging children is strong. Workers must prepare for such sessions by making available such toys or drawing and modeling material that will enable the children, especially the younger ones, to participate at a comfortable level. Paradoxically, it also involves allowing a child not to join in, if that is his wish, and helping the parent cope with her wish for the child to "perform" for the workers.

Although one might expect these parents to resent children receiving attention or having fun, many seem to have a desire to understand their children and find family sessions conducted at the child's level acceptable. We therefore try to involve the children, even toddlers, continually encouraging parents to seek their opinion or interpreting the messages the children are giving in their play. We find that an assumption that even two or three year olds are not aware of major issues in the family is usually misplaced, and parents can be quite moved by the child's feelings as expressed verbally or in play.

> Mr. and Mrs. Main varied between overindulgence and callous discipline and set few consistent limits for their children. Wayne, 3, began self-destructive behavior, including swallowing cleaning fluid, but the parents would not accept from the author and his coworker that Wayne was unhappy or needed help. "He is just an adventurous boy, into everything." In one family session Wayne identified some toy men as those present in the room. The model he identified as himself he threw on the floor and stamped on and then tried to chew up. This was a much more effective way for the parents to be helped to understand the needs of their son than would have been obtained in a dry discussion. When the author said to Wayne that he must feel bad about himself, he began to communicate in a freer way than he had managed before, presumably relieved that his inner pain had been acknowledged.

With some families where there is little knowledge of play and few positive experiences, the play therapist is used to help the parent, usually the mother, to learn play skills and begin to enjoy her children. Often the parent, not having had such an experience herself as a child, will want to join in the play alongside, or even at the expense of, her own child. It may only be after an experience of being played with that the parent can begin to be the instigator of play with her child. Another model which has had some success is for the play therapist to see the children while their parents receive individual or marital work from colleagues nearby. The family will arrive at the unit together, thus expressing some motivation for family unity, and then receive separate inputs. After an agreed period the session ends with the children and therapist rejoining the parents and their coworker for a brief family session which again expresses symbolically the aim of togetherness. This model is especially useful where the individual needs are so strong as to render family therapy on its own unworkable.

Statutory Work

Most of our work is aimed at keeping families together, but there are times when the goal must be to enable a child to receive alternative care (temporarily or permanently) and for the family to come to terms with this. We have found that the interdisciplinary team has been of assistance in managing this type of case, both in assessing the placement needs of children and in providing a consistent therapeutic relationship for children going through the uncertainties of fostering or children's homes. We have found that giving the child someone to relate to in addition to the social worker responsible for the case management has helped the child express feelings in a way that could not be done to someone carrying decision-making powers.

> Sally, 4, had numerous caretakers before being statutorily removed from her mother after injury and failure to thrive. Her personality was severely damaged by such deprivation. Weekly psychotherapy at the unit for 2½ years, helping her make sense of her confusion, anger, and despair about her life's experiences became the anchor which helped her survive the move from hospital to a children's home, an unsuccessful rehabilitation with father, a return to the home, and finally a successful, and hopefully permanent, stay with her father.

At one time it was thought that "parents cannot bear the stress of ambivalence in a relationship in which they are beginning to invest their trust and affection. Any necessary legal proceedings should not be the responsibility of the primary supportive worker."[45] We now feel that where legal proceedings are necessary it is counterproductive to create such a split and that by being both supportive and controlling the social workers are "reflecting reality through an integrated therapeutic person."[46] No parent will find this easy, but resolving this basic paradox of caring is the focal point of work with abusing families. Where parents cannot begin to resolve this dilemma, this may indicate that the child is in need of permanent alternative placement rather than that the therapeutic strategy is inappropriate.

Decisions about court action to take a child into care or to ensure supervision at home are very difficult, and subsequent decisions over rehabilitation are even harder. Working for a child-focused agency like the NSPCC makes these decisions only fractionally easier, for the intensity of involvement with all family members makes one painfully aware of the impact of separation on parent and child alike. A child abuse team like that at the Haringey Unit, would have some members who are not involved with the family and their more objective assessments are invaluable in focusing on the best interests of the child.

SUMMARY

As one aspect of the National Society for the Prevention of Cruelty to Children, a specialized interdisciplinary child abuse team provides a challenging forum in which a variety of ideas and treatment techniques can be examined. The advantages of having so many perspectives under the auspices of a single agency are many, but these will only remain if the team is prepared to explore continually the complex issues of management and philosophy such a combined operation will present. As a treatment facility alone, the impact will be limited to the small number of cases handled, but the consultation and teaching that can be offered from the experience of those cases considerably widens the sphere of influence.

The author wishes to acknowledge the consultation provided by NSPCC Director, Dr. Alan Gilmour, and NSPCC Child Abuse Consultant, Ray Castle, in the preparation of this chapter.

REFERENCES

1. Parton N: The natural history of child abuse: A study in social problem definition. *Br J Social Work* 1979;9(4):431–451.
2. Kempe CH, Silverman FN, Steele BF, et al: The battered child syndrome. *JAMA* 1962;181:17–24.
3. Helfer RE, Kempe CH (eds): *The Battered Child.* Chicago, University of Chicago Press, 1968.
4. Skinner AE, Castle RL: *78 Battered Children: A Retrospective Study.* London, NSPCC, 1969.
5. Jones RA: Battering Familes. *Health Social Serv* 1973;313–314.
6. Okell C: The battered child: A tragic breakdown in parental care? *Midwife Health Visitor* 1969;5:235–240.
7. Castle RL, Kerr AM: *A Study of Suspected Child Abuse.* London, NSPCC, 1972.
8. Parton N: The natural history, pp 431–451.
9. Tunbridge Wells papers: in White-Franklin A (ed): *Concerning Child Abuse.* Edinburgh, Churchill Livingstone, 1975.
10. Department of Health and Social Security (DHSS): Report of the Committee of Inquiry into the Care and Supervision Provided in Relation to Maria Colwell. London, HMSO, 1974.
11. DHSS: Report, pp 88–115.
12. DHSS: Memorandum on NAI to Children. LASSL (74) 13 CMO (74) 8. London, HMSO, 1974.
13. DHSS: NAI to Children: The Police and Case Conferences. LASSL (76) 26, HMSO, London, 1975.
14. British Association of Social Workers. Birmingham, BASW, Children at Risk — BASW's Code of Practice. Reissued 1981.
15. Hallett C, Stevenson O: *Child Abuse: Aspects of Inter-Professional Cooperation.* London, Allen and Unwin, 1980.
16. Sutton P: Child abuse: Suffer the little children. *Social Work Today* 1981;12(43):10–11.
17. Morris A, Giller H, Szwed E, et al: *Justice for Children.* London, Macmillan, 1980.

18. Creighton SJ: *Child Victims of Physical Abuse, 1976.* London, NSPCC, 1980.
19. Jones C: Meeting the needs of abused children. *Social Work Today* 1978;9(26):9–14.
20. Creighton SJ: *Child Victims.*
21. Essex Area Review Committee: Malcolm Page. Chelmsford, Essex County Council, 1981.
22. DHSS: Child Abuse: Central Register Systems. LASSL (80)4 HN (8) 20. London, HMSO, 1980.
23. BASPCAN: Child Sexual Abuse. London, BASPCAN, 1981.
24. Creighton SJ: *Child Victims.*
25. Allen A, Morton A: *This is Your Child: The Story of the NSPCC.* London, Routledge Kegan Paul, 1961.
26. An NSPCC Inspector, 1912, The Cruelty Man. London, NSPCC.
27. Outram PJ: NSPCC special units. *Social Work Serv* 1975;8:8–11.
28. Baher E, Hyman C, Jones C, et al: *At Risk: An Account of the Work of the NSPCC Battered Child Research Department.* London, Routledge Kegan Paul, 1976.
29. Jones CO: The critical evaluation of the work of the NSPCC Battered Child Research Department. *Child Abuse Neglect* 1977;1(1):111–118.
30. Bourne R, Newburger EH: Interdisciplinary group process in the hospital management of child abuse and neglect. *Child Abuse Neglect* 1980;4(2): 127–135.
31. Schmitt B (ed): *The Child Protection Team Handbook.* New York, Garland STPM Press, 1978.
32. Steele BF: Experience with an interdisciplinary concept, in Helfer RS, Kempe CH (eds): *Child Abuse and Neglect: The Family and the Community.* Cambridge, Massachusetts, Ballinger, 1976.
33. Schmitt B, Grosz CA: Ground rules for effective team conferences, in Schmitt B (ed): *The Child Protection Team Handbook,* New York, Garland STPM Press, 1978.
34. D'Agostino P: Strains and stresses in protective services, in Ebeling NB, Hill DA (eds): *Child Abuse: Intervention and Treatment.* Acton, Massachusetts, Publishing Sciences Group, 1975, p 44.
35. Gustaffson LH, et al: Collaboration in practice. *Acta Paediatr Scand* 1979;68(Suppl. 275):126–131.
36. Trowell J: Child abuse: The role of a consultant psychiatrist in a specialist institution. *Child Abuse Neglect* 1979;5(1):23–26.
37. Trowell J: Child abuse, pp 23–26.
38. Trowell J, Castle RL: Treating abused children: Some clinical and research aspects of work carried out by the National Advisory Centre of the NSPCC in The United Kingdom. *Child Abuse Neglect* 1981;5(2):187–192.
39. Martin HP (ed): *The Abused Child: A Multidisciplinary Approach to Developmental Issues and Treatment.* Cambridge, Massachusetts, Ballinger, 1976.
40. Baher E, et al: *At Risk: An Account,* Chapter 8.
41. Pickett J, Maton A: Protective casework and child abuse: practice and problems, in White Franklin A (ed): *The Challenge of Child Abuse.* London, Priory Press, 1977.
42. Trowell J, Castle RL: Treating abused children, pp 187–192.
43. Martin HP, Beezley: Resistance and obstacles to therapy for the child, in Martin HP (ed): *The Abused Child.*

44. Martin HP, Beezley: Therapy for abusive parents: Its effects on the child, in Martin HP (ed): *The Abused Child.*
45. Court J: Psycho-social factors in child battering. *J Med Wom Fed* 1970;52:99–104.
46. Pickett J, Maton A: Protective case work, in White Franklin A (ed): *The Challenge.*

16 Child Abuse Treatment in Liverpool, England

Judith K. Williams
Ann J. Gegg

In this chapter, we describe the way in which child abuse is dealt with in Liverpool and try to put this into the context of the local and national framework of legislation and provision of services to the abused child and the abusing family. Liverpool has a large number of nonstatutory social work agencies (including the NSPCC). However, they make up less than 10% of the fieldwork force. The majority of investigations into child abuse are carried out by the local authority social workers, and they deal with all children made subject of a care order (see below).

What then is a local authority? Briefly it is a number of professional and administrative staff employed by the local city or county council to administer and provide certain services, some of which are prescribed by national legislation. The city council is elected by the citizens who live within its boundary. The city councillors decide the level of provision of these services, eg, housing, education, recreation, and they raise this money from the rates, a tax on both residential and commercial properties. There is also financial input from central government.

THE SETTING

Liverpool today embodies many of the problems associated with contemporary cities in Britain and throughout the developed world. It is a city of contrasts—the grandiose symbols of opulent colonialism dominate the city center, and yet next to them are areas of urban wasteland.

The city grew up as one of the premier ports of Britain's mercantile past, the fulcrum of a slave trade triangle which linked Liverpool, West Africa, and the Americas in a circuit that created fabulous wealth for a few and untold misery for many. The Industrial Revolution led to both the expansion of its port and the growth of related industries. As the port flourished, so did the city but, with the decline of trade and the Empire, there was a gradual but persistent erosion of Liverpool's economic structure. This was interrupted but not reversed by World War II and the postwar boom. Since the war, unemployment has usually been at least double the national average and sometimes four times that of the southeast of England. Within some areas of Liverpool, eg, Toxteth, there is an unemployment rate at the present time of 46%.

During Liverpool's prosperity, in the city center lived the city merchants in their grand houses and the laborers in their back-to-back dwellings. With the coming of better transport facilities, the merchants moved out to the country areas. In this century private housing has been built on the outskirts of the city. This, together with Liverpool's economic decline, has led to the depopulation of the central areas. The slums that subsequently developed have been cleared and new local authority housing estates on the outskirts of the city have accelerated the central depopulation process. The old large houses have been occupied by many families at once in some cases, allowed to fall to pieces in others. There is now very little housing available for private rent in the city center, and much of the council housing is old and substandard. In common with many other cities in this country and throughout the developed world, we have the inner city problem: here live the most disadvantaged groups within our society—the old, black, poor, and homeless.

It is an area in which people who have the choice do not wish to live, and thus even the newly built council property is not improving it to any great extent. The central area of the city has one of the highest rates of child abuse in Liverpool. This is hardly surprising in terms of the enormous stresses that people are under—unemployment and poor housing are, after all, the primary stress factors.

Liverpool has a poplulation of 570,000 and a child population of some 115,000, of which 30,000 are under 5. The child abuse register had 1213 children identified at the end of 1980. Recently in the Liverpool region there have been two government inquiries[1,2] into children (Paul Brown and Darryn Clarke) who have died at the hands of their caretakers. This has had a substantial effect on both the professional workers and the public at large. Any government inquiry into a child's death has an enormous impact because of the media coverage. National press, radio, and television extensively cover these reports. The fact that we have had two of them locally has led to a high level of anxiety among the various professionals involved. Increased public awareness means that there is a rise in the rate of referral. Many of the practices on child abuse have developed from the recommendations of goverment inquiries into the deaths of abused children,[3] although not all recommendations have been implemented.

CHILD CARE AS PART OF THE PERSONAL SOCIAL SERVICES

Child care may be defined as the "blend of legislation and practice which inspires the social care of children and young persons under the age of 18."[4] This goes back through many centuries, developing through the Victorian era when philanthropists such as Dr. Barnardo took in "waifs and strays." In Britain the death of a child at the hands of his foster parents led to the Curtis Committee's report[5] in 1946. This was followed by the Children's Act[6] in 1948 which established a service specifically for children who for one reason or another could not live with their own families. The child care officers working in the Children's Department (part of the local authority) became concerned not only with children in their care but also with trying to prevent the breakdown of families and the abuse of children in their own homes. "Preventive work" was encouraged by the Children and Young Persons Act of 1963 which allowed local authorities to spend money on this area of work. The 1969 act brought juvenile offenders within the scope of the Children's Department.

In 1970 the Social Services Act combined the Children's, Mental Health, and Welfare Departments into one large organization following the Seebohm Report.[7] This was intended to improve communication, provision, access, and adaptability and to provide a comprehensive family service for all (but not including income maintenance) from the cradle to the grave.

Thus, most of the child care provision, from day nursery to residential care and mothers' aides to social work counseling, was gathered under the roof of the Social Services Department. This improved communication led to problems of knowledge for the social workers who suddenly became "generic" and were supposed to have knowledge of all areas of work of the department. As time has gone on, there has been encouragement to specialize, but most social workers in Liverpool carry a case load which includes clients with all kinds of problems.

Access to social services is through the 11 district offices in the community,the eight hospitals (two of which are exclusively for children), and the four specialist teams which the Social Services Department provides. Most of the district offices now have an intake team which we found to be the most effective way of working for a busy central office.

INTAKE

The intake team consists of a group of workers who deal entirely with new referrals to the department. They are used to eliciting information from the public and the other professional agencies in the area. In an alleged case of child abuse, working as a group they can carry out the initial checks on a family quickly and effectively. They will then have the maximum information before they visit the house. Two members of the team may then visit together, depending on the availability of the staff and their knowledge of the family. There has been much debate about the effect on the family of such a visit, but the districts where child abuse is most prevalent have found it particularly useful to have two people in order to notice the reactions and different responses of the family that may be forthcoming to the different workers. It also means that it is possible to talk to the members of the family separately.

LEGAL FRAMEWORK FOR CHILD CARE

In the United Kingdom the legal framework for the protection of children is enshrined in several acts of parliament. England and Wales have a separate legislative system to Scotland and Northern Ireland. There are also government guidelines called circulars, which are issued in order to keep a relatively uniform system. There is no mandatory reporting of child abuse as there is in the United States, and child abuse registers have been ill-defined until a recent circular laid down guidelines. However, it is for each area to decide the categories of children that they wish to include.

The Children and Young Persons Acts 1933[8] and 1969[9] allow courts to intervene in the situation where they are satisfied in the case of a child that

a) his proper development is being avoidably prevented or neglected or his health is being avoidably impaired or neglected or he is being ill-treated; or

b) it is probable that the condition set out in the preceding paragraph will be satisfied in his case, having regard to the fact that the court or another court has found that that condition is or was satisfied in the case of another child or young person who is or was a member of the household to which he belongs; or

bb) it is probable that the conditions set out in paragraph (a) of this subsection will be satisfied in his case, having regard to the fact that a person who has been convicted of an offence mentioned in Schedule I to the Act of 1933, is, or may become, a member of the same household as the child; or

c) he is exposed to moral danger; or

d) he is beyond the control of his parent or guardian; or

e) he is of compulsory school age within the meaning of the Education Act 1944, and is not receiving efficient full-time education suitable to his age, ability and aptitude; or

f) he is guilty of an offence, excluding homicide,[9]

and he is in need of care or control which he is unlikely to receive unless the court makes an order. The orders which the court can then make may involve hospital orders under the Mental Health Act or require the parents to exercise proper care of him. However, the majority of orders that are made are care orders and supervision orders.

Care Order

The effect of this is to pass the care of the child to the local authority until the child is 18, and it is the social workers who decide whether the child is placed in a foster home, in residential care, or returned to his parents. At any time the local authority can decide to move that child without reference to the court.

In cases of child abuse, it is generally accepted practice that it is better to work with a court order than on a "voluntary" basis (see below). This then gives the social worker and others working with the family some measure of control.

Supervision Orders

These orders can be made to the local authority or the probation service, but in the vast majority of cases, it is the former. The effect of the order is that the relevant person has to supervise the child, and the child and the family also have to be supervised. There are powers that can be included in the order which insist that the child should live in a certain place with a certain person and that the child is medically examined from time to time.

Voluntary Reception into Care

Under the provisions of the Child Care Act 1980,[10] parents can ask for their children to be cared for by the local authority, if they are unable to do so themselves. The social workers decide whether it is in the interests of the child to be received into care. If they refuse, they may be able to help the parent by offering other resources, eg, mothers' aides, nursery facilities, "mobile housemothers."

If, for any reason, when the child is in "voluntary" care, it is felt that the parents are unfit to resume care of the child, then the local authority may decide to take over the care of the child (as detailed in the 1980 act). If the parents object to this, then the matter is heard in juvenile court.[11]

NONACCIDENTAL INJURY SECTION

In response to the concern regarding child abuse and the 1973 government circulars, Liverpool Social Services Department decided to set up a central system for nonaccidental injury, and a section has developed which now consists of two principal social work consultants (nonaccidental injury) and the administrative and clerical support. This section is responsible for organizing and chairing case conferences and taking and circulating the minutes. The organization of such a conference is complex because a suitable time and date has to be found for a large group of people usually within 48 hours. The people who attend include hospital staff, social workers, nursing and medical staff, and may also include the consultant involved with the parent (if, for example, they were having psychiatric treatment), district social workers, the senior social worker, health visitor (if the child is under 5), midwife (if it is a newborn baby), general practitioner, police, NSPCC, head teacher, school nurse, school doctor, educational psychologist, and education welfare officer (if the child or siblings are of school age). The probation service, voluntary agency (if they are involved), day nursery, residential home or foster parents may also be there; in fact anyone having a professional interest in the child and his family.

The administration of the register, including the reviews, updating, and destruction of information after a set period of time, is carried out in this section. Destruction of records normally takes place two years after the child's name has been moved to the dormant section of the register. Here, too, inquiries as to whether a child is known are answered, as are questions professionals may have about a problem about identification or what step to take next if they are worried about a child.

The section is easily identified, and through the case conference system the principal social work consultants are known personally by social work staff and professional staff in other agencies. This aids communication. The social work consultants are also involved in training of staff, both within and without the department, and therefore meet most of the professionals who work with abused children and their families.

In acting as advisers to the Social Services Department and other agencies, the social work consultants have a citywide perspective and are able to carry out a continuous assessment of the procedures, policies, and provision. Training is both consolidatory and innovatory. Research is yet another area which this section is encouraging, as there is a good deal of material which could be used to improve the service that is offered to the abused child.

AREA REVIEW COMMITTEE

All matters of policy to do with child abuse are referred to the area review committee, eg, registers, case conferences, training. The area review committee has now been condensed to a group of 20 representative professionals from the various disciplines in the city. The committee meets at least four times a year, and once a year there is a special larger meeting to include those that might have a particular professional interest. The committee is responsible for the procedures to be followed in child abuse cases in Liverpool and has produced a manual[12] that contains guidance as to the responsibilities of each of the different professional groups that may be involved with the abused child. Problem areas such as communication, overlapping, and serious errors are considered by this group. There may be plans of mutual interest, and agencies may combine to provide services for children. Interdisciplinary training is organized through the area review committee, and members of it cooperate in helping other disciplines with their training program.

THE REGISTER [13]

The Liverpool Area Review Committee decided on the criteria for registration of children. Originally it was a nonaccidental injury register, but there was a rather vague definition of "at risk" and any professional involved with the child could ring up and ask that the name of a child or his family should be included. From 1976 on, this was done only after a decision was made at a case conference. By then the register had been extended to include children who had failed to thrive for nonorganic reasons, newborn babies where there had been a sibling subject to nonaccidental injury, and a first-born child where there was very serious concern about the mother's ability to cope.

Government guidelines in 1980 suggested that registers should also include children who have been persistently and severely neglected and whose behavior had thus been severely affected: situations where an adult who has been convicted of an offense against a child lived in a household or regularly visted. The Liverpool Area Review Committee also felt the register should include a separate category of children who have been subject to sexual abuse.

The Liverpool Register is available 24 hours a day, during office hours in the nonaccidental injury section and at night with the emergency duty team. When someone checks the register, they are phoned back and a senior person is spoken to. This is in order to preserve confidentiality and to ensure that the professional who first called needs the information. Extensive use is made of the register, especially at night when other agencies have closed.

CASE CONFERENCE

The British system for dealing with nonaccidental injury and child abuse has relied on the multidisciplinary case conference for communication and coordination between the services involved.[14] The various inquiries into child deaths have highlighted this, and government guidelines have encouraged this even further. Case conferences are held at the beginning of concern regarding abuse, eg, nonaccidental injury presenting at the hospital or the child alleging incest to the police. Immediate decisions are made at this conference: Should the police become involved? Should the children be returned home? Who should investigate the facts of the situation and the background of the parents?

If the family is well known to most agencies, then long-term decisions may be made, such as should the Social Services Department apply to the court in order to obtain a care or supervision order? Should we work voluntarily with the family? Are there any other facilities that we can offer? Who should become the keyworker?* Should the child's name go on the register? How and when should the parents be told about that? If the family is not known, then it may be necessary to reconvene the conference in order to make these decisions.

Case conferences are also held to review a family's progress when this is required by the key worker or other professionals. However, there should always be a case conference to look at the overall situation when there is an intention to return a child to the family, dispense with a court order, or take the child's name off the active part of the register.

In Liverpool we hold around 400 conferences a year, and the number is rising. These conferences consist of a number of professional peo-

---

*Within the child abuse procedures in Liverpool, the term *keyworker* denotes the person who coordinates the management of the case and is the person to whom all others involved should relate (ie, health visitor, school teacher, even the police). Thus, the keyworker is not necessarily a caseworker within the social understanding of the term.

ple with different perspectives, depending on their responsibility for the child or the family. Much debate takes place at these conferences because those involved with the family do not always agree about the direction that should be taken because of their professional viewpoint. For example, social workers are often reluctant to take children into care because they know their resources are limited and the damage that care can sometimes do. Other professionals often see local authority care as providing the ideal family situation for the child and therefore are more enthusiastic about it. However, these debates would seem to be one of the strengths of the system because they allow for decisions to be made looking at every angle and every resource that we can offer to the family. Having described the setting, the national and local framework, the procedures and policies, we now turn to look at how they are put into practice.

IDENTIFICATION OF CHILD ABUSE[14-18]

Identification of child abuse is a complex problem,[15] and the following discussion mentions some of the criteria that are used in Liverpool to identify children at risk. Many children come to attention after having sustained an injury. However, there are other situations that give cause for concern, particularly when children appear at the hospital regularly with trivial injuries, with repeated minor illnesses, and illness reported by the mother but not identified in medical examination. Small babies represent a particularly vulnerable group in this category, and such babies, attending regularly, whose mothers report constant illness, irritability, or sleeplessness with no medical findings, should be referred for social work assessment. In addition, certain children are thought to be particularly vulnerable, especially low-birth-weight babies and those who have been separated from their mother in the first few weeks,[16] children with mental or physical handicaps, and children whose parents perceive them as being "different," strange, or overactive in their behavior. Furthermore the child who appears tense or unhappy and whose relationship with parents and other adults is strained indicates that all is not well.[15] This may be reflected in poor growth and development.[17,18]

Apart from these factors observed by the worker, research carried out at the Royal Liverpool Children's Hospital in 1973–1975[19] identified certain social problems as representing stress factors in families where abuse of a child had occurred. They were placed into four general categories: problems in daily living including financial, unemployment, and poor housing; stress and violence between the parents; difficulties between the parents and the child; and problematic histories of the parents themselves including psychiatric histories, criminal records, and unhappy and disrupted lives as children.

When one or, more usually, a combination of these factors is observed to be present, the child and the family will normally be referred to the social worker for further assessment. The referral may come from medical and nursing staff (hospital or community-based), day nurseries, school, police, or the public at large.

Within the hospital setting it is not uncommon, as part of relieving parental stress, to admit the child to a ward and allow time for further assessment, both medical and social, and the mobilization of the appropriate resources.

REFERRALS

Referrals alleging child abuse are made from many different sources. There is no mandatory reporting of child abuse in the United Kingdom, but public awareness of the problem is high. The way in which a referral of abuse is taken has been found to be of crucial importance, and an immediate response should always be made. It is practice to see the child within 24 hours of the referral if the child is reported, from any source, to be injured, and the police will, if necessary, be called upon to help trace the child.

INVESTIGATION

Of paramount importance is the safety and well-being of the child, and the following discussion relates to circumstances where the child is thought to have been subject to abuse, for example, nonaccidentally injured, sexually abused, emotionally abused, neglected, or ill-treated.

A medical examination is performed in the early stages of investigation. In Liverpool this is normally carried out by a paediatrician at one of the children's hospitals. Where abuse is suspected or in evidence, the child will be admitted to hospital for further medical investigations. At the same time, a social work assessment will take place. Provision is made in child care legislation for the protection of children, if necessary, by application to the magistrates of the juvenile court who can issue a "place of safety order" ensuring that the child stays in a safe place for up to 28 days.

The investigations will normally be carried out by the multidisciplinary team and should always include the following: (1) a full medical examination including x-ray and blood tests; (2) interview of parents/caretakers of the child by both medical and social work staff (separately or jointly) as to the history of the injuries or the abuse; (3) observations by the nursing and social work staff of the child, parents, and their relationship on the hospital ward; (4) a visit by the social worker to the family home if the family is not already known.

The initial interview is crucial in determining the way that we work with the family. Workers in this situation need to be honest with the client, clear as to the etiology of child abuse, aware of children's normal growth and development, and confident in their own professional ability.

In the home situation, physical conditions can be directly observed, and it is here that the worker can begin to assess the family circumstances. A full family history should be obtained, including the medical histories of all family members, composition of the immediate and the extended family, family movement, etc. It is important to observe the way that the parents relate to each other, obtain a history of their relationship, and observe the place of the abused child within the family. The perception of the child by his parents and their expectations of him are also significant, and the behavior of the child in his parents' presence must be observed. The well-being of the siblings must also be considered and, where one child in the family is found to be abused, the other children in the family are normally medically examined as soon as possible and, if necessary, also protected by the juvenile court.

Mismanagement by the social worker at this stage can be damaging for the child and his family, not only at the time but also for anyone trying to work with them in the future. The social worker will also liaise with professional staff in the community and other institutions to gather information about the family. This will normally involve the general practitioner, the health visitor, the school and their nurse and doctor, and possibly the probation and aftercare service. The police are occasionally contacted. The multidisciplinary team approach in the handling of a child abuse case is thought to be important in Liverpool, and it is often a combination of medical, nursing, and social work opinion that leads to confirmation of an allegation of abuse.

MANAGEMENT OF AN INCIDENT OF CHILD ABUSE

If, after the inital investigation, it is considered that the child is subject to abuse, has been in the past, or may be in the future, then a case conference will be called. This decision in the hospital setting is made after discussion between medical and social work staff. In Liverpool this will cover most cases of child abuse, as these children are referred to the hospital for assessment in accordance with the area review committee guidelines and allow the majority of cases to be handled by a team experienced in child abuse. The case conference is an important step in the procedure, and its purpose is to collect and share all relevant information and to make decisions as to what action should be taken and how the child and family should be managed in the future. Any major deviations from the case conference decisions must be taken back to, and sanctioned by, the case conference. In most cases the parents are aware that the case conference is taking place and are involved at some stage and informed of the decisions taken.

The long-term aim in resolution of the problem must begin with identification of the needs of the abused child and of the individual family members.[18,20] This may or may not involve the return of the child to its parents, and it is becoming increasingly clear that the earlier that a firm decision can be made, then the better for all concerned.

For the child who is to return home, a considerable input into the family is often made prior to discharge from hospital. Medical and nursing staff will counsel parents as to the appropriate methods of child care including the basics, such as a regular feeding regime, the needs of small children, and their expectations of their parents. Parents are encouraged to see the hospital as a place to turn to for help if necessary. Discharge home is carefully planned and is carried out in consultation with the parents as well as the community team — social workers, health visitors, schools, and general practitioners.

Once home, support in the community can be considerable. In Liverpool the local authority day nurseries are used to support the child and the parent. There can be a full psychological assessment of the child, and advice for the parents about the child's management is available from the nursery. Mobile housemothers are used to visit the home on a daily basis, if necessary, and they will provide both practical help and advice on child care, financial management, etc. Mothers' aides and groups of specially trained volunteers may also be used to provide support of a practical nature. At the same time the family may be offered counseling sessions with a social worker, psychologist, or psychiatrist, depending on the assessment of the problem. In Liverpool it is the individual community social worker who carries the responsibility for the majority of cases.

If the condition of the child and the family circumstances are such that the child should not return home, then application can be made to the juvenile courts for a care order. The circumstances in which this can take place are defined in the legislation, and rightly so as the child can thus be removed from the parents' care until the age of 18. Two key factors emerge in the successful management of the child in care: First, full and proper assessment of his needs, recognizing the severe damage that abuse by an adult of a small child can cause and, second, deciding where that child belongs, ie, whether rehabilitation to his family is possible. If so, this must be actively worked toward so that the child is not out of the family for longer than 12–18 months. If rehabilitation seems unfeasible, it must be decided whether a long-term substitute home should be found or the child needs to become a full member of a family through adoption. While institutional provisions are available, it is normal practice to place children in substitute family homes, even if this is only for periods of assessment and rehabilitatiion.

CASE HISTORY

The following case history was chosen to demonstrate some of the procedures followed and highlights the importance of the multidisciplinary team in the investigation and management of child abuse.

The referral was made by the doctor in the accident and emergency department to the hospital social work department. Ann A., aged 2 years, had been brought to the hospital by her mother with a head injury, and it was suspected on clinical grounds that her skull was fractured. Mrs. A. had brought Ann to hospital because she had noticed a "soft" area on her head, but at this stage, she could offer no explanation for the injury.

Ann had a history of an accidental injury at the age of 6 months and was attending the hopital outpatient clinic on a regular basis because she was seriously delayed in her development. This was considered by the consultant paediatrician to be due to lack of stimulation in the home environment. In view of the injury and Ann's medical history, she was admitted to the ward for further investigations. Mrs. A. was happy about the admission, presenting in the accident and emergency department as a pleasant, intelligent, and caring parent.

The family had been previously known to the hospital social work department. Ann was the younger of two children; her older brother Jon, aged 3 years, was born before Mr. and Mrs. A. had married. Jon was also attending the hospital outpatient department, having had febrile convulsions. He had also been admitted to hospital six months previously, having ingested an unknown amount of hair shampoo. A social work assessment at that time indicated a complex family history with considerable friction between the parents and within the extended family. Mrs. A. had a history of psychiatric problems and was thought to be a vulnerable personality. There was no evidence of child abuse at this stage; a case conference was not convened, but social work intervention was felt to be necessary. The family, however, refused any contact with the social work department, and so the health visitor and family general practitioner were advised of the problem and agreed to maintain contact with the home.

The medical investigation revealed that Ann had sustained a fracture to the skull, and Mrs. A. by this time had deduced that the child might have fallen onto a stone fireplace within the previous two days, as she had been found lying on the floor and crying. The paediatrician felt that this story was unlikely, but it did fit the injury and there was such a fireplace in the house. Thus it was not possible to confirm nonaccidental injury.

The initial social work investigation interview with the parents took place 24 hours after Ann's admission to hospital. The parents were aware that there was concern about Ann's injury and how it had occurred. They were tense and defensive, but presented a united front of a caring couple providing a good home for their two children. Liaison with other professionals in the community indicated considerable problems. Mrs. A. was the subject of a probation order having committed an assault on a barmaid the previous year, and the probation officer was aware of difficulties in the marriage. A combination of this history together with the injury to Ann and her developmental delay led to a case conference being called.

A case conference, of which the parents were aware, was called. The conference was attended by the hospital doctor, probation officer, ward sister, hospital social worker, health visitor, police inspector (CID branch), and community social worker and was chaired by the principal social work consultant for nonaccidental injury. Information at the case conference revealed marital problems, housing and financial problems with Mr. A. unemployed for seven months, and a mother with a psychiatric history, having attempted suicide four times during her teens.

The case conference group felt that insufficient evidence was available to remove Ann from her parents' care and that the family could be worked with in the community. Nevertheless, the skull fracture was inadequately explained, and Ann's name was therefore placed on the child abuse register. The parents were informed of this and of the group's concern about the child. A day nursery place was to be found for Ann to offer her increased stimulation and assist with her development, and both parents were to be involved in the admission procedure and the nursery activities. The social worker was to be the caseworker in the family and attempt to assess the family further and offer the necessary counseling.

Ann started to attend the day nursery, but work with the family was very difficult as the parents were convinced that the "authorities" were waiting to "pounce" and remove the children. When, after some weeks, this did not happen, Mrs. A. began to talk to the social worker and gradually the following history emerged.

Mrs. A. had had a very unhappy home life, seeing her father as an all-powerful man who shouted at her and criticized her constantly. She had attempted suicide three times during her teens and once during her first pregnancy. She was unmarried at the birth of her first child, Jon, and lived at home with her parents after the birth until she married, when she set up home with her husband. Her father refused to let her take Jon with her and only grudgingly allowed her access to him. She consequently conceived Ann to fill the gap in her life. By the age of 3, when the social worker met Jon, he was still with the maternal grandparents, and Mrs. A. left him there, feeling that the child should decide when he was ready to leave his grandparents to live with his mother. Her expectations of Ann were equally unrealistic. The marriage was unstable and violent, and the couple frequently separated and then reconciled. Mrs. A. was very dependent on her husband and could not see herself as a separate human being with an identity of her own. Mr. A. spent much of the family income on himself, sometimes leaving insufficient finances for the family to eat. Mr. A. refused to cooperate at all with the social worker. He had had a strange upbringing at the hands of his grandmother and had lived in a large city center tenement block fending for himself from a very early age. Marital therapy was offered to the family jointly by the social worker and the probation officer, but this was refused. Any attempts to sort out the financial situation were likewise refused, and the housing problem increased when the family moved out of their home and became squatters in an old tenement block, owing large amounts of rent.

Ann, however, began to make progress and suddenly blossomed, catching up with her peers very quickly. She and her mother began to develop in their relationship, and Mrs. A. began to appreciate the needs of a small child and the fact that her daughter should be allowed to be a child.

At a nine-month assessment, it emerged that Ann had in fact progressed well. It was also clear that the marital relationship was deteriorating. There was increased violence, and the social worker had to consider helping the couple to separate. Jon remained with the maternal grandparents. The housing and financial problems had not improved. The need for psychotherapy for Mrs. A. was apparent, and she had reached a stage where it would be acceptable to her. At this stage, the future of this family seemed to lie with her and her daughter and the progress that they were beginning to make. Mr. A. was constantly made aware of the help available to him, should he choose to take it. While the risk to the child was reduced, it remained clear that further violence could always take place.

As this is an ongoing situation, there is no "happy ending," but the child remains with her parents and work continues with the family.

CONCLUSION

We have tried, in this chapter, to describe the policy and practice of child abuse in Liverpool. In some ways every city and its problems are unique and hence the response to them will also be unique. However,

Liverpool has, in common with most areas of the United Kingdom, had to deal with its problems at a time of financial constraint, eg, the Social Services Department has been affected by a 16% reduction of field social workers. There have also been cutbacks in the health services and in education and housing which have seriously affected people.

Child abuse in the United Kingdom is a highly emotive subject, and it raises moral and political issues about which everyone holds an opinion. This leaves the social worker in an invidious position, and both public opinion and the media react strongly in cases that come to their attention. Social workers are seen to make a mistake, either by cruelly removing a child from loving parents or leaving the child at home with cruel and sadistic parents, thus causing the child serious damage or death. In this situation it is very difficult to stop these pressures from having an effect on the professional judgment of those making very difficult decisions. It is easier to play safe and know that by doing so, you will receive the support of the employer. The element of risk in decision-making in the field of child abuse remains as yet largely unaccepted in this country.

The attention paid by the media to the abusing family is likewise unhelpful. It is only the more serious cases that are reported, and there is seldom any discussion about the nature of child abuse or acknowledgment of the fact that most parents feel desperate about their children from time to time. A local paper called the child abuse register the "list of shame." How then can we convince parents that this is not a blacklist of parents, but a list of children who need our help?

The difficulty of assessing and meeting the needs of the abused child will be known to all those working in the field of child abuse, and an awareness is needed of the damage that can be caused by the procedures themselves, for example, a traumatic admission to hospital. This knowledge serves to reinforce the need for sensitive handling of the abused child and his family. Sometimes mistakes are made in the diagnosis of abuse, and we prefer to acknowledge this to the parents honestly, but we are also aware that ignoring a cry for help can be more disastrous than the unnecessary labeling of someone as an abusing parent.

With the growth of experience in the field of child abuse has come an increased awareness about the problem of sexual abuse. We are still looking at ways to deal with the devastation that it causes within the family and to improve the methods by which social workers and all professionals in the field, including the police, approach the problem.

In this problem, as in other problems of child abuse, we are increasingly confident about the investigation. We are, however, concerned about the long-term effects of social work intervention on both child and family. When is it advisable to separate a child from his family? How and when should he be returned home? What can we offer the child if he is not returned to his parents? How can we prevent the abused child from becoming an abusing parent? These represent fundamental questions in our practice that can only be assessed in individual cases when the child has become an adult and a parent.

REFERENCES

1. Report of the Committee of Inquiry into the Actions of the Authorities and Agencies relating to Darryn James Clarke. HMSO Cmnd. 7730, November 1979.
2. Report of the Committee of Inquiry into the Case of Paul Steven Brown. HMSO Cmnd. 8107, December 1980.
3. Report of the Committee of Inquiry into the Care and Supervision Provided in Relation to Maria Caldwell. HMSO, 1974.
4. Leeding AE: *Child Care Manual for Social Workers,* ed 4. London, Butterworth, 1980.
5. Curtis Committee Report on the Care of Children. HMSO Cmnd. 6922, 1946.
6. Children's Act, 1948. HMSO.
7. Seebohm Report on Local Authority and Allied Personnel Social Services. HMSO Cmnd. 3703, 1978.
8. Children's and Young Persons Act 1933. HMSO.
9. Children's and Young Persons Act 1969. HMSO.
10. The Child Care Act, 1980. HMSO.
11. Jackson J, Booth M, Harris B (eds): *Clarke Hall and Morrison on Children,* ed 9. London, Butterworth, 1980.
12. Child Abuse Manual. Liverpool Area Review Committee, January 1981.
13. The Central Child Abuse Register. Birmingham, England, BASW Publications, 1978.
14. Hallett C, Stevenson O: *Child Abuse: Aspects of Interprofessional Co-operation.* London, George Allen and Unwin, 1980.
15. Kempe RS, Kempe CH: *Child Abuse.* London, Fontana, 1978.
16. Lynch MA, Roberts J, Gordon M: Early warnings of child abuse in the maternity hospital. *Dev Med Child Neurol* 1976;18:759–766.
17. Lynch MA: The prognosis of child abuse. *Child Psychol Psychiatry* 1978; 19:175–180.
18. White Franklin A (ed): *Child Abuse Prediction, Prevention and Follow-Up.* London, Churchill Livingstone, 1977.
19. Sills JA, Thomas LJ, Rosenbloom L: Nonaccidental injury: a two-year study in central Liverpool. *Dev Med Child Neurol* 1977;19:26–33.
20. Okell-Jones C: Meeting the needs of abused children. *Social Work Today* 1978;9(26):9.

17 Preventive Services for Children in Clwyd, North Wales

Mary Scott
E. G. G. Roberts
Peter L. Appleton

DESCRIPTION OF GEOGRAPHICAL AREA

Clwyd (population 330,000) is one of the eight administrative areas of Wales (population four million). Prior to 1973, it comprised two counties, Flintshire and Denbighshire, which bordered the English counties of Cheshire and Shropshire. It is the most industrial area of northeast Wales and functions as two separate districts (north and south), with Wrexham as the main town (population 35,000) of South Clwyd. The density of population in this district is 100,000 within a five-mile radius.

Clwyd is within 40 miles of the large English ports of Liverpool and Manchester. Although culturally Welsh, there are only small pockets of communities where Welsh is the first language.

Strong family ties and an obsession for educational excellence are social attributes of the communities. Traditional work-oriented lifestyles, mainly linked with the local mining and steel industries, are evident. Recent factory and mine closures have resulted in one of the highest unemployment rates in the United Kingdom.

STATISTICAL BACKGROUND

Detailed study has been made of verified cases of child abuse and failure to thrive occurring in the south district of Clwyd, ie, in the catchment area of the Child Development Centre.

The total population of Clwyd in 1980 was 386,500 of which 23,000 were under 5 years old and 82,000 under 15. The population of the south district was 215,000, of which 14,000 were under 5, and 50,000 under 15.

During the period 1975–1980, the rate of abuse per year (including failure to thrive) was consistently close to 0.5 per thousand child population under 15 and 1.0 per thousand under 5. The figures are remarkably similar to those found in a large-scale British survey.[1]

When analyzed by age, 18.8% of the cases were under 1 year and 56.4% were under 5 years. These percentages are also very similar to the NSPCC studies and a small-scale (N = 55) study in Norfolk, England.[2] The age data clearly indicated that specialist services for families with very young children should receive priority.

Analysis of socioeconomic class data demonstrated a highly skewed distribution toward low social class. Furthermore, certain neighborhoods produced relatively high rates of abuse. In-depth study of one of these neighborhoods led childcare professionals to reexamine conventional ways of working, improved interdisciplinary communication, and catalyzed voluntary community developments in the locality.

EVOLUTION OF
STATUTORY SERVICES

It was not until the late 1960s that the problem of child abuse was given recognition in the United Kingdom, and this was due mainly to the work of Joan Court,[3] sponsored by the NSPCC. Locally, concern was mounting, and individual professionals were becoming more aware of signs of child abuse. Where actual injury had occurred, cases were dealt with in the hospital setting, and social workers were not involved until court or care proceedings were necessary. Where suspicions were aroused, there was no forum for sharing of concern.

This was remedied in January 1974, when the then medical officer of health for Denbighshire set up a working group of professionals from all interested disciplines. Their terms of reference were "to consider in depth both the preventive and rehabilitative aspects of non-accidental injury in children and to recommend at a later date, improvements or additions to the Service already in existence."

In April 1974, major reorganization of local government and the National Health Service took place, and health service social workers were transferred to the local authority. Prior to this, social workers in the health service were not involved in statutory duties, and this area of professional responsibility and accountability had to be resolved at the local level. Also in April 1974, the Welsh office issued a circular (123/74) recommending the setting up of an area review committee whose prime function was to "ensure regular joint reviews by all involved agencies, of the management of cases of non-accidental injury to children."

The Clwyd Area Review Committee, which comprises representatives of the medical, nursing, and social work professions, as well as local authority, NSPCC, police, and probation service, has fulfilled this task since 1974. Functioning through two district working groups (one of which was similar to the group already mentioned), the committee has been engaged in a review of procedural policies, relating to the management of child abuse cases, seeking to clarify anomalies and improve the effectiveness of the services offered in coping with complex problems.

The Clwyd definition of child abuse in 1977 was "any abnormality occurring in a child under the age of 16, where the nature of the abnormality is not consistent with the account of how it occurred, or where there is a reasonable suspicion that the abnormality was caused, or not prevented by any person having charge of the child."

After several years of experience, the professionals concerned felt that the terms of reference did not incorporate other forms of abuse. The following criteria are now used: (1) persistent severe neglect; (2) unexplained failure to thrive; (3) sexual abuse; and (4) emotional abuse. Sexual abuse is now being studied in more depth.

PROCEDURES

In September 1977, the committee published a manual of guidelines to be followed when dealing with suspected cases of child abuse. This brought together the individual procedures of the various agencies engaged in the identification, investigation, and management of cases. It included information regarding the legal framework and social factors associated with the problem. However, with the broadened definition, the manual is now being revised.

In the original circular, the Welsh office advised that a central record of information be set up in each area to promote communication between the many disciplines involved in the management of cases. A further circular of guidance in 1976 recommended that "information from all relevant agencies be fed into a central register, which should be kept by a designated officer." Because of the many difficulties which had to be overcome, particularly relating to confidentiality, a central register was not set up until 1977, although the social services department have held their own register since 1976.

340

Procedures Adopted When Dealing
With Supected Cases of Child Abuse

The following flow chart shows the procedures to be followed when the referral is received, right through to the decision-making stage.

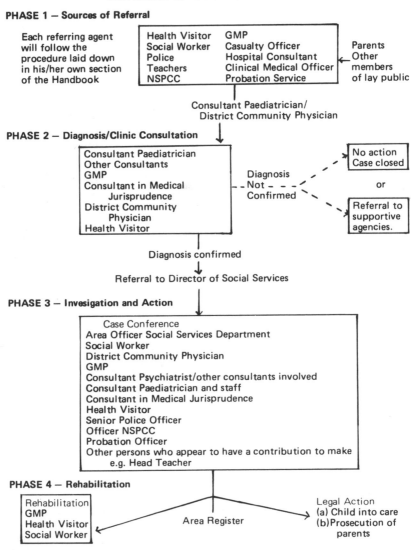

SUSPECTED MALTREATED CHILDREN

PHASE 1 — Sources of Referral

Each referring agent will follow the procedure laid down in his/her own section of the Handbook

Health Visitor	GMP
Social Worker	Casualty Officer
Police	Hospital Consultant
Teachers	Clinical Medical Officer
NSPCC	Probation Service

Parents
Other members of lay public

Consultant Paediatrician/
District Community Physician

PHASE 2 — Diagnosis/Clinic Consultation

Consultant Paediatrician
Other Consultants
GMP
Consultant in Medical
   Jurisprudence
District Community
   Physician
Health Visitor

Diagnosis
Not
Confirmed

No action
Case closed

or

Referral to supportive agencies.

Diagnosis confirmed

Referral to Director of Social Services

PHASE 3 — Invesigation and Action

Case Conference
Area Officer Social Services Department
Social Worker
District Community Physician
GMP
Consultant Psychiatrist/other consultants involved
Consultant Paediatrician and staff
Consultant in Medical Jurisprudence
Health Visitor
Senior Police Officer
Officer NSPCC
Probation Officer
Other persons who appear to have a contribution to make
   e.g. Head Teacher

PHASE 4 — Rehabilitation

Rehabilitation
GMP
Health Visitor
Social Worker

Area Register

Legal Action
(a) Child into care
(b)Prosecution of
   parents

NOTE:
(a) The flow-chart in no way replaces the need to act in accordance with the specific instructions relating to the individual discipline concerned.
(b) Any deviation from the defined procedure will inevitably become the responsibility of the individual concerned.

Referrals to Social Worker

The referral route to social workers differs according to whether they are community- or hospital-based.

Community social workers in Clwyd are based in six area offices and operate in teams supervised by a senior social worker. They receive their referrals from other agencies and also the lay public. Suspicions may also be aroused when dealing with other problems, eg, finance, housing, marital disharmony, etc.

In some areas there is a team of specialist social workers who deal specifically with child abuse cases, and the leader of the team also coordinates the service. This does not apply in Clwyd at present. Recently, however, it has been decided that the appointment of a coordinator is essential and, when financial constraints are relieved, this will be regarded as high priority.

Hospital social workers rarely receive referrals directly from the public: their main source is from pediatric staff. Many suspected cases of child abuse are identified in the casualty department. The parents are told that further medical investigations are necessary and that admission to the pediatric ward is advisable. This is usually accepted and thus gives the social worker an opportunity to meet the family while the child is in a safe environment.

The role of the hospital social worker is much more intensive in the field of prevention, particularly with the unborn child, the very young baby, and the handicapped child.

Case Conferences

Once information has been received from an agency about a possible case of abuse, the area social services officer follows the procedure shown in the flow chart. After consultation with the district community physician regarding the medical evidence, a case conference is called. This must take place as soon as possible after notification, but not later than three days after hospital admission, wherever possible.

The membership of the case conference is laid down by the area review committee (see flow chart) and is chaired locally by the area officer or deputy. Its terms of reference are: (1) to decide on the immediate action to be taken; (2) to name the agency to be primarily responsible for the management and supervision of the case and to name the caseworker; (3) to decide on the method and frequency of communication of workers involved; (4) to make recommendations regarding legal procedures, whether civil or criminal; and (5) to decide whether the child's name is to be put on the central "at-risk" register and the frequency at which the cases will be reviewed.

The caseworker may be a social worker, health visitor, or probation officer and is usually either already known to the family or would be acceptable to them. This worker is responsible for the actual management of the case, is recognized as the one through whom all information is channeled, and is responsible for ensuring that it reaches the other participants. Such an arrangement does not relieve the other professionals of their responsibility but facilitates the swift and ready exchange of information between those concerned. Any member of a case conference is able to convene a further meeting of all participants at any stage, if there continues to be serious cause for concern or if there are any developments which indicate a need for the agreed plan to be reviewed.

It is acknowledged, however, that the decision of a case conference cannot be binding on the representatives of bodies with statutory powers and duties in relation to children. Where a consensus view cannot be reached, any participant may, after consultation with senior officers, take action contrary to that recommended by other members of the case conference. Where this occurs before action is taken, other members should be notified of the proposed action and the reasons for it, unless an emergency demands otherwise. It is only within the last year that the value of case conferences in the field of prevention has been recognized.

In these cases, the hospital social workers may become the primary referring agent, particularly in the perinatal periods.

The terms of reference are exactly the same as stated previously, but the aim is primarily to establish a supportive network for a family considered to be high risk. In extreme cases, it has been necessary to remove children from their mothers at birth by using statutory powers, but this is only done when the known behavior of the parents is so extreme that the child would be considered to be at grave risk. Such examples have occurred when the parents had already pleaded guilty to serious life-threatening abuse to a previous child and in a case where the unmarried mother had a long history of psychiatric disorder without responding to treatment.

These actions are not taken lightly. Meanwhile, intensive work is undertaken with the parents who, in some circumstances are allowed to keep in contact with their child, pending court decisions. The length of time between the removal of the child and the court hearing is a cause of concern for professionals who are attempting to treat the family.

The case conference decides whether parents should be told that their child's name has been put on the at-risk register. This is done in most cases. Occasionally, when it is thought that the parents may react adversely, thereby putting the child at greater risk, the information is withheld. The caseworker, as designated by the case conference, is usually selected to inform the parents and does so immediately after the conference. In most instances, parents have already been told that a meeting of concerned professionals has been called to try to decide the best way of helping them with their problem. This is usually accepted without malice, and the various concerns are appreciated.

Use of At-Risk Register

The case conference decides whether or not the family should be put on the register. It is usual to register all cases of established abuse. The advantages of having a child on the register are that the case will be reviewed at intervals of six or 12 weeks, as decided by the case conference, and agencies can find out quickly, through nominated representatives, whether a name is on the register and which agency reported it initially.

It has been found, however, both locally and nationally that the register is infrequently used in this capacity. Most agencies prefer to use their own informal methods by making telephone contact with colleagues in other agencies and sharing information which could be useful in determining action to be taken.

Reviews

The cases considered to be high risk are reviewed at six-week intervals. Other cases are reviewed at 12-week intervals. The review panel consists of a social services officer of senior management level, a local area officer or his deputy, and a senior community physician (child health).

The caseworkers must attend reviews. Others who may have something to contribute may also be invited. Evidence can be submitted either in writing or by telephone. The ongoing work with the family is fully discussed and, where appropriate, suggestions may be made about the further management. The review committee also has the power to remove names from the register. Problems associated with the register and review system arise mainly in relation to the increasing number of children registered and the amount of time taken by reviewing.

EVOLUTION OF CHILD ABUSE PREVENTIVE SERVICES

In 1973, the Wrexham Hospital Child Developmental Centre (CDC) was opened as a multidisciplinary diagnostic unit, grafted onto the existing children's department. All handicapped preschool children, whether they have obvious mental, physical, or behavioral problems, are assessed. Treatment programs are initiated to meet not only the needs of the child, but also those of the family. Referrals are screened by the consultant pediatrician, and the nature of the various problems is usually revealed over a period of four to six weeks. In this exercise, all medical and other diagnostic agencies are employed from the hospital and community resources, which are now well integrated. In some instances, linkage with Liverpool and Cardiff regional centers has extended the service, especially for genetic and chromosomal disorders, and where medical tests requiring highly specialized equipment can be dealt with.

In addition to the pediatrician, the CDC staff includes social workers, play specialist, speech therapist, physiotherapist, psychologists, and nurses. This team functions as the district handicap team.[3] Diagnosis and treatment of children and their families, including those at high risk of child abuse and neglect, is being developed in line with national policy. Intervention schemes involve various combinations of staff who have worked together for over five years. Their work is brought together at weekly staff meetings, and final assessments are collated after six weeks.

Diagnostic Roles of Doctor, Social Worker, and Psychologist

In dealing with the child abuse problem, we have, for the protection of children, developed a philosophy of "ever concerned — always aware." We know that isolation and frustration are an integral part of the dynamics of abusers and that a crisis, or an accumulation of small crises, usually precipitates the actual incident of abuse.

In the setting of the admission room, the doctor's index of suspicion is aroused in cases where children, especially under the age of 3 years, have injuries which are not compatible with the history. This is reinforced where there is evidence of general health neglect. Suspicions mount when there is (1) a history of previous similar episodes; (2) frequent change of doctors; (3) a prolonged interval between trauma and presentation; (4) the child is brought to hospital by persons other than parents; (5) alleged self-inflicted injuries in an infant; (6) unexpected location and amount of soft tissue injury. Where such a situation arises, the social worker is asked to probe further into the reasons offered.

Medically, the child is fully investigated. It is now possible to date old fractures by using routine skeletal isotope scans, and this procedure is carried out on all injured children. Documentation of children admitted to the pediatric wards with suspected abuse include color photographs and accurate measurements (using infant grid) for failure to thrive; serial head measurements are recorded if subdural hematomas are suspected. Blood surveys exclude leukemia, scurvy, and thrombocytopenia.

During the period of hospitalization, the behavior of the parents is also noted. Inappropriate concern and/or anger and frequency of visiting are recorded. After discharge from hospital, wherever there is cause for concern, a medical follow-up program is always arranged, with referral to the CDC and other community-based resources.

Where the case is referred to the CDC the family first meets the social worker, who usually visits them at home. The purpose of this visit is to describe the Center, its staffing, functions, etc, together with the various procedures which will be followed, to obtain background information about the child and his family which will be useful in the multidisciplinary assessment.

Although it is expected that the social worker will bring back specific and factual information, retrospective to the time of birth, it is the way the parents felt about events, and their perception of what happened, which are important.

During the interview, which is semistructured, parents are encouraged to talk freely. Taking one example, it is interesting to see how often a birth which has been described in the medical notes as normal is recounted with great feeling, by the mother particularly, as having been a horrific experience. One gets clues about interference with bonding and early feeding difficulties which lead to problems in the mother–child relationship. Undiagnosed depression in the mother is frequently identified. Skillful interviewing should also reveal family interaction, attitudes, etc, thus providing the social worker's colleagues with a fairly comprehensive picture of how the family functions.

Referral to the CDC is usually acceptable to parents, as the hospital is seen as an acceptable place to bring one's child. By using the same procedure as for any other child referred, help in both a preventive and rehabilitative sense can be offered to parents who would otherwise be untouchable.

This form of history is the social worker's first tool, and the nonthreatening method used helps the parents to ventilate their feelings at a time when they are most vulnerable. If the child is still at home, this can act as a safety valve and reduce the risk of injury. In cases where the social worker feels that the child is in extreme danger, admission to the pediatric ward is offered and can be speedily arranged through the family's doctor and the consultant pediatrician. The use of the hospital as a place of safety thus avoids the introduction of statutory procedures at this stage, although they may be introduced later.

The clinical psychologist may make two contributions during the diagnostic phase. First, he can do a developmental assessment of the child. This assessment is likely to involve formal tests and direct observation of behavior. Rodeheffer and Martin[4] have discussed the special problems in assessing abused children. The psychologist, using a variety of sources of data, should aim to specify the conditions under which an individual child is able to positively engage in active learning. Second, the psychologist can use systematic observational methods to study parent–child interaction patterns. By definition, the abused child has suffered disturbed interaction patterns; it therefore follows that scientific observation of these variables is indicated. Such observation can form baselines for behavioral interventions[5] aimed at helping the parent(s) relate to the child more effectively and manage noncooperative behavior.

In our work, the psychologist's findings are carefully integrated with the findings of the social worker, pediatrician, play specialist, speech therapist, and physiotherapist.

Intervention in Response to High Risk

As previously stated, the early warning signs for child abuse in a family are now well recognized.[6] In the CDC our practice, in relation to child abuse, has been based on the recognition of those signs and provision of appropriate help. Two trends have been apparent in the development of these services during the last decade: first, intervention at an increasingly early age, culminating in the recent antenatal work, which is described later; and second, an increasing awareness of the necessity of provision at a community level and progressive decentralization of work.

Early intervention is regarded as crucial with families having a handicapped child. Family support and center-based or home-based child development programs have reduced the stress in such families.

Early referral from the community of parenting difficulties has been strongly encouraged by the center. Failure to thrive, feeding problems, sleeping problems, the crying child, behavior control problems, and bonding failure are recognized as worthy of immediate intervention. Babies who have received special care after birth are followed up, both in the community and in the hospital when necessary. The facilities of the CDC are available for children with developmental problems and families with parenting problems. Immediate admission to the pediatric wards is offered to parents under acute stress, the admission acting as a place of safety.

Our treatment of families who are at high risk has followed certain key principles.

1. The therapists must recognize the strengths and limitations of the particular family and its social network. This analysis is based mainly on the social history.

2. The parent(s) are helped to play at an age-appropriate level with the child. Instruction and demonstration techniques are used.

3. The parents are taught new control (handling) methods. The therapists are aware that high-risk families have extreme difficulties in being consistent and thereby respond to noncompliant child behaviors on an intermittent reinforcement schedule. It is known that behavior learned under an inconsistent regime is highly resistant to change. Parents therefore need a great deal of support and reward from the therapists for very slight improvements.

4. The parents are helped to reduce the frequency and intensity of negative interactions. The range of interactions is first defined by interview and direct observation by therapists and/or parent. The parents are helped to recognize how to divert both themselves and the child from escalating into a coercive exchange.

5. The mother and child are helped to make new relationships outside the family. For the mother, social isolation may be a major cause of the presenting problems. Direct counseling on friendship formation may be necessary with women who have a history of relationship failure. For the child, very early introduction to parent–toddler group, play group, or nursery is important for the child's own developmental needs. There is some evidence that abused children have later difficulties with peers, and therefore early experience of peer relationships may be regarded as preventive work. Quite apart from the importance of the new relationships, high-risk mothers and children need the break from each other.

6. Direct help for marital problems is frequently necessary and is offered. It has been our experience that the families who have made greatest progress have been those in which the husband or cohabitee has been willing to make an equal contribution to family change.

Finally, as our work has increasingly been with younger children and, closer to the community, we have recognized that we are involved with "the tip of the iceberg" of parenting problems. In one sense the now well-established emphasis in child care on detection and prevention of physical abuse misses the point. Emotional abuse, in the context of parenting difficulties, may well be far more common than actual physical abuse. Indeed, physical abuse may be subsumed under emotional abuse as one possible outcome. A brief section at the end of this chapter outlines our ideas on how primary preventive approaches to emotional abuse should be based on extended preparation for parenthood and community development.

Intervention in the Antenatal Period

Within the last 12 months, attention has been focused on the antenatal and maternity departments of the hospital.

It was notable that at case conferences, the early warning signs of possible abuse had been present in the perinatal stages. Facts about the parents' life-style and observations on patterns of behavior, had been well documented in the case files by expert observers, but the importance of these facts, in relation to possible child abuse, had not been recognized, and the information had not been passed on. Reasons for this were the lack of specialist social work attachment to the maternity department and lack of understanding of roles.

A pilot scheme was therefore set up by a nursing officer and social worker, both at senior level. The terms of reference were to explore the problem and set up lines of communication so that confidential information could be collated and used in the interests of the family to protect the fetus by possible intervention and support during pregnancy and to provide a communication network for therapeutic intervention in the perinatal period.

Using previously identified areas of concern, criteria for referral to the social worker were formulated: (1) late bookers; (2) persistent defaulters at antenatal clinics; (3) single parent, especially if under the age of 16; (4) previous termination of pregnancy for various reasons; (5) history of psychiatric illness, drug dependency, alcoholism; (6) request for sterilization or abortion refused; (7) previous children on child abuse register held by social services; (8) previous children in the care of the local authority; (9) severe marital problems; (10) major housing problems; (11) prolonged unemployment with financial problems; (12) cohabitation; (13) second marriage if associated with other risk factors; (14) already known to a social services department, but not on child abuse register.

One isolated factor would not always be a valid reason for referral. For instance, to be a single parent is now sometimes a carefully made decision, and interference would rightly be resented. A constellation of factors usually emerges, and most cases referred have at least three areas of concern, with as many as nine in several instances.

Patients are asked if they would like to see a social worker, but many refuse during the antenatal period. Nevertheless, they frequently refer themselves during the lying-in period, when the realities of coping with a baby dawn on them.

Should someone with a number of concern factors refuse social worker help, the staff in the antenatal clinic keep a close eye on them. The local health visitor is also informed. When she receives a birth notification, the health visitor is already well informed about possible difficulties and visits the mother soon after discharge from hospital. If her anxieties about the safety or welfare of the baby are aroused, she would then follow the procedures as laid down in the guidelines.

On several occasions, anxieties about the circumstances surrounding a newborn infant are so acute that a case conference is held before the child is discharged. In one such case, a previous child in the family was already in care because of child abuse. In another, the psychiatric state of the mother, who was also a single parent, resulted in the child being made a ward of the court.

The removal of babies at birth from their parents is exteme action, but a recent survey of social services departments in the United Kingdom showed that between 1973 and 1979 a total of 160 babies had been taken statutorily into care immediately after birth.[7]

At the end of our local pilot scheme, which ran for four months, from 820 live births, 63 mothers were referred to the social worker. The geographical distribution of these referrals showed that the majority lived in neighborhoods which were already identified as presenting numerous problems to social services and other agencies. The rising number of single mothers is a cause for concern and now accounts for about 22% of the total maternity bookings in South Clwyd.

As the value of preventive work is always difficult to evaluate, no firm claims can be made that child abuse has been avoided, but good communication and a supportive network system have been established. This is still operating with an increasing rate of referral to the social worker and should be the basis of a treatment plan involving health, education, and social services. A community development project for families with young children in one high-risk neighborhood is at an early stage of formation.

Health Education

It is recognized that the effectiveness of preventive treatment in child abuse and neglect could take many years, or even a generation, to assess. This problem is shared by educators and health personnel at administrative level. The health education needs of three groups of children could be met by using different techniques and topics appropriate to students aged between 10 and 13 years, 13 and 16 years, and 16 and 20 years. Courses are now being planned to include (1) normal child development and its variations; (2) parentcraft, including family planning; (3) hygiene and maintenance of healthy environmental standards; (4) the value of play, play groups, and nurseries; (5) the role of grandparents; (6) dangers of drugs; (7) early diagnosis and prevention of disease. These topics need careful handling by experts, who would include not only teachers, but health and social service personnel.

CASE STUDIES – PREVENTION

Case A

To prove that any form of intervention has prevented child abuse is extremely difficult. However, in cases of developmental delay, where it is thought that the cause lies in the child's faulty environment, some manipulation of that environment should produce positive change. The following case not only illustrates this, but shows how a multidisciplinary team functions and how several different agencies work together.

Gwyneth and John were brought to the attention of the CDC staff when John, 14 months old, was referred to the pediatrician by a community health physician. His mother was a Welsh-speaking girl who had attended the infant welfare clinic sporadically. John was found to be severely undernourished, had lost weight since his last visit, and was noticeably retarded in motor development.

After examination, John was admitted immediately to the pediatric ward for treatment of a chest infection. The doctors described the parents as being of limited intelligence, showing obvious concern, and mother slightly depressed. Initially, John was lethargic, with little interest in his surroundings, and functioning at about the 7-month-old developmental level. During his stay of six weeks, he gained weight significantly and responded to play stimulation. Meanwhile, the social worker had visited the parents' home and found that John's sister, who was just 11 months older, also appeared delayed in her overall development.

The physical standards of the home were very poor. Furniture was sparse, and mother seemed to have few domestic skills. The only food in the house was of the convenience type, which did not require cooking. Mrs. Jones, who came from a large family, had attended a residential school for educationally sub-normal (ESN(M)) girls. One of her sisters was severely physically handicapped and known to the social worker. The council estate on which the family lived is six miles from the hospital. Houses are modern with good physical amenities, but the area is rapidly becoming known for its social problems. Mr. and Mrs. Jones had applied to be rehoused in the town, so that the children could attend a Welsh-speaking play group and so that Mr. Jones would be nearer his place of employment. This wish to have their children brought up as thoroughly Welsh, seemed to be the only ambition of the parents, who appeared to be incapable of caring for their children adequately and who could be considered as causing delayed development by neglect. This was not thought to be willful at this stage, and as the parents were cooperating with the suggested treatment, a statutory case conference was not convened.

Attendance of both children and their mother at the CDC was arranged on a three-days-per-week basis for a period of three months. During this time, using play as a medium, the children were helped with development of motor and social skills. Both children responded quickly to this treatment. Mrs. Jones was included in all the activities, and through the acceptable medium of play, she was taught basic skills such as bathing, washing, and cooking. She did not learn quickly but, because of her warm personality, was well liked by the staff.

At the end of three months, the multidisciplinary team collated their findings. By this time, both children had made rapid progress developmentally, and John had reached the correct weight for his age. Nevertheless, it was evident that intensive family support would be needed to maintain progress. The family were offered a home help to assist Mrs. Jones with domestic tasks. Admission of the children to a day nursery was also to be arranged, and the social worker and health visitor would also remain involved with the family.

Surprisingly, the parents refused to cooperate with the suggestions. Although Mrs. Jones' own health was poor, she was adamant that she would not allow anyone into the house to help with housework — even a Welsh-speaking person was unacceptable! Concern grew when telephone calls were received from neighbors and relatives, alleging that the children were being left alone in the house while the parents went out drinking. It was now decided to call a statutory case conference.

At this meeting it was revealed that the police had also received complaints which had been investigated. Because of the home circumstances and the physical condition of the children, they were considered to be at risk of child abuse and neglect. It was now felt that a firmer approach had to be adopted. The parents' behavior reflected less concern than had previously been thought. Developmental delay in children caused through ignorance was one thing, deliberate neglect was much more serious.

Mr. and Mrs. Jones accepted the recommendations of the conference with little fuss. The children were admitted to the local authority nursery on a day-care basis, and social work support was transferred to the community-based team, who would give statutory supervision. The children were put on the at-risk register, and reviewed at 12-week intervals.

About six months later, Mrs. Jones contacted the hospital social worker. There were problems with the new council house which they had been allocated. After these had been dealt with the underlying reason for the cry for help became apparent. Mrs. Jones was quite severely depressed and could not cope. The weather was bitterly cold, and she had very little bedding for the children. Her husband was now unemployed and, as neither of them were good managers, they were unable to manage on a reduced income.

The children has also been arriving dirty and hungry at the nursery, and their overall progress had slowed down. The case conference was therefore reconvened. Discussion centered around whether or not the children should be removed from their parents. Eventually it was decided that another attempt would be made to increase support at home and to bring the children back to the CDC on a daily basis. Again the children responded well, but Mrs. Jones gave repeated excuses for not attending in spite of transport provisions being made. Mr. Jones also resisted, as he did not consider it to be a place for fathers!

Other tactics were then employed. The hospital social worker took over the main supportive role and spent more time in the home. Furniture, bedding, and clothes were obtained from various sources, and as the physical standards of the home were raised, so also was the parents' morale. Both parents talked freely, and their own feelings of low self-esteem became apparent. Mr. Jones accepted his wife's limitations and began to take over many of the household tasks, even though this was against the cultural pattern in which he had been reared. He cooked simple meals, did the shopping, and really took care of his wife. As her health and morale improved, the children responded.

Eventually, Gwyneth was admitted to a Welsh-speaking infants' school and is of average intelligence. John is still a slow learner but is under the careful surveillance of an educational psychologist.

Conclusions   This family will no doubt continue to have problems and will need some measure of ongoing support, but they bear no resemblance to when they first presented to the hospital. The lessons to be learned from this case are that at different stages of breakdown, parents respond to different methods of intervention. Initially, the accepting, nonthreatening ethos of the hospital produced cooperation. When this was withdrawn, attitudes changed, and statutory intervention was necessary. They then managed to get the children back into the hospital situation, declining to become involved themselves. When more attention was focused on them as individuals, they again responded positively.

This case also highlights the necessity for social workers to adopt an individual approach for each family and to exercise flexibility in moving between agencies until a balance has been achieved and a method of intervention acceptable to each family is found.

Case B

One of the highest risk factors in predicting child abuse cases is now acknowledged as the baby who cries persistently despite all parental efforts to stop him. In many proved cases of physical abuse, the parents have admitted that it was the child's crying which drove them to snatching up the child and shaking him violently. They had been to the family doctor and to the health clinic, but with repeated failures of trying suggested remedies, their own despair grew. They became increasingly tired and depressed and finally their flash point was reached.

The health visitor and community physicians had the problem brought to their notice at infant welfare clinics, and the attention of the staff at the CDC was alerted.

A number of families have been referred and, through a combined approach of behavior modification and counseling techniques, most of them were helped. The following case illustrates the approach and methods used at the CDC.

Sara's referral to the CDC was atypical and illustrates the awareness of staff in other departments of the hospital.

A nurse in the antenatal department heard a casual remark indicating that Sara's mother was not at all pleased about her second pregnancy. Her daughter, now aged 2½, had cried incessantly at night, and they had not had a complete night's sleep since she was born.

Her mother was asked if she would like to see a social worker. On doing so, she revealed not only her extreme ambivalence toward her daughter, but she also demanded an abortion, stating emphatically that she would not be responsible for Sara's safety if this was refused. Sara's birth had been bitterly resented because her mother had just obtained an interesting job. She had stopped taking the contraceptive pill when a smear test revealed suspicious results. She feared she had cancer, but when she went for the result of a second test, she was told she was pregnant. Her words were, "I didn't know which was the worse."

Within days of discharge from hospital after Sara's birth, feeding problems started. She took hours to take a few ounces, then vomited. Admission to hospital at 3 months revealed nothing organically wrong, thus reinforcing her mother's feelings of inadequacy and guilt.

The young parents were advised to let Sara cry and did so. They stood it for an hour; then the crying stopped suddenly. Mother rushed to look at the baby and found she had inhaled vomit and had stopped breathing. She responded to immediate resuscitation, but this method of dealing with the baby's crying was abandoned. This method of intervention was tried again one year later on advice of the health visitor and doctor, but the child had a febrile convulsion and was again admitted to hospital.

Their confidence was by now completely shattered. Sara now slept in the parents' bed every night—between them. She also refused to eat, and the only way her mother could get food into her was by pushing a spoonful into her mouth while the child's attention was distracted by the television. The social worker felt that the mother was as desperate as she claimed to be and took the threat to harm Sara seriously.

The pediatrician and general practitioner were alerted, and both offered early appointments to see the child and mother. The general practitioner telephoned to say that he had visited the home and, as help seemed available, found that the mother's attitude had modified and she was no longer talking about abortion. The clinical psychologist and social worker from the CDC visited the home. They talked with both parents, assessed their attitudes, and described possible ways of help. Above all they observed the child's behavior at play in her own environment. Sara was a delightful toddler, obviously very intelligent, extremely manipulative, and knowing exactly how to provoke her mother.

Discussion with all the professionals who had been involved with the family concluded that the parents were now sufficiently motivated for the sleep problem to be tackled again. The psychologist planned a management program for the parents, which would be strictly adhered to. Their fears of implementing it would undoubtedly be related to the possibility of vomiting, convulsions, and the fear that the child could die. To counteract this, both doctors agreed that the child should be put on an anticonvulsant drug during this trial period, and the general practitioner would respond personally to any cry for help.

The program was that a normal bedtime routine was to be followed. Sara must firmly be told that she had to stay in her own room, and thereafter her behavior was to be totally ignored. The psychologist explained to the parents that if they gave in, even after four or five hours, they would only reinforce the undesirable behavior pattern. Practical details were also discussed, such as fitting of a half door on Sara's bedroom so that she could not get out of her room, leaving the landing light on, parents speaking briefly and reassuringly to the child as they passed, but certainly to ignore all demands, etc. They were given charts to record factual details, and it was arranged that the social worker would call each morning at 9:00 AM to review progress of the night.

At this stage the social worker also had to come to terms with her own doubts about the likely success of this form of intervention. She was not entirely convinced about the lasting value of behaviorist techniques, as it was very much against her own patterns of child-rearing to allow a child to cry for hours. She also had doubts about the mother's ability to tolerate prolonged crying and wondered if the child's safety was being even more acutely threatened. However, in view of the urgency of the problem and the fact that the child's father seemed stable and sensible, she agreed to participate.

After four terrible nights, during which the child had discovered many ways of provoking her parents — almost wrecking the bedroom, throwing everything in sight onto the landing, wetting on the carpet, etc, the parents began to recognize how they were being manipulated.

By now, the length of screaming time had reduced from four hours to one. The social worker's morning visit was crucial. She was the crutch on which the parents leaned. On the first three days, she returned in the afternoon to give the mother an opportunity to air her feelings. During these visits, much of the antagonism which she had felt toward the child was ventilated, but although Sara heard every word, the relationship between mother and child was visibly improving. She was now praised more than criticized and she in turn frequently cuddled up to her mother.

By the end of the second week, Sara was going to bed at 7:00 PM and sleeping 12 hours. Everyone was much happier.

Contact by the CDC staff was maintained with the family, and early admission to nursery school was arranged for Sara when the new baby was born.

Other problems continued to exist, all of which appeared to arise basically out of the mother's dissatisfaction with her own life-style. Now at least she knew where to obtain help and seemed to benefit greatly by merely ventilating her feelings to sympathetic listeners.

This method of intervention was successfully used in several instances where young children were seriously at risk by interfering with parents' sleep. In every case, it was found to be essential that counseling was offered, along with a planned management program, thus meeting the parents' own needs and to some degree modifying the existing disturbed relationships between themselves and their children.

REFERENCES

1. NSPCC: *Child Victims of Physical Abuse.* London, NSPCC, 1975, 1976.
2. Norfolk Social Services: Non-Accidental Injury in Norfolk, 1977.
3. Court D: *Court Report.* 1976, Chapter 7, p 735.
4. Rodeheffer M, Martin HP: Special problems in developmental assessment of abused children, in Martin HP (ed): *The Abused Child.* Cambridge, Ballinger, 1976.
5. Jeffrey M: Practical ways to change parent–child interactions in families of children at risk, in Helfer RS, Kempe CH (eds): *Child Abuse and Neglect.* Cambridge, Ballinger, 1976.
6. Kempe RS, Kempe CH: *Child Abuse.* London, Fontana, 1978.
7. Fairburn AC, Tredinnick AW: Babies removed from their parents at birth: 160 statutory care actions, *Br Med J* May, 1980;987–991.
8. Scott M: Social work in a multi-disciplinary setting. *Social Work Today* 1978;10(2):10–11.

APPENDIX

SUMMARY OF PROPOSAL PROHIBITING
CORPORAL PUNISHMENT IN SWEDEN

In former times it was held in Sweden, as in the majority of other countries, that it was quite self-evident that parents and other caretakers had the right to beat their children.

The law of 1920 relating to children born in wedlock stipulated that parents had the right to punish their children. In the 1949 Parenthood and Guardianship Code the word "punish" was replaced by "reprimand." It was stated there that parents, in order to reprimand their child, were entitled to employ those expedients available to them as parents which were suitable. The removal of the word "punish" indicated that the legislature held that the more violent forms of physical beatings should be avoided. Until 1957, the Penal Code also contained a provision as to exemption from punishment in the event that a person, in the course of exercising his or her legal right to beat the one under his or her guardianship, causes it injury of a minor nature.

In 1966 the right of parents to beat their children laid down in the Parenthood and Guardianship Code was removed. This means that if a parent strikes his or her child, the act is judged on the same rules which apply when adults commit acts of physical violence on adults or on other people's children, that is to say, the provisions of the Criminal Code decide whether an offense has been committed or not.

The Commission on Children's Rights now proposes that an explicit ban on subjecting children to physical punishment or other degrading treatment should be introduced into the Parenthood and Guardianship Code.

This provision does not represent any extension to the punishable area. It is still the provisions of the Criminal Code which decide whether an action shall be subject to penalty or not.

The proposed provision is already found, inter alia, in the Education Act and in the Constitution for Child Welfare Institutions.

The commission holds that the same concept should be expressed in the Parenthood and Guardianship Code. The proposal would mean stating explicitly that children may not be punished by means of blows, beatings, boxing the ears, and by other similar means, and that children may not, for any other reason or cause, be subjected to acts of physical or mental coercion.

The commission maintains that physical punishment is a form of degrading treatment; mentally humiliating and dismissive treatment is another. Their effect can be identical, that is to say, creating a lack of self-esteem, and a personality change which may leave its mark on the child throughout its childhood and adolescence, and which may affect it as an adult. Even mild physical reprimands should be avoided, in the opinion of the commission.

The primary purpose of the provision is to make it clear that beating children is not permitted. In fact, there are many who are unaware that it is not permitted. Secondly, the commission wishes to create a basis for general information and education for parents as to the importance of giving children good care and as to the prime requirements of their care. The proposed provision should, in the long term, contribute towards reducing the number of cases of acts of physical violence on children.

Child psychologists and child psychiatrists have long agreed that it is improper to punish children physically and that physical violence may cause physical as well as mental injury. If the caretaker accepts violence and imposes it on the child, the risk exists that the child will also use violence in the future in order to achieve its ends.

In conclusion, the commission stresses the importance of the public being informed that it is not permitted to beat children for the purpose of disciplining them and the importance of a recurrent general parental education program being set up as soon as possible. The commission notes this because there are many immigrants in Sweden who come from countries where beating is a part of children's upbringing.

English translation
courtesy of
Ruth Wächter,
Stockholm